PENGUIN BOOKS

THE TERRIBLE TEENS

Critical acclaim for *Life After Birth*

'A sanctuary of revelation about the bafflingly contradictory experience of becoming and being a mother . . . In places I laughed out loud in relieved recognition' Rebecca Abrams, *Independent on Sunday*

'Vital reading for parents-to-be . . . Sensible, with a lot of helpful details thrown in' *Time Out*

'[I] salute Kate Figes's sensitive book which, admirably, helps redress the balance between the plethora of pregnancy manuals and the ridiculous paucity of advice on how to cope after' Leonie Miller, *Mail on Sunday*

'Work out your maternal worries with this practical, deep and therapeutic book' *Baby Magazine*

'Should be compulsory reading for every first-time mother' Rosemary Carpenter, *Daily Express*

ABOUT THE AUTHOR

Kate Figes was born in 1957. Her previous books are *Because of Her Sex:
The Myth of Equality in Britain* (1994), *The Cosmopolitan Book of Short
Stories* (1995), *The Penguin Book of International Women's Stories* (1996) and
Life After Birth (1998).

The Terrible Teens

What Every Parent Needs to Know

KATE FIGES

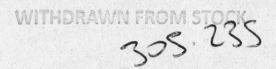

PENGUIN BOOKS

PENGUIN BOOKS

Published by the Penguin Group
Penguin Books Ltd, 80 Strand, London WC2R 0RL, England
Penguin Group (USA), Inc., 375 Hudson Street, New York, New York 10014, USA
Penguin Books Australia Ltd, 250 Camberwell Road, Camberwell, Victoria 3124, Australia
Penguin Books Canada Ltd, 10 Alcorn Avenue, Toronto, Ontario, Canada M4V 3B2
Penguin Books India (P) Ltd, 11 Community Centre, Panchsheel Park, New Delhi – 110 017, India
Penguin Books (NZ) Ltd, Cnr Rosedale and Airborne Roads, Albany, Auckland, New Zealand
Penguin Books (South Africa) (Pty) Ltd, 24 Sturdee Avenue, Rosebank 2196, South Africa

Penguin Books Ltd, Registered Offices: 80 Strand, London WC2R 0RL, England

www.penguin.com

Published by Viking 2002
Published in Penguin Books 2004
2

Copyright © Kate Figes, 2002
All rights reserved

The moral right of the author has been asserted

The permissions on page 422 constitute an extension of this copyright page

Printed in England by Clays Ltd, St Ives plc

For both my daughters . . .
. . . and both my parents . . .

The young are in character prone to desire and ready to carry any desire they may have formed into action . . . They are changeful, too, and fickle in their desires, which are as transitory as they are vehement; for their wishes are keen without being permanent . . . they are passionate, irascible, and apt to be carried away by their impulses . . . Youth is the age when people are most devoted to their friends or relations or companions, as they are then extremely fond of social intercourse and have not yet learned to judge their friends, or indeed anything else, by the rule of expediency. If the young commit a fault, it is always on the side of excess and exaggeration; for they carry everything too far, whether it be their love or hatred or anything else. They regard themselves as omniscient and positive in their assertions; this is in fact the reason of their carrying everything too far . . . their offences take the line of insolence and not of meanness.

Aristotle, 4th Century

I would there were no age between sixteen and three-and-twenty, or that youth would sleep out the rest; for there is nothing in the between but getting wenches with child, wronging the ancientry, stealing, fighting.

Shakespeare, *The Winter's Tale*, 1611

He can, for example, wearily congratulate himself on the fact that his children do not – as far as he knows – steal cars or bomb buildings or inject themselves with drugs; that they have not got themselves arrested by the police yet, or pregnant. Sometimes Brian wishes they had done so; then at least they would be somewhere else – in jail or an unwed mother's home – and someone else would be responsible for them.

Alison Lurie, The War Between the Tates, 1974

Contents

Acknowledgements

The idea for this book came from Fanny Blake. Fanny edited *Life After Birth* and as she signed off the last chapter said, 'Now you have to do the same thing for parents with teenagers.' She has given me acres of advice on our dog-walking excursions and has edited this book with her usual determination and care.

Thanks are also due to Jeannie Milligan and Sue Stuart Smith at the Tavistock Centre in London and John Coleman as well as all his staff at the trail-blazing Trust for the Study of Adolescence in Brighton. Lindsay Mackie and Colin Edgley helped enormously at the grass roots level. The librarians at the National Children's Bureau and the British Library have been inordinately patient.

I am deeply grateful to Felicity Rubinstein, Sarah Lutyens and Susannah Godman at Lutyens and Rubinstein for everything they do for me, not just as agents but as true friends indeed. Thanks also to Juliet Annan, Kate Barker, Lucy Chavasse and the sales and marketing team at Penguin for working so hard to publish this book well.

I have had some good times and some bad times during the tortuous process of writing this book. But the best times have been the countless hours I have spent in the company of parents and teenagers, discussing the issues that matter to them about living with adolescence. I met many wonderful people and some of their stories are contained in this book. As their names have been changed to preserve their privacy, I cannot thank them individually here, but they know who they are. Thank you all so much for your honesty, generosity and hospitality.

My own family have put up with years of grumpiness, exhaustion and obsession during the writing of this book, for which I can only apologize. Christoph and our daughters, Eleanor and Grace, are owed all the love and gratitude in the world, for without them, there is nothing.

1. The Terrible Teens

I'm fit to burst, to burst I tell you, when I think I'm only sixteen! All the years ahead – years of exams, matric, professional training, years of messing about and groping in the dark. Oh, how I detest this moment in my life, Vinca! Why can't I, all at once, be twenty-five!

Colette, *Ripening Seed*

It was as I staggered out of a restaurant one spring afternoon, clutching a large bunch of flowers, that another woman leaving the restaurant said something that seemed to speak for an entire generation of troubled parents: 'Well if you think this bit's hard, just wait until they hit adolescence.'

She had been celebrating her birthday; I, the publication of my book *Life After Birth*, which chronicles the upheavals of new motherhood and seeks to reassure mothers when they feel miserable or inadequate that they are not alone. This was a book founded on my own experience of new motherhood, which mercifully was now history. Adolescence seemed like a long way away, except that it wasn't. My daughters were barely out of nappies before they were wearing nail varnish, worshipping pop stars and singing, 'If you wanna be my lover' or 'Picture this, we were both butt naked banging on the bathroom floor'. I'm regularly told to 'get a life', and rows in our house have long resembled those that parents are supposed to have with teenagers as my children express their opinions and assert their autonomy while I try my best to socialize them for adult life and stay in charge. Middle childhood, that calm oasis between toddler tantrums and the teenage years, seems to be contracting. Puberty begins earlier, drugs are now found in primary schools and teenage culture is being marketed to younger and younger children.

Adults almost always assume that their child's teenage years will be terrible; angst-ridden for teenagers as their hormones turn them into irrational and moody monsters, and terrible for parents as the rows accelerate and adult vices beckon. Adolescence looms on the horizon of childhood like a dark cloud. Friends with small children ask me nervously what it's going to be like. Other mothers quiz me at the school gate with, 'Must it be dreadful?' or 'Boy, do I need that book now,' as the ructions of early puberty begin. Parents dread the approach of adolescence, yet have little idea how to manage it. Countless parents find the adolescent years difficult. One study found that nearly two-thirds of parents described adolescence as the hardest stage of being a parent.[1] Yet they rarely get advice or support because their problems are not so extreme as to draw them to the attention of the education or social services. Many parents find that their traditional support systems disappear, for the networks of earlier motherhood can vanish as children go to secondary school. Like new motherhood, adolescence is often a taboo subject, since many parents find it impossible to admit even to their closest friends that they are finding aspects of living with teenagers hard.

The sanctions of middle childhood become weaker when children begin to develop the mental ability to question adult reasoning and fling back resistance or insult. The emotions aroused by adolescent children can be far more intense and disturbing than anything parents have previously experienced. It's shocking when your angelic child shouts, 'I HATE YOU!' for the first time, or, 'Fuck off,' before storming up the stairs. It's infuriating and frustrating when they become solipsistic, inconsiderate and morose. Living with adolescents means having all of one's middle-aged insecurities, presumptions, prejudices and weaknesses pointed out, for nothing escapes the new-found analytical eye of the teenager. It means having one's waning physique and sexual prowess overshadowed by their growing sensuality.

Daily life may be a great deal easier for parents compared to when their children were little – teenagers sleep, so you can too; they don't need watching over every minute of the day; space opens up at the weekends as they go off and do their own thing; they are even capable of getting their own meals. On the other hand, new depths of anxiety emerge as adolescents begin to negotiate the risky world outside without parental protection. When young people make mistakes as teenagers, they can have lasting consequences for their health and welfare. Alcohol and drugs are easy to obtain, pregnancy and sexually transmitted diseases common and failing GCSEs or A levels really matters. Powerful feelings of loss also complicate the emotional toll of being a parent to an adolescent. There is the loss of the perfect child who has now mutated, almost without you noticing, into an adult with adult characteristics – spots, rough skin and smelly armpits. There is the loss of physical closeness as they withdraw and sit slouched in front of the telly, apparently deaf and mute to the outside world. There is the overwhelming loss of family togetherness as the child that was once such an integral part of one's being begins the slow but inexorable process to independence. 'There's a sense of time speeding up, that he's only got a few years left with us,' says Martin, father of three sons, the eldest of whom is thirteen. 'A lot of the sixteen-year-olds I teach don't go on family holidays any more. Have we wasted the time we've had together and should we have had more good times together before it's too late?'

Martin's partner, Andrea, also feels the passing of time more keenly now. 'It's exciting moving into a new era which is so different, a time of fast-moving change, but it is also the end of an era. When they were little I thought this is never going to end. Now I have this sense that it is and I actually feel quite positive about it. It makes me appreciate them more and I think I've got to get it right, otherwise they're never going to speak to me again. When they're little you think, "Oh well, I'll get it right next time." Now you sense that there are few next times left.'

While there are plenty of handbooks with blanket solutions on 'living with your teenager', there is next to nothing about how parents and teenagers feel about living with adolescence. Intelligent discussion on the nature of adolescence is also missing for the parent who wants to understand what their children live with as they grow up today. It seems important to me that we see the problems from both sides before we try to work out how to deal with them. Understanding adolescence also enables parents to differentiate between the normal ups and downs of adolescent development and abnormal behaviour which needs greater attention. Parents often overreact to normal behaviour and make it worse, and under-react to abnormal behaviour, also making it worse.

The foundations of adolescence are laid in childhood. When the teenage years are difficult for parent and child it is almost always because parents overreact or misunderstand in some way and not simply because rampant hormones have taken over or their child has been influenced by a delinquent group of peers. If children have grown up feeling able to express their negative emotions and feel empathy and support they are far more likely to be able to deal with the heightened negative emotions of adolescence. The higher the self-esteem in childhood, the higher it remains in adolescence. Effective communication is crucial to healthy family life but if that hasn't begun in childhood, it is far, far harder to establish during the teenage years. When there is neglect, abuse, emotional trauma or unsupported loss at home during childhood, young people are far more likely to 'go off the rails' in adolescence, when the brain matures and literally wakes up to the stark reality of their lives. Many delinquent, violent adolescents displayed aggressive behaviour and signs of neglect as younger children. Attitudes to health, diet and fitness established in childhood underpin the adolescent years, when teenagers stray from the family meal table and indulge in more risk-taking. There is even mounting evidence that without a sound basis of literacy and numeracy established during the primary years, adolescents find it harder to develop the more advanced intellectual skills essential for adult life.[2]

Adult society lets down young people in numerous ways. No other age group is so consistently misunderstood, feared, reviled or defined by stereotype, as typified by the Harry Enfield character Kevin. When teenagers drop out of school or leave with no qualifications at sixteen and face the prospect of unemployment, society is at fault for failing to modernize education and equip young people with the requisite intellectual and practical skills for adult autonomy and economic independence in a rapidly changing world. When teenagers get pregnant, adults have more often than not failed to equip them with adequate sex education, easy access to contraception or sufficient self-worth to value themselves enough to delay motherhood. When adolescents get depressed, as they often do, adults underestimate the genuine difficulties they face and the speed with which depression can spiral down into problem behaviours such as drug or alcohol abuse or self-harm. When adolescents develop eating disorders, adults are to blame for creating an environment in which emaciated women are considered beautiful and sexy. When adolescents become obsessed with material goods and feel inadequate because they haven't the financial means to pay for the goods which the media tells them are essential, adults are to blame for creating that market in the first place and for failing to equip young people with intellectual defences against such an onslaught.

Adolescence is the most radical period of development human beings live through. The tasks of adolescence are in many ways Herculean. They have to mature physically, emotionally, psychologically, socially and sexually in order to become effective adults capable of independent economic survival and reproduction. Young people need to develop adult intellectual functions, their own sense of identity, moral and ethical standards, and independence from their family, and be able to form intimate relationships with other adults. While there has always been 'youth', the nature of contemporary adolescence has inevitably been moulded by the force of history and social change. At the beginning of the twentieth century, when most young people left school before they reached puberty, they entered adult society as apprentices or servants and learned how to be adult from a wide range of examples. Now, with compulsory education, young people grow up in schools, learning more from their peers and the television than they do from the adults they meet. Extended economic dependence on the family, with more and more young people having to live at home until their early twenties, has prolonged the period of adolescence and exacerbated conflict between generations. At the same time, youth culture in fashion, music and style has mushroomed since the 1950s, defining the teen-ager as different to both child and adult, and dangerous.

The notion of adolescence as a time of protracted space, uniquely different to both childhood and adulthood, did not exist until the 1950s. Young people used to look like miniature versions of their parents rather than like teenagers with their own distinct sense of style. There were no shops specifically targeted at young people before London's Carnaby Street exploded onto the fashion scene. Now entire industries survive by marketing products to the young. Life was simpler, change was slower and more easily assimilated than it is today. Some historians and sociologists believe that the concept of the teenager emerged because there was such a substantial loss of young lives during the two world wars that young people were owed something in return. It may also be that the swift pace of change and the increasing complexity of our world has extended adolescence by creating concepts of generation. Each of us is now the product of a distinctly different time.

This book will show how it is harder these days for our young people to grow up and cross the milestones to maturity, and how parents need to adapt the way they bring up their children in order to support them through the challenges they face. It is also a book about how adult society fails in its responsibilities to the young and in doing so gets the youth that it deserves. We need to know what adolescence is and understand the increased pressures and difficulties that young people live with today, in order to be able to manage those years effectively, keep them alive and stay on the same side. By drawing on the monumental amount of academic research that has been conducted on adolescent development since the 1980s as well as interviews with parents, teenagers and experts, I have examined the nature of teenage emotions and attitudes towards parents, friendships and their futures. A chapter on the psychological development of adolescence shows that it is not hormones that determine teenage behaviour but radical changes in thinking. Chapters on sexuality, school and risk-taking will, I hope, surprise and reassure parents by challenging some of the many myths that have surfaced with the concept of the teenager.

The media portrays teenagers as sexually promiscuous or pregnant, when most under-sixteens are terrified of the prospect of sexual intimacy with another human being and not sexually active at all. Raging hormones are almost always blamed for the sudden moods and angry outbursts, the 'otherness' that seems to take children over at puberty. Yet the hormonal changes create far less difficulty for adolescents than parents imagine. Their impact is slow and the physical changes of puberty easily assimilated provided the teenagers are prepared for them. 'It just happens,' a group of sixteen-year-old boys told me. 'It's no big deal.'

'It wasn't as big a deal as everyone made out,' says Karen, aged sixteen.

For every nervous, uncertain moment there are three excited ones as children contemplate the prospect of growing up, longing for breasts and shaving smooth cheeks in the hope of facial hair. 'I'm just waiting to implode with sideburns,' says Nick, who is sixteen.

When adolescents seem down, their moodiness is often attributed to hormones, just part and parcel of being that age, while more serious problems such as depression are overlooked. But it is not so much hormones as the radical change in the way that the mind works – enabling young people to think in more adult ways, with enhanced powers of perspective, criticism, abstract thought, hindsight and memory – that creates difficulties for teenagers and affects their behaviour. Recent research into adolescent brain development indicates that changes in the mind are far more unsettling than anything that takes place in the rest of the body, for unfamiliar, powerful concepts of existential aloneness and self-consciousness emerge. These changes are slow. The tendency is to treat teenagers as adults once they appear to have matured physically. But it takes many more years for the mind to mature, and while they are adolescent, teenagers really do think differently to adults. They don't understand what their parents are on about unless it is painstakingly pointed out to them time and time again.

There is also a tendency to blame peer pressure for seducing innocent, happy children away from parental influence. But research shows that it is troubled and emotionally unsupported teenagers who become over-dependent on the peer group and that the vast majority of young people are sensitive and intelligent enough to be able to assess different sources of advice.[3] They may want and need to follow the crowd when it comes to fashion, music or leisure pursuits, but they still listen to their parents on the more important issues of health, safety, education and career. Friends are important. They offer a vital source of support as adolescents begin to sever links with their family and have yet to find emotional nourishment from a mate, but they rarely corrupt a young person who was not well on the way to corruption before the onset of adolescence.

Family life with teenagers is always assumed to be tumultuous as adolescents fight and rebel. Inevitably there is some upheaval as parents adjust to the needs of their changing child and most families do experience greater conflict at this time. However the vast majority, roughly 80 per cent, ride out the storm successfully and remain close and friendly throughout.[4] When there is a serious breakdown in relations, or when adolescents seriously go off the rails, this tends to be because of problems that were present way before puberty. Adolescence is not some great uncontrollable monster that springs out and turns a happy and contented child bad. It is a slow continuum, which builds from early childhood when the emotional foundations are laid with a sense of security, stability, love and protection. If that is lacking, the great changes of adolescence are harder to deal with for both parent and child. When there are violent rows at home they are almost always based on gross misunderstandings and lack of communication between generations. Feeling misunderstood is part and parcel of growing up, but I have been staggered to find great oceans of misunderstanding between parents and their children when there should only be streams between them. Often, parents and adults stop talking to teenagers because they stop talking to us. But it is parents who have to reach out and try to understand the rising number of problems their children face by listening, empathizing and helping them to develop effective solutions and ways of coping. Parents have the intellectual maturity, children do not; and parents have to be the parents long after the children have stopped considering themselves children, for adolescents are still children in so many ways.

This is a book which will hopefully reassure parents that they are not alone when they are finding life with adolescent children challenging and emotionally difficult. Just like *Life After Birth* this is a 'hybrid handbook' which does not tell parents how to parent but suggests how to improve under-standing and communication between generations by being better informed. There are no easy answers, just common mistakes, and by reading about the experiences of others we can avoid a great many of them. With appropriate boundaries, trust and respect for children's right to their own emerging autonomy as well as masses of love, empathy and understanding, parents are more likely to have an easier time of it. But when things go wrong, when life is imperfect and unfair, rather than feeling a sense of failure and despair parents can improve things a great deal by acknowledging that bringing up teenagers in the modern world is hard and by reaching out to others for help and support.

Sometimes when we experience difficulties with our own children as teenagers, the answers lie embedded in our own experience of childhood and adolescence. Adults tend to forget the agonies of growing up, the embarrassments, uncertainties and anxieties, and they romanticize the good, the exuberance and vitality of youth. We compare their lives to our own upbringing and think they should consider themselves lucky to have so much when we had so little. We transfer our own failed hopes and dreams to our children and expect them to achieve more than we did, or become that doctor, pianist or footballer that we always wanted to be. We justify the short sharp shock with 'if it was good enough for me it was good enough for him'. Or conversely we try to eradicate the traumas of our own childhoods by doing it differently with our own children. We move on and grow up again through our children.

I launched into research for this book, hopeful that I would find myself better prepared for the inevitable fights and inexorable separations of living with two teenage daughters. What I wasn't prepared for was the way that my own adolescence would come back to haunt me and that so much of what I discovered offered explanations for my own teenage life. Memories of my childhood are episodic and haphazard: holidays in Cornwall; clearing the snow off the car with my father and brother when I was five during the great winter of 1963; the day my little brother pulled a paving stone leaning against the garden fence onto his big toe. Huge areas of daily life have been forgotten, perhaps because they were uneventful. But my memories of adolescence are still vivid and complete, largely, I now realize, because of the monumental leaps the mind makes at this age.

It was a time when the black–and–white world of an unhappy childhood erupted into full glorious technicolour as I found greater freedom to live my own life. Travelling around London on my own, earning my own money through babysitting, the thrill of getting into pubs under age, and the supreme satisfaction that came from being part of a strong gang of girls empowered me, for adolescent friendships are as passionate as love affairs. Children begin to break free from their parents with puberty, they need to spend hours alone in their bedrooms listening to music or staring at themselves in the mirror in order to come to terms with who they are becoming. Reading about this psychological need took me straight back to my own bedroom, to the tiny, mono, box record player that belted out Bob Dylan and the Rolling Stones repeatedly and the extreme emotions lived out in that small square room.

But I also have answers now for so many of the other darker moments of growing up and I've lost count of the number of times I've read something, looked up and said, 'So *that's* why!' All those insecurities about my body and boys were not peculiar to me, but typical of the teenage experience for girls as they struggle to keep hold of some sense of self-worth. My parents divorced when I was five and I missed my dad, and as with most divorcing couples my parents found it hard to stop their anger and argument from affecting me. The emotional wounds were deep and led, as psychologists now recognize, to a diminished sense of self-worth. In a child's mind, the child is divorced too. I was not loved enough for my father to stay and the consequences of that lack of self-worth affected my adolescence, for the whole concept of counselling or minimizing the impact of divorce on the child was non-existent then.

Hampstead, north London, during the 1970s was hardly a suburban backwater and I did all those things that parents nationwide now fear their children doing. I smoked too much dope. I got hold of the pill at fifteen and approached sex as an interesting experiment rather than as the romantic consequence that older people still maintain it should be for the young and uninitiated, and I had an abortion before I was eighteen. I drifted, uncertain as to what it was I could or wanted to do in life and failed French A level not once, but twice. I argued so vehemently with my mother that I felt an emotional rift between us for years subsequently, left home after a row with her at seventeen and moved in with my father. First love, is, according to the psychologist Erikson, essentially narcissistic. Teenagers fall in love with an image of themselves that reflects well on them, rather than with the real person within. I fell in love with a beautiful young man, flattered perhaps by the fact that he wanted me at all. Crucially, he was someone that both my parents judged unsuitable.

At the time I considered myself bohemian, original, and life was exciting. It is only now that I have researched the nature of adolescence that I understand how much I anaesthetized my pain by being stoned whenever possible, and confirmed my worthlessness through my promiscuity. I survived adolescence, shaped irrevocably and sometimes negatively by my experiences, but not destroyed by them. Perhaps it is the irrevocability of so many of the activities that adolescents indulge in that makes them so important. For adult life without the protection of parents can be very risky and young people have to live with the consequences of their own actions and mistakes. As my elder daughter embarks on puberty I have to face a painful truth. My love for her is so strong that I will do anything to make sure she reaches maturity unharmed. Yet I also have to accept that she may do everything I did and more in order to break free. Letting go just enough to accommodate her difference, her separateness and her need to do things her own way, without burdening her with my own emotional needs or leaving her emotionally stranded with the genuine difficulties inherent to growing up today is, I now see, one of the trickiest aspects of being a parent.

Like countless other parents who had a difficult time during adolescence with their own parents, I want to avoid the mistakes of my own upbringing and do things differently. I want to repeat the good and eliminate all of the unhappiness, isolation and that deep sense of abandonment which destroyed so much of the magic of childhood for me. I want to maintain good relations with my daughters and make them feel so loved and secure that they will always be able to turn to me for advice and support, however old they may be.

'I was brought up in a very old-fashioned way where nothing

was ever discussed in front of the children,' says Bianca, a single mother with a thirteen-year-old son. 'You knew that there were awful things going on, but nothing was ever explained to you, you were never involved or allowed an opinion. So I've made a point of talking to Hugh about everything. I've kept him informed because we've been together on our own for so long.'

Joan grew up in a staunchly Catholic household in Ireland. 'I felt, growing up, that I lived a different life to my parents, where the main fear was that they would find me out. But that's such a huge barrier. I've invested so much in my three daughters and I don't want them to have this whole life out there that they can't feel they can talk to me about. I remember once saying to my parents that some boy had a twitch when he was asleep and there was this appalled silence, I wanted the ground to swallow me up. But that wouldn't happen with my kids, it's better that way.'

'I felt like I was an extension of my mother at that age, the way she wanted me to be, which wasn't uncommon then,' says Philippa, a single mother with two sons aged eighteen and sixteen. 'They're their own people, they don't have to bust out of that mould in order to find out who they really are and that's wonderful, much better.'

'My life would have been different had I not settled down so early. I don't think you understand the pull a person has over you at that age,' says Stella, who has three daughters and married young. 'I tell them that it's not a good idea to have sex young because you're then biologically programmed to want that person to like you even if he's a total dickhead. I want them to stay free for as long as possible.'

While we may be trying to avoid the mistakes and misunderstandings of previous generations, new sources of conflict have inevitably surfaced between parents and their young, many of which are influenced by social change. We now have parents who insist that they are such firm friends with their children that they are equal, yet children throughout their adolescence need to feel that their parents are still in charge. Rising numbers of children live with family breakdown and stepfamilies and feel abandoned by a parent, but children need to feel their parents are stable rocks from whom they themselves leave when they are ready. Two leading American academics, E. Mavis Hetherington and Judith Wallerstein, have spent their lives studying the long-term impact of divorce. Both believe that family break-up can be a major predictor of adolescent difficulties

Others, particularly the growing numbers of only children, live with overprotective parents. They feel concern and parental input in every area of their lives and have to fight even harder to break free. Child poverty has increased threefold in the UK in the past twenty years at the same time as an unprecedented rise in materialistic values and job uncertainty for the young. Others live in cash-rich, time-poor households, where every material need is met but hard-working parents are rarely around for support and guidance. There are heightened pressures these days to succeed academically, and greater material demands as youth culture and a specific youth market have mushroomed. All of these socio-economic trends have had a profound impact on the emotional development of young people and inevitably bring them into new types of conflict with their parents.

Childhood influences adolescence and they both haunt and define us throughout our lives. We all retain elements of adolescence as adults. Understanding who we are, or what we want from life, from members of the opposite sex and relationships are ongoing concerns which begin in adolescence but are not necessarily resolved then. Countless responsible and successful adults still grapple with many of the conflicts and conundrums of life which first emerge in adolescence.

Distinguishing oneself from one's parents can be a lifelong ambition. Being competent at work, coming to terms with aspects of loss and death, forming lasting intimacy with another person and reaching a modicum of self-confidence over one's abilities and physical appearance are landmark achievements singularly; rare, indeed, collectively. We all regress at times of stress or poignant milestones and long occasionally for Mum or Dad to sort out our difficulties. We all take unnecessary risks for that adrenaline rush, or drink too much when we need to escape temporarily from the torments and responsibilities of adulthood. When people live through mid-life crises, they often demonstrate much of the selfishness and narcissism which is quintessential adolescent behaviour. They long for some of the trappings of youth to make them seem more youthful. Driving a red sports car with room for only two, or taking off with a younger lover, helps convince the middle-aged that they are still young at heart. Obsessions over appearance, fitness levels, heightened egotism, difficulty in putting their child's needs before their own, and a general refusal to accept responsibility for their own actions by heaving the blame onto others, are adolescent tendencies which persist in numerous adults.

There is no blueprint adolescent experience but diverse experiences, because adolescence is deeply influenced by the social and cultural environment children grow up in and is affected by their gender and ethnic background. Consequently parents and teenagers will identify more with some voices than with others. By presenting the range, I hope to be able to build a composite picture of life for parents and their teenagers today. *Life After Birth* succeeds as a book because it reassures countless new mothers with detailed research and with the voices of other new mothers. *The Terrible Teens* is in many ways its natural sequel. Both new motherhood and adolescence force major changes in our attitudes and in the nature of family life. Both create powerful feelings in parents and can at times reduce them to the depths of despair and exhaustion. It is only by truly understanding adolescence and what young people live through as they grow up, as well as listening to the experiences of other parents, that we have a chance of managing it effectively. Does adolescence, by definition, have to be tumultuous as young people begin to break away and forge their own way of life, or are there other, cleverer ways of managing the transition so that parents and their children manage to stay on the same side? What happens to children mentally, emotionally and physically as they grow up, and what do teenagers have to say about the hurdles they face as they move into adulthood?

When I talked to teenagers, and their voices pervade this book, they describe a very different world to the one that parents imagine. They talk of great pressure and boredom at school as well as immense uncertainty and fear over who they are and what their future will be. They describe the immense pain and difficulties of forming social and sexual relationships, the self-loathing they feel when they make mistakes, and deep inadequacies over the way they look. They talk of feeling sidelined, living in a border-line state where they are denied the sanctity of childhood without the greater privileges of adulthood. They feel marginalized from a society that does not seem to care or acknowledge their needs, offering few affordable places to go with their friends outside the home. So they take to the places where they will be left alone, left to perpetuate the stereotype that society says is teenage life – parks and cemeteries at night, supermarket car parks. They scream their pain silently through the starvation of eating disorders, the nick of the razor blade against their young flesh, and through drug abuse, depression and suicide. The rates of all of these psychosocial disorders have risen disproportionately amongst the young in recent years. When troubled teenagers talk, they crave greater support and understanding from their parents and seem to want such simple things. They want parents who have the time to stop and listen to what they have to say, to really hear them and trust them to look after themselves. They want parents who will remain constructive and non-judgemental when they confess to the minor misdemeanours and mistakes that are crucial to healthy development as adolescents learn how to negotiate the real world as they find it outside the artificial protection of the family home.

Many of the teenagers I talked to had nobody to confide in. They couldn't talk honestly with their parents either because they felt their conversation would produce shock, disapproval or outrage, or because they needed to preserve the privacy and distance between them. Talking to friends about how difficult life is with parents can be immensely helpful, but adolescents desperately need to keep up appearances with their peers, so discussion about their deepest fears and inadequacies rarely happens. Teachers in secondary schools often don't have the time to build up proper relationships with pupils and while there may be counsellors, school nurses and elements of 'pastoral' care, few teenagers trust that system without a sound relationship with the staff involved. There is also a perception that counsellors are there for children with serious difficulties rather than typical teenage turmoil. When teenagers exhibit serious signs of distress they are often scooped up and helped. But the trouble is that typical teenage turmoil can quickly descend into extreme distress expressed through alcohol and drug abuse, eating disorders, cutting and suicide, almost without adults noticing.

As parents we generally tend to view adolescence in our children as negative because there are so many negative aspects for us: the squabbles, mess, noise levels, anxieties and the sad realization that this once precious baby, who has been so central to our lives, is gradually moving away. But for adolescents themselves, these years can be as exhilarating, passionate and highly creative as they are difficult emotionally, provided that they still feel nourished and supported at home. It is a time when teenagers feel great surges of energy, joy and enthusiasm, enjoy 'having a laugh' with friends and exploring their new-found freedoms. There is a vigorous, raw energy to the spirit of youth, forcing human society on to find new ways of doing things, to embrace new concepts and hear new sounds as their culture floods the market – if we are prepared to listen. The intellectual development and intense new emotions of adolescence provoke great idealism, vital new ideas as well as age-old ones dressed up in new clothes for a new generation, and the passions triggered easily translate into industry if they are tapped and nurtured. Countless young people long to set the world to rights as they begin to understand the wider inequities of the world. Adolescence is a time of great health and vigour, when people rarely feel the effects of staying up until four in the morning, and yoga or meditation techniques are unnecessary because teenagers are grand masters at the art of chilling out. They know that the whole of life is ahead of them and have a right to feel optimistic. They also know that time is limited before the real responsibilities of adulthood set in. They only have these years in which to let rip, enjoy themselves and explore the boundaries of their tolerance, fears and desires. Adolescence is by its very nature a highly creative time when the body, mind and soul crystallize over a decade in order to form a fully-fledged adult being, and if there is one thing that I hope this book shows it is that we do not consistently view that transition as crucial to healthy adult life.

Adolescents can be difficult to understand. They lack logic or consistency and can be outgoing and compulsive one minute, shy and inhibited the next. They can be maddeningly self-centred and then display astonishing feats of altruism. They can be lazy and rude, and then helpful when you least expect it. Teenagers are neither all good, nor all bad, merely human.

Their cockiness often masks feelings of inadequacy and usually it is the extraordinary, complex and protracted psychological transformation from childhood to adulthood which lies at the root of so many of the difficulties and conundrums of adolescence. In recent years we have been overwhelmed by research and literature which helps adults understand the needs of very small children in order to enable them to be better parents. There are now dozens of activities for parents to choose from to help them occupy, stimulate and educate their children, from indoor soft play to music, drama, art and French classes for the very young. Research is now beginning to tell us that the adolescent years are just as crucial to healthy child development as the early years, but where is the literature, where are those activities and challenges and where is the investment in their welfare that our teenagers need so badly?

The changes that take place in the adolescent mind are just as important and seismic as the changes that take place in the minds of the very young as they learn to talk, read and write. Nursery education and early learning through play are now considered every child's right but we haven't even begun to change the way we teach or challenge adolescents at school to make the most of their capacity to learn and flourish as young adults. Our children now spend more time as adolescents, from the onslaught of puberty at ten to true economic independence in their twenties, than they do as children. The tasks we face as parents in order to raise them successfully have never been greater or more difficult. The more we understand about the way that adolescents think, act and feel about things, the more likely we are to be able to surf the inevitable conflicts, stay friends during the teenage years and keep them alive through the most profound changes in the human lifespan.

2. Emotional Parents

I have had worse partings, but none that so
Gnaws at my mind still. Perhaps it is roughly
Saying what God alone can perfectly show –
How selfhood begins with a walking away,
And love is proved in the letting go.

   C. Day Lewis, 'Walking Away'

As my elder daughter grows taller and more independent, I cling onto the last remnants of childhood in the younger one. I hug her as often as possible to feel those small, soft chubby arms around my neck and the neat way her body still sits in my lap. I watch her little ways, the way she plays, and marvel at her ability to find laughter in the tiniest thing because I now know that in just a few years' time much of that innocence and simplicity will be gone. Our home has been the home of their childhood and the artefacts and souvenirs of those precious years lie all around us: photographs, pottery, pictures and paintings, cards and their toys. I stare at this legacy and try to remember the sound of their voices, their mannerisms, the feel of their bodies in my arms, but much of that is gone, replaced by the urgency of today's needs. When they were small, time seemed to stretch ahead of us with so many years to do all those things we dreamed of. Now there is a sense that there are only a few years left.

All of the parents I met expressed some sense of sadness and frustration at living with adolescent children. For the small number of parents like Rosamund who suffer a complete

breakdown in relations, the sense of anxiety, anger, anguish and loss is acute. Her son has been truanting from school, made friends with someone she considers a bad influence and discovered a passion for smoking dope in his GCSE year. Communication has broken down between them. They no longer eat together and he will not tell her where he is going or when he is coming back. 'The last six months have been simply horrible. I haven't told him that he's made me think of jumping under a train, but I feel anguish, rage, misery, humiliation and, yes, suicidal at times – everything you can think of intensely. This is a dangerous time because not everybody gets through it. Relationships can break down for ever in adolescence and if you don't handle it right, you can lose your child. They've got a perfect right to go.'

Others have more stable and less tormented lives with their children, but the sense of loss, anger and anxiety is still there. All parents tend to feel more anxious about their children's welfare as they lose control and influence over their lives. They also often find that levels of anger and frustration rise as children begin to resist and rebel. There is great loss, too; loss of the child and those unrepeatable times together, loss of power, loss of a sense of place and purpose as a parent and loss of a definitive chapter in our lives as their young adult physiques and ambitions force us to realize how much older we have become. However, I couldn't help but notice that there were differences between those who found these new frictions in family life easier than they imagined they would be and those who found them disabling and oppressive. Parents who were strong enough to take whatever their teenagers hurled at them and not show shock or hurt, those who were able to separate their own emotional needs from those of their children, those who set boundaries within a climate of democratic discussion, and those who understood how vulnerable their children were emotionally and found ways of supporting them, coped much better with their children's adolescence even when there were serious difficulties. Adolescents produce intense, negative feelings in their parents and it is understandable that many withdraw, hurt and wounded by their behaviour. But retreat and emotional distance are not in a teenager's best interests. Somehow parents have to find the strength of mind not to feel insulted or intimidated by adolescent outbursts and find gain buried deep amongst the acute and painful sense of loss.

The first sense of parental loss comes with the physical changes of puberty. Puberty can be profoundly shocking for parents. The small, cute child mutates in front of our eyes into a gangly giant as childish innocence clashes with the onset of adult sexuality, and both inhabit the same body at the same time. Their skin is no longer silky smooth but coarser in parts, the odd spot appears but their flesh still retains that plumpness beneath. They begin to wear adult shoe sizes and the oddest combinations of clothing, and accentuate their sexuality through dress but they still hug teddy bears at night. Socks and armpits begin to smell and baths become crucial for personal hygiene. I notice how my daughter's back is suddenly broader, her hips are widening and her voice is deeper, more responsible and adult in tone. There is no longer a childish whine to her yelling, 'Mum!' When I look at photographs taken just a few months ago, I can see that her face is longer, less chubby. As the budding begins and I begin to get used to the idea that she will one day have breasts, I suddenly notice the first dark signs of pubic hair and stare incredulously at the pudenda I wiped so meticulously when she was a baby and thought I knew so well. She still wanders naked into the bathroom with the lack of self-consciousness that is so precious to childhood. And yet all of the darker signs of adult sexuality lurk ominously there too.

When puberty begins as early as nine or ten, parents feel

the loss more keenly for it seems so premature. Alexandra has three children and her eldest daughter began menstruating at ten. 'She sat huddled in sweatshirts, very embarrassed about her body and wouldn't be seen naked. She wasn't happy about her body from the age of nine because she felt so different to her friends and that was a great shame because it just felt too soon for all that. I felt she deserved a little more time as a true child.'

With puberty, children begin to distance themselves from their parents and seek greater privacy in order to grow into their new selves. They hibernate in their messy rooms with their music, their moods and their heightened solipsism as they change slowly into adults and find the courage to face the world. They push parents away, emerge from their festering rooms only to express their vehement criticism of your attitudes or conduct or their utter contempt, without the tact that comes with maturity, and many parents understandably feel deeply hurt by the rejection. 'I miss hugging him,' says Helen, whose son is fifteen, 'but it's very important that I don't force it upon him. We used to snuggle up on the sofa in front of the TV but now if I hug him he goes all sort of stiff.'

'I do try and put my arms around him,' says Sally, whose son is now nineteen, 'but he doesn't melt into me any more. He doesn't really want it. I think that's one of the hardest things because the closeness that you had with your kids when they were little just gets eaten away.'

When our children are small we notice their physical similarities to us, the way their features and expressions resemble our own, as confirmation of the umbilical bond between us. But with puberty we begin to notice their differences more and more, and how unlike us they look as they grow up. As parents we think we know our children and can usually predict their reactions or attitudes. But with puberty all that begins to change. We feel that we know them less as they become reluctant to divulge information, have external lives they exclude us from and close the door when they are on the telephone to their friends.

'It's interesting realizing how different she is to me. It's all perfume, make-up, nail varnish and shaving her legs and I've never been interested in any of those girlie things but she is. It's like she's a foundling,' says Annie, a single mother with a thirteen-year-old daughter.

Barbara's son is fourteen. 'It's quite hard to see the same person that he was when he was little. He's not jolly any more, he's quite silent and very intense and preoccupied with not doing any school work.'

Jill's son Michael has always resembled his father and now that he is becoming a man she finds it harder to see the boy she once knew. 'I look at him and think, where on earth did he come from? It's quite difficult making the connection between this person and the little baby. But in many ways you don't know them, you don't know what they are thinking, especially boys.'

Caroline realized how separate her sixteen-year-old daughter was, when she drove past her and didn't recognize her. 'The other day I saw this adult standing at a bus stop and then I realized, "Oh my God. That's Anna!" It's very strange seeing them as separate.'

'The worst bit for me was that there was absolutely no communication and I felt that I'd lost him, that was horrible,' says Sally. 'When he was little we were really close but as a teenager he wouldn't tell me anything. If I asked whether he had a girlfriend, he'd say, "If I did you'd be the last to know," which is hurtful because I'd like to know everything. He'd come in slamming doors and criticizing and that's a bit hard to take because we've all got things that can be criticized and you don't really want it rubbed in.'

Adolescents wound us deeply because they are now more

able mentally to strike at our most vulnerable points. When my husband was at a turning point in his career, facing his own mid-life crisis, the words 'Dad, you're such a loser' over the breakfast cereal rendered him speechless and he looked deeply hurt. The only time I have ever felt that I just wanted to run away because I was no longer needed, came after I collected my elder daughter from a weekend away from home with a friend. She was eager to see her father. 'We couldn't manage without him, you'd fall apart without Dad,' she said. I agreed reluctantly but then when I foolishly asked the question as to whether they could do without me, she was adamant that they could, striking a blow at the heart of my need to be needed. She felt stronger and more powerful than ever because she had spent such a good weekend away from home alone. But I sat sobbing in the car in the dark after she rushed in to hug her father, questioning the whole point of my existence in an adolescent sort of way. We give and we give, we love and we love, and when they no longer reward you in the same way with their childish devotion it hurts, physically, for there is nothing that you can do to stop the inexorable process of them pulling away. At the same time, they idolize others, seek out other adult role models, other ways of being, and seemingly reject our own. Somehow we have to find the strength of mind not to feel hurt, insulted, rejected or to blame for whatever they throw at us.

'For a year she was really quite upsetting,' says Mark of his sixteen-year-old daughter. 'We went to Centreparcs for a holiday last Easter and were treated like dirt. She wouldn't sit with us but sat with her friend and there was this general feeling that we were beneath her contempt, and she was very, very rude.'

Christmas, like holidays, can highlight loss for parents because these are times that families traditionally spend together. 'We had this mega-row last Christmas and I sobbed into my pillow and thought, that's it! It's all over,' said Caroline who has two teenage daughters. 'Actually she was right. I'd made some comment about one of her friends and she said that it was none of my business and she was right. But it felt so significant to me because it was Christmas and she hadn't wanted to be involved with any of the Christmassy things. She stayed in her room while we put up the tree and decorated it, whereas in previous years we'd have done it together.'

Rosamund's son is an only child, so she feels the loss that much more keenly. 'We read together a lot until he was nine, we swam together and we had a lot of good country holidays together and all of that's completely gone. He used to say that he loved me until about a year ago. I've cried a lot every single day for the last six months. He has been unbelievably foul and abusive, really horrible, saying anything and everything that you can imagine, and you keep saying to yourself that this is a horrible patch and we'll get through it but at the time it's pretty ghastly.'

Teenagers often hurt parents badly through their aggressive criticism and rejection, but they rarely mean to be quite so offensive. They need to stop idealizing their parents as they grow up in order to develop their own distinct identity. They are also only just beginning to develop the capacity to think about the effect of their behaviour on others and to see life from other people's perspective (as we shall see in Chapter 4) and rarely have the linguistic tact that comes with maturity. Parents have to find the strength of mind not to take this rejection or criticism personally. We also have to remember that as parents we have played a crucial part in nurturing their manners and attitudes towards others. Children who from an early age have been indulged or rarely reminded of the need to consider other people are likely to find it that much harder to consider them once the shutters of teenage narcissism and solipsism fall. 'As small children we encourage them to go out and find experiences for themselves and not to think of others except in terms of "Be kind" or "Don't hit me",' says Jeannie Milligan, psychotherapist at the Adolescent Department of the Tavistock Centre. 'It's not on, then, for parents only to think about how hurt they are by their behaviour or not considered once they become teenagers. You can't suddenly expect them to behave very differently as adolescents.'

It's very easy to love small children and be seduced by their charm. But as they grow into great, galumphing, opinionated, noisy and selfish adolescents parents easily find that there is much more to dislike – the lethargy, the mess, the way they raid the fridge when you've just struggled round the supermarket for the third time that week, their inability to focus or assume greater responsibility without a fight and the way that they bore on about their latest obsessions and expect you not only to listen intensely, but exude excitement. They impose their needs on every other member of the family. When they are unhappy, nobody is allowed to forget it. An entire Saturday can be ruined when a girl feels she has nothing to wear for a party. She may stomp around the house for hours in deep despair, pulling out the contents of her mother's wardrobe as well as her own, and then accuses her of being mean when she won't give her any money to buy something new. The peace and quiet of every other family member has to be sacrificed to her needs. Yours no longer matter and any gentle suggestion that she could adapt something in her existing wardrobe, or that she might be kind enough to put all of the clothes lying in a heap on the floor back into the cupboard is likely to be met with vitriol and rejection. 'I hate you, why are you so horrible to me?' You can see from the fiery anger in her eyes that she really means it and – you know what? – you hate her too for ruining everybody else's day, for being so unreasonable and selfish. It's a deep and very real hate, an emotion that mothers are not supposed to feel.

Alison Lurie describes this common but rather unnerving feeling in her novel *The War Between the Tates*:

In her whole life she cannot remember disliking anyone as much as she now dislikes Jeffrey and Matilda. In second grade she had briefly hated a bulky girl named Rita who ate rolls of pastel candy wafers and bullied her: in college freshman year a boy with a snuffle and yellowed nylon shirts who followed her around everywhere asking her to go out with him. She had, in the abstract, hated Hitler, Joseph McCarthy, Lee Harvey Oswald etc., but never anyone she had to live with and should have loved – had for years warmly loved.

Gita finds it similarly wearing appreciating her sixteen-year-old twins at times. 'Trying to be nice to your children when they're not very likeable – that's the hardest bit, because they're not people that you want to be around.'

'All of the usual things irritate me. Being calculating, never working, moaning about having to do things, saying she'll do something and she doesn't, the fact that you go into her room to ask for washing and she gives you all of last week's clean washing that has been sitting on the floor and got creased. We do get on but that's today. There are times when I have very, very strong feelings of loathing because she is so self-centred,' says Caroline, whose elder daughter is sixteen.

'The worst thing is the sheer self-preoccupation and selfishness, and I hear myself saying the same things as my mother,' says Annie. 'I ask her hundreds of times to do the simplest things and I've just cottoned on to the fact that she doesn't hear me because of her own self-absorption. There's this feeling that she has a right to things. She looks at me sometimes as if I were something dirty under her foot, the looks are worse than all the rowing. The expression on her face just says, "Crawl under a stone and die, you scum," and that hurts deeply.'

'It's normal to be at boiling point,' says Helen, who runs the Manchester branch of Parent Network, an organization which runs parenting courses and group counselling. 'Often parents come to us saying, "I had no idea that I'd feel this negative about my children. I hate them at times." These feelings can be very frightening and they accelerate as the child gets older and more able to fight back.'

Annie feels that things have settled down now but for about a year, when her daughter was twelve and thirteen, 'We'd have rows for week after week where she wouldn't speak to me over really daft things, it wouldn't matter what it was, it was as if she was feeding off the conflict. On two occasions she left the house after dark and I felt like murdering her, in fact once I threw a chair at her. I was in such a state wondering where she was. I subsequently discovered that she'd gone round to the chip shop and was sitting on the doorstep eating chips until she felt ready to come back in. It's a deeply passionate anger, I feel challenged to the very core of me, but when we get through these rows things are much better. It's so intolerable sometimes living with that strop that I push it to the limit just to burst the bubble, it makes me tired just talking about it!'

When children present more serious difficulties through adolescence and parents feel unable to cope with them, parental anger can erupt so frequently that it becomes self-defeating. Rosamund told her son at one point that she was not prepared to give him any money for the summer unless he was prepared to be civil. 'He said he could make more money dealing drugs than I could ever give him, at which point I just wanted to hit him.'

Antonia became guardian to her nieces when her sister died of cancer. When the eldest hit adolescence she became argumentative and promiscuous, began to take money and alcohol, failed most of her GCSEs and continually lied about her whereabouts. When Antonia challenged her over the lying, her niece packed her bag and ran away to stay with a friend, and relations deteriorated to an all-time low. 'I used to lie in bed tossing and turning through anger, anger at her. I'd done so much for her and she'd just thrown it all back in my face and said, "Fuck you, I'm going to do my own thing." I run quite a tight ship here but I can't stand lying. I'd always lose my temper and she'd burst into tears. It was all, "Me, me me. I've been through a bad patch," and never anything else. Never, "How are you?" And then when she wanted to speak to her younger sister on the phone I developed this neurosis that she would poison her into leaving as well. Of course that wouldn't happen but the anger and frustration within me was so intense that it made me think of stupid things.'

Karen has two teenage children and a son who is now in his twenties. 'I remember we had trouble with both the boys when they turned sixteen. With the eldest one it was probably lucky that I was driving the car at one point because if I hadn't I would probably have gone for him. He was pushing the boundaries and I wasn't bending.' Karen and her husband had always said that their children had to come away with them until they were sixteen, after that they could do what they liked. They were on their way to their static caravan on the Norfolk coast for the weekend. Her son wanted to stay at home. It was the weekend before his sixteenth birthday. 'It was bang, bang, bang, "You're ruining my life! You don't understand!" The knuckles on my hand were going white round the steering wheel as I yelled back. I was so angry and it was difficult because I wanted the other two in the back to know that I wasn't about to be pushed over the edge, and hurtful too for him to think that I had no thoughts at all for his feelings.'

The issues that trigger hostility become more complicated, important and adult. Gita's sixteen-year-old son is bright and highly capable but he is idle at times, relying on friends and his twin sister to 'hook him up' to earning opportunities. 'Yet another job had come up and he had asked a friend for the number but he's been reluctant to give it. I said, "Acknowledge his power. If you go and do something yourself it puts you in a better position." He was in such a strop, his whole attitude just completely narked me, I wanted to strangle him. I shouted, "Why are you always waiting for other people to do things for you when you can do them for yourself?" He replied, "Because it's easier," and I screamed back, "BUT SOME THINGS AREN'T EASY!" I could have burst a blood vessel, I just wasn't getting through.'

Often the resentments that parents first experienced through the constraints of the early days of family life resurface with adolescent children. The frustration parents feel when they cannot coax a recalcitrant toddler into a coat or a buggy becomes even more intense when you cannot physically persuade a child who is bigger than you to do something. That ghastly sense of feeling trapped at home resurfaces as parents sense that they need to be there far more to detect difficulties. Some feel this sense of being trapped has an extra loneliness to it because the adolescent doesn't actually want them around.

'Sometimes I feel as if I'm completely chained to the house and left alone with these walruses,' says Jill, who has three sons, the eldest of whom is fourteen. 'They don't even want me to be here except that if I'm not here nothing gets done because I have to nag them about their homework or get a meal for them or chaperone them, so they're in that in-between stage. It's what I call sentry duty. You've gotta be there marching around the house like an automatic soldier saying, "Do your homework/piano practice/get in or out of the bath/turn the television/computer off/come and have supper/put your plate in the dishwasher." It drives me completely round the bend but if I didn't do it there would be complete and utter chaos.'

Like many exasperated parents, Jill has in some ways

imprisoned herself in this role. Early adolescents need to be encouraged to manage their own time and learn from their own mistakes. Too many commands communicate the message that you don't trust that the adolescents are capable of doing it for themselves, and tend to foster resentment rather than motivation. If they fail to do homework on time or regular music practice, that should be picked up by their teachers rather than parents. They need more subtle reminders with consequences attached rather than orders, which are never really appropriate for a child of any age, since children and adolescents need to be talked to with the same civilities and respect that adults afford other adults. Autonomy has to be granted gradually from childhood, with a steady easing out of the reins when parents feel their children are ready to be trusted with greater responsibility for their own welfare. Plans for evenings and weekends need to be laid out so that there can be a discussion as to what homework, instrument practice or chores have to be done and when they are going to be fitted in around television programming and meals. And, just like toddlers, teenagers can push their parents to extreme levels of frustration and anger, but as with toddlers it is often far, far better to walk away when they are driving you mad than to risk making the situation even more volatile by trying to maintain authority over something which probably doesn't matter that much at that moment anyway.

There are some surprising parallels between the behaviour of toddlers and that of adolescents. Toddlers try the patience of even the most saintly parents, and teenagers can be just as wearing because they are going through an equally seismic life stage. The toddler struggles away from babyhood and complete dependency with his first steps. Frustration and rage often characterize his attempts to explore his own immediate environment alone in order to learn from it, and it is parents who inevitably bear the brunt of that. The adolescent begins the slow process of walking away from childhood into the wider world beyond in order to learn more. Both stages provoke tantrums and fights as children discover where their new boundaries lie, and produce ambivalent emotions in parents as well as their children. Both toddlers and teenagers regress at times when they find growing up too difficult, and both need the extra security that comes from loving parents so that they are able to experiment and make mistakes without losing love.

Teenagers fight and lash out angrily in order to test those new boundaries. Arguments flare up out of nowhere when parents try to encourage responsible behaviour because teenagers find it hard to see this as anything other than nagging or blatant infringements of their new sense of autonomy. They are also grand masters at the art of heaving the responsibility back onto their parents. They now see their parents' weaknesses more clearly and can therefore wound more effectively when it comes to attack. When you forbid something, they are likely to hit back with, 'You just want to keep me young because you're too old to have another baby.' Barbara has two sons, aged fourteen and twelve: 'It drives me insane to be told, "Fuck off," because it seems so unprovoked and completely irrational. He does things like wanting me to give him a sick note for swimming when he's not sick so I won't do it. He actually manages to make me feel guilty about not lying for him and then he tells me to "Fuck off".'

Teenagers hurl insults and throw their new-found weight around to make contact with their parents, not to sever links with them entirely. They need to be able to explore what they really think and feel about things within the safety of the family at the same time as asserting their emerging individuality. They fight and throw tantrums because they cannot deal with the new spectrum of intense and often stressful emotions which surface during adolescence. Through their awkward behaviour they struggle to keep parents close as well as push them away, and this 'push–pull' dynamic is integral to the process of growing up.

Comparing toddlers and adolescents Jill says, 'There are lots of things that are very similar, like "I want to do it myself!" But often they don't have the knowledge or the emotional maturity to do whatever it is that they want to do. Then when they do it, they don't like it or they get frightened or they feel they're out of their depth and they want parents to come and rescue them. It's a bit like a toddler who climbs to the top of a climbing frame and then gets scared and can't come down. My son will say, "Mum, I'm stuck with my homework," so I'll go to his room to help and then he'll say, "I've done it now." When I go away, he'll say, "Don't go away." On the one hand he wants support and on the other he doesn't. If you tell them to do their homework then you're in trouble but if you don't tell them to do their homework then it's your fault when they get into trouble for not doing it. Whatever you do gets twisted round and used against you. I found toddlerhood pretty wearing and this is similar.'

As we grow older, as our bodies sag and the aches and pains of middle age take hold it would be inhuman not to feel a little envy. To a grown-up, teenage bodies and futures are taut with health and sexual promise. Life stretches ahead of them like a blank sheet of paper, while ours are full of mistakes and wrong turnings as well as all those dreams which we now realize may never be achieved. As people delay having children until their thirties, adolescence increasingly dovetails with parents' menopause or mid-life crises. While most parents avoid a full-blown psychological crisis at this time, the majority do indulge in greater introspection and self-assessment during their forties, questioning their choice of careers or relationship.

'I'm aware of how envious I am of her,' says Annie whose

daughter is thirteen. 'There's this blooming, sexy girl and I'm in the middle of the menopause with a severe crisis of confidence, and how dare she sit there looking so good with it!'

'I found the boyfriend issue difficult because it makes you extremely nostalgic,' says Joan, who has three daughters aged seventeen, fifteen and twelve. 'I feel very nostalgic for my youth, for all that excitement and the newness of it all. It brings up a lot of stuff for you, your chance has gone unless you're gonna go out and have four affairs. I wouldn't want to be that age again but I do think they're so lucky, being out and about.'

Envy is, inevitably, integral to a great deal of parental hostility to teenagers. It can be hard to view teenage emotional needs as distinct from our own emotional milestones, and all too often parents misinterpret or underestimate the importance of teenage angst as a result. It is easy for parents to view their children's lives as fortunate. While all of these new intense emotions of anger, envy and even hatred may seem disturbing to parents who have always felt such undiluted and intense love for their children, in many ways they serve a useful purpose, for we relinquish crucial aspects of control over our children when we are angry, and afford them greater autonomy. When we loathe them we walk away and give them greater space. When we find ourselves exasperated and tired of having done all their washing for the past fifteen years we find it easier to insist that they do it for themselves from now on. When we are angry there is less room for anxiety or worry about their welfare, for at that moment of extreme hostility it is hard to care and it is easier to let them go.

Joan's eldest daughter has been out a lot socializing with friends for the past year and is now busy making plans to leave home for university. 'I found last year that when she was out a lot, I didn't really like her. She was really getting on my nerves even though she really wasn't doing anything awful and

I knew that she had to do it. Last year when she was doing her GCSEs and I was putting out the milk bottles, she followed me out and I thought, would you get out of my face? It's not surprising that you feel that way – it's so that when they go away you don't miss them as much.'

Hostility and envy can be disturbing and ugly new emotions for parents when complete love and generosity is what is expected. Anxiety is, however, recognizable, although the intensity of these anxieties can reach unbearable heights when children begin to move away from our protective eye and we imagine them jaywalking across dual carriageways and consuming more alcohol and drugs than nutrients. There is a great deal more sleep to be lost over teenagers than there is over small children. Worries about whether they were still breathing in the middle of the night as new-born babies are mild compared to the prolonged and paralysing fear parents feel when they sit up for hours at night because their children have failed to come home and they have no idea where they are. 'There's a whole new set of anxieties now,' says Andrea. Her eldest son of three is now thirteen. 'I'm worried about him going on a school ski trip and getting alcohol poisoning, or the coach crashing on the way.'

It is utterly normal for parents to be anxious about their children's welfare. We worry because we care, because we are programmed to tend to their needs, and because children are vulnerable, immature and innocent of life's dangers. However, anxiety levels among many middle-class parents have soared well out of proportion, making the inexorable separations of adolescence harder perhaps for both parent and child. We perceive the modern world to be so much more dangerous, so we keep them under constant surveillance, discouraging the spirit of adventure in case they should come to any harm, often compromising their self-confidence and their ability to develop sound judgements as a result.

The modern social ethos which controls children's environment and monitors their every waking moment may seem sound and manageable when our children are small, but with adolescence children have to learn how to take care of themselves more and more. They need to be able to distinguish between high and low risk, they have to fend more for themselves and find ways of coping with their own rising levels of fear and anxiety as they negotiate the wider world alone. These are skills which children ought to be developing in middle childhood. Learning to deal emotionally and practically with life's dangers is essential if young people are to cope with the real world away from the safety of the family. Children have to be allowed to fail, to face risk, even danger at times, in order to recognize the emotions triggered by those events, find ways of coping with them and develop their own sense of judgement.

When young children lack opportunities to develop their own internal controls through experimentation and adventure, because they have always been organized, supervised and driven everywhere, the dangers inherent to adolescence may be less easy to navigate. Parents cannot stop teenagers from drinking too much or taking drugs; they have to learn their limits for themselves. 'Taking risks is part of growing up and doing things that you've never done before, and so may be creative,' says Jeannie Milligan, psychotherapist in the Adolescent Department of the Tavistock Centre. 'But you also need to develop a sense of when pushing those boundaries stops being creative and becomes disturbing or self-destructive. You need to develop the confidence to know that you don't have to go along with a whole range of things on offer where you have to trust your own instinct: from whether to go out with a boy to resisting heroin. If you are used to having everything done for you, how do you leave home, cross the road alone or cope with the painful fact that a friend has let you down or betrayed you?'

'It's harder for overprotected teenagers,' says psychotherapist Asha Phillips, 'partly because they feel that their parents know and control everything and partly because they actually need them more. If you've been protected all of the time you don't want to lose that sense of safety through conflict or rebellion.' Overprotected teenagers are also likely to be far more secretive about their activities and find it harder to confide in or seek guidance from parents in case openness provokes upset, misunderstandings or rejection. Children who have been allowed out alone from a reasonable age or who have travelled regularly on public transport learn how to navigate the world as they find it. Children who have learned how to cope with and survive failure from small and harmless mistakes find similar emotions easier to deal with during adolescence. Resilience develops in children when they are allowed to cope successfully with small risks, not when they avoid them entirely. The children who have never been allowed to walk along a wall in case they should fall off, or to swing dangerously high in the playground, have never tested the extremes of their physical or emotional beings. How then are they able to develop the judgement necessary as to their own limits when the risk stakes increase with adolescence? And if we as parents have little experience of trusting that our children will survive without accident, how much harder it then becomes when they venture out alone as teenagers.

The acute anxiety I felt when my eldest started secondary school was for all the obvious reasons – would she like it/make friends/find her way around and manage the new workload and expectations? But my main concern was not over what happened within those locked gates. It was the fact that she had to take two buses through central London and King's Cross on her own with just a few practice run-throughs with an adult beforehand. She loved the challenge and quickly made friends with others using the same bus route, but I was left with a resounding sense of anxiety. It felt as if she was out there drifting between two safe posts as she travelled between home and school, with little experience of travelling alone through London. I would have no sure way of knowing that she had got to school that morning until she came home again that night. How much easier that transition would have been if she had had more experience of travelling alone. If we seek to control so many aspects of our children's lives, the inevitable loss of control integral to the separation of adolescence merely exacerbates our anxieties about their welfare. We cannot watch over them every minute of the day and are left only with our imaginations, fuelled by the latest horror stories in the news.

As our children grow older and more sophisticated, our anxieties become more general and entrenched. We have the power as parents to kiss most things better when our children are small. But the problems our teenagers face are not so easily solved. You cannot lift a daughter out of a depression with an ice cream. We can find playmates for the young child who does not have any friends but the adolescent has to make his or her own friendships. The young child who finds aspects of school life or the curriculum difficult can be helped at home or use his parents as a go-between, but that is harder for parents of older children because the adolescent expects and is expected to motivate himself. Life gets more complicated and less easily appeased and that can leave parents feeling disabled, and impotent, disconnected from the role that they have played for so long. We long to prevent them from making the same mistakes that we made, but those warnings fall on deaf ears. They have to learn for themselves.

'There are things that I feel general vague anxiety about,

like the job and employment situation because it's just so difficult nowadays and that has made schools so much more competitive. There is enormous anxiety about what GCSE grades you get,' says Jill. Her son has not done very well in his end of year exams and she worries that he will not put in the work required to get through his GCSEs.

Rosamund's anxiety about her son's future is that much more acute because he has just sat his GCSEs and she feels his future will be limited by few passes. He says he wants to go to agricultural college and does not want to sit A levels, but Rosamund does not trust him to know his own mind. 'What happens at the end of week one when he phones up and says that he doesn't like it?' She finds it hard to trust him generally, which is a source of great anxiety, and, 'At his very worst I've looked at him and thought, you could get seriously on the wrong side of things and become so anti-authoritarian you could become a criminal. I have had fantasies of him going to prison.' She worries about where he is and whether he's safe because he never tells her where he is going or when he is coming back, and underpinning all this acute and nerve-wracking worry is one central concern: their relationship has deteriorated to such an extent that he might leave home on bad terms and then she wouldn't know where he was at all. 'After a really bad time with him I have tremendous fantasies of him coming home to a bolted door, a suitcase on the doorstep, his cannabis plants in a black plastic bag and the name and address of a social worker. That's what I feel at my absolute lowest but I'd never do it. I have a lot of support, but I can see why people kick sixteen-year-olds out and why they end up on the streets. That's why we have this whole crisis of youth, masculinity and crime. I can see the whole thing. I think if I'd been completely unsupported with a boy as difficult as this, I'm quite sure I'd have kicked him out and then what do you do? It would be complete torment not knowing where he is.

Or I could come back and find that he's gone. I don't know how people survive that.'

Living with common adolescent scrapes and difficulties can make parents deeply anxious because they feel so helpless and unable to support their children or effect change. Mark and Sharon were worried at one point that their daughter might be developing anorexia. 'She was extremely fashion conscious and very thin. She would eat tiny amounts and at weekends she would make a point of being out at meals. We knew we shouldn't talk about it but after years of being a mum you can't help it, so I'd buy little snacks she liked and left them on the stairs. For about a year it was a real worry.'

Karen's second son was badly beaten up one night when he was fourteen and eighteen months later he was held up at knifepoint at 7 p.m. walking to a friend's house to do some homework. 'It affected him badly, made him much more introverted, insular and aggressive actually because he's angry. There wasn't much we could do for him except drive him around more which was a bit wearing. I'm terribly protective of all three of my kids, and letting go of them is very difficult, but this has definitely made us more protective of our youngest child, particularly as she's a girl.'

Studies have found that parents of adolescents are much more likely to feel less adequate and more anxious about the way they parent than those with younger children. They can look back over a decade of their child's life and pinpoint factors which may have destabilized him or her such as divorce, changing schools, or being bullied. They begin to see cracks in the foundations of their parenting and feel that it is too late to put them right. Often this happens in early adolescence, when children first challenge their parents' authority. Barbara's son started refusing to do his homework and got excluded from school when he was fourteen. 'Suddenly it all felt very different, as if everything was on a knife-edge and about to explode. It's the most difficult bit about being a parent because it makes you feel rather inadequate as a person. You feel that you ought to be able to deal with it. It throws everything into relief which is very scary. All your faults, the faults in your marriage magnify because you feel that they must be to blame for your adolescent's problems, when perhaps they're not.'

Elizabeth, an unemployed single mother of two daughters, looks back and realizes that in trying to give her daughters everything and denying her own ambitions she has been too liberal. Both daughters have been heavily involved in drugs, flunked school and indulged in unsatisfactory precocious sex. 'There was very little discipline in my house. Looking back I know that was a mistake. I did not know how to stand up for myself nor how to set limits and boundaries without feeling like a tyrant. I was not going to repeat the inconsistent and petty rules forced on me as a child. Why didn't somebody tell me that as a woman, mothering girls, it is not what you give them or do for them that counts in the long run? It is who you are and how you feel about yourself that matters. You are their main role model.'

Laila is a Somalian single mother with two children, who came to Britain in 1986. Her elder daughter is seventeen and has not been attending college. She spends long periods of time alone in her room and comes down at two or three in the morning to eat by herself. Laila tries to talk to her daughter but doesn't know how to reach her. 'She left the house once for two weeks and I didn't know where she was. I cried all day long. She is so confused, even with clothes she is confused. All her savings went on a jacket that cost £130 but she said that if she didn't have that jacket she would die. She wore it once and then said she didn't like it. When you're seventeen and that confused something is wrong, but I don't know how to help her. I'm there, waiting for her to tell me her problems but she doesn't come. Sometimes I think that this is all because she doesn't have a father.'

Rosamund attributes some of her son's problems to the fact that his workaholic father has not been around enough. 'One of the things that I've thought over and over again is that you cannot lay strong enough foundations because it gives you some kind of hope that they will return to them. But if you didn't, you see the cracks and think, that's why. Lots of times I feel as if I've handled it quite appallingly, but then I guess everybody does. What is the right way? You're feeling your way, particularly with an only child. I had a mother who made me feel fantastic all my life and somehow I haven't quite succeeded in the same way with Karl. I can be quite sharp and sometimes I look back and think, you've been too confrontational, you have been too negative, you haven't made him feel good about himself. He's been told endlessly that he's good-looking and funny and clever, but he has also had a lot of negativity from me at different times when I've basically been exasperated by his behaviour. It's better now that I'm learning to bite my tongue.'

Gillian knew that her eldest daughter was showing signs of anorexia months before she was prepared to admit it. People would comment on how thin she was. 'I didn't know how it had all gone wrong, whether it was just dieting gone wrong or whether our family was totally dysfunctional without my knowing it. I thought I must have overfed her, or I must have been too focused on food. Why else would she want to react in this way? She knew it was deeply hurtful because I've always been the provider, the feeder. Am I such an overwhelming Jewish mother with food left right and centre? Then I thought, no, I'm not. It did worry me and made me doubt my wisdom as a mother. The crunch of those apples used to drive me wild! She'd eat about eleven a day and I could see this body crying out for bread or some pulses and there she was with another apple.'

When parents can identify tangible sources of their child's difficulties, such as divorce or adoption, or the fact that both parents worked long hours during childhood and simply weren't there enough to set the ground rules, feelings of inadequacy mushroom into guilt. 'Most parents will say that the hardest stage of being a parent is adolescence. But separating parents have even more trouble,' says Nicky, a Relate counsellor. 'There's this burning worry of, "How can I reach them and not lose them completely?" as the family begins to fall apart.' In a moving collection of writings, *A Stranger at my Table*, several single mothers lament the absence of a father in their child's upbringing. 'I chose to be alone,' writes Diana Mason. 'I closed the two-parent door for them and denied them a choice. Their anger is real, born of incomprehension and frustration and mine is compounded by guilt.'

Sarah adopted her second child when she was nine weeks old. She is now twenty-four and dying of multiple sclerosis. During her teenage years she rebelled badly, began taking drugs and self-mutilating. 'She was a very angry young lady with a lot to be angry about. I wish we'd known more at the time of the adoption about the way that sense of loss and abandonment might resurface during her adolescence because it just wasn't talked about. The thinking was that if you give them enough nurturing it'll work out. But no matter how much you do, you cannot undo that message that I'm not wanted, I'm not good enough. Had we been more aware of how that might manifest itself we would have got her involved with others who were also adopted so that she could talk things through.'

When parents experience this cocktail of intense emotions provoked by their child's adolescence they can find it hard to cope. Often they feel unable to discuss their difficulties with other parents, for the casual network of parents, where advice and anecdote can be freely swapped in relative confidence, tends to evaporate as children go to secondary school and no longer need picking up. They also begin to feel they shouldn't discuss their children's difficulties because it feels somehow like an act of betrayal now that they are old enough to understand. 'I couldn't even admit to my closest friend and neighbour that we were going through such difficulties because I was aware that others would be deeply critical,' says Sarah. 'I didn't want us to be deemed as having failed as parents and I didn't want my daughter criticized at such a sensitive time.'

Without help, many parents have nothing much to go on when it comes to dealing with teenagers other than their own experience of being a teenager. 'It was just different then,' says Ian. 'I would never have turned around and used a rude word ever! Never! I know I was sulky and slammed doors but it was more like dumb insolence, not screaming matches and using the worst words that you can think of.' Often one's own parents are still around to remind one of the fact that they handled adolescence with greater aplomb and that books aren't necessarily any help. Rosamund felt deeply the loss of the family sense of home when her only son refused to be there for meals. She found a light handbook on adolescence reassuring in that she felt 'part of the swim. But then you read things like, "Of course, it's unacceptable for him to come home late for the family meal," and you think, excuse me, what family meal is this? We don't have family meals any more, it's all broken down.'

'When I was going through it, I didn't know anyone with children the same age.' Karen has three children, the eldest of whom is now twenty. 'I could talk about my feelings with those who were really close to me but there was no one there to say, "There is light at the end of the tunnel."'

But there is light even though the tunnel may seem inordinately long at the time, for adolescence is a phase of child development just like all the others. Just when you begin to think you can't stand the sight of another nappy, they begin to potty train. The emotions of early parenthood can be intensely disturbing, but they stabilize eventually as both parent and child get used to life as it now is. The emotions triggered by living with an adolescent can be even more distressing but they do settle down as children mature and parents learn how to trust them. However, because of their intensity, those parental feelings do need to be contained and controlled far more than they ever were when the children were younger to avoid unnecessary confrontation, for adolescents can be equally emotionally volatile.

There are subtle and effective ways of managing the emotional vortex for parents of adolescents. As our children grow older, we have to learn gradually how to distinguish and separate our own emotions from theirs in order not to damage their development. Anger in adults has a powerful impact on children and can make them highly distressed and more aggressive. Teenage behaviour can provoke unparalleled levels of anger in parents, but nine times out of ten it is better to walk away and cool down rather than to express it at the time. When we get angry we become irrational, are more likely to alienate our children and are therefore less able to deal with the situation effectively. Teenagers tend to focus on the fact that they are not liked at that moment so parental hostility merely confirms all their own feelings of worthlessness. They are also far less likely to hear what you are saying and amend their behaviour or attitudes, which they might if the matter was discussed calmly and more thoroughly after the event. We can be much more adept at wounding because we have greater intellectual capacities at our command, but the danger is that the mildest criticism can be perceived as hostile by a sensitive teenager. They may swear, rant and rave, but that is because they are still children struggling with a whole range of new pressures and intense emotions, as we shall see in the next chapter.

'It's perfectly all right to be angry if it's done in a constructive way, by saying what you need as a parent. Teenagers like to be consulted in that way,' says Philippa, a single mother with two sons aged eighteen and sixteen. 'My mother was physically abusive and I was scared to have kids in case that should come out in me. It did come out and I had to deal with it and move on. A lot of that anger I now know comes from being tired and having too much on my plate so I try to be kinder to myself and we have found different ways of coping. We talk about things a lot more, I get away from them when I need to and send them away sometimes to avoid confrontations. Horsing around also helps get rid of some of that frustration.'

It also helps to remember that parents are supposed to be the mature ones; they're still kids. 'Looking back now I wish that I'd backed off more in confrontations where I've pushed things,' says Mark, father of sixteen-year-old Karen and a son aged thirteen. 'Pride comes into it, I suppose, false pride or a determination to win which means that arguments come up which needn't have.'

The increased anxiety that comes from being the parent to an adolescent can also be eased through a conscious separation of one's own emotional needs from theirs. Helen is a single mother living in Manchester with a fifteen-year-old son. 'I remember when he went to his first concert at the age of fourteen, I sat on the edge of my chair all night. I knew it was ridiculous. I know what goes on at concerts but I still couldn't control my anxiety. But it's my anxiety, not his, and he's clear now about the fact that I need him back at a particular time to suit my needs. A lot of the time I have to sit on my emotions so that he's not constrained by them. I'm also more accepting now of his other emotions when they are different to what I think they should be.' Her son is at a very tough school in Moss-side with an undercurrent of gangland violence where a boy accidentally shot himself recently. The whole school was traumatized about this and special assemblies were held, but Helen's son just felt, good riddance: 'He was an evil bastard and I wish he'd shot a few of his friends as well.' 'Previously I would have tried to put the alternative view, that the boy was severely disadvantaged, but all I could say was that I could understand why he felt that way. It's important to let them have that separateness.'

Constant rescuing from parents undermines a teenager's sense of self-esteem, and in order to avoid rescuing we have to learn how to relinquish pointless areas of worry. 'If they got back late I used to imagine paedophiles running them over and *then* abusing them,' jokes Judith who has a sixteen-year-old daughter and a thirteen-year-old son. 'But then with my son I had to consciously decide not to worry – he's as big as me now, he's at senior school, he goes everywhere on his bicycle, he's good at getting back on time – and I just don't have that ferocious worry any more. It's like a letting go, and the parents who don't do that really worry me – they say they love them so much but love is letting them go. I love them as much and as passionately. It's not an emotional withdrawal because you would still die for them, it's more of a drawing back of emotion and involvement, a feeling of "sort yourself out" a couple of steps removed, not in a cold way but in a recognition that they are going to move on.'

'Basically I've learned to let go and in letting go I actually keep them closer,' says Karen who has three children aged twenty, eighteen and fifteen. 'I trust them and give them that respect and consequently I get trust and respect back.'

By sitting on our own emotions, separating out our own anxiety from their needs, we give them space to breathe and explore aspects of the adult world they are so keen to join. If we are more considered and less emotional in our responses we communicate valuable messages about our respect for them as growing individuals and we also force them to take more responsibility for their actions. 'It's physically liberating as well,' says Andrea. Her eldest son of three is thirteen. 'He broke a glass recently and I just said, "Can you clear it up, please?" When he was younger I'd have rushed there and said, "Don't touch it, you might cut yourself! I'll do it."' We may feel desperately anxious about their welfare, but by slowly letting go, we let them know that they have control over certain areas of their lives and know best. After just two weeks at my daughter's new school, road works and severe traffic congestion made her very late one morning. She took her own executive decision. She got off the stationary bus, walked down to King's Cross and got on another bus. 'If I'd had a mobile,' she said, always keen to push her need for one (I'm resisting for as long as possible, anxious about the health risks), 'I'd have been able to ring you and ask what to do.' But because she couldn't ask me she had to work it out for herself. She had made a good decision and now felt more confident about her own ability to travel alone. Without that mobile I was also blissfully ignorant of her plight.

When parents worry excessively about the dangers their adolescent children face in the wider world, it is worthwhile remembering that the statistics do not necessarily back up their fears. There is a great difference between the experimentation with danger that is crucial to healthy adolescent behaviour and the use of drink or drugs as an emotional prop. Drugs are rarely a problem for happy children and, in spite of the ubiquitous presence of hard drugs as well as their low cost, rates of use have barely risen since the 1960s. The Leah Betts of this world are, mercifully, extremely rare. It is the use of drugs sanctioned by some adults, such as alcohol and cannabis, that have mushroomed, enabling young people to feel more grown-up as well as have a good time. What young people want and need is greater discussion and honest information about drugs so that they understand the true risks, know what to do if they are with someone who has drunk too much, and do not feel inhibited to ask for help should they get into difficulties themselves. 'One of the hardest things is trusting that the way I see things is really the way it is,' says Philippa, who has two sons. 'Some parents say that everyone is taking drugs. It is going on but I don't think they do it, but if you just focus on that element in their lives you miss everything else. There may be lots of teenagers taking drugs but there are also lots that aren't. You have to realize that these are your worries and that maybe they are sussing things out better than you give them credit for. Kids are putting their own morals together and they don't do that in a vacuum.'

The seeds of adolescence are sown years before the arrival of breasts and a torso. All of the advice, guidance and preparation necessary for healthy adolescent development has to be inculcated well before teenage narcissism and false bravado take hold. When parents have laid reasonably solid emotional foundations in early childhood, their children are far less likely to go seriously off the rails as adolescents because they have a secure base at home from which to separate through the transition. When children have grown up with positive experiences of intimacy, they are more able as adolescents to form intimate and solid relationships with friends and potential lovers. When children feel loved and valued, they are more likely to value themselves, take care of themselves and develop the capacity to endure frustrations more easily during adolescence without becoming demoralized. 'I worry about drugs, of course I do,' says Clara, a psychologist with three children, two of whom are teenage. 'But I think you've put it all in by now to some extent. You can't do anything more than say, "I'm going to accompany you everywhere you go." It's almost as if you've done your bit and you just hope that they'll have enough inside them to see them through all the temptations.'

By learning how to ease off unnecessary control from an

early age, we learn how to trust our children. That withdrawal may develop naturally. Many working mothers haven't the time to be as involved with every aspect of their children's lives as those who stay at home. They encourage their children to get themselves something to eat when they get home from school and insist that they do their own cleaning and washing because there is no one else to do it for them. Often it is the children themselves who ask for greater freedom when they feel that they are ready for it. When children are allowed out alone locally within specific boundaries, from the age of nine or ten, say to the local newsagent, library or bookshop, with a set time to return, they will learn valuable coping skills about being out alone within a neighbourhood they know. Parents also communicate the valuable message that they trust their children and get more used to the idea of them being out and about on their own.

Often the increased anxieties and anger aroused by living with adolescents force parents to set new ground rules which help both parents and teenagers understand where their new boundaries lie. 'We needed some serious new ground rules,' says Philippa. 'I wasn't going to worry about them when they were out and I needed to know where they were. We worked these things out together and there was a lot of angst over it but they understood that I couldn't fret about it. I've been quite tough because I couldn't stand the worry.'

Gillian learned eventually that the best way to appease her own anxiety was to set some ground rules and is now calmly realistic, resigned almost to the inevitability of her girls, aged eighteen and sixteen, going out away from her watchful eye. 'I made lots of mistakes in the early days. Several times I waited up for them. I'd assume that they'd be back by four because I couldn't believe that anybody would want to be out later than that and then I'd be in a total state by five. Well, either they were having a really good time, or they'd fallen asleep somewhere, and it was only when other parents said that I really had to set some times that I was able to go to sleep without worrying. We had no going out in the week, unless it was the eighteenth birthday party of a friend – which happened surprisingly often – and the eldest was not allowed to stay with her boyfriend other than at weekends because of the work. The two girls go out with a vengeance on Friday and Saturday nights and then they are mostly in bed on Sunday, but they are always with friends and never alone so actually I've now come to accept that they're quite safe.'

Most families maintain good relations throughout and the vast majority of children grow more independent without becoming emotionally detached from their parents, provided that parents find ways to adjust to their children's changing needs and continue to put them first. Teenagers may be less physically demonstrative with their affections, but they still need to know that they are loved. Jill felt the loss of physical touch with her eldest son keenly, but managed to devise new forms of contact. 'At his final year in primary school, when he came home from his school trip he said that I wasn't to hug him or kiss him when I came to pick him up. So I asked, "What am I allowed to do?" "You're allowed to say, 'Hello, Michael.'" So now we almost have this code where if I say, "Hello, Michael," it's as if I'm saying that I'm feeling quite fond of him because I'm not allowed to hug or kiss him at all. I can playfight with him at home, or tickle him, rough housing, that's acceptable.' Helen too has managed to find other ways of getting her emotional needs met now that her teenage son resists her embrace. 'Adults invade children's space far too much and as they grow older the intimacy changes, but as an adult I now get more adult needs met because we talk about things more.'

Letting go successfully means relinquishing images of our child's perfection, and accepting human frailty. 'I remember reading somewhere that adolescence was a time of real disappointment when you suddenly realized that these extraordinary children were going to be ordinary people just like yourself.' Alexandra has three children, two are teenage and the youngest is nine. 'But I don't find that too bad, in fact it's rather reassuring, thinking of them as ordinary, interesting human beings even though there is this loss of the perfect physical child.'

Letting go successfully also means relinquishing them to life's risks and allowing them to pursue their own interests as distinct from yours. It means accepting their tactless criticisms and rejections. Their growing intellectual clarity enables them to see their parents as individuals more clearly and often their comments can be more insightful than we care to admit. 'Life changes with a teenager around,' says Andrea. 'They're not so cute, but they are funny in a much more subtle way. I quite like the way they take the piss out of you and give it back. It challenges you.'

'We have some good laughs. They take the mickey out of me, the way I look or say things, they just play it back to me and we laugh,' says Philippa. 'I don't mind that, they do it so well. They're their own people and by being that they help me to see that much of the sadness I have about things is actually nothing to do with them.'

Many of the parents I interviewed found that they were more able to deal with their emotions once they had attended a parenting course run by organizations such as Parent Network and Parentlink. Bianca found it reassuring to know that she was not alone in finding it hard. She was the only single mother amongst 'all these middle-class women with their husbands there coming up with exactly the same stuff. I thought, wow! I'm not this abnormal person who shouts and has this child shouting back, "I hate you. I hate you." I used to be really hurt when he said that, I could never have said that to my mother and father. I wasn't allowed an opinion or feelings! But the fact that they were having the same problems even though they were two-parent families with resources was very comforting.'

Philippa found a course helpful in managing her anger. 'Parentlink helped me realize that kids don't make you angry, they're just kids. It's the way you cope with it that matters. It's also useful just to talk to other people in the group because then I come home and see things differently.' She is American and has no family in this country but a firm band of friends with children who stretch back twenty years and who, she says, have helped her enormously when things were really tough. She also found her elder son helpful in that he reminded her to think before she reacted when the younger one began to rebel. 'He'd say things like, "It's really important for him to be able to go out with his friends," and I'd be a little more tolerant as a result.'

Some parents try to ease the feelings of loss by retaining some semblance of control. 'I remember standing in the shower crying one day,' says Barbara. 'They both came back from this camp that they'd been on and they were surly. It was as if they'd left us. It was very, very obvious and very upsetting but in a way perhaps it was a good thing because I saw what it was going to be like. You readjust but you can't really stop it being upsetting. I cling onto things like *I* put the older one's clothes away even though I think he'd probably be happier if I just dumped them outside the door, but I think, oh, they'll get all mixed up, you can't have that. So I go in and put them in the drawer and feel I'm keeping some kind of control over things.'

Others cope by realizing that it really is better sometimes not to know the full truth, that the distance teenagers create by withdrawing helps protect us as parents, as well as affording them greater autonomy over their own lives. Staggering numbers of parents assume that it is other adolescents who get into trouble. By not knowing the full truth, our anxieties as parents are eased and our children develop a sense of their own world, their own privacy, as they experiment with mild dangers. Caroline has finally learned to just about trust her sixteen-year-old daughter although there have been hurdles along the way. 'There was this in-between period when we had to adjust and learn how to feel confident about her. We were into new territory. She was once involved in a fight where the police wanted statements and that was all a bit worrying, but she's never come home roaring drunk or stoned out of her brain. She doesn't ever stay at her boyfriend's so I don't worry about regular sex and I think I am learning to trust her.' Caroline is a child psychologist who has given up working with adolescents because it felt too close to home with two teenage daughters. She discovered that parents and their teenagers are in fact protected by the gap of ignorance that opens up between generations. She once went into her daughter's bedroom which was full of boys and found one of her clients amongst them. 'I do know some things about some of their friends and I hear about some of the things that have been happening and just think, oh my God! I think it really is better for us as parents not to know everything they get up to.'

The truth is usually never quite as bad as imagined, but a great deal worse than our children are prepared to let on. This gap is crucial to preserving good relations between parents and their children. It alleviates parental anxiety and affords adolescents greater autonomy. Parents who do not overreact emotionally to life's seductions and dangers and give sensible and honest advice about drugs, sex and social pressures are more likely to keep essential channels of communication open and are therefore better placed to deal with genuine difficulties as and when they arise. What matters is that relations continue to be sufficiently good, without too much blame or hostility, so that children feel able to turn to their parents for help when they do encounter difficulties, when they feel out of their depth and genuinely need guidance or rescuing.

As a mother, I completely identify with the intensity of anguish, uncertainty and inadequacy expressed by so many of the parents I have met, particularly when things begin to slide out of control or go dangerously wrong. But I also understand now that finding the strength to manage one's own emotions is crucial to the equation and that it is just a phase, however ghastly, which passes, eventually. Memories of our own adolescence inevitably surface as we watch our children growing up. We remember how boring and middle-aged we found our parents and have to accept that we have now become just as boring and middle-aged. We identify in some way with what our children are going through but those memories inevitably conflict with our need as parents to keep some semblance of control over our children's welfare. All too often our emotions come into conflict with their needs as growing children; there is a tendency to overprotect them because of our own anxieties and then paradoxically to abandon them at other times when we fail to take charge and be the parent in difficult situations. But adolescents need their parents to be boring, stable and unemotional in their responses. More than anything else they need to feel that their parents are still in control, that there is a firm framework around them as everything else in their lives begins to change. 'It is very hard being a parent to teenagers,' says Julie who has two grown-up daughters and has taught teenage girls for the past thirty years. 'You feel so rejected by them after all you've done for them but you also have to realize that it'll be all right in a year or two if you hang in there and that it's terribly important to stay in charge. It's a disaster when some of the younger mums try to be sisters with their daughters. If it works when they're eleven, it backfires by the time they're fifteen because they have no control over them whatsoever. People tend not to like the word control, but when I say I control my class, it's about being in charge. Teenagers don't like to feel as if they're on their own.'

Everything we feel as parents, adolescents feel too, as we shall see in the following chapter. The hurt that adults feel when their children point out their weaknesses or reject their help, teenagers feel in spades whenever they face the mildest criticism from parents, peers or teachers. They also feel humiliated whenever they have to ask for help because they feel that they ought to be able to do it for themselves. The hostility, guilt and self-blame that adults feel, adolescents feel too because of their impotence, their inability to provide for themselves financially or materially and general teenage stereotyping. Parental anxiety over their children's future is more than matched by teenage anxiety over their appearance, bodies, sense of self and place in the world and that first date they are so desperate for. Even loss, that omnipresent emotion which dominates over all of the others, teenagers feel too – loss of childhood security, protection, loss of innocence without the full advantages of adult society. We are expected to be grown-up enough to take the strain of this final hurdle of being a parent. They are still children, innocent and emotionally needy, desperate for the same sense of flexible but solid support around them that they may have enjoyed as younger children if they were lucky.

While we may feel that we lose a great deal as our children begin to grow up there is also great gain. I do not feel any less close to my daughter now that she is almost thirteen than I did when she was small, if anything I feel closer, because her understanding and language is so much more sophisticated and we talk about things. When we haven't seen each other for what feels like days, and she looks as if she's feeling fragile, we go to bed early together, lie side by side with our books and talk about things between paragraphs. We've replaced childish play with shopping trips where I am allowed to indulge myself as well as her, and a shared penchant for renting weepy movies from the video shop.

Stella has three daughters, the eldest of whom is fourteen. When they were on holiday, her daughter had nothing to read and asked if she could read one of her mother's books, *Captain Corelli's Mandolin*. 'I said I thought she'd find it very dull, but she loved it, read it solidly from beginning to end and we had a really adult and interesting conversation about it. That brought us a lot closer as I was so pleased to have a conversation with her about a book. I feel the opposite of losing her, it drives you closer. And in those moments of closeness you do feel genuine affection for one another which is different to the way you felt when they were children. There are so many pleasures.' Stella took her eldest daughter to work with her on 'take your daughter to work' day and both of them loved it. 'I was so proud of her, she was so self-possessed. She's dipsy and vacant sometimes at home, it drives me nuts – but there at work, when we stayed for drinks, she was fab, so interested in other people, so socially confident, adoring every moment and I really loved being with her.'

Often parents discover a new lease of life in their relationship and greater freedom to pursue their own interests once their children become teenagers.

'Suddenly there's time at the weekends to do things that we want to do,' says Clara. 'If they're out with friends I might go to an exhibition or we have drinks with friends at six o'clock and you suddenly discover each other again.'

'We've got a lot more time on our own now,' says Joan. 'It's the usual story of him building a career while they are small but now we go away more on our own.'

Judith and her husband found that they had to consciously do something pleasurable for themselves to fill the space. 'The children are so busy now on the weekends that we thought we'd make a point of doing something for ourselves on a Friday. Rather than sitting here alone, all middle-aged, we go out or have people round.'

'Tom helped me by reminding me that the boys were getting bigger and that they didn't necessarily want me to take them places. I needed him to say that,' says Karen. 'I needed him to be strong enough to say, "You can't be with them all of the time."'

For Gillian, 'It's much more balanced now. Peter's totally involved whereas before it was much more of me with the children. As a family it feels more stable now, we're growing more equal and it's fascinating having the eldest one coming home from her first lectures at university. They're bringing their own angle on the world into the home and it's very rich.'

Nobody can get the job of being a parent entirely right. We try our best and sometimes our best isn't good enough because life is imperfect and often unfair. Adolescent children provoke powerful feelings in their parents and parents have to find ways of expressing those emotions, without damaging their child's development. Often that means looking deeper into ourselves, questioning why certain behaviours trigger such an extreme reaction. When our children wound through their criticism or rejection, perhaps it is time to do something that we enjoy for ourselves to enhance our own self-confidence. When we get angry, does their behaviour really warrant such a reaction or is it that we are actually feeling something else – hurt at the rejection or worried at the way our authority is now so easily being pushed aside? Talking about how you feel in less emotional moments will help teenagers to understand that their own mixed emotions are common to human experience rather than particular to themselves, and will bring you closer together. And when things go wrong, when parents explode with rage, become over-anxious, regretful or cry because they feel to blame for something, it is perhaps comforting to know that it is never too late to put things right, through apology or explanation as well as through reassurance that they are still loved. Adolescence, as I hope the rest of this book will show, is a deeply malleable age, when children can be surprisingly resilient and forgiving, as well as capable of great change.

3. Emotional Children

Sad and terrible happenings had never made Frankie cry, but this season many things made Frankie suddenly wish to cry. She was afraid of these things that made her suddenly wonder who she was, and what she was going to be in the world, and why she was standing at that minute, seeing a light, or listening, or staring up into the sky: alone.

Carson McCullers, *The Member of the Wedding*

Adults often view adolescence as an idyllic time full of promise and free from responsibility which is somehow wasted on the young. But when I spoke to teenagers a very different story emerged. For every parent troubled by their adolescent, I met ten troubled teenagers. As the mind matures, teenagers begin to come to terms with an entire new spectrum of negative emotions for the first time in their lives. They sense their vulnerability now that they see more of the dangers inherent to the modern world. They become more self-conscious, anxious, and develop a sense of inadequacy and insecurity, which they never had as young children.

Adolescents face change in every aspect of their lives at roughly the same time. They move to secondary school, a much larger institution than their primary school, which produces heightened expectations and pressures, as puberty kicks in. A new sense of existential aloneness emerges as the wider world with all its difficulties zooms into focus and teenagers begin to understand that they have to make something of their lives on their own. Every teenager I spoke to expressed emotional difficulties with some part of their lives, with friendships or their love lives, school or their parents. 'You get more involved with things, there's so much more to be emotional about,' says Vicky, who is seventeen. 'I don't get upset too easily now but if you see someone crying there are about ten different things that could be the matter. It's not like when you were four and had just fallen over. You could easily cry from thirteen to nineteen because so many things go wrong and can upset you.'

Feeling misunderstood, particularly by one's parents, is a common aspect of adolescence as children strive for autonomy and assert their individuality. But all too often those feelings mushroom under the sheer weight of parental criticism, hostility, argument, stereotypical assumptions and lack of trust. Teenagers need to feel different as they grow up, but they also need to feel the strength of parental support beneath them as everything else changes. So many of the teenagers I met expressed a distressingly high level of pain and confusion over their lives and a deep sense of abandonment at losing the greater love and support of the parents they felt they had had when they were smaller. The emotional toll of growing up can be great indeed but it is almost always within the power of parents to lessen that burden substantially for the young, provided they are prepared to listen, reach out and understand what their child may be going through. With so many stresses inherent to growing up in the modern world, children need their parents to teach them from an early age how to express negative emotions such as anger and frustration in ways which do not hurt others. We also need to help them develop ways to soothe their anxieties in healthier ways, through exercise, yoga, massage and deep breathing.

With puberty, children begin to feel the loss of childhood. Increasing hormones circulate through their bodies from the age of eight and are only partially responsible for the moodiness and emotional volatility of adolescence. It is not that the body changes are difficult in themselves, although they can be, but what causes teenagers such grief is the way the changing mind now sees this new body, and the growing awareness of the need to fit in and feel accepted by the wider world. With puberty beginning earlier, children become much more aware of their emerging sexuality and the way others react to it before they may be ready for it. 'I developed breasts at junior school which was very embarrassing because there was only one other girl like me and I felt monstrous,' says Amanda.

'I was eleven when I started my periods,' says Vicky, 'but at the same time I wasn't nearly an adult. Your mind is behind your body, you're starting on this road to adulthood and your brain isn't quite ready for it yet. And you can't stop it happening, you can't go back to being a child any more and that's quite scary.'

As the mind begins to focus on the body in order to come to terms with the new emerging self, teenagers inevitably have to contend with disappointment. I remember very little about my own body as a child, but the feelings that emerged with adolescence and the growing realization that I was too plump for clothes to look good on me are still with me. My shoulders hunched in order to cover my breasts and stomach, and the agonizing search for something that was both flattering and socially acceptable to wear became an obsession. The same emotions are now surfacing in my daughter even though she is physically very different – very beautiful with a smile that lights up the world, rake thin with an athletic body, and blonde. 'I don't like my knees and I'm too skinny,' she said glumly one day during a shopping trip for her birthday. 'Today's been a good day,' she commented just a few weeks later, 'because I didn't think about how I looked once.'

Similar sentiments were expressed by many other teenagers when I asked them how they felt about their bodies.

'I'm fine with the top half of my body except for my nose and my spots but my legs are fat. I hate them so much and I didn't feel like that before,' says Emma, who is fourteen, black and deeply attractive.

'When I suddenly got muscles, I thought, what's going on? I hadn't been working out but my shoulders got bigger.' Colin is sixteen. 'I looked in the mirror the other day and saw this thing growing on my lip and thought, ugh! Gotta get it off. I haven't shaved yet but I'm going to start because my friends all take the mick.'

Denise is also sixteen. 'Puberty has been mad, the spots, the hair and trying to get it to go your way, which is especially hard for Afro-Caribbeans. I hated the way I looked from about thirteen. I hated my legs and my glasses, but from this year I have begun to accept them more. Sometimes I do still feel that there are things that I'd like to improve about myself. I'm always comparing myself to other people and I hate that because it makes me jealous and very low.'

'I'll be really pleased when puberty is over and done with. Everyone I know thinks that some part of their body is fat,' says Carol, who is twelve. 'You feel really self-conscious. Little pimples that you think everyone can see and you make it worse by fiddling with it so much.'

Now that Vicky is seventeen, she is able to look back over her adolescence with greater perspective. 'You don't want to have to confront your body or to have to think about it, so you wear baggy clothing and it takes you a while to get used to it. Breasts were a bit of a problem. I remember feeling that I just didn't want any right then and it does take a few years to feel comfortable about the new you and to feel able to talk about things. Now I can have a conversation with my friends about anything, but then, when those physical changes were happening, you wouldn't have said a word about it.'

Studies show that teenagers worry more about the way they

look than anything else. The body is everything, the prime source of identity for early adolescents because they are still too young to be able to root their sense of self in other ways, whether through their social and intellectual strengths or by the force of their personality alone. Girls worry about looking or being fat, and noses or breast size are common obsessions. Boys worry about their squirt-like height, lack of muscle, penis size and their inability to control their voices, or their erections, both of which can go up and down at the most embarrassing moments. Teenagers need regular assurance that breasts and muscles will eventually come (see Appendix 1 for details of physical development), and regular reminders of their internal strengths to distract them from these fixations and offer temporary relief even for just a few moments.

Teenagers need to withdraw to their bedrooms and stare at themselves for hours in order to establish for themselves who they have become. Dress, hair and body art allow teenagers to take control over their bodies and express their individuality. They spend hours dressing and changing, intent on presenting the right image of themselves to a world which their narcissistic adolescent mind feels only has eyes for them. They can be utterly contradictory, needing to distinguish themselves, but also needing desperately to feel as if they fit in. They squirm with embarrassment at the thought that anything about their appearance could be remotely out of sorts. They genuinely think that they need that £35 nail job, their ears pierced for the third time or trainers that other teenagers will know cost £80 in order to deflect attention from all the other bits of the body they feel so unsure of. 'They are preoccupied with being "cool" simply because they feel so "uncool" most of the time,' says adolescent psychotherapist Jeannie Milligan.

As teenagers begin to mature psychologically, they see their parents' inadequacies more clearly and find that many of their emotional needs are no longer being met by them. The loss of the perfect parent, who instinctively does the right things and creates feelings of being loved, respected, trusted and understood, is deeply painful to the adolescent. 'Why can't my parents be how I need them to be?' is a common and distressing wail of discontent amongst teenagers. Yet paradoxically the discovery of those differences and deeper failings in one's parents is an essential step to establishing one's own sense of autonomy through those very differences. As the world becomes that much more vast and dangerous in their mind's eye, their sense of place in it shrinks and their ability to protect themselves feels wanting. Their inexorable drive for independence means that they are reluctant to rely on their parents for support and yet they know that they are not yet able to fully take care of themselves.

'There's no one really looking after me.' Karen is sixteen. 'There's my mum and my dad and they look after me but they don't tell me what to do any more and while that's good I miss it as well. I was going to change courses and I just wanted someone to say, "You should change," or "You shouldn't," because it felt like such a big decision, instead of which they were saying, "It's completely up to you."'

'I started to worry more about everything, stupid things like diseases,' says Amanda who is eighteen. 'I think you become more aware about getting ill and being vulnerable whereas when you're young you feel protected from everything by your parents.'

Edward, sixteen, was far more aware of how vulnerable he became as a teenager alone on the streets. 'You get assaulted more. When you're ten you don't think that anyone is going to attack you.'

Seventeen-year-old Claudia finds the prospect of accepting responsibility for her actions daunting. 'It used to be that the big problems in life were the things that your parents could kiss better, but as you get older it's just not like that any more because if I make mistakes now there is nothing that my parents can do about it.'

And for children who have had a traumatic childhood, the loss of support is felt even more keenly. Jamie is fifteen and spent several years in care. 'I think when you turn fifteen, that's when you realize how shit the world is and that no one is going to take an interest and help me.'

Teenagers are able to look back on their childhood and perceive that some of that magic is lost for ever. The irrepressible excitement of impending birthdays or Christmas begins to lessen, presents begin to disappoint and what or how much is given now measures love or the lack of it. Days that once seemed so special because of the rituals and parental attention now lose some of their shine. 'Christmas changed,' says Karen. 'It used to be that I'd look forward to it all of the time and then when I was about thirteen the day came and it wasn't as good as I'd remembered it. It wasn't the day that changed, that stayed exactly the same year in year out, it was me. Holidays weren't as much fun either, being with my parents for a whole week with no escape!'

When parents are critical or unable to sit on their own intense emotions of frustration and loss, teenagers tend to interpret that parental animosity as lack of love. Insults of any sort really hurt and as criticisms mount over their appearance, attitude, laziness, lack of application or bad manners, those feelings of aloneness are compounded. Teenagers often feel as if they no longer have any real sense of place at home, they no longer feel as if they fit in or are valued. They sense the hostility and lack of trust in these criticisms and feel that they may not be liked and loved as much as they were when they were smaller. 'My dad doesn't live with us and if I do anything wrong, like get home at nine when I said I'd be home at eight, she'll say, "You're so stupid, you're just like your dad,"' says

Trish, whose mother is Turkish. 'If I reply, "Well if I'm stupid, you must be as well since I get half my genes from you," she'll get cross and say, "How dare you say I'm stupid?" But it's all right for her to say horrible things like that to me.'

'My mum's really over the top clean, like everything has to be spring-cleaned each Saturday and when I question the need for this she just calls me lazy,' says Emma. 'She called me a liar the other day and when I said, "Don't talk to me like that," she said, "I can talk to you any way I like. Your attitude stinks."'

Adolescents live in a half world, a transient state where they are not yet able to enjoy the full privileges or assume the full responsibilities of adulthood, yet they are also denied much of the emotional security of childhood that they used to enjoy – affectionate hugs on laps, spoiling with toys and praise for their creative efforts often diminish as children assume more adult physiques. Writers such as Simone de Beauvoir and Anne Frank have eloquently described the pain of this rejection as they grow older. 'For years he had done nothing but heap praises on my head,' writes Simone de Beauvoir of her father in *Memoirs of a Dutiful Daughter*:

But when I reached the awkward age, he was disappointed in me: he appreciated elegance and beauty in women. Not only did he fail to conceal his disillusionment from me, but he began showing more interest than before in my sister, who was still a pretty girl.

Anne Frank complains in her diary:

They criticize everything, and I mean everything about me: my behaviour, my personality, my manners; every inch of me, from head to toe and back again, is the subject of gossip and debate. I'd like to feel that Father really loves me, not because I'm his child, but because I'm me, Anne.

I also remember feeling a deep sense of isolation and emotional abandonment in the flat that had once felt like home, as I began to grow up. As the boundaries expanded outside with greater freedom to travel on buses to school, to the homes of friends or to my father, the boundaries within my own home seemed to shrink. As a child every room felt welcoming. But as an adolescent I became more sensitive, and much more aware of the emotional dynamic between my mother, my brother and myself. Whenever my opinions or my new emotional sensibilities were criticized I felt personally attacked and diminished. I felt that the bigger I became, the less I was respected or loved. The home of my childhood was still my home but somehow it was only within the walls of my bedroom that I felt able to be myself and find sanctuary from disapproval. That adolescents need to feel misunderstood in order to forge their own independent path may be a truth, but in the fragile adolescent mind that can so easily translate into a sense of emotional abandonment.

Teenagers surveyed in Glasgow in 1995 who said they felt misunderstood by their parents wanted them to listen more and dismiss their feelings as trivial less. They wanted someone who was there 'and not say they were too busy', someone to 'guide me through the difficult stages but let me make the decisions', someone to 'help me sort my feelings out instead of just laughing at me and telling me not to be silly'. Far too many of the teenagers I have talked to expressed a powerful and articulate longing for greater understanding from their parents.

'I think she should try and understand what I'm going through and listen more instead of going on about how I did this or did that,' says Emma, aged fourteen. She feels her mother favours her younger sister; she longs for a room of her own, for her own space to mood and brood on herself, but has to share her bedroom with her six-year-old sister, while her parents have separate bedrooms. 'My mum is always telling me that I'm horrible to my sister and she's read my diary. Have I no privacy at all at home? I said, "I don't have to explain myself. It's my diary and I can put anything I want in there." She says she doesn't want me to feel so alone and wants me to be able to come and talk to her but I can't. She's so moody, you have to pick the right time to ask her things. She was so much nicer to me when I was smaller, like she is with my sister now. I'd like her to be more supportive of me. She ought to explain why I can't do things and be more understanding of me instead of all this you can't do this and you can't do that. Sometimes I do things just to annoy her and I don't know why. She makes me so unhappy, I just want to make her unhappy. She doesn't need to be so horrible to me.' When Emma expresses her opinion or complains about something, her views are criticized. 'Sometimes I think I hate my life, it's so rubbish, so shabby and I don't get to do this or that and Mum just thinks you're lucky to get to do anything at all with that attitude. It's all school and home and I hate school but she says I should appreciate it and then I hate being at home because it doesn't feel like a refuge. My younger sister is really close to my mum. Last time she went shopping in Harrods she came home with all these bags and bought stuff for everyone else except me. She said she didn't see anything for me but how can that be, in Harrods? If I didn't have my friends or like listening to Eminem I think I'd crack up.'

Denise feels that her parents have labelled her as the 'bad seed' of the family because she has got into trouble at school for swearing and being rude to teachers. 'They think I'm just one way because of the music I listen to and the places I go, but that doesn't make me who I am. They don't realize that I have feelings.' Denise was waiting to hear about her GCSE results when I met her. She has two older sisters who have been successful and she wants to be able to make her parents as proud of her as they are of them. Her parents are staunch disciplinarians and Denise used to be regularly beaten as a child. They demand to know exactly where she is going when she goes out but do not match their concern over her welfare with good communication. 'They don't see the sensitive, caring side of me and you have to work hard to make my parents proud. I'd just like to know that my parents are there for me should something happen, that they'd talk to me sympathetically and say, "You tried your best" if I don't pass my exams rather than just shout at me. My mum goes completely off the rails if I don't do well, but what good does that do except make me feel worse?'

Many troubled teenagers do not talk to their parents about their problems because they already perceive them as stressed or exhausted and do not want to burden them any more. Emily is fifteen and was deeply distressed when I met her because she had had a big row with her parents the previous evening, felt that she couldn't go home and had gone home after school with a friend instead. She has had multiple problems through early adolescence – eating disorders, learning difficulties (she was recently diagnosed as dyslexic) and she has found puberty difficult with acne, disabling period pains and PMT. She considers school pointless, longs for a boyfriend and seems depressed. But what seemed to distress her most during our conversation is that she feels that her parents do not understand her and are unable to provide her with the essential emotional sanctuary that she needs. She longs to be able to talk to them about the more serious aspects of her life but, 'That's something that's just not done in my family, they put on a fake face about everything and laugh it off.' When her school realized that she had an eating disorder, Emily asked them to contact her aunt, the one family member she felt able to talk to. 'My auntie came down and explained it all to my parents and they just cried a lot and I really can't deal with that. Parents are supposed to be the strength that you rely on. If they're upset, it's kind of hard to cope with. I just feel they're the adults, they're not supposed to let me down here and be upset because this is my problem not theirs and I'm upset as it is and don't want to have to support them through this. I need them to support me. They feel that they've let me down which just makes me feel worse because I feel guilty, they make me feel as if I've let them down. My mum's constantly saying, "I'm not a good enough mother, I've been a terrible mother." But it's not like that at all.'

Emily's problems would be a great deal easier to deal with if she felt she had more understanding and support from her parents. She is smart enough to be able to identify that honesty and serious conversation will bridge the emotional divide between them. 'I just want to be able to explain some of the things that were said yesterday. I've been in a lot of therapy in the past year and talking to my auntie has made me feel better, but Mum could never come up to me and say, "Hey, I've been in therapy too," which I know for a fact she has. I just feel that if she just said, "It's all right to open up," and trusted me then maybe I could trust her too.' Instead, Emily is left with a burning desire to get away from home. Every question directed at her hopes for the future came back to her longing to travel. 'Getting away from it all completely would make it all better.' She sat on a sofa next to her friend Sal, who in stark contrast found teenage life far more fulfilling. Puberty was less difficult, she had a boyfriend and felt that she was achieving her potential at school. But the one thing that Emily really envied was the fact that she had a good relationship with her mother. 'I am lucky,' Sal agreed. 'While there are things that I wouldn't want to talk to her about, I do feel that I could talk to her if I needed to.'

When parents interpret their teenagers' behaviour as merely typical of the teenage stereotype, their children feel even more isolated and misunderstood. 'Sometimes when my parents make me angry, they'll mock me and make out that I'm this stroppy teenager, the Harry Enfield stereotype,' says Claudia. 'It really frustrates me when they tell me how I must be feeling because it's not based on me but on what they think because of general teenage stereotypes. They don't base it on you but on the rowdy, rebellious teenager that doesn't want to be told what to do.' Claudia also resents the way that her mother puts everything down to peer pressure, which means that she underestimates her daughter's ability to decide things for herself. 'My mum has this age-old idea that I do things because it makes me look cool. She thinks that I smoke because my friends do it but that isn't even plausible because I have friends who don't do it, it's not even an issue. It kind of depresses me that they think so little of you, that they know you so little and think that you could be so easily pressurized.'

'People are always saying, "She's fourteen. She's at that stage now, it'll pass,"' says Emma, 'but *what* will pass? I hate it when people say that because they act like they know, but they don't really know ME at all.'

Teenage stereotypes communicate the message that they are not generally liked, at a time when young people are at their most self-conscious and vulnerable to other people's perceptions and criticisms. It's easy for teenagers to be influenced by these assumptions. If so many people hate teenagers then maybe there really is something loathsome about me? If teenagers are presented so universally as criminal or difficult, how far do children feel that they have to live up to this image in order to be real teenagers? Adolescents are often blamed for a great many of society's ills, for lack of respect for authority, for street crime and violence and for weakness in the face of drugs. Adults commit crimes as individuals but in the case of adolescents an entire generation is often tarnished with the same brush. 'The general public blame everything on the kids,' says Colin. 'Last night I was standing on the street corner talking to my friend and this old lady picks up the phone and calls the police.'

'Crime, it's always a young person; drugs – it's always a young person; or it's all those teenage mothers who get pregnant all the time,' says Neil, who is nineteen. 'Basically everybody blames young people. The nearest I've come to any sort of drug-pushing is chucking some Panadol to a friend with a nasty headache.'

Many of the teenagers I have interviewed are dismayed by the way their parents suddenly mistrust their motives when they become teenagers and question their ability either to take care of themselves or to do the right thing, a mistrust which results from these general stereotypes or their own anxieties. When parents discover that their daughters are at sleepover parties with boys, many imagine grotesque orgies. Sophie's father went 'skits' when she casually mentioned, as she was recounting a story, that she had spent the night with a friend at a boy's house after a party because there wasn't enough room at another friend's. 'I couldn't understand the problem. Parents have this impression of teenage boys as some awful predatory "thing", as if they're all spotty sex maniacs, but these are my friends. If you're sleeping in a room with lots of other people, you're not going to wake up in the middle of the night with someone lying on top of you. It just doesn't happen. So now if I sleep on the floor at a boy's house I consciously lie about it, not because I'm guilty of something and trying to cover it up but because I can't be bothered to have an argument about it.'

'I'd just like a bit more trust and freedom at home,' says Denise, 'freedom for boys to be able to come over to the house without them thinking that something's going on, for a boy to ring up and for them not to think that they are my boyfriend straight away.'

Parents easily belittle their teenagers' concerns when set

against their own more adult ones. 'They think having to do some geography coursework isn't anything compared to paying the mortgage, but then it's all relative, we've only been on this earth a few years,' says Amanda, who is eighteen. But their problems are real. All of the teenagers I interviewed described emotional difficulties in at least one but usually several aspects of their lives. Many of them felt great loneliness, and were eager to replace the security and love they felt they had lost from their parents with the reassurance and affirmation of a lover (a subject which is fully explored in Chapter 7).

Like countless other teenagers, at sixteen Denise from Brixton feels more angry, more anxious and more fearful of her future than at any other time in her short life, yet expression of these new thoughts and feelings provokes responses from her parents which make her feel even less supported. 'Grownups seem to think that this is the best time of your life, but I don't find that. Basically, you're getting to be more responsible but everything is harder; going for exams, the struggle to be in with the in-crowd, and trying to be someone that everybody likes, and trying to fit in with the world so that the world likes you better. It stresses me out. Money, that's another problem. You can't earn it. I'm looking for a job but that's hard without the qualifications, so I'm always scrounging off my parents and wanting stuff, which doesn't feel nice. If you've got everything like education and good grades, you're getting on with your family and you've got loads of friends who'll stand by you through anything and you're able to go out and have fun, then you can say it's easy being a teenager. But people who are struggling in school and not getting on with their parents or having trouble with their friends, then it's hard. I want to go the right way and do the right things. I don't want to mess up my life by getting pregnant. It worries me, I worry so much about the future and where I'm going to be and what I'm going to be doing, and that makes me feel insecure, I wonder whether I can do it.'

The education system exacerbates adolescent emotions by piling on the pressure and failing to cater for their wider developmental needs, a subject which I explore in greater detail in Chapter 8. Many found school boring or the work hard, and felt intimidated by particular people there. They felt overwhelmed by the pressure of exams and the need to do well and deeply anxious over their futures when they felt they had yet to really know themselves. A survey of nearly 40,000 teenagers conducted annually by Exeter University found in 1997 that 30–40 per cent of those aged eleven to fourteen felt dissatisfied with their lives and that their anxiety increased through early adolescence between Years 7 and 10 when GCSE coursework begins and interest in sex mushrooms. More young people worried about their schoolwork than they did in 1992, indicating that academic pressures are rising.[1] 'There's quite a lot of pressure,' says Trish, who is fourteen. 'I do quite well in class but the teachers expect so much from you in your tests. When we had our mocks for SATs, I was really worried and came up in big rashes all over my face.'

'The worst thing is the pressure, I guess, academic pressure and the pressure to succeed when you're young,' says Amanda. 'I was never that worried about schoolwork until my GCSEs, but A levels were really horrible. I would think of things like recession and knew that I had to work really hard. You've got to really put your head down and work like a lunatic if you want to get good grades. Everyone has to succeed these days and the schools are so worried about results and league tables that you're more of a statistic than a human being. Every year in my school there is some sort of psycho case due to the pressure of A levels. Last year there was a girl who was anorexic. I was put onto antidepressants. I remember Mum telling me that I could take a year off and do my A levels the following year and me saying, "I can't, they're my life!" That's how much they are drummed into you.'

'With each year there is less and less that you can get away with,' says Claudia. 'When you're a child you can get away with a lot by looking confused and being sweet. I find it really daunting that I'm only just sixteen and yet we're being told to write CVs at school and we have to think about GCSE results in order to get into university, and I don't really want to think about that at the moment. Things like getting a job and getting out of my parents' house as soon as possible are a strain and then there's choosing A level subjects. You don't want to make a mistake and find after A levels that you really loathe your subjects. The pressure is on now to make a decision about what you are going to do in five years' time. But what if you don't know?'

Adolescence is notoriously a time of great emotional volatility. Those great mood swings exist because teenagers, like children, find it difficult to understand why they feel the way they do and find it hard to control their emotions. They erupt angrily, swear and lash out and smash things, or burst into uncontrollable tears because they still lack the adult restraints and controls that we now know take a great many years to develop. Without adult perception, adolescents find it hard to judge the significance of a difficulty. Claudia and her friends used to have major battles with her Latin teacher when she was fourteen and she used to get really upset about it. 'My dad said, "If *this* is screwing you up, then you're really not going to cope with life." And I went up to my bedroom and thought about what he said and he was right. In the week we argue with a teacher, he's a tosser, so what?'

In Larson and Richards' study *Divergent Realities*, family members were bleeped at random times of the day and asked to write down how they felt. Young teenagers of twelve and thirteen swung more quickly between the extremes of euphoria and depression than their parents. They were easily bored in lessons and then felt their spirits rise sky high just minutes later when they joined their friends in the playground. Now that social relationships matter so much more to their sense of well-being, falling out with their friends can be deeply painful but they can be mended in a trice. 'You get miserable about the same things as you get older but those feelings become so much more intense,' says Karen. 'Arguing with someone is such a big deal, you get really stressed and paranoid about it and let it grow into this huge problem because it's so upsetting and frustrating, and then you wake up the next morning and remember what happened and it doesn't seem like such a big deal any more.'

Small events can trigger great reactions. Kissing someone with a big 'wow' factor can make an adolescent euphoric for hours and unable to think of anything else. 'Compliments from people, getting good grades or doing well in sports make you feel so much better about yourself. When boys pay attention to you or even just a wolf whistle can make you feel much more confident for a while,' says Trish. But the mildest criticism can also make them deeply despondent. 'People annoy me a lot quicker than they used to and I get fed up really easily,' says Emma. 'I've become much more moany about things and get upset quickly, and not bothering, I don't care as much as I did before, I don't care if my mum's not talking to me.'

These mood swings are not chaotic, or a sign of pathological disorder, but a normal consequence of growing psychological maturity and exposure to greater challenges and emotional experiences. Hormones may play a part, but the impact of the teenagers' immediate environment and individual circumstances are far more influential now that they can see all the minuses as well as the pluses in their lives. As a result they may lack confidence in their ability to surmount these hurdles in order to make something of their lives. The environmental impact on two teenage girls I interviewed could not have been more clear. Karen is sixteen, slim and pretty and has not found puberty difficult to deal with. She has always been popular at school, lives in a quiet, middle-class area of Brighton and has a weekend job which produces money for her material needs. She also has two loving parents who have always tried to consult her on her views. 'I get down sometimes, and I do worry about the future, and I hate the way that my parents still treat me like a child. They expect me to sit there at dinner time until everybody's finished and then clear the table, but basically things could be worse.'

Kim is at the other end of the spectrum – black, younger at thirteen, and living in Hackney, London. She lives in a tiny house with both her parents and younger brother and her sister who is severely physically and mentally handicapped with whom she shares a bedroom. The house is dominated by winches and pulleys to move her sister around and there is only just enough room in their bedroom for both of their beds, no floor space for the dancing which Kim says is the one thing which cheers her up. She was tearful when I met her, unable to describe why or put words to her feelings. She skips breakfast most mornings, feels unattractive and spotty (she isn't) and longs for greater acceptance by her peers at school where she is consistently picked on. Now that she is becoming more aware, the poverty of her immediate environment has come into focus. 'When I was little I didn't think about what was going to happen to me when I grew up, I just played around with my friends, but now I have to think about getting a good job. I don't want to be in Sainsburys and have to put my food back at the till because I can't pay for it. It seems to me that so many other people have better lives than we do and that makes me angry. They have proper sisters. I'd just like a proper family home.'

To dismiss these mood swings as hormone-related can be a mistake because they may be masking genuine problems such as depression, which lies behind so many other teenage problem behaviours, as we shall see in Chapter 9. Many teenagers are depressed without their parents realizing it because the symptoms of child depression are often different to those of adults. It's perfectly normal for teenagers to withdraw more to their bedrooms, become surly and kick the walls occasionally. But an adolescent who is withdrawn for long periods of time, is not integrated within a peer group or has no friends is showing signs of distress. Other signs may include extreme inaction/passivity, a persistent dark mood and complete avoidance of any adult company. Difficulty concentrating, dreading being alone, promiscuity, permanent exhaustion, frequent headaches or stomach aches and quick shifts from one activity to another, in a desperate search for new stimulation to relieve boredom, are other indications of depression in teenagers. More obvious symptoms, such as a sudden drop in marks, loss of weight, running away from home or school, getting into fights, frequent alcohol or drug abuse or talking about suicide, are serious danger signs, and indicate that a child needs outside help.

Adolescents experience depression not just as sadness, but as sadness mixed with a great deal of anger.[2] They lash out and argue when they feel bad about themselves, or when they feel restricted by their circumstances, as Anne Frank vividly describes in her diary:

Both Peter and I are struggling with our innermost feelings. We're still unsure of ourselves and are too vulnerable, emotionally, to be dealt with so roughly. Whenever that happens, I want to run outside or hide my feelings. Instead I bang pots and pans, splash the water and am generally noisy, so that everyone wishes I were miles away. Peter's reaction is to shut himself away, say little, sit quietly and daydream, all the while carefully hiding his true self.

Depression is a serious condition for young people that can swiftly mutate into far greater dangers such as suicide and self-harm, or drug and alcohol abuse. Teenagers often lack the emotional coping skills or the sense of complete perspective that comes with experience and more adult maturity and if they feel that their problems are being either belittled or ignored by their parents, feelings of isolation and depression easily become entrenched. 'We suspect that the current epidemic of adolescent problems partly reflects individual teenagers' desperate attempts to deal with feelings they cannot control,' writes Reed Larson in *Divergent Realities*.

Psychologists can pinpoint several factors which enable people to feel good about themselves – appearance, a sense of achievement, feeling accepted by others and a sense of control or value to the wider community. Teenagers find it particularly hard to feel positive in even one of these areas and are therefore far more vulnerable to low self-esteem and depression. In addition there are other more subtle pressures on young people in the big wide world – the pressure to be happy, attractive, successful and thin, the pressure to have the right type of material goods, the latest designer names. When adolescents lack the ability to place these pressures within a wider context or to rationalize them effectively they respond emotionally and easily feel inadequate and depressed. When teenagers sense that they are not trusted they feel they have nothing to lose when the pressure mounts; they need to release some of these new and pent-up emotions through activities which bring immediate gratification or the adrenaline rush that comes from danger. After the pressure of SATs and some major maths investigations, which they had found hard to accomplish and left them falling behind the rest of the class, Trish and her friends decided on impulse to scrawl their initials all over the walls of the music room. 'The teacher came in and made us wash it all off and asked us why we did it, but I really don't know, I just had the urge, you don't think why, it just happened, it just sort of boils up from nowhere.'

Depression often surfaces during adolescence when children have experienced more significant trauma such as neglect, abuse or a messy divorce. Far too many young people still grow up in families where they may be the victims of parental neglect, left alone, poorly fed, or expected to cook and care for younger siblings as well as themselves. Large numbers of parents do appalling things to their children. They can be violent, aggressive, alcoholic, autocratic and overprotective, or they abandon their children completely without explanation. In the case of re-marriage, step-parents and stepchildren are expected to live harmoniously together. Parents can be blatant in their favouritism or use a child as a scapegoat. They may see their children as possessions, extensions of themselves, and place expectations on them which are often based on their own failed hopes rather than on their child's actual abilities. 'I see a lot of kids who have distorted views of life because something traumatic has happened to them, and that interferes with their capacity to develop sound judgement,' says Jeannie Milligan, adolescent psychotherapist at the Tavistock Centre. 'If they've had too many odd experiences without an adult supporting them or talking with them about what is going on they get stuck. They haven't necessarily got the means to recover from something that has gone wrong in their lives, and without someone helping them by putting forward solutions or new ways of seeing things, that often remains a paralysed area.'

Far too many well-meaning parents underestimate the

shattering emotional effects of divorce or separation on children. Countless young people now live with what is considered to be the acceptable face of family breakdown, with mushrooming rates of divorce or separation and the formation of new family units, often without adequate preparation or consultation. Parental behaviour and divorce have far more of an impact on adolescents' development and their interior emotional world than parents generally like to acknowledge. The modern emphasis on happiness in relationships, rather than staying together for the sake of the children, has to be right, but in our need to justify our own actions as adults we often deny the very real damage done to children through family break-up. Where there is divorce, there is conflict, and adolescents need home to be a stabilizing influence at this time of great change. Major decisions affecting the whole family are usually taken solely by the parents, but the impact of these changes usually has a disproportionate effect on the young. Divorcing parents are usually distracted parents, absorbed by the separation and their own emotional pain at the breakdown of the relationship. Consequently they may have less time or patience when it comes to supporting their children who are in even greater need of patience and understanding as they cope with their own loss of a parent at home. Where there is hostility and anger between parents, some of that anger invariably gets unleashed upon the child. Anger begets anger in the child. 'Divorce brings out very primitive emotions and often knocks the parent back into a very childlike state,' says Kate Wilcox, a counsellor for children of divorced and separated parents. 'Inevitably that has an effect on the welfare of the child.'

All children are likely to be concerned about the practical aspects affecting their stability. Where will we live? Will I have to leave my school and my friends? Will I still see both parents and will I have to choose between them? Will there be enough money? These are questions which, not surprisingly, regularly run through children's minds when they have neither the experience nor the power to effect change. Younger children are to some extent protected from long-term concerns by their limited ability to think far into the future, but adolescents are only just beginning to understand the long-term implications. There is also the additional stress of feeling abandoned by the parent just at the time when they need their parents to be a stable rock in order to move away from them effectively. 'The worst time for parents to split up is when their children are adolescent,' says Nicky, a counsellor who works with separating families, 'because there's such a lot of other things going on for them at that time to do with growing up. They need that solidity there so that they can push away and rebel, knowing that they can come back. When that's disrupted with one parent disappearing and perhaps forming a new sexual relationship, their whole view of relationships changes. They see them as more transient. With small children you can talk to them and make sure they know that you are still there for them but with older children that is harder to achieve.'

Judith Wallerstein is a psychologist who has been studying the effects of divorce on children since 1971. 'Divorce seems to shake the child's confidence in the existence of a morally ordered, meaningful world . . . The shaky family structure of the newly divorced family and the loosened discipline of the transition period combined with parental self-absorption or distress diminishes the available controls.'[3] Divorce and family break-up can also radically alter and upset the natural gradual separation between parent and child that is essential to adolescence.

'Many adolescents seem to have problems with the father,' says Kate Wilcox. 'If he left some time ago he may find it harder to know how to talk to them. They tend to think the child is still the same age as when they left and can't adapt.

Teenagers need to be able to talk to their fathers about how they are feeling but often that's not possible. They are frequently very angry about the divorce but don't want to talk about that and push them so far that they are rejected totally. They also often want to retain an idealized version of their father, which is very sad.'

When Kate and I discussed the emotional legacy of divorce, my own difficulties as an adolescent suddenly made sense. I adored my father and missed him badly as a small child, indulging in fantasies of being rescued from my attic bedroom and escaping to his flat as I grew older. I had been left by someone I loved and did not want to do anything to antagonize him and push him further away. It wasn't until I was twenty-three and fully independent, living with friends and earning a good salary in my first proper job that I felt able to say all of those things that had made me so angry and unhappy as a child. I rang him up and demanded that he drove a hundred miles that day to see me so that we could talk. He did. He sat in my living room and just listened for hours as anger and impotence over my unhappy childhood poured forth. He couldn't really say much and left the house looking sad while I cried buckets and then felt better. My father was not there for me at home when I grew up and therefore avoided all of the animosity, rejection and criticism that normal adolescents heave onto their parents through the teenage years and which my mother had to bear alone. In just one evening I had made up for an entire decade of lost time.

Colin's mother and father split up when he was sixteen. 'That was hard and it was probably one of the main reasons why I failed my GCSEs. I just went off the rails and did nothing for two months, just mucked about and had a good laugh. I was angry but hid it inside and just went out and did what I wanted. If he could do that then so could I. I knew six months before they told me, I could tell and that's what hurt the most, when they didn't tell me what was going on.' When Colin's father eventually told his sons, he told Colin last, which hurt him even more. He felt that as the eldest he ought to have been told first, because he knew already and because he wanted to be able to support his younger brothers. 'I've got a lot more pressure now 'cos I've gotta look after my brothers and my mum as well. I feel that she's got a life to lead, she needs to go out and when she does I stay in and look after the boys. A lot of my friends' parents have split up and my friend helped me out a bit. He was just there, he said, "It happens, you've gotta get over it. It gets better." And it has got better.'

Gita has twins, Keith and Stella, who are now sixteen. Their father left when they were small and Gita remarried when they were fourteen and she was pregnant. 'All the anger came out of Keith then. Everything he could do to wind me up he did, coming home late, not getting a message to me, and then he ran away when we went shopping for clothes two weeks before the wedding. I wasn't prepared for the strength of feeling. The three of us were always so close but it turned to real anger. When I had the baby the twins came to the hospital and Keith refused to look at the baby or go near him and that hurt me so much. I thought, well you can be angry with me but this is your little brother. Now they're happier with him but there are huge gaps and always this feeling of, "You've got a new family and where am I in all this?" On reflection I don't think that I could have given them the reassurance that they needed, I was stressed to the eyeballs. If we had the space to be together then it might have been possible. One time he was so angry he was leaving home, but he walked out the back door rather than the front and his stepfather stopped him, put his arms around him and when he'd calmed down left us alone together. I asked him why he was so angry. But he couldn't answer. I asked him if he knew why I had split up with his dad and he didn't. In all this time he had a perception of events that was far removed from the reality. He thought I had left him, that I didn't want his dad. I just sat there and hugged him. It was really hard.'

Gita's daughter, Stella, reacted very differently. She pretended that she wasn't upset by it and absorbed the change emotionally so that she could grow up and help look after the others. 'The split was pretty easy, it never really affected me, it wasn't like they didn't love me, although I don't see my dad these days. My stepdad's OK but I hated him at first. You know how people come into a house and have to make it theirs in order to feel as if they live there? It wasn't like he was taking Daddy's place because we'd got used to the idea that Daddy had left it but it was the things he tried to change in the house. We used to wash up the dishes and lay them on the surfaces but he bought one of those racks that you stack them up on. Why? Go away.' She finds it hard to believe that boys might find her attractive and longs to feel loved by someone in order to feel valued. She is emotionally detached from sex and has argued publicly in class that she sees nothing wrong with prostitution. 'You might as well get paid for it.'

The emotional legacy of divorce and the models of relationship established subsequently can be profound and long-lasting, but the negative impact on children can be minimized if parents are able to find the strength and have the financial resources to put their children's needs first. Young people need stability in as many aspects of their lives as possible. If they can stay living in the same home and can keep their friendships by going to the same school when their parents separate there is less stress for them to deal with at the same time. When parents are able to conceal their hostility towards each other and allow the children to express their own hurt and confusion, they are better placed to be able to explain the reasons for the break-up and reassure them. What matters most to a child's welfare however is not so much the make up of the family they grow up in, but the quality of the love, support and understanding they receive within that family. Research shows that the quality of the relationship between children and their parents matters much more than whether there is one parent around or two, it's just a great deal easier and less tiring to be attentive to a child's needs with two.[4]

The importance of good family life in protecting or buffering adolescents from the increasing pressures and risks to which they are exposed cannot be overemphasized. Parents and caring adults still matter and exert a profound influence over teenagers, even though they may fight and hurl abuse and general loathing as they struggle to break free. Teenagers who say that they feel close to their parents score higher than their peers on measures of psychosocial development – they have higher self-esteem and a sense of well-being, seem to do better at school and are more self-reliant. They are also less vulnerable to psychological and social problems such as depression and drugs.[5] Research shows that parents have a crucial role to play in helping to bolster teenagers at this sensitive time.

When children are younger, many parents never stop telling them how clever they are, praising their splodgy paintings and their physical achievements and they find it easy to tell them how much they are loved. But as children grow and withdraw more, expressing their acute embarrassment and disdain for everything that parents say or do, parents tend to find it harder to reach their children, and withdraw too. But teenagers desperately need the affirmation that comes from being praised just as much as they did when they were younger. They still need to be told regularly how much they are loved because they feel the loss of childhood security keenly and lack more adult emotional resources to help them to cope. They need their talents, strengths, achievements and inner qualities pointed out to them as often as possible to divert attention away from the supreme importance of body image and to relieve anxiety, even if that's only for a few moments. 'They're very fragile in their teens,' says Mary, a single mother with two grown-up sons. 'They need a lot of bolstering because they have to build up enough self-confidence to be able to deal with the world. You have to tell them when things are going well and I think it is also important to try and be as open as possible so that they always feel that they can come and talk to you. Also, we do a lot of hugging.'

Research shows that self-esteem tends to plummet during early adolescence as the more negative aspects of growing up come into play. Low self-worth in teenagers is often at the root of such behaviour as bitching, name calling and teasing; inappropriate touching or avoiding physical contact altogether; constant excuses for failures; excessive bragging; self-deprecation; lack of expression of opinions and a generally submissive attitude; or loud, dogmatic tones of voice.[6] A low sense of self-worth is far more likely to lead to giving up, avoiding or delaying tactics, denying, cheating, blaming others or playing the clown.[7] The sense of having parents there to support, encourage, guide and understand is crucial to a teenager's sense of self-worth. The higher the baseline of self-worth established during childhood, the higher it is likely to remain during adolescence. High self-confidence, with a strong sense of self-worth, buffers a child against stress, increases motivation and means that they are more likely to be able to resist peer pressure and say 'no' to things they feel uncomfortable with. They are also more likely to have developed internal judgements and coping mechanisms at an earlier age to help them deal with life's difficulties as they arise during adolescence.

Young people develop self-worth through their athletic and scholastic achievements, through social acceptance and their physical appearance, but also through approval from parents which is not contingent on their own high expectations. They enjoy active challenges, which produce feedback that can affirm their emerging sense of self, and the concentration needed to perform these tasks enables them to become less self-conscious for a while, to lose track of themselves within a larger, more powerful system with specific rules, goals and challenges such as competitive team sports or dance and drama. All of these activities as well as hanging out with gangs of friends and listening to music connect the emotionally volatile and self-preoccupied adolescent to some sense of a wider community, and offer valuable relief from the angst of solipsism.

Children need to have their emotions labelled for them from a very early age in order to understand them or accept them as normal. Parents who explain their own negative emotions make them seem less frightening to a child. When parents encourage their children to express negative emotions and say, 'It's fine to cry,' rather than, 'Please don't,' children grow up less ashamed about feeling down when they have a right to be. 'We don't allow them expressions of anger or real sadness because it upsets us too much,' says Kate Wilcox. 'We allow the good ones of conformity and happiness but by denying the spectrum we deny them the ability to learn how to cope with them. Then when adolescence hits and emotion comes to the fore, they get really pent up and don't know what to do with all these new bad feelings, and that puts tremendous pressure on them.' When there have been family or childhood difficulties, young people need these discussed so that they understand that they are not to blame and their intellectual understanding of cause and effect is enhanced. When things go wrong in a child's or a young person's life, when they suffer from hurt or injustice, psychologists believe that they can be helped a great deal by an 'enlightened witness', someone stronger and more powerful who feels angry for them, assures them that it wasn't fair or their fault and allows them to express their feelings.

Adolescents need desperately to find ongoing, stable emotional nourishment from their parents in order to value themselves enough to be able to find emotional nourishment from others. While parents may feel that they do everything they can — 'we gave her everything and look how she treats us' — what matters is the teenage perception of the level of support they get rather than the reality from an adult perspective. Parents of teenagers have to tread a fine line between enforced benign neglect when young people need to make decisions or venture out alone, and rock-like emotional support in the face of all difficulties. Overreaction to the normal highs and lows of adolescence can push teenagers further away as they try to hide their distress, fearing they may hurt or upset their parents. Shock may cause withdrawal and offering comfort or reassurance too soon can communicate the message that this adult cannot take any more upset. Criticism demoralizes rather than motivates and when something really bad happens any expression of parental anger or disappointment only makes them feel worse. When Kevin slept through an important chemistry exam because he had set the alarm clock for p.m. rather than a.m. his father screamed at him and called him a loser. 'I felt bad enough that day without him telling me that I'd never come to anything.'

Parents provide the scaffold for adolescents to grow against and mature successfully, like the plumpest vine, and if that scaffold is not strong enough to take the pressure as the weight of that vine increases, then growth can be impaired and untrained. Branches extend in every direction, reaching out for other sources of support. Teenagers need to feel greater trust and autonomy over their lives as they grow older but they still need to feel that their parents are in charge and continue to empathize with their needs as they did when they were younger. Intellectually they want to be treated more like adults, but emotionally they are still children. Whenever I talked to teenagers I was struck by how open they were and keen to talk to someone in confidence because there was often no one else to confide in. Counsellors at school were almost always dismissed as useless and parents either wouldn't or couldn't understand. Girls found it easier to talk to their friends but often didn't want to divulge their deepest fears and secrets because they couldn't be entirely trusted to keep them. When I asked parents why they didn't discuss difficulties or talk more openly with their children, they tended to say that their children didn't want to talk to them. Yet when I talked to teenagers, I was struck by how self-aware so many of them were, how conscious they were about the particular psychological dynamics of their own family and how much more support and understanding they felt they needed from their own parents.

Adults do not hold a monopoly on feeling stressed. Teenagers face an array of frightening emotional difficulties because of the physical and psychological changes of adolescence. They have to come to terms with a new body and a new sense of aloneness, which can easily develop into loneliness if they have to contend with cruelty and ostracism from their peers. They face greater pressure at school over exams and uncertainty over their futures. They are desperate for the security and affirmation that comes from having a girlfriend or boyfriend and have to contend with rejection when things go wrong. They feel more intensely as a result, and their emotions become much more complex, more adult and less easily appeased. 'I just wish I could learn how to be happy, happy with what I have,' Denise told me as we left a café in London's Brixton. But happiness is not so easily achieved as an adult. Concepts such as attaining happiness, knowing who you are or what you want from life and establishing lasting and nourishing sexual relationships are still difficult for countless adults. Imagine then how much harder they must be for teenagers.

It can be hard for parents to find ways of reaching their

teenagers emotionally. Their behaviour can be so unpleasant at times that many parents do find them harder to love. But when adolescents fight, scream abuse or flout resistance to parental wishes they are usually trying to force their parents to see them for who they are. 'Here I am,' they scream. 'Different to you and your aspirations for me but important nevertheless. Love me for who I am now because if you can't love this changing, confused, complex new being, if you can't trust and respect me, how can I ever learn how to love my new self?'

Teenagers need their parents more than ever at this vulnerable time even though they pretend that they don't. They need tolerance, understanding, guidance, empathy and a sense that their parents are there for them, to explain emotional difficulties in adult terms and enable them to find ways of coping with problems when they arise. Young people need to feel trusted, they need to feel respected as individuals rather than the products of some redundant teenage mould and they need to be able to express their volatile emotions within the safety of their own home. But above all, they need to feel loved, that they haven't lost the love of their parents with the loss of childhood and that there is still a haven there for them to return to, for as long as they need it.

4. Me, Myself, I

The first half of '43 brought crying spells, loneliness and the gradual realization of my faults and shortcomings, which are numerous . . . the second half of the year was slightly better. I became a teenager, and was treated more like a grown-up. I began to think about things and to write stories, finally coming to the conclusion that the others no longer had anything to do with me.

  Anne Frank, *Diary of a Young Girl*

Like countless others, I always assumed that the emotional upheavals of adolescence were caused by hormones. But new research from America suggests that it is the profound change which takes place in the mind that creates such turmoil.[1] During adolescence the brain evolves through the rough and tumble of teenage life and matures with more adult ways of thinking. It is this slow change in the way that an adolescent thinks and perceives his or her place in the world which creates typical teenage behaviours such as narcissism, idealism, impulsiveness and tactless confrontation. If we understand the way that the adolescent mind works, we stand a better chance of understanding why teenagers can be so sensitive and irrational. We are then less likely to overreact or blame them when they appear to be unreasonable or contradictory, and more able to prevent conflict from escalating towards irretrievable breakdown.

  Scientists are only just beginning to explore and understand the subtle but seismic shifts in an adolescent's mind. Neuroscientists have always assumed that the brain was fully formed by late childhood, but two research projects of the late 1990s have found that different parts of the brain mature at different rates.[2] The ability to plan or evaluate arguments in order to make sound judgements, and the skills necessary for controlling our emotional responses only begin to develop in early adolescence. Teenagers are emotionally volatile because they have yet to develop the mental ability to control their emotions, not just because their hormones are all over the place. They are still driven like children by the things they see and want and find it hard to delay fulfilment of their desires and expectations. Adolescents have yet to master the intellectual skills to be able to see things in the same way as adults. They cannot see the full picture, because they have to develop the wisdom that comes from experience. They cling to the certainties inherent to idealism and narcissism because they cannot deal with the uncertainties they are now beginning to see all around them.

In adolescence we move slowly from the innocent abandon of childhood to the responsibilities of adulthood. As we move from complete dependence to self-sufficiency our brains are radically changing specifically to expand our range of skills and develop an accurate sense of our own identity complete with individual strengths and weaknesses, in order to increase our chances of survival in a competitive adult world. It's a slow process because adult human life is so complex. In pre-industrial societies, children work alongside their parents and grow up quickly because they pick up the skills they need for adult survival at a very early age. Puppies grow into dogs in little more than a year because there is next to nothing to master about adult canine life (particularly in our house where dinner is chopped and served without having to be caught and killed first). But for human beings growing up in the modern West, the process takes a great deal longer. For the best part of a decade, adolescents learn how to master the mental skills essential to survive on their own and it is often a tortuous process.

All too often, adult society misses opportunities to educate and guide adolescents when their intellectual skills are at their most malleable. When children are small, we patiently teach them how to read and write, how to count or tie their shoe laces because we know that these are essential skills. Yet when our children reach adolescence, we often withdraw and offer less guidance because they are so much more capable physically of doing things for themselves. But this new research tells us that adolescents are just as needy intellectually as small children. It is a time of great mental plasticity, when young people need exposure to a broad range of experiences and challenges specifically so that they can develop adult intellectual maturity. If they are not stimulated adequately at this highly creative time, when the brain is at its most capable of absorbing new skills specific to adult survival, they may miss that slot in their development. Learning may then be less easy at a later stage, in much the same way that it is harder to teach an illiterate ten-year-old than a five-year-old how to read.

This new research has huge implications for the way we teach children in school, for they need far more challenge and active learning than they currently get (a subject which is fully explored in Chapter 8). It could also give rise to a whole new emphasis on stimulating adolescents psychologically, in much the same way as we now stimulate our under-fives, if they are to achieve their best. But the most enlightening aspect of this research for parents is the knowledge that teenagers can't help it when they are at their most difficult or infuriating. They really do think differently to the small child they once were and the adult they have yet to become and they need constant challenge and dialogue to help them up the ladder to psychological maturity.

In childhood we tend to see things in absolute, black-and-white terms. Young children are passive victims of their senses and emotions and they find it hard to judge their abilities. Knowledge comes primarily from what they see, hear and feel and they accept reality without question as a given construct. As young children we tend to worship our parents as omnipotent gods, our love for them is uncompromising, their ability to soothe and reassure unfailing. Children have a precious ability to live in the present. What matters is now, today, the fact that Mummy or Daddy is near, the prospect of that immediate treat and they are blissfully unaware of the future. But as our intellectual horizons expand gradually through adolescence, we begin to develop a sense of our own individual future, a future which we have to determine ourselves and one that is perilously vulnerable to fate or chance as the paradoxes and pressures of the wider world begin to come into focus.

Through adolescence we slowly begin to understand that knowledge and reality are not absolute. We begin to think in more abstract terms and grasp the significance of perspective and hypothesis. We develop greater logic and a sense of strategy and can now see that our actions provoke consequences. We are more able to question our place within the wider world. Our sense of memory develops, enabling us to look back over our short lives in order to construct a clearer image of who we really are. We begin to see faults and weaknesses in our parents, and are now more able to define ourselves as distinct and different to them. We begin to understand that there may not be clear-cut answers to problems and that other people may see things differently. This new and emerging sense of perspective affects our social and sexual relationships, our attitudes to parents, family life and school. 'When you're a child the things you really care about are getting a new pair of white jeans,' says Claudia, who is seventeen. 'It wasn't that maybe people don't like me because I'm stuck up.'

It is this gradual widening horizon from childhood to maturity which explains many of the conundrums and contradictions of adolescence. Teenagers are still children in so many ways and yet they want to be treated like adults. Psychologists are now able to pinpoint three stages to the process of achieving adult intellectual maturity – early, middle and late adolescence. In early adolescence, teenagers are only just beginning to come to terms with the implications of perspective but are unable to prevent themselves from responding emotionally to events and criticism. They may apply logic to one area of their lives and not to another. They are quite likely to bore on about the need to protect the environment and then drop litter onto the pavement. They will argue fanatically about the evils of Western capitalism one minute and then moan about not having enough money to buy a new computer game or a ludicrously expensive only-wear-once dress the next. Memory is selective, capable of remembering the lyrics of each song on Madonna's latest album as well as every single nuance of the last six episodes of *EastEnders*, but failing utterly to remember to do their homework, or even to bring it home. Early adolescents can be egotistic and narcissistic. One mother of four children aged from nine months to twelve years told me with some amusement that when she asked the eldest to hold the baby for a moment while she did something, her daughter replied, 'I can't. I'm eating an apple.'

Teenagers are idealistic, hypocritical, easily prone to obsessions and often prone to contradictions as the psychologist Anna Freud astutely points out: 'Adolescents are excessively egoistic, regarding themselves as the centre of the universe and the sole object of interest, and yet at no time in later life are they capable of so much self-sacrifice and devotion. They form the most passionate love relations, only to break them off as abruptly as they began them. On the one hand they throw themselves enthusiastically into the life of the community, and on the other hand they have an overpowering need for solitude.

They oscillate between blind submission to some self-chosen leader and defiant rebellion against any and every authority. They are selfish and materially minded and at the same time full of lofty idealism.'[3]

It is only with middle to late adolescence that teenagers become more rational and consistent. Middle adolescence begins roughly when the physical changes of puberty have settled down and teenagers have replaced the security they used to gain from parents with the sense of containment that comes from a gang of friends. Late adolescence, at seventeen or eighteen, begins when teenagers feel self-sufficient and confident enough to break away from a tight-knit peer group and form relations with others as individuals. The older adolescents are, the more likely they are to be aware of the risks and future consequences of a decision. Some move through these stages quickly, most are still in late adolescence in their late teens and early twenties. The evidence from research suggests that approximately 30 per cent of sixteen-year-olds have reached what the child psychologist Piaget defined as 'early adult thinking' and only 10 per cent have reached near-adult maturity.[4] It's a slow process but one that can be egged on with the right sort of intellectual and social challenge. A fifteen-year-old who has been encouraged to behave responsibly and independently from an early age often shows more maturity than a cosseted twenty-year-old. A twelve-year-old who has parents patient enough to consistently point out over the years the need for manners and consideration of others will be more polite and less inconsiderate than a fifteen-year-old who hasn't.

Adolescence is a highly creative and exciting time intellectually. We become more interested in abstract concepts such as relationships, politics, philosophy, religion and mortality, as well as much more reflective and self-aware. Command of language becomes more sophisticated with more complex sentence structure and a new ability to grasp the significance of metaphors, puns and analogies. Working memory improves and we also get quicker mentally. One study found that ten-year-olds were approximately 1.8 times slower in processing information than adults. Twelve-year-olds were 1.5 times slower, but fifteen-year-olds were almost as fast as adults.[5] Storytelling improves and lies become much more convincing for we become more adept at predicting other people's reactions and at applying new skills of logic to our advantage. Many of the intellectual functions with which children struggle, such as calculating, reading and writing, are processed automatically in an adolescent's mind, freeing it up for more complicated tasks and for wider breadth of vision. A child can only focus on one problem at a time, but with adolescence thinking slowly becomes multidimensional. 'Somehow as you get older you seem to be able to take in so much more,' says Claudia, who is seventeen. 'I'm so much more perceptive, I spend my whole time noticing things, analysing things, daydreaming about things, thinking the whole time rather than just floating through life.'

But this new intellectual equipment also enables teenagers to see life's difficulties more clearly. Chance happenings could now upset the simplest plans. They become aware of new dangers and risks that they were blissfully unaware of before and have to weigh up choices with potential consequences. 'You could go to Oxford Street to buy a dress that you really wanted and then something would happen to you on the bus and it wouldn't be worth it,' says Louisa, aged twelve. They also begin to understand that often all that stops us from death or injury is ourselves. My children sit either side of me on a chair lift at a ski resort. The adolescent now understands that she could push herself off to her death, while the seven-year-old kicks snow off her skis and sings, blissfully unaware. When things do happen to teenagers and other people fail to react in ways they expect, the duplicitous nature of morality hits them fair and square. 'I got mugged by some blacks on a bus at knifepoint,' says Colin, who is sixteen. 'They asked for some cigarettes, I said I didn't have any so they put a knife to my face and I gave them my fags. Nobody on the bus said or did a thing. I was dead scared, but I learned something from that. If I saw that happening to someone else I'd speak out and try and help. That was what really annoyed me, people sitting there and doing nothing, just staring.'

The naivety of small children protects them and allows them to feel bigger. They are the centre of their parents' universe, contained within the stability of a house which they know intimately. But with adolescence they paradoxically begin to feel much smaller as they shoot up in size and notice how big the world is out there. 'Putting everything into perspective, that's a big problem,' says Claudia. 'You have to put yourself into perspective, like I'm nothing in the whole universe, yet I'm everything within my whole life and it's hard to try and reconcile the two.'

The wider inequities of the world begin to come into focus and turn early adolescents into fierce and dogmatic defenders of vegetarianism or world peace. Concepts of honesty and morality become less clear-cut too, as young people begin to realize that fairness doesn't just mean dividing things up equally and that sometimes adults have to choose between the lesser of two wrongs in order to do the right thing. For a child stealing is always wrong, but an adolescent begins to understand that there may be times when it can be justified. The following hypothetical scenario used in an experiment by the psychologist Lawrence Kohlberg illustrates the difference. A man's wife is dying of a special kind of cancer and a pharmacist has devised a cure but sells it at a very high price. The man has borrowed money from everybody he knows but still cannot afford to buy it. When the chemist refuses to sell the drug any cheaper, the man steals it. When children are asked whether the man should have done that, their answer is usually unequivocally no. Stealing is always wrong. But the adolescent begins to understand that there are more complex issues of conscience and morality involved. How could a chemist charge so much and let people die simply because they are poor? Is stealing the drug a lesser crime when the man is faced with the prospect of his wife dying if he stands by and does nothing?

As their perceptions widen, early adolescents become more acutely aware of unfairness in their own lives. They begin to question parental judgement when they are denied something they want and argue their case vehemently, and they are apt to notice familial discrepancies more and interpret denial as lack of love. They begin to see the arbitrary nature of rules and the way they are bent and that authority figures can be inconsistent in the way they legislate or punish. 'There's all these silly rules at school, like you have to tuck your shirt in. But I don't see the difference if it's in or out,' says Trish, who is fourteen. 'You can't wear two pairs of earrings but you can wear one. But if you can wear one why not two? Sometimes they say no high heels but some girls wear four-inch heels and never get into trouble. I had a little chain on around my neck and the teacher told me to take it off but there was this girl sitting there in the same class who wears big earrings and loads of make-up and jewellery and when I pointed her out she said, "I can't see anything"! That girl's always dressed like that but because her mum's always hassling the school and saying leave her alone they do, so she's allowed to wear bangles up to her elbows and make-up and I can't wear one chain. It's just not fair.'

With greater perception, teenagers begin to understand that other people do not necessarily see things in the same way as they do. Then they begin to wonder what they think about them. It is this new realization which makes them so self-conscious at this age. 'How can you know what someone else thinks about you when you don't even know yourself?' says

Louisa. 'I want to be seen as a teenager but how do I know that they think I am one?'

This slow expansion of intellectual horizons is crucial for the development of individual identity. For a child, identity is given. You are who you are. Children know that there is a difference between themselves and other people but they cannot yet conceive of the fact that those people may have different thoughts and feelings. Children assess themselves and others through their physical attributes, by hair colour, height and whether or not they can swim or climb a tree. Their all-or-nothing thinking leads them to overestimate their abilities in an unrealistically favourable light. Once they can doggy-paddle a metre before sinking, they can swim. When they can't solve a maths question for homework they chuck down the pencil with a hefty, 'I can't do maths.' There is little analysis of the underlying causes of their behaviour and emotions.

It is only as we grow older through adolescence that we are able to make comparisons between present and past performances and begin to describe others in terms of interest and personality rather than physical attributes. We begin to realize that identity can change and be moulded by circumstance and context and therefore begin to question who we are. The ability to think more laterally and with greater perception and depth also helps adolescent children to build a stronger sense of self. They begin to consider what they actually think about things, rather than just accepting notions handed down from parents or authority figures. They become increasingly interested in understanding their own personalities, in how they differ from when they were younger and why they behave the way they do; they ask questions which connect and differentiate themselves from their immediate family – 'Am I more like my mum or my dad? How am I different to my sister?' – as they begin the inexorable but slow and sometimes tortured process of establishing who they are.

Our emerging sense of self is defined primarily through the physical changes of puberty. Children give little thought to their physical welfare. But as breasts bud and limbs lengthen, we are forced to focus on our changing bodies in order to establish just who we are becoming. Adolescents stare at themselves for hours in mirrors and shop windows. Girls experiment continuously with clothes and hairstyles, and narcissism takes hold because young people are now so much more aware of how they come across to an outside audience than they ever were as children. They become acutely self-conscious and more aware of their physical failings as their bodies change in ways which fail to match up to the images of physical perfection on advertising billboards and television. Once teenagers understand that other people assess each other differently, it is not uncommon for them to presume that they are constantly the focus of everybody else's interest, which is why they spend so much time getting ready to go out and easily get upset over one seemingly insignificant spot. 'It is only in the last few months that I've been wearing trousers, not to hide my body, but just not to show it off so much, and you don't think of things like that when you're a child,' says Emma, aged fourteen. 'I see my little sister wearing socks and tights together or odd socks and it looks so wrong and then I see photos of myself when I was younger wearing similar things and think, how could I have done that? When you're young you don't think about odd socks and make-up. When I used to prance about in my aunt's dressing room in her high heels it was like fancy dress. Now it's all about self-expression.'

As teenagers grow older and become more self-confident through middle to late adolescence, they are more able to look back on their earlier teenage years and assess them more accurately. 'I can remember when I was about thirteen, I would think more about the way I was dressed because it was more of an issue, you had an idea of how you wanted to look,' says Anna, aged sixteen. 'Whereas now, I just buy stuff that I like and wear it as I like. It's probably because I feel more confident about myself now.'

'I feel much happier about myself and I've come out of a really dark patch. I once dyed my hair really red and now when I look back at those photos when I had haircuts like curtains across my face and wore really baggy clothes, I know I looked crap, but I guess I was just trying out how I looked,' says Claudia, now seventeen. 'But everyone goes through that, you always feel as if you don't fit in, you were too young and didn't have the right clothes.'

Teenagers play around with clothing styles or body art to make a public statement of their maturity and to feel a sense of belonging. 'You don't just sort of wake up one morning and think, I know, I'll get piercings and dye my hair and look weird,' comments Dixie, who is sixteen, has a lip ring, and likes the artificial extended family of the Crusties and travellers. 'You identify with the way other people who look like that think.' Young people assert control over their own bodies through piercings or tattoos. By choosing to wound, inflict pain and draw blood they declare responsibility for their bodies and extinguish elements of childhood innocence. Crying is no longer appropriate and they have to tend to the wound to ensure that it heals properly. They also have some physical reminder that they have crossed a significant threshold towards adulthood. 'I feel more grown up somehow,' my daughter said as we returned home after having her ears pierced, the long-awaited fulfilment of a promise. She felt elated and proud. I felt sick and giddy. I could still hear the sound of that gun puncturing her soft and perfect little ear lobes and felt so ill as I sat there holding her hand that I chickened out of having my own ears pierced, even though I had the most perfect pair of expensive earrings – a Christmas present – at home waiting to be worn.

Often teenagers spend an inordinate amount of time contemplating having their bodies pierced as a way of camouflaging what they consider to be imperfections. When they feel deeply inadequate about the way they look, just the thought of such a powerful act diminishes feelings of helplessness. 'It offers the rare experience of permanence, even if that permanence is illusory,' writes Marilee Strong in her book on self-mutilation, *A Bright Red Scream*. 'For someone who feels not only physically but psychologically adrift, these indelible markings may be as grounding as the anchor tattooed on a sailor's arm, which helped him keep faith that one day he would make it home.'

When young people can more easily recognize the differences between themselves and their friends or their parents, they begin to develop a sense of their own uniqueness. They also begin to see weaknesses in their parents and find aspects of their attitudes or behaviour irritating, helping them to develop a clearer sense of who they are through their differences. We assume, as children, that we know our parents. But it is only with adolescence that we begin to see their faults and weaknesses, we see aspects of their personalities which we do not necessarily like and make conscious decisions now to mould ourselves differently. 'I think I liked my mother more when I was younger,' says Trish, 'because little things didn't get on my nerves so much, but now everything she does is so annoying. In school I'm not really moody but when I get home, if my mum says anything, the littlest thing really annoys me. She's just passed her driving test and she can't park and I sit there really embarrassed while she takes twenty minutes trying to. When I say, "Can you let me out while you park?" she says, "No, you sit there," and I have to with a red face. It's so awful. She's the same really, it's just me, things annoy me more and I feel less affectionate towards her, which makes me feel guilty, because I ought to feel closer.'

'I've always had problems with my mum, mostly with how

much she loves me. She smothers me. I've had some nasty thoughts, being ashamed and pitying my mother, but that's mostly just because she's your mum that you think that. I never wanted her to be perfect,' says Rebecca, who is twenty. 'When I was quite unhappy, I remember I didn't want her to know or assume anything about me, her questions felt like such an invasion. I remember once she was talking about something that was going to happen the following summer and she said, "You'll be seventeen then." I just thought, how dare she assume I'll be seventeen. I realized afterwards that was quite funny really.'

With greater powers of memory teenagers are more able to know themselves, for memories provide each of us with our own personal stories and it is only when we are able to look back over our pasts, however short, that we are able to construct a narrative of the self. 'I don't remember much of my childhood except that I was very happy and very unaware,' says Rebecca. Childhood memories are fleeting and usually associated with great extremes of emotion – great happiness at receiving a special present or trauma and loneliness. Adults' memories of childhood come principally from adolescence simply because that is when the brain begins to mature enough to be able to retain the information. 'I do have vivid memories about being a child but they are isolated incidents,' says Judith who has two children. 'You can remember yourself at fifteen, but not at five because when you're fifteen you start analysing and thinking about things, writing turgid diaries and saying, "It's not fair."'

'I can remember things from two years ago much better than I could remember things when I was eleven about being nine,' says Claudia, aged seventeen. 'When I re-read my diary, everything is terrible, really embarrassing and I feel like I've changed from being the old me to being the real me even though I haven't changed that much in essence. I've changed a lot in the way that I look at things, my perception of things, but I haven't changed myself and I can read anything I've written since then with comfort.'

I have vivid memories of sitting alone on the school play-ground bench during playtime at the age of five because I had no friends and didn't know what else to do. I can remember that my mother was discussing hairdryers with our next-door neighbour over the garden fence when my two-year-old brother squashed his big toe by pulling over a paving slab that was leaning against the fence. But I have no memory of day-to-day life. It vanishes because it is unremarkable and often hard to disentangle true memory from the stories we are told about ourselves. But with adolescence we gain perspective over our whole lives. 'Remembrances came sudden and swirled, each coloured with its own season, and for the first time she looked back on all the twelve years of her life and thought of them from a distance as a whole,' writes Carson McCullers in *The Member of the Wedding*.

Ideas of what constitutes a 'man' or a 'woman' are crucial to an adolescent's emerging sense of self. As children we differentiate between boys and girls in very simple ways, through the obvious differences in genitalia and preferences for toys. But through adolescence, children look to their parents first for clues as to how to be a man or a woman and begin to understand that there is depth and complexity to gender differences. The easy androgyny of childhood begins to disap-pear for ever as each child now looks more to society in general for accepted models of masculine or feminine behaviour. Boys feel that they have to be strong, assertive and self-reliant in order to conform to macho imagery. It is no longer acceptable to cry, hug Mum in public or show one's feelings. Helen's fifteen-year-old son goes to a tough school in Moss-side and has been mugged, like countless other teenage boys in Manchester. 'I see a passivity in him and his friends. They're frightened of going out and he says he has to tense his body and wear a mean expression in school just to fend off what's coming. There's a loneliness to being a sensitive boy in a tough community and he gets by, by pretending to be different to the person he actually is.'

Girls can be equally confused as they try to suppress their needs in order to conform to society's expectations of femininity. American psychologist Carol Gilligan has found that all too often, confident, opinionated and happy ten-year-old girls turn into guarded, confused and nervous creatures in early adolescence who say, 'I don't know,' every other sentence. An internal struggle develops between being true to themselves and doing what they perceive is required of them now as young women: looking good, being nice, kind and sympathetic, and not being outspoken in case they find themselves isolated from the relationships that they long for in order to feel validated. They begin to struggle with the contradictions that numerous adult women still find hard: wanting to look better, but knowing that beauty is only skin deep; wanting to eat but also to lose weight; wanting to fulfil their own career aspirations but not to seem so smart that they frighten off the boys; wanting to be sexy, without being tarty. 'I'm scared of being weak and a lot of that is to do with being female,' says Rebecca. 'For a long time I thought it would be better to be a boy and even now I actually despise the way many women are.'

During early adolescence, teenagers' new and emerging sense of self is heavily fragmented. They have many 'selves' – a childish one at home with their mother; another side to their character entirely with their father or siblings; a more mature and intelligent self with teachers or other adults; and a completely different one again, more playful and cheery, with friends. Colin was always highly articulate about his problems and his emotions when I talked to him. When I asked him if he was able to talk this way with his friends, he said, 'No' without hesitation. 'I'm articulate when I need to be, that comes from my mum but I don't talk like that to my friends. It's like two personalities really. I shorten the words, swear a lot, but if I talked like I talk to you with my friends, they'd think, what? Where you from? Every now and then I pick a big word and it's, "Oh! Smart boy!" I'm not afraid to say what I feel and I'm not scared talking to adults. Meeting my mum and dad's friends made that possible.'

Teenagers are playing around with who they are, and are often unable to detect the inherent contradictions in their behaviour. They cannot yet integrate all of these different aspects of their personality into one cohesive sense of self. That comes with maturity. With heightened powers of perception as well as an embryonic sense of self, the opinions of outsiders become crucial for definition. Other people act as mirrors; 'through others' reactions we learn whether we are competent or clumsy, attractive or ugly, socially adept or tactless,' writes the psychologist Laurence Steinberg; 'we learn from others what it is we do that we ought to keep on doing, and what it is we do that we ought not to do.'[6] The desire to know the self is integrally linked with learning how to relate to others, and during early adolescence, teen-agers go out of their way to conform to wider peer pressures because they feel that rejection more keenly without the certainties of knowing who they are. 'You don't really have a defined self when you start secondary school,' says Vicky who is seventeen, 'but now I'm much more confident and if people don't like who I am that's fine. But I used to keep quiet about things. If I didn't agree with people I wouldn't have said anything but now I'm much more prepared to say something and feel that my opinions are valid.'

'When I was about eleven and went to secondary school, I feel I was easily influenced until I was fourteen,' says Rebecca, who fell out badly with her best and only friend when she was fifteen. 'I wanted to be friends with all the people who were really cool and couldn't understand why I couldn't be popular like them. I was different to them but I wanted to be the same as them. When she stopped talking to me I stopped talking to everybody else. That's the age when your mind starts waking up to things and being who you are. The fact that such an important friendship broke down at that time meant that I thought that was how I was, someone who didn't have friends. So I isolated myself. It's a protection thing because at school you're always scared that people won't like you, so it seems easier if you say that you don't care, if you don't try. It's only now that I'm older and I can look back and begin to work out who I really am and what I really want that their opinions matter less.'

Teenagers can become very introspective and preoccupied with what other people think of them because so many different versions of 'me' crowd the landscape as they grow older and life gets confusing. They begin to detect the contradictions in their behaviour (which one is the real me?) and the need for social recognition gathers momentum as they become increasingly aware that their sense of value cannot come from being praised and adored by their parents alone. Numerous coming of age novels describe what became known during the twentieth century as the identity crisis of youth. 'Doesn't it strike you as strange that I am I, and you are you?' asks Frankie in *The Member of the Wedding*. 'We can look at each other, and touch each other, and stay together year in, year out in the same room. Yet always I am I, and you are you and I can't ever be anything else but me and you can't be anything else but you. Have you ever thought of that. And does it seem strange to you?'

Many typical adolescent behaviours are reactions to this confusion of selves. Idealism, egocentrism, dogmatism and even adolescent love enable teenagers to pinpoint who they are by association. It helps when you're not sure who you are to be able to say, 'I'm a vegetarian,' or 'I'm a member of Greenpeace.' Cults or totalitarian doctrines are attractive because they offer adolescents something strong, almost familial, to identify with, and simplistic, easy answers to life's problems and paradoxes. Teenagers become passionate about issues such as the environment, homelessness or poverty because these are clear-cut moral issues with obvious answers. There should be no homelessness if there are empty houses. Pollution is wrong and poverty unacceptable when the rich get richer. But if you were to ask teenagers how to right these wrongs in detail they may find it hard to answer, for they have yet to face the challenges and disillusionment of reality or the many absurd paradoxes of the modern adult world. Their idealism is inevitably naive. Gillian's son is fourteen and has found a transient sense of boundaries outside the home through his membership of the Cadets. 'He didn't like being a child and he doesn't know what to do with himself as an adolescent except for the Cadets, which gives him a clear role and a uniform and structures and he loves that. The army has given him a real sense of belonging and purpose.'

Often teenagers become obsessive in their new-found beliefs. There is no room for criticism or doubt because that raises feelings of uncertainty which adolescents find particularly difficult to deal with just as all their childhood security is beginning to disappear. Narcissism is integrally linked to adolescent idealism because teenagers are less interested in how the world is than how it ought to be to match up to their expectations. And they may not have ever experienced the emotions that actually go hand in hand with their new-found beliefs. Gillian's fourteen-year-old son recently became very categoric about death. 'He was telling me how he isn't afraid of death and I thought, goodness, he's thinking about all these things and I had no idea. But he said that he wasn't afraid, it was just a fact, that people live and then they die and there was nothing to worry about or dread. We knew someone whose child had died in a road accident and that was on my mind and he was trying to make me feel better by saying that this was just a fact of life. I said but what about all the emotional ties and the mourning. His answer was, "Yes, but in the grand scheme of things it doesn't really matter." I suppose that is partly his age because he hasn't made those emotional attachments yet, or really experienced death, other than the rabbit.'

Teenagers often start arguments with parents to help them establish what they really think about things. I remember countless hours of argument with both my mother and my father over current events. My arguments were never well prepared and both my parents easily picked holes in what I had to say with the benefit of adult experience. But still I would keep on, flinging back alternative stances and ideas at them to see how they would react, while establishing what I really did think about issues as diverse as the Common Market and drugs. They enjoyed the spats, interested perhaps by this new thinking person within their midst. Perhaps they even enjoyed being able to win against such a weak and inconsistent opponent. But I found it hard to understand that when they attacked my argument, they were not attacking me personally, what I stood for and believed in even though I wasn't quite sure what that was yet. Inevitably they would reduce me to tears. I would limp away, wounded by their accusations, wipe my eyes and then come back for more.

As parental security vanishes, teenagers have no choice but to focus more intently on themselves. Early adolescent girls in particular attempt to establish who they are by starting diaries, writing their name on every available surface and experimenting with handwriting styles. Adolescent love can also be seen in some respects as an aspect of this essential quest for identity. 'My inner life took full shape around such a love,' writes Mary Karr in her memoir *Cherry*. 'I learned to imagine around his force. Before such enchantment takes us, there are only the forces of parents, other kin. Those are doled out to us; they *are* us in some portion. These first beloved are other. And we invent ourselves by choosing them.' First love is often narcissistic. No one has ever loved so deeply or lost so much.

Young people tend to seek out lovers who will make them look good or 'cool'. They are not yet emotionally mature enough to be able to recognize that genuine relationship accepts difference as well as another's faults alongside their strengths. But adolescent love is also useful, enabling the individual to pull away from the exclusivity of the group, and the obsessional, passionate, all-consuming nature of that relationship allows teenagers to both lose and find themselves within the couple, through more intimate and honest conversation. Early sexual contact is crucial for exploration of their new adult physiques. The exquisite sensations that come from being touched by another confirm a teenager's mental picture of his or her changing body. The knowledge that another gains pleasure from their body can push adolescents closer towards adult acceptance of its imperfections. Finding love and approval from another human being outside one's immediate family helps to build confidence and sometimes this is enough to break the last threads of complete dependence on family life.

Adolescents oscillate between childish ways and their chronological age. At times they feel omnipotent, punch drunk on their new powers, but often they don't feel up to the tasks they face and easily feel helpless and inadequate. Their true age seems transient, hovering daily somewhere between three and twenty-three. When teenagers are talking to other adults they seem so grown-up and yet they can be like small children when they are ill or don't want to do things and need to regress into the play of childhood when things get tough. The constant performance of adolescence, the effort involved in being 'cool' and the emotional consequences of all this new perception can be exhausting at times and teenagers find it deeply relaxing to be allowed to wallow in childhood again. Through play with younger children, water fights or football they are able to relive that carefree certainty of childhood.

'I was sixteen then, and I'm seventeen now and sometimes I act like I'm thirteen,' says Holden Caulfield in J. D. Salinger's *The Catcher in the Rye*. 'And yet I still act sometimes like I was only twelve. Everybody says that, especially my father. It's partly true, too, but it isn't ALL true. People always think something's ALL true.' Adults are so much more aware of the certainties of their own age that they often forget that teenagers never quite know exactly how old they are. They feel older than we think they are when they want greater freedoms or more money, and younger than we tell them they ought to be when it comes to taking greater responsibilities. And sometimes they feel a mixture of young and old, when they want to go to a party but feel such excruciating self-doubt that they can't think how to summon up the courage to go and long for a parent to tell them that they can't. Adults inevitably contribute to this ambivalence over their real age.

'If I want to stay up late, my mum says, "You're only thirteen,"' says Emma. 'But when it comes to tidying my room she says, "You're nearly fourteen." When she wants me to help, I'm old, but when I want something, I'm too young.'

'We're part adult when they want you to pay for things – how can you stop being a child and pay full fare on aeroplanes at the age of twelve? I could have two million pounds on Saturday by winning the lottery but I still can't vote, it's dumb,' says Stella, who is sixteen.

'We're considered adults when it suits but not when it doesn't,' says Karen, aged sixteen. 'We have to pay adult prices, but we're not allowed to vote. We're adults, but we're not. We're sort of nothing.'

We tend to expect rational, consistent adult thought from teenagers simply because they look so grown-up physically. But it can take years for this great upheaval of physical, psychological and social change that is adolescence to gel. They have a tendency to be extreme or over-generalize because they still see things in black-and-white terms as children do and have difficulty connecting their own actions with their beliefs. As they grow older, egocentrism fades and adolescents begin to accept the possibility of uncertainty and relativism. 'There have been times when I've thought that nothing has any meaning at all,' says Rebecca. 'I just saw the absurdity and uselessness of everything. But once you realize that I have no meaning and the world has no meaning, you then begin to understand that you're still human and things make you happy and that if you're going to be happy then you have to find things to do which have meaning for you.'

Adolescent contradictions and self-centred hypocrisies may be infuriating, but they are healthy, normal, and integral to teenage charm. These are not deliberate, premeditated acts designed to drive adults mad. When teenagers seem to be single-minded, completely failing to understand the meaning of the word 'compromise', that is because they cannot yet grasp the full significance of perspective and that other people may see things differently. If you ask teenagers how they feel about something and they reply in simplistic terms – 'like shit' – that is probably because they can't be bothered, don't want to talk about it or can't yet understand why they feel so bad. Claudia finds this uncertainty over what she actually thinks and feels deeply disconcerting. 'I find it so hard to understand myself that to try and understand other people is just impossible. Sometimes my boyfriend says something that upsets me and I try to explain why and could come up with twenty different reasons but I wouldn't know which one was the right one, or actually if any of them were right. They're like educated guesses rather than actually knowing and that's quite scary. I didn't worry about that sort of thing when I was a child.'

Aspects of adolescence are inevitably harder these days, for teenagers grow up with a whole range of conflicting pressures which previous generations did not have to deal with. These new pressures can inhibit psychological maturity. Teenagers need adults to understand their confusion and support them far more than adolescents did in the past as they struggle for clarity and a stronger sense of individual self. Puberty tends to begin earlier now than it did in the past. The average onset of menstruation is twelve or thirteen today in Europe and America; at the beginning of the twentieth century it was between fifteen and seventeen. There is no conclusive evidence as to why, however, psychological development appears to be linked more with chronological age rather than with the stages of puberty. This may mean that it is harder for early maturing adolescents to understand or come to terms with what is happening to them. There is considerable research evidence to show that early maturing girls in particular are more likely to feel out of step with their peers, more likely to feel negative about their bodies and more likely to develop eating disorders and psychosomatic symptoms than those who start puberty later. Earlier puberty does not mean that they become adult earlier, in fact there is some evidence to suggest that it takes longer.

The ubiquitous visual impact of firm, fat free, perfect bodies on advertising hoardings and television has a profound effect on adolescents at this vulnerable stage of their development. They still respond as children do – emotionally – to these images. The visual imagery of beautiful young people and the extensive marketing of products to young people is as powerful as the advertising of toys to children before Christmas, but goes on all year round. When adolescents lack understanding of the way that their emotions are being played on and that these images of perfection are manipulated, all they are left with is a resounding sense of disappointment with their own physical inadequacies. 'Our national infatuation with "hard bodies", combined with the idea that bodies are perfectible, heightens the pressure on adolescents and complicates the business of adjusting to a new sexually maturing body,' writes Joan Jacobs Brumberg in her powerful history of American Girls, *The Body Project*. Rates of cosmetic surgery amongst the young are now soaring as they strive for the body they want, rather than learning how to accept the body they have. Having exactly the right image, the right trainers, nails or hair colour defines who they are but can be extortionately hard to achieve now that business has successfully nourished a flourishing and lucrative youth market. 'In the twentieth century, the body has become the central personal project of American girls,' continues Brumberg, 'because they believe that the body is the ultimate expression of the self.'

Adolescents need sensitive handling. They need constant reassurance, to have their inner qualities as well as their physical strengths regularly pointed out to deflect attention from their insecurities about their bodies, even if that is just for a few moments. When girls despair that they will ever have breasts to fill out their strappy little vests, they need reassurance that they will come with time. When they loathe the fat on their thighs they need to be told that a certain amount of body fat is essential for menstruation. When boys feel inadequate because their height leaves them shorter than most of the girls they fancy, they need to know that boys tend to have their growth spurt towards the end of puberty, whereas for girls it is often one of the first signs. Boys also need to know that they might develop tender swellings in their breasts during early puberty but this does not mean that they have cancer or are turning into girls. As the hormones begin to settle down the swelling subsides. Adolescents need plenty of open discussion about the way that beauty is used to sell products and the way branding hikes up the price of the goods they want so badly. And when they moan about a spot or not having the right thing to wear to go out in, they need that anxiety to be understood as important rather than dismissed as trivial. Parents know that that spot is barely visible, and that in the grander scheme of things it doesn't matter, but to say so risks alienating the adolescent who retreats and feels misunderstood. Empathy and a spot concealer are far more constructive solutions.

Emma's mother is thin and beautiful, her younger sister is also slight and Emma considers herself big in comparison. (I thought she looked lovely.) 'The way I look is one of the main things that gets me down. My mum used to be a model, my aunt is a model, they're all really tall, slim and perfect and then there's me! She'll say things like, "It's good to be big," but I don't want her to say that and she can't see why that's insensitive. When I'm jumping around she'll say, "It's like having an elephant in the house." I feel more self-conscious about my body than I did when I was younger so it takes ages to get ready to go out, but my mum doesn't understand that. She says, "When you're going out with your friends you're fast, but when you're going out with me you take ages." But it's more fun with your friends and when you're by yourself it's harder to decide. You think, I've got nothing to wear, but all Mum says is, "You've got all these clothes."'

Teenagers also grow up now with a host of new media and are bound to be affected when they lack the mental maturity to understand it. Television advertising bombards teenagers with fast messages that trigger emotional cravings, the control mechanisms for emotions we now know to be underdeveloped in the teenage brain. These messages are sent in such a short period of time that there is little opportunity for the adolescent brain to employ rational or reflective thought in order to be able to make sound judgements. Emotional aspirations are triggered rather than fledgling reason, and sometimes the messages given are so confusing that it is easier not to think at all. Video games are often violent and teenagers actively engage in this screen violence without consequence. They do not have to think about their actions from the perspective of the victim and do not develop empathy as a result.

The search for identity is also made harder by aspects of the modern world. What does regularly moving house and the resulting absence of community links do to a young person's emerging sense of identity when our sense of self is so clearly defined by history and place? When your father's trade or class determined who you were and how you earned your living, when your gender or birth place as either the eldest or youngest child determined so much of your future, struggling with the essential adolescent question of 'Who am I and what do I want to do?' was far less significant than it is today. When poverty was more widespread, earning any sort of a living was paramount and the modern emphasis on happiness, fulfilment, job satisfaction or a sense of purpose and achievement from work wasn't the prime motive. Now, growing numbers of educated young people expect all this as well as sufficient income to feed their growing consumer needs. There are few prescribed paths, and the modern emphasis on self-determination means that they feel they have to achieve all this alone, with no clear picture as to what the future holds, or what is available, other than that it is riddled with risk and uncertainty. Young people lack adult role models to help them, apart from teachers and television presenters. They want to be pop stars and doctors because they rarely come into contact with the rest of the working adult world within the confines of school and rarely have any idea about the diverse and changing nature of work.

When I was a student I had no idea who I was and therefore

what I wanted to do. I drifted through an arduous degree in Russian and Arabic because I enjoyed them and thought, foolishly perhaps, that the unusual nature of my choice might help me to earn a living. But I didn't really mind, life was for living and having fun. My daughter has a far more focused and anxious attitude to her future at a much earlier age. She wants certainty, security, but now knows as an adolescent that there are no guarantees. She has to think about and plan her future carefully in order to maximize her chances of success in ways which my generation never bothered to even consider when we were growing up. 'There are such high expectations these days,' says Polly, aged nineteen. 'We have teenagers growing up with adult issues and they're without the emotional resources to deal with them. You're still a child in so many ways; you don't have the stability, the self-confidence yet, but you're forced to deal with things. There's nothing sacred about being a teenager any more – you grow up so fast.'

With few role models or career focus at school, adolescents need their parents to introduce them to the different, individual worlds of other adults in order to widen their intellectual horizons at this vulnerable and highly creative time. Parents can also do a great deal to help shunt their child up the ladder to greater psychological maturity. Schools tend to cram teenagers with facts in order to get them through exams, rather than teaching them how to think. There is rarely the time for the extensive discussion, analysis and experimentation that is essential at this age to develop their powers of critical thinking and judgement and their ability to make decisions. Now that schools are, as we shall see in Chapter 8, failing so badly to meet the specific intellectual needs of teenagers in order to prepare them for adulthood, we have to take greater responsibility for their welfare. My parents did not have the faintest idea what I was learning at school and I do not remember being helped with my homework. But we need to play a more active part with our own children to help them flourish and mature. We need to take an interest in their homework in order to pinpoint areas of misunderstanding. We need to remind them to stop and think, stick to the task and approach things systematically, and we need to teach them how to study, for basic study and revision skills are rarely taught in our schools. If teenagers are having difficulty with something, sitting down with them and pointing out the areas which do not make sense or fit in helps them to identify the problem so that they can work out a solution, and develops their intelligence. Telling them *how* to work out the problem does not. Just enough help, usually in the form of questions, urges them on to find their own solutions: solving it for them does not.

We also need to develop their powers of reasoning and argument through questioning and discussion about current events, philosophy, history, the law and morals in order to help them understand that there are different kinds of knowing. By directing them more towards the outside world, we deflect attention from themselves temporarily. Teenage idealism can be given greater depth through conversations where alternative scenarios are posed, and context is added to argument so that adolescents develop their powers of perspective at the time when their brains are crying out for this kind of stimulus. They need to go on outward-bound courses where they have to work in teams and test the new boundaries of their physical and emotional abilities with controlled risks. They need active involvement with organizations outside school which connect them to the wider community and give them a sense of value and place.

The sense of self-interest rather than community that tends to dominate modern culture inevitably makes it harder for adolescents to emerge from the solipsistic phase of their development. Why consider others when it is the self and self-gain which seem to matter most? 'Adolescents find it extraordinarily difficult to understand that other people actually exist in the world beyond themselves,' says Adam, who has taught English to teenage boys for thirty years. 'I have noticed that basic consideration for others within the school environment has got worse because this isn't one of the primary ideals which parents instil in their children. Initially there is this idea that the sheer achievement of the child has been the most wonderful thing, which it is. But this develops into the idea that the child is somehow delicate and needs to be protected, which therefore means indulging. His love needs to be purchased. The child then grows up with this negative idea of his own specialness and then comes to school and belabours the rest of us, leaving his things scattered about the classroom for others to pick up or pushing and shoving on the stairs and corridors.'

More than ever, when they are being selfish, teenagers need to be reminded of the imperative to consider and respect the needs of others. When parents are prepared to point out repeatedly how their children are being inconsiderate, they help them through the tunnel of solipsism, even though it feels at times as though they are merely banging their head against a brick wall. When adults challenge, support and encourage in the right way, teenagers are more able to integrate socially with their peers and elders. They will also be better equipped to deal with the risks inherent to adolescence. The more mature the child is, the more self-protective he or she will be and, given the easy availability of drugs, this cannot be a bad thing. Early adolescents find it difficult to connect their actions with consequences. They genuinely find it harder than adults to link sex with pregnancy, or drinking alcohol with damage to their health. They are also at their most vulnerable to peer pressure and do things, which they may later regret, to fit in with the crowd. It is only when teenagers are in situations where they have to use their powers of judgement or weigh up consequences that they begin to develop the area of their brain which exerts control over their emotional drives. Challenges from middle childhood onwards that allow children to make judgements in the face of minimal risks encourage that development and move them swiftly through the mental stages of early adolescence when they are most vulnerable. 'When you talk to young people they often say that being a teenager is awful, but then when you talk to them a year later they often say it wasn't so bad. I survived it. Something happens to move them along,' says psychologist Jeannie Milligan. 'When you're feeling unformed and uncertain about your identity it's exciting to be part of a huge blob at a rave bouncing up and down. But as you get older you need that less and less. Observing others more means that you begin to notice aspects of their behaviour that you loathe and then see those aspects in yourself and want to change them.'

The mind changes of adolescence make teenagers vulnerable emotionally and their fragile self-esteem is easily damaged. We need to listen to them closely in order to understand what they are living through and we need to tolerate their inconsistencies as normal at the same time as gently pointing them out. Sarcasm, ridicule, patronizing attitudes or demoralizing statements are likely to alienate or antagonize the young adolescent who takes this as personal criticism and does not yet have the resources to bounce back. Adults have a tendency to want to puncture adolescent idealism and narcissism with cynicism. When teenagers talk with absolute certainty about things they know little about, adults feel uncomfortable and find it hard to resist putting them straight by saying, 'I know better, I have the wisdom which comes from age.' But idealistic visions are the privilege of youth and without those flights of fancy and hope, society stagnates. 'I have scarcely reached the age of eighteen, and I already hold the key of history in my hand,' wrote Napoleon, with the arrogance of youth, in his autobiography. 'I possess that enthusiasm which a deeper study of human nature often destroys in our hearts. The venality of a riper age will never smudge my pen.'[7]

Adolescence is a time of dynamic energy and families who cherish this very special and creative time by allowing teenagers to express themselves freely, encourage them to flourish and move on. Families where everyone has a voice 'characterized by both separateness, which gives the adolescent permission to develop his or her point of view, and connectedness, which provides a secure base from which to explore options outside the family encourages the child to look to their own futures with greater courage and confidence and without fear of retribution or disapproval from their parents,' conclude Shirley Feldman and Glen Elliott, editors of a monumental academic collection of articles assessing academic research on adolescence, *At the Threshold*. As the eldest child reaches adolescence, parents begin to understand that they have to tread a fine balance between allowing their children to make their own mistakes in order to learn, and bailing them out to let them know that they are still supported by family and loved. Often just talking about this balance with children helps them to voice where they feel they need help and where they don't. 'There are times when they want you to be the parent and just sort it out and other times when they want to be able to make their own mistakes,' says Andrea, whose eldest son is thirteen. 'Last summer on holiday, Julian got concussion and the hospital wanted him to stay overnight but I couldn't stay with him because he was on an adult ward. I wanted him to make the decision as to whether he should stay. I said that I thought that he was old enough, but he didn't feel that way. He wanted me to as the parent because he couldn't judge what was the right thing to do, so I told him he should stay.'

'An adolescent who never questions what she is taught,

never wonders where she is headed and never explores different identities is likely to be inflexible, dogmatic and overbearing – or, shallow and conforming as an adult,' writes the psychologist Laurence Steinberg in *You and Your Adolescent*. However, when parents manage to reach out to their adolescent children and find more sophisticated and adult ways of communicating with them, the rewards are great; a more interesting person evolving at home, someone who thinks differently and has valuable insights on new emerging generations and the changing nature of modern life. We do not lose control when our children become more critical and need more provocative challenges. We are bringing up independent thinkers who are capable of saying 'no' and standing up for themselves, who have enough critical capabilities to believe in themselves, and who are less likely to self-destruct because they believe, through parental approval and acceptance, that they have intrinsic merit. Research has found that when this type of child-rearing is practised through adolescence, teenagers are more able to mature psychologically, and develop that firm and confident sense of self that is so crucial to healthy separation from parents.[8] 'I think they need you more when they're in their teens, because when they are little they just bubble along and they are not aware of how everything interacts,' says Mary, who is a single mother of two sons who are now in their early twenties. 'But as they mature they see ramifications, they see how life is rounded and if it gets a bit rough at this edge or that, they need someone to help smooth it off again.'

More often than not teenagers muddle through this extraordinary psychological transformation to maturity relatively unscathed. But coming to terms with who you are and what you might want from life takes time and provokes a struggle with parents as well as with themselves. Inevitably, when adolescents think differently to adults and children, conflict escalates, which is the subject of my next chapter. Many parents believe that their children become more argumentative as teenagers, but in fact they just get better at arguing and will argue for the sake of it in order to develop their thinking skills. They no longer accept facts as absolute truths without question. The child that once obeyed you because you said so is no longer there. Home should be a safe place for adolescents to practise their arguments, play with identities and be able to change their minds without losing face. And as time passes, parents see them change and mature, shedding the selfishness of early adolescence for a more mature perspective which is considerate of others. 'They begin to understand about responsibility and how their behaviour affects other people, that you can't just rampage down the street and knock people flying,' says Mary. 'You can see these mental changes happening. I used to look at them and think, good God, why are they behaving like that? But then they matured and behaved differently. They do eventually realize that they are not the centre of the universe.'

5. Conflict

The best way to keep children home is to make the home atmosphere pleasant – and let the air out of the tyres.
  Dorothy Parker

When the eldest child embarks on adolescence, the whole dynamic of family life begins to change. With younger children, parents assume the lion's share of decision-making and the family muddles along as a cohesive unit. But with early adolescence children begin to resist doing familiar things. They kick up rough at the prospect of going to the park or their grandparents on a Sunday if that means missing their favourite television programme. They moan at the prospect of eating pasta *again* or at the fact that it is cold when they have taken ten minutes longer than anybody else to sit down at the table. Weekends and holidays begin to get complicated when everyone wants to do different things but may not be old enough to be allowed to do them or to be left at home alone for long. Tagging along with parental decisions provokes a storm of rebellion. Even the way that the home is used begins to change. 'We used to go for walks and bike rides together,' says Caroline, who has two teenaged daughters aged sixteen and twelve. 'Now we're just four different people in four different rooms.'

With greater responsibilities at school as well as greater independent mobility, teenagers are often home late because of sports practice, homework clubs or skateboarding in the park. It becomes harder for parents to know what homework their children ought to be doing and harder to monitor it when whole days disappear without anything more than a few words muttered between telephone calls and television programmes. When they're in, if not as a brooding presence upstairs, they make themselves felt by eating their way through the fridge, sprawling across the sofa in front of the telly, hogging the phone or skateboarding up and down the hall. They don't need to go to bed, they can stay awake for hours after exhausted parents feel their eyelids drooping, and those rare moments of middle-aged sexual congress have to be conducted in complete silence.

'It puts great pressure on your relationship because there's absolutely no space for you two,' says Stella who has three daughters, two of whom are adolescent. 'The eldest goes to sleep at midnight and then she's up at six to start her ablutions and make herself look beautiful for whoever she is going to see at the bus stop. We try and take time off because we need it, but the difference is that now there's no time in, because they're always there.'

Noise levels rise as the relative calm of middle childhood evaporates. You may find yourself crawling into the airing cupboard to get away from the constant thumping of pop music. There's the hoarse and persistent yelling of 'Phone' or 'Supper's ready', or 'I hate you'. There's the unseemly screaming at each other when tempers are frayed and parents simply haven't the energy to be understanding, and the violent roars of angry, frustrated teenagers when they are refused exit visas until midnight on a Tuesday. Rows with siblings are common during adolescence, far more so than rows with parents. Sisters and brothers who previously got on now begin to squabble daily as competition between them increases with the eldest asserting superiority and venting some of their new and intense emotions by needling and teasing the younger. As younger siblings enter adolescence, fighting between them intensifies. They now fight over clothes, CDs, space on the sofa in front of the TV, what's on the TV, who gets what.

'I argue more with my younger sister than I do with my mum,' says Sophie, aged sixteen. 'Mum doesn't go out of her way to antagonize me and she doesn't care if I take her own clothes.'

Rising levels of conflict are inevitable when both parents and teenagers are so emotionally volatile, when teenagers need to assert themselves and genuinely find it hard to see priorities in the same way as their parents do. The average family squabbles at least two or three times a week over minor domestic matters such as tidying bedrooms, money, clothes or curfews.[1] These battles usually hurt parents far more than teenagers who feed off the adrenaline. 'I enjoy the arguing, it helps you keep your distance,' says Ed, who admits to fighting sometimes out of laziness. 'Sometimes when they want you to do things, you could, but you can't really be bothered. When my mum goes, "Do your work," and I can't because it's quite difficult, I storm around the house. It usually works. My tantrums are brilliant when I want to get out of things.'

Parents, however, come home tired from work and resent having to exert so much energy over something so seemingly trivial. Living with an adolescent means having all of your deepest fears and weaknesses exposed to scrutiny. Nothing escapes the eye of a teenager: the colour of the walls, styles of hair and clothing, the fact that Dad loves Mum less than he should or that Mum doesn't let Dad out enough to the football now become legitimate subjects for general conversation and criticism. When there are weaknesses in family set-ups, with mothers over-dependent emotionally on their children because their marriage is spent or because they have nothing else in their lives, or when fathers are too harsh and judgemental or abusive of their children, the conflicts of adolescence escalate as teenagers struggle even harder to assert their difference and their own needs and parents shake their heads in despair, wondering where it all went wrong. 'But we gave her everything . . .'

Teenagers need small victories over the right to dye their hair pink or have their ears pierced because these victories establish important principles of autonomy over the way they look and the sense that their bodies are entirely their own. Teenagers argue to establish what they really think or want and to test parental boundaries or force them to adapt to their changing needs. Sometimes teenagers fight because they know of no other way to make contact with their parents and make them hear what they really think or feel about things. They may forget about the whole incident moments later, while their parents nurse their wounds for days afterwards. If there is great conflict and bickering at home, this merely reflects the more murky internal conflict between an adolescent's needs for support and for independence, or parental inability to adjust to the changing needs of their child. Teenagers fight for space or a voice, but they also scream abuse because they feel let down. 'I hate you' all too often means, 'Why can't you understand me better?'

Many of the families who live with high levels of conflict had problematic relations during earlier childhood, even though they may not have recognized them as such, for with shaky emotional foundations, children are more likely to go off the rails at adolescence.[2] Sometimes the emotional alienation between parent and child is so great that parents are afraid of confronting their own children. Their teenagers seem so withdrawn or emotionally volatile that they become reluctant to challenge behaviour or negotiate rules and boundaries. Others do not recognize how big a part parents play in exacerbating conflict with their teenagers through their reluctance to embrace change, treat the new young adult in their midst with the same courtesies and respect they would afford anyone else, or accept adolescents' ability to take responsibility for themselves.

I remember having vicious rows with my mother when I was a teenager. We screamed at each other sometimes for so long that my throat went hoarse. I cannot remember what we argued about, but I do remember feeling that whenever we rowed the animosity of argument compounded my sense of emotional alienation within my own home. The detail of what we rowed about seemed insignificant in my intellectually naive mind, although clearly in hindsight they must have been important issues for my mother. What mattered to me were the emotions behind the arguments; criticism meant that I was disapproved of, or not trusted enough to take responsibility or to do the right thing; anger meant that I wasn't loved enough and sarcasm told me that I wasn't liked. I responded emotionally to these confrontations, as children do. I withdrew to protect myself and sought solace elsewhere when I needed it, from a strong and supportive group of friends, from my father and stepmother, as soon as I was free to move around London on my own. I now understand from researching this book that my mother and I engaged in a power struggle when we argued, one that neither of us could ever win.

Such a breakdown in effective communication is common in families and is typified by regular and fierce fighting, and I met parents and teenagers who had reached a similar impasse in their relations. However I was staggered by the numbers of far healthier households I was welcomed into, where parents and their children maintained good relationships in spite of the bickering over chores and boundaries. Harmony in teenage homes is far more common than the myth of adolescent turmoil suggests. The vast majority of adolescents say that they stay close to their parents and respect them, with some three-quarters of families maintaining warm and conciliatory relations throughout adolescence.[3] Teenagers stop idealizing their parents as they should, but this does not necessarily mean that they become emotionally detached. They still desperately need the constancy and security of family life. They may find it boring and long to be out and away but it is that boredom, that stability, that offers them valuable relief from all the self-consciousness they feel in the public eye. They need to feel that home is somewhere they can hide safely, a buffer against so many of the more extreme difficulties of growing up, with parents who empathize and give them room to breathe.

Most families muddle through successfully, enjoying the new emerging individual in their midst and sensitive enough to bend with the changes their teenagers provoke rather than to resist them. Mary, a single mother with two grown-up sons, found the experience far better than she imagined it would be. 'They were very amenable, we did have arguments but all in all it was never that bad. We never seemed to have terrible hormonal turbulence and they were never like Harry Enfield's Kevin.'

Aspects of modern living have inevitably exacerbated and prolonged the nature of conflict in family life. More and more teenagers are either unemployed at sixteen or moving into higher education, still economically dependent on their parents. With this prolonged dependency, parents are more likely to feel that while they are subsidizing them they have a right to determine when and where their children go and what they spend their money on. Teenagers naturally feel constricted psychologically and socially by their inability to achieve economic autonomy and integrity. They rightly question why their ability to take responsibility for their decisions has anything to do with their inability to earn their own money. 'Usually it's about teenagers demanding a degree of independence that the parents are not comfortable with,' says

Helen, a Parent Network counsellor in Manchester and single mother to a teenage son. 'Their efforts to keep children in their control push them further away and there's a spiral of alienation. They impose more and more limits, tighter screws which the child doesn't adhere to and eventually they may run away or experiment with drugs. It's really important to keep the channels of communication open before it's too late.' Adolescents have a tendency to feel that they are ready for adulthood years before their parents are ready to accept that. There's a mismatch between the two, which helps keep children safe but inevitably produces struggles over power and responsibility. Parents feel that the greater freedom that teenagers demand has to be matched with more adult responsibilities and a sense of order at home, while teenagers couldn't care less about the fact that half the contents of their wardrobe are lying scrumpled in a heap on their bedroom floor or that several coffee cups are sprouting mould on their bedside table. This is their territory.

Rising rates of children being brought up in poverty may mean that these children become that much more argumentative and difficult as materially needy adolescents, fuelled by relentless product marketing and the changing fads dictated by television. 'Thou shalt honour and obey thy parents' is a commandment rarely adhered to in modern homes where more liberal and democratic sentiments dominate. A warm and loving family is now the ideal and conflict levels rise as adolescents answer back without fear of retribution. It also takes longer to arrive at decisions when several different family voices have to be heard and argument naturally flares. The modern tendency to keep our children close now that they are the chosen, cosseted and emotional centre of our lives may also exacerbate conflict as they begin the process of breaking away. Parents feel the loss more keenly, while adolescents have to fight that much harder to assert their own needs, to prove that they are capable of getting from A to B safely without being driven and of meeting the deadline for that university application form.

Changes in the nature of family life with rising rates of divorce and the adoption of step-parents have also inevitably raised levels of conflict. When parental relations break down arguments soar not just between the adults but between all family members, for warring parents often have less energy for and patience with their children. Access and money easily become regular sources of argument in households impoverished through divorce or where the split has been acrimonious. Adolescents become skilled at playing one parent off against the other now that they see their weaknesses that much more clearly, and single parents have to bear the brunt of arguments with teenagers on their own. Conflict with step-parents and step-siblings is also understandably common as teenagers are forced to accept new circumstances usually without consultation. 'There are some very explosive households around with not enough time for anybody,' says Kate, a Relate counsellor.

Felicity first met her stepchildren when they were sixteen and eleven. She remembers one furious row on a beach when they had walked miles from the car for a picnic but forgotten the water. Her husband asked his then thirteen-year-old son to get the water and he wouldn't go. 'So we sat there and ate our lunch without anything to drink. We all refused to go and it was frightful.' She later battled with her stepdaughter when she was twenty-two at her brother's eighteenth birthday dinner, an awkward evening because the children's mother was also present. The daughter announced that she wanted to go to El Salvador.

'I don't think that's sensible because it's terribly dangerous.' (Felicity)

'I think it would be interesting.' (daughter)

'I suppose it would be if you like looking at decapitated corpses.' (Felicity)

'I'm not going to be patronized by you.' (daughter, before storming out of the restaurant.)

Felicity's stepdaughter wrote a letter to her father months later in which she said that she felt Felicity was very opinionated, that they would never see eye to eye and that he wasn't to show her the letter. 'He said I can't do that because if you're married to someone you have to share. She replied by saying that she felt as if he had divorced her when he divorced her mother. It is obviously difficult because when you have a second family inevitably your new family are going to take priority. You say the word "Step-parent" but the only time when things went wrong were the times when I did behave like a parent. That's why she said I was patronizing. I should just have shut up and let her father say it.'

Parents are now solely responsible for the socializing and upbringing of adolescents. During the 1930s, roughly half of all households in the US and the UK had at least one other adult member besides the parents. Now that figure is less than 5 per cent.[4] There were servants, lodgers and other family members around to help with negotiation and discipline. 'The family handed over production to offices and factories, religion to the churches, the administration of justice to the courts,' writes Joan Lipsitz in her book on adolescence, *Growing Up Forgotten*. With apprenticeship, adolescents learned from their elders a great deal more than just how to do a particular job. Now there are fewer caring adults around to help. 'Most of my family live either abroad or too far away to be involved much in Hugh's upbringing,' says Bianca, a single mother. 'We went to Germany last summer and he met some of his cousins and uncles for the first time. That helped a lot, having older men to kick a ball around with, who could act as role models.' Schools find it almost impossible to cater for much of the adolescents' other emotional and psychological needs because of the driving need to get them through their GCSEs. Even wider society can no longer be relied on to discipline or look out for a teenager's needs. How many people would reprimand a thirteen-year-old for dropping litter or question why they are not in school?

Understandably, many parents feel at sea, with few guidelines as to how to raise and support their adolescents in the best way possible. Often they have little other than their own experience of adolescence to fall back on but that can only be partially helpful when their children are now growing up in very different circumstances, with very different pressures. 'When I was fourteen, I had to do what they said,' says Barbara, whose eldest son is fourteen and very argumentative. 'I could be sulky and miserable but there wasn't any question that they were in charge, but that is no longer the case, that's what's changed, I don't feel completely in charge. There's always the possibility of having to negotiate about something and there aren't so many rules about things so you don't know really what is the right way to do things, it's not fixed any more. I have a rule that he has to ring at six o'clock if he's not home, and those rules work, but it's other things like he doesn't want to come on holiday with us this year and we've said that he can stay here with a friend for a week, which feels like an enormous thing. He's not coming on holiday with us at fourteen years of age, but with some other people there wouldn't be any question about it – he'd have to go with them. Maybe we've been too wishy-washy, perhaps it would have been better if we'd had more family rules, or an extended family with more people in it to share the load.'

Often conflict escalates because parents have no certain knowledge or confidence as to how to deal with issues, they don't know how much to involve themselves and often resort to a knee-jerk policy that shifts with the sands and their energy levels. Judith has two teenage children and finds it hard to marry her own daughter's dependence on her with her own self-sufficiency at the same age. 'I've talked to lots of mothers who were teenage themselves in the 1950s and 1960s and there is this general feeling that we were expected to do more at this age. They hardly help at all, but then I came from a family where my mother was on tranquillizers and basically a bit of a mess, as was my older sister. I realized from about thirteen that I was going to have to take care of myself, as well as the rest of the family. But it is different for my children. Their support system is good, we're a strong couple with no money problems or illness. Generally amongst the middle classes there's less need for them to help. They know that a cleaner comes and that I'm here, so it feels slightly artificial to say, "No, you get your own deodorant," if I'm going into town anyway. I don't know what the answer is but I do slightly feel that when they're out on their own they'll have to do it anyway. When she had glandular fever I used to bring up some toast and a glass of milk to make sure that she'd eat. I still do that now because I feel better knowing that she's had a good breakfast, although she's nearly old enough to get married!'

Joan, like Judith, finds it hard to tow a firm line with her three daughters when she is at home full time. The overriding need to maintain some sense of emotional equilibrium presides. 'At one point when I wasn't feeling very well I said, "Could you just help? Could you pretend that I was really, really ill and just help? When I was young I had to do everything in the house." The middle one said, "Well you hated that, didn't you? And you hated Granny for it, didn't you?" I said, "Yes, I did," and she said, "There you are then."' Joan laughed when she related this conversation to me and while I could see that some child development experts might see this as indulgent, there was no doubting the warmth and happiness of her home. It is perhaps much more important to be on good terms in order to be able to deal intelligently and calmly with the really important things in life, rather than to risk alienation by battling over trivia. The healthiest families have parents who pick their fights carefully.

The first tensions and fights between parents and their children are usually over clothes and their appearance with the radical physical changes of early puberty. 'I remember one of the earliest clashes of control was over clothes,' says Claudia. 'The issue was always that if I looked nice it would make my mum look good. After I had done my entrance exam for secondary school there was this At Home where you met all the other kids. I wanted to wear my jeans and this cardigan I really liked. She made me wear this disgusting dress that I didn't like but she thought I looked nice in. We had this huge row about it and I put the dress on and then when I turned up everyone else was in jeans, so I didn't take my coat off the entire time and sat there sweltering.'

'Mum'll say things like, "Is it necessary to wear such a short skirt?" or "That makes your bottom look so big,",' says Emma. 'If I wear a vest top she'll say, "You're going to wear a cardigan over that or change." So I put on a cardigan and then take it off when I get outside.'

When parents were brought up in other cultures the fights over clothes and what parents consider to be an appropriate image can be even more intense. Trish's mother grew up in Turkey and came to live in Britain before her daughter was born. 'We do argue a lot, sometimes every day, about going out. She is so old-fashioned and ignorant. She thinks there's something wrong with men who are gay and I say, "Mum, how can you think that?" She tells me to stop cutting my hair and let it grow but it's none of her business what I do with my hair. I asked if I can dye it and she said no, but she let my older sister dye her hair, that's what we mostly argue about, my sister being treated differently.'

With wider perception, teenagers rightly question the connection between how they look and their parents' ability to parent. 'My mum has this problem with my trousers,' says Esme, who is sixteen. 'They're a bit ripped and I wear them around my hips as opposed to my waist. She says I'm naive to be going out with my trousers down my bum, but I don't walk around the streets with it so far down that it could be provocative because it would just look stupid, but she doesn't see it that way. I say, "Look, if I go out looking scruffy, people won't know that I'm your daughter so what's the problem?" But I don't think she's even listening to me.'

Esme's friend Anna feels the same way. 'I can't imagine judging other people's children by the state of their trousers, but that's what Mum does. Mine get ripped around the bottom because they're long, not because I rip them on purpose because I think it's cool which is what she seems to think. I understand that when I go and see my grandparents I should make an effort because they don't understand how things have changed since they were bringing up their own children – my sister takes out her nose ring when she goes because it wouldn't be worth the discussion – but you kind of expect your own parents to be able to deal with it.'

It may be upsetting to see one's precious daughter dressed like a hooker or a slob but any unsolicited comment or attempt to make her change meets with resistance and rightly so. This is their body to dress as they please and criticism easily translates into feelings of being unsupported and misunderstood in a fragile teenage mind. Parents who remember their tussles with their own parents find it easier to button their lip, but even then it can be hard. Stella has three daughters aged fourteen, twelve and seven. She remembers a major battle with her own mother when they were about to go out for lunch with formal friends. 'I spent ages getting ready and came down the stairs on a boiling hot summer's day in a full-length, black Victorian dress with black make-up, lacy gloves and tie-up boots. Mum said, "I really don't want you to go out like that." I ran upstairs sobbing and then Mum relented and never said a word about the way I looked afterwards. I used to dress outrageously and remember overhearing someone saying to my father at a Christmas drinks party, "How can you let her go out looking like that?" I was so shocked that it could be used against my father. My father said that it was of no relevance to him how I chose to dress, and I knew that that wasn't true. But it was brilliant to hear him supporting me like that.'

With her own two eldest daughters, Stella admits to finding it hard when they dress inappropriately and occasionally tries to get them to change. 'But usually I give in because they've got to do it really. The girls joined me at a party after work and the eldest was dressed like a streetwalker. Had I been there I would have tried to damp it down a bit, but she had such fun with the way she was dressed and everyone knows that it's a teenage girl dressing up and I shouldn't be so precious about it and try to control them.' As teenagers grow older, more aware and accepting of their new physiques they tend to tone down the more extreme aspects of their appearance. They emerge from the chrysalis of early adolescent slobbery and begin to take care of themselves. 'Certainly there was a point, and it wasn't too long ago when I realized that I should be washing more,' says Claudia. 'It wasn't that I was smelly, just that I only had baths about once a week and I'd wash my face and that was it. There hadn't been anyone saying, "It's bathtime" for years and then suddenly I thought, this is gross, what am I doing? So I started buying really nice smelly bath stuff to make myself feel better.'

Sometimes parents become exasperated by aspects of teenage

behaviour over which they have little control because they are caused by the major physical changes of puberty. Early adolescents genuinely need more sleep and more food at such a time of rapid growth, which is why they raid the fridge at odd hours of the day and find it hard to get out of bed before 11 a.m. Their sleep rhythms also change. They feel more awake late at night and least alert first thing in the morning. If they were left to regulate their own sleep schedule, they would sleep from midnight to approximately 10 a.m. Studies show that adolescents are least alert between 8 a.m. and 9 a.m. and most alert in the afternoon, which does not dovetail neatly with the demands of the school day. It also means that many of the arguments that develop over food consumption and sleep patterns are pretty pointless and best avoided or saved for the really important occasions – early nights are imperative before exams and that delicious chocolate pudding in the fridge is for guests coming for dinner tonight, not for you right now.

Arguments over cleaning up and tidying bedrooms also tend to dominate countless households during early adolescence. 'Fourteen was a tricky age for both of them,' says Philippa, a single mother whose sons are now eighteen and sixteen. 'I had serious rows particularly with the oldest one over staying out and clearing up. I find it hard coming home from work to find things in a mess. I'd say, "Why didn't you clear this up?" and they'd feel unjustly accused, and that was what a lot of the rows were about, them being slapdash around the house and then wanting to go out and me having to say, "There are certain things you have to do first." I had to do endless chores when I grew up but they seem to feel that their after-school time is theirs, that they have a right to free time which is a complete anathema to me.'

Antonia, aunt and guardian to her nieces, argued regularly with the fifteen-year-old over cleaning up. 'If I knocked her for one small thing like leaving something unwashed in the sink, she'd barge out and slam the door, the music would go on and she'd be very off for quite some time. It's her room but my house and I'm paying for a cleaner to come. She can't clean in there if it's in a mess and anyway who wants to live in sluttish surroundings?'

'There are clothes trodden into the carpet and that infuriates me but I won't do anything about it because he gets very upset and angry if I go in,' says Barbara. 'I go in about once a week and pick things up and wash them, which seems to be OK but if he can see that I've moved papers or picked things up, he is furious.'

The early adolescent mind, always intent on perceiving things as personal insult, and preserving the new sense of privacy and autonomy, sees things very differently. They see through pointless comparisons with what their parents had to do at their age. 'My mum's always saying that I'm lazy,' says Trish. 'But I'm not. I'll hoover up and then she'll say, "Thanks. Can you wash up?" I'll say, "But I just hoovered," and she'll say, "You're so lazy. In my day I used to have to use a dustpan and scrub the carpet. I got married when I was eighteen and I used to wash all my own clothes by hand." But I think, good for you, but we've got a washing machine now. Why do you want us to carry on like that? You should be happy that we don't have to live like that any more. But she just goes on and on about how we've got too much and have an easier life. I reckon they're just jealous.'

Teenagers react immediately to what matters at that moment and find adult obsession with cleanliness and tidiness deeply frustrating and superficial. They find it hard to plan ahead or think strategically and there appears to be no connection between the fact that if a pair of trousers lies scrunched up at the end of their bed, it won't be clean or neatly pressed for that party tomorrow night unless they do something about it. They tend to think about things when they are full of anticipation about something or when things go wrong, when they are locked out or dumped by a boyfriend. Parents place all of this irresponsible behaviour within wider adult codes of morality and perspective because of their maturity. Early adolescents do not have these skills, they need them highlighted gently and at appropriate moments. 'My dad really annoys me because he nags me about everything, about my school work or bringing my bin down when the dustmen are coming,' says Karen. 'But when he doesn't remind me to bring my bin down I forget and I end up with piles of rubbish in my room. But he always asks me to do things when I'm in the middle of something, and then I forget. If he just waited until *EastEnders* was over then I'd be able to do it.'

Sometimes the mess in their room gets so bad that they cannot begin to think how to tackle it alone. We had been nudging our elder daughter gently for weeks to tidy up her room, which was so messy with clothes, books, papers and CDs that you couldn't see the carpet, before we realized that it was actually too much for her to do alone. Christoph and I looked at each other after supper one evening and announced that we were going in. 'Don't,' she wailed, her eyes glued to the TV. 'It really doesn't matter, it's not important.' I took the clothes, he tackled the books and music, and half an hour later it was clear, with just a huge pile of pens and pencil cases on her bed for her to sort through before school the next day. When I went down to announce that the deed was done and that we had found about a hundred pens (she had been complaining that she had nothing to write with at school), as well as ten quid in a purse she managed to shift her eyes from the television screen, smiled with relief and said, 'Thanks, Mum.' Just a few days later she felt able to continue the tidying process alone, sorting her jewellery and grading her nail varnish by colour.

Teenagers are far more likely to respond to genuine need

(in their terms) rather than constant nagging (to conform to yours). Stella has nurtured a culture at home where her three daughters, two of whom are twelve and fourteen, have always been expected to help from an early age and do so. 'My mother didn't have a mother really when she was young and only worked part time. So she did everything for me and I left home unable to cook. But they have to help me in the house because I work full time and we can't afford a cleaner. I've always said to them that we either go on holidays or I can employ a cleaner. So on Saturdays and Sundays we clean together and they know how to cook. Maybe you just do things in reverse. But I am amazed by how many people spend their lives ferrying their children around. I now say that if they want to do something they have to organize getting themselves there. They have bus passes and have to work out how to get there. It's made them feel older, more responsible and freer.'

In families where children have always been encouraged to do simple chores from an early age, the move to greater domestic responsibility is a great deal easier. Those who have always cosseted their children and done everything for them are perhaps being a little unfair in expecting their children to turn magically into thoughtful, considerate and helpful teenagers around the house just because they are older. From the teenager's perspective, the sense of abandonment and emotional loss of the securities of childhood are even greater and resistance is bound to flare.

Teenagers resent conforming to adult goals when they are so busy trying to ascertain and establish their own. Being told what to do by an adult, whether it's tidying their bedroom or clearing the dinner table, makes them feel that they are still controlled by their parents. It pre-empts their own initiative and sense of self-control, when to a parent this is just an emotionally uncomplicated practical necessity. Teenagers are intelligent enough to be able to differentiate between their own personal concerns and those which may affect others. They feel affronted if parents feel they have a right to comment on the state of their bedroom or their dress, or to criticize their friends when they feel these are their own personal concerns. But during early adolescence they do tend to understand and consider it within their parents' rights to know where they are going and when they are coming back, because these are issues couched in safety, for which they still hold their parents accountable.

Teenagers develop a keen awareness of the need for personal privacy, dignity and respect through early adolescence and this is easily offended within the family home. Emma is fourteen and resents the fact that her mother makes her play with her younger sister who is six. Her privacy is rarely respected. She has to share a room with her sister, while her parents have separate bedrooms. She resents the way that her physical boundaries are invaded as if she were still a small child. 'I hate the way they make me see relatives I don't even know. They kiss you everywhere, and they're all sweaty and I have to kiss every single one of them. And then when I do something wrong, she tells the whole family instead of keeping it to herself. So when I walk into my nan's house they're like all staring at me, and Mum's going, "It's her hormones. They're all over the place." I just wish she'd shut up. On the weekend, if I'm larking about with my friends then I'll have fun, but most of the time I'm constantly arguing with my mum. If I say, "I'm tired," she'll ask, "Why?" When I say that I've been at school all day she'll say, "Well I've been at work all day and you've been out all over the weekend while I've had to cook and clean." If I say, "Well at least you get paid for going to work," she'll say, "Don't get cocky."' Sometimes Emma's mother hits her. 'The other day I was so angry with her that I wanted her to hit me so that I could hit her back. I don't think you should hit children. What can it achieve? It just makes me angrier.

She should just talk to me rather than hitting which just makes me ruder and angrier.' There have also been times when her mother has kicked her out of the house. 'Last time she told me to get out of her house. "Go! Get out of my house," she screamed at me. I said, "Where do you want me to go?" "Wait outside the door, if I see you I'll kill you, I'll go mad." So I went outside and because it was raining I sat in the car for a while. When I went back inside she told me off for doing that, said I had to wait outside, but what is the point of that?'

Feeling unwelcome at home and as if one is merely a lodger in one's parents' house, is common amongst adolescents who row a great deal with their parents. 'Get out of *my* house,' Emma's mother screamed at her when she forced her to stand out in the rain simply because she was furious with her. 'It's her room, but my house,' Antonia maintained throughout their prolonged confrontation over territory and responsibility. As teenagers' needs from their living environment change, they are forced to retreat to their rooms for privacy and for some sense of control over their own space. The kitchen and the living room only feel like theirs if they are encouraged to use them, and if they are constantly chastised for leaving a mess they easily interpret this as feeling unwelcome.

Claudia's mother had just embarked on her first affair six years after her divorce and asked Claudia to be out of the house on the rare occasions when he was able to come round. 'My sister asked the same thing when she had a party so I feel like the only nice person in my family. I'd never do that to them because it's so hurtful, but when I say so, Mum's view is that I just want to prevent her from having a nice time. She doesn't see that it's alienating to be asked to leave your own home.'

Trish's mother doesn't understand how important it is for her daughter to feel that what goes on in her own bedroom is private. When she had two friends in her room one day, she opened the door and found her older sister eavesdropping. 'I was so angry and told Mum, but she just said, "She's your sister, she has a right to know!" I screamed at her, "She doesn't have a right!" She has no conscience about those sorts of things, about my own need for privacy.' She also feels that her mother often abuses her power within the family home by treating her like a servant and blaming her for her own mistakes. 'My mum is so lazy. She'll shout for me so I come into the room and she'll ask me to turn on the light. She'll call me into the room to do that rather than get up herself. One time I was actually sleeping and she was cooking some soup and I woke up hearing her screaming for me. When I ran in the soup had boiled over and spilled all over the cooker and she said, "That's because of you. If you'd been here earlier you could have turned it off." When I said, "Mum, I wasn't even in the room, I was sleeping," she replied, "I don't care. When I call you you should come. Now clean up the cooker. It's because of you."'

Fights over these sorts of issues appear to be greatest in families with overbearing, dogmatic and stubborn parents. In multicultural homes there may be a clash between the far more traditional upbringing of the parents in their country of origin and the more liberal expectations of their children. 'It's very difficult for me to accept that a woman can go out and come home at twelve o'clock, and not say where they've been or that it's none of my business,' says Laila, who came to Britain from Somalia in 1986. Her daughter is seventeen. But children who grow up absorbing British youth culture develop a keener sense of their own individual rights. 'They are the kind of parents who just tell you how it is,' says Denise, who is sixteen and has West Indian parents. 'They don't ask me what I think and that has made the fighting worse. Their argument was that you just can't have it, basically.'

When there are too many fights over these basic but rather superficial aspects of growing up, teenagers feel alienated within their own family home, the only security they know.

Then as they grow older and more serious issues surface, over homework, playing truant, experimenting with too much alcohol or drugs and staying out too late, parents discover that they have even less influence. The atmosphere is already so sour, the teenagers so silent and unforthcoming because they have learned that putting a foot wrong or volunteering any information about what they get up to only gives them grief, and parents are left either in ignorance or over-anxious about their children's welfare. Antonia became permanent guardian to her two nieces when her sister, a lone parent, became a chronic alcoholic and developed terminal cancer. She found it easy to give them both the love and support of a stable home when they were younger, but as the eldest changed, the rows escalated and good communication evaporated. When she found a packet of contraceptive pills in her room, 'I felt this great surge of, "Oh my God, she's only fifteen," and took her to task for it. Then she failed eight out of nine GCSEs so her place at sixth form college fell through. Then I noticed strange things like the vodka was disappearing when I didn't drink it and she was taking money, nicking my cigarettes.'

She discovered that her niece had been lying about where she had been, claiming that she was babysitting. 'When I finally got hold of her on her mobile I told her to come home. She came in ten minutes later and packed her bag without telling me where she was going. I told her to leave her keys and her mobile [a Christmas present, with a strict arrangement over free time over and above which her niece had to pay] and two weeks later I got two bills for £400 each.' The entire tone of their exchanges was non-conciliatory. Antonia wasn't interested in explanations, merely in her niece conforming to what she considered to be house rules. She found it hard to reach out and listen to what her niece might have to say. There also appeared to be little understanding or empathy for what her niece might be living through emotionally, as an orphan, living with an aunt who loved her but could never replace the mother and father she had never had. Emotional neglect inevitably resurfaces during the emotional upheaval associated with adolescence. Looking back on those times Antonia has two regrets. 'She's a very lovable girl, perhaps craving more love than I was able to give. I'm not a very tactile person, I didn't put my arms around her a lot, which I think perhaps a mother would do more. I also wonder whether it would have been different if I had made her feel that this was more her home.'

It can be exhausting, emotionally traumatic and hard to navigate the fine line between allowing them some of the greater independence they crave and maintaining some semblance of authority. 'In many ways it would be easy just to let them go at thirteen, because they really are so awful,' says Sally, whose eldest son is now nineteen. 'When I hear of children running away I really understand that parents can't cope with the stuff that's thrown at them, when most parents only want what's best for their children. When they are awful to you, you just want to say, "Piss off." But it's harder because they're so good at arguing their case and they make you question yourself all of the time. You have to be quite strong and stand firm, but you do have to listen to that child, but one easily conflicts with the other and that's really difficult. It's very hard to get the balance right.'

When parents are tired they are less patient when it comes to listening, they are more likely to issue commands which meet with resistance rather than asking courteously, and they are much more likely to react precipitously and get angry over minor transgressions. When parents are feeling negative they are far more likely to see their children's actions as wilful, premeditated acts and respond punitively. Hypersensitive, self-preoccupied adolescents then easily feel picked on and misunderstood, and an entire evening can be ruined by noisy rowing because of minor, thoughtless criticism or over-harsh words from a harassed or preoccupied parent.

All this change and heightened conflict places a new series of strains on parents' relations with each other. 'It throws everything into relief, which is very scary. All your faults and the faults in your marriage suddenly appear magnified,' says Barbara. Marriages and partnerships go through two distinct blips with parenthood: first during the first two years, when parents have to adjust to such a major upheaval in their way of life, with less time for each other and their own personal interests; and secondly with adolescence, when the child forces change on the whole nature of family life. Some couples find that they begin to argue seriously at this stage, often for the first time in an otherwise healthy partnership, as each remembers his or her own experience of growing up and takes a view as to how they should manage their own child's teenage years. 'Adam says it's her life, she has to live with her mistakes,' says Clare whose eldest daughter is revising for GCSEs. 'Whereas I'm trying to keep all the frameworks in place and insist on the importance of study. If we were any further apart on this we'd probably fall apart.'

When Mick's eldest child reached thirteen, he began to get argumentative, rude and difficult for about a year, throwing his weight around the house and tormenting his two younger sisters. He wouldn't do his homework, was getting into trouble regularly at school, which eventually led to expulsion from a progressive and liberally minded school, and there were big fights nightly. 'We had no sanction. If you said, "Do your homework," he'd say, "Fuck off. You gonna make me then?" You'd try to think of some threat such as, "If you don't do it then you won't be going to the football," or something else that he wanted to do at the weekend and in the end he would do it but it was so exhausting. It was never going to threaten a good marriage, but nonetheless it was a very difficult period.

It produced the worst and most sustained bad chapter in what is now twenty years together. His mother would say something like, "Did you hear what he just said to me?" and I'd refuse to get involved, saying that it wasn't my fight. We'd try and play the good guy/bad guy routine because there was no point in both of us ranting at him and I used to hit him when I got really cross; that would upset her and she'd start crying and then I'd get irritated by that because it seemed to me that crying, just like hitting, showed him that he had won. Then we'd argue about that, and then the little one would get out of bed and say, "I can't sleep, please make it up with Mummy."'

Power struggles easily degenerate into unseemly squabbles when parents try to use the same methods of control habitually used with younger children. 'I don't think that even with a small child it's appropriate to stamp your feet and say, "Do it because I say so,"' says Martin. 'But it's even more important not to do it with a thirteen-year-old.' Adolescents know that no one can make them do anything. Grounding them focuses children's attention on the futility of the punishment and on the waning power of their parents, for they know that they could walk out of the door if they really wanted to. Physical punishment is an act of desperation. Parents hit out when they don't know what else to do. But for an adolescent it is also a physical, sexual insult because parents violate the distinct new physical boundaries that teenagers erect between themselves and their parents. Punishment deflects a child's attention away from his or her behaviour; good communication and democratic discussion focuses the developing mind of an adolescent on his or her relationships and responsibilities towards other people.

Over-control is a hasty form of abuse stemming from the misguided belief that parents are merely doing their best for that child. But teenagers find means of escape, often unhealthy ones, from parental clutches, like the five timid and lonely

Lisbon sisters in Jeffrey Eugenides' chilling novel *The Virgin Suicides*. They were never allowed out alone, except to attend one party, chaperoned by their father, a teacher at the same school. When they returned, Mrs Lisbon stood like a prison guard at the front door, checking her daughters' breath for signs of cigarette smoke and when she smelt tobacco pulled all her daughters out of school completely. Throughout the novel, peripheral characters express sheer disbelief at the fact that five young girls could take their own lives. But Eugenides is clear about the reasons for their mass suicide. They died because they were denied the right to live. I felt a similar shiver of gloom when one of the many teenage girls I interviewed described the life of one of her close friends. 'At the age of thirteen she was still having her clothes laid out for her at the end of her bed, telling her what she was going to wear the next day. She is taken to school every morning and picked up, she's not allowed male friends and letters have to go via a friend because her mother reads her post. Can you imagine living in such conditions?'

Gita had always told her children since they were little that she hated smoking and would force them to stop by radical means if they took it up. When she discovered Stella's cigarettes, she went out and bought a packet of the strongest cigarettes she could find, took her daughter out into the garden and made her smoke one after the other until she went green. 'I wasn't going to let her make my house smell so I took her outside. By the time she got to the second one she wasn't taking it down properly, so I told her to really inhale and not to waste my cigarettes. It was awful, tantamount to child abuse but it worked.' Except that it didn't. All Stella has learned is that she needs to hide the evidence more effectively from her mother, because she smokes in order not to eat and to alleviate her anxiety. 'If someone gave me one now, I'd smoke it. I used to smoke a lot, like ten a day, because it's cheaper than eating and it feels nice and I like the way cigarettes feel in your hand. If you're working it gives you a break.'

It's better perhaps to accept that teenagers may smoke, and stay on the same side. Express disapproval and all the health arguments by all means but also show understanding for some of the reasons why they may be taking these risks. 'I allowed him to smoke in his bedroom and I knew that he had smoked cannabis,' says Sally of her teenage son who is now nineteen. 'I haven't said that's OK but I'd rather he felt able to tell me things, which means that I have to be reasonable. If I hit the roof he wouldn't tell me anything. It's sort of a game really, you mustn't be too closed in case you shut the doors, so you've got to look reasonable and then you discover what they are doing even if it isn't what you want to hear.'

Parents often give contradictory messages to their teenagers. They encourage them to confide in them but then counter it negatively with shock or disapproval – 'Tell me everything, but I'm not sure that I want to hear it.' When teenagers sense this, they simply withdraw. Girls in particular would rather remain silent if they know from former experience that expressing their opinions could damage their relationship with their parents. Parental disapproval will not make them reform their ways if they do not believe they are doing anything wrong in the first place. It will give them something concrete to think about but the danger is that it will also alienate them from more benign and supportive parental influence. Parents have to be considered and measured in their responses and reactions when their adolescent children disclose information that shocks or concerns them. Trust is a crucial aspect of good communication and when parents overreact to the news that their child has a friend who smokes, or has spent the night at a boy's house, they transmit the destructive message that he or she is not trusted. When teenagers feel misunderstood or think that their honesty will provoke disapproval or anger, they tend to shut down completely or lie. Zoe is sixteen, lives in Bromley but goes to school in central London. She enjoys the distance between these two lives because 'it means they really can't keep tabs on me as much as they might do if I was at school in Bromley. It's not that I'm guilty of anything, or trying to cover things up. You just can't be bothered to have the argument because you know that what you've done isn't bad and they'll never really believe that. You listen to what they have to say and then you go. I find it frustrating that if I were to be true, that just gets me into trouble.'

Her friend Emily agrees. 'If something really frustrates me, I just tend to keep my head down and leave the dinner table quickly. It's better than getting into some massive row about an issue that they really find contentious but that I don't have a problem with. You can try and see it from their point of view, but you know that they are never going to see it from yours and as soon as you start arguing you become this difficult teenager with all the usual excuses. But if you're quiet, you appear guilty. That makes it better for my mother because you're already remorseful. If parents learned to deal with things better, then their kids would tell them more. If they knew that if there was something really wrong, they could turn to them because they wouldn't take things personally or be so overprotective of you, then life at home would be a great deal easier and happier.'

Parents have to adopt far more subtle methods of manipulation and more sophisticated adult modes of communication if they are to stay on the same side as their children. We need to think more before we react to adolescents and ease up on the structures of discipline and control, ensuring all the time that the children still know that the framework of rules, expectations and support is still there. Adolescents need guidelines that help protect their health and safety rather than rules and they need the reasons for these guidelines explained.

'There were definite rules but I always took great pains to explain why I felt certain rules were necessary because I remember my father always saying, "Because I say so," when I asked, "Why?" That used to drive me mad, it's the most inane excuse that an adult can ever give to somebody who is growing up because they are intelligent enough to take on board a reason,' says Mary. 'Giving them reasons tends to work. They valued the fact that I treated them as equals. When they were younger I used to sit them down and say, "This is a committee with the three of us running the house, each with our own responsibilities – I pay the bills, you tidy your rooms." Of course there were times when they didn't do things and we'd end up having a screaming match, but I don't remember any out and out rebelliousness.'

Andrea and Martin have regular house meetings to discuss their family life. 'It tends to bring out the worst in everyone, delinquent behaviour in them as they sit there tearing paper to shreds. They say they want them, but actually they see that it's a chance for Martin and me to have a moan about the same old things and try to force them to do things under the pretence of consent. It is absolutely exhausting, but I am also absolutely clear that I am not doing chores for five people. We all do chores and my cross to bear is to have to hassle them. I don't expect them to happily empty the dishwasher, just to do it. I'm not going to be a mother of three sons who expect women to run around for them.'

Psychologists tend to agree that establishing good communication where parents actively listen to what their children have to say and speak to them with the same courtesies as they would use with another adult reduces conflict with early adolescents and eases the motions of family life. Adolescents are particularly sensitive to criticism because they are so self-conscious. When parents insult or ridicule their children, when they tease too much or use sarcasm, adolescents easily see themselves as the 'problem', as someone who can't help breaking curfews, leaving a mess or telling lies. Even the mildest criticisms can provoke powerful responses.

'Our arguments have been about him wanting more independence about things like clothes-buying while I've been more authoritarian about things like, "You will wash every day with soap." We joke about it,' says Helen. 'But when I overstep the mark, say about using a facial wash, he reacts by saying that all that pressure does is make him feel bad about himself.'

Lectures, unsolicited advice and dismissal of an adolescent's worries with light reassurance – 'things will turn out all right, you'll see' – can trivialize teenage concerns and convey the message that they are powerless to effect change. Orders and commands will now bounce back and need to be replaced by questions, which emphasize the need for and encourage cooperation. This may not work as a strategy for achieving your objective (the dirty clothes still lie in a heap on the floor and the table still hasn't been laid for supper), but who really cares if that means that there is some semblance of constructive conversation over the dinner table?

Wherever possible parents need to really listen to what their teenagers have to say and make time to talk. Teenagers tend to want to talk at unexpected moments, and often at just those times when busy, overworked parents haven't got the time to stop and talk. But often just ten or fifteen minutes of good conversation can iron out weeks of misunderstanding. When parents are regularly open, honest and understanding in their conversations, when they volunteer anecdotes from their lives about how they have handled something badly or well, they teach by example and encourage adolescents to be more forthcoming and communicative.[5] Essential criticisms need to be positively phrased by being sandwiched between two positives because adolescents, just like small children, need constant affirmation and praise for the smallest achievements in order to keep their confidence levels high. And when there is a genuine difference of opinion over appropriate boundaries the question 'What would you do if you were in my position now?' will widen the discussion as well as their intellectual horizons, encouraging them to think about things from the parents' perspective and involve them in the setting of rules.

Separating one's own emotions from their behaviour is one of the hardest aspects of being a parent, but it is a crucial skill when dealing with adolescents. Taking responsibility for our anxiety or anger by saying, 'I get worried when you're late and haven't phoned,' is far better than venting relief through confrontation. 'Where have you been?' will produce either a row or withdrawal. Walking away from them when you are feeling angry is far more constructive than pointless confrontation. Teenagers are far more likely to change their behaviour and mature psychologically by thinking about the effects of their behaviour on other people if parents focus on the fact that whatever they have done has cost them money, created extra work or interfered with their own right to privacy, and if they say this at a time when no one is feeling angry or moody. Communication has to be specific: 'I don't like your attitude' tells them absolutely nothing about the effects of their behaviour.

'There hasn't been huge conflict, I think because I'm non-judgemental,' says Joan who has three daughters, two of whom are teenagers. 'I had a mother who was like the thought police. She let us out but we were told what to think and it was horrible, so I don't show shock even though I have been shocked at times.'

Parenthood has to evolve around a child's needs. With adolescence, the child grows more complicated as he or she assumes the mantle of adult conflicts and contradictions. But so too does the task of being parents to that adolescent. They have to accept and tolerate contradictions and a sense of incompleteness in their child, 'without treating the adolescent like a child or prematurely forcing upon him the burdens of adult responsibilities. It requires an ability to tolerate a border-line state,' writes the psychologist Richard Frankel in his book *The Adolescent Psyche*. It also means that parents have to scale new heights of self-sacrifice, self-denial and to silence their true feelings of loathing or disapproval in order to maintain good relations with a child in transition.

'It's really hard,' says Clara who has three children, two of whom are teenage. 'There's nothing that works at the time. It's like potty training, you wonder how you'll get through it and then you look back two years later and you have. It's a bit like that with arguments with my daughter about how late she can stay out and how they come back, and it's knowing that what works with her is negotiation. She knows that I trust her to be sensible when she makes her own decisions about sex or drink and to know when these things are appropriate.' When there is trust, empathy and good communication within fam-ilies, adolescents are far more likely to confess their doubts, disturbances and confusion and parents are able to reassure as well as ascertain when their children are really beginning to go off the rails and need help. Once communication has broken down, it is even harder for parents to break through to their recalcitrant, troubled teenager. 'It's really tricky trying to find a line where we still have some authority and he still has his independence, when we can't even discuss these things because the shutters have just gone slam,' says Rosamund, whose sixteen-year-old son went seriously off the rails by smoking far too much dope in his GCSE year. 'He says he just wants us to live independent lives. I could sort of hack that at seventeen or eighteen but at sixteen I still think he needs us around. We play it by ear, day by day, and it changes all the time. He won't talk to us or do anything with us like eat and that's dreadful, he just takes his food to his room.'

Caroline, a child psychologist, discovered the painful reality that rowing with her sixteen-year-old daughter merely pushed her further away when she found evidence of dope-smoking in her bedroom. 'We had rows about where she was, because she wanted to go to lots of sleepovers. And then we discovered that if we stopped her from doing things she just lied to us and did them anyway so we decided to let her do what she wanted provided that she told us. The only thing that we now insist upon is that she rings to tell us where she is and when she's coming home and it's been really good now. That was quite a moment when we discovered that she was lying. We'd rather know where she was. They've both been terribly good, they haven't done anything really wicked and we'd much rather know that she's safe.'

Liberal sentiments in family life tend to work; authoritarian ones tend to provoke insurrection, animosity and great unhappiness. Tough and repressive regimes at home force teenagers to flout authority more as a means of defiance and in ways which will most aggravate their parents. The hot-housed child of an over-ambitious parent is more likely to reject education. The children of an overly prudish and abstemious mother are more likely to flaunt their drunkenness, to scream their own inimitable right to an independent life in a way that their parents just might hear. Many psychologists believe that over-control of young people in families can be one of the main causes of some of the more serious difficulties young people face, such as suicide and anorexia, subjects which are fully explored in Chapter Nine.[6]

When we understand that we can never completely control teenage behaviour, but have to influence it more subtly with active participation from our children in decision-making, family life muddles along, thrown here and there by circumstance, but it is basically sound, and most importantly it remains a source of refuge and confidence for teenagers when they are troubled. 'My friends think I never get angry but Mum and Dad say the exact opposite because I take it out on my family, because they've got to put up with me,' says Karen. 'I know that my family don't deserve it but if I were to take it out on my friends they could walk away. They also always get me at the end of the day as well, when I'm tired.'

Conflict is often a positive aspect of family life. It provokes expression of feeling, shakes people out of their complacency and forces people to change and find new solutions to problems. 'I feel he's able to stand up for himself and argue back, which are good qualities,' says Martin of his thirteen-year-old son. 'He's finding a way of not being pushed around by his parents by arguing and although it's infuriating at the time, when you stand back from it, I'd rather he was doing that than being a pushover. It's the tension between being in authority and wanting them to stand up to it. So I say, "I don't mind you answering back, but try and do it with a little respect."'

Sometimes simple fights mask other deeper concerns. Imogen found herself embroiled in a row with her sixteen-year-old son when he wanted to go to a friend's house on a Monday night when he ought to be at home revising for his exams. She simply grounded him. Later on, when she asked him why he needed to go there so badly he told her that this particular friend was going through a bad time and that he had promised to help, and then quite uncharacteristically he burst into tears, saying that he was going to do terribly in his AS levels anyway, before storming up to his room. Imogen realized then that going out was a diversionary tactic. She followed him up to his room and was able to have a far more constructive discussion with her son about helping him by getting a tutor, perhaps. They then agreed on a compromise, that he would do two hours' work and then go out and be back by 10.30.

When conflict is harming family relationships by taking the form of power struggles or attacks on each other personally, the most constructive solution is to try to resolve these problems together as a family in such a way that everyone feels they have gained. Put a moratorium on the subject until everybody has cooled down. Start with a clean slate and a new policy. Establish ground rules, for example that everyone has to be treated with respect, without sarcasm, name-calling or put-downs. Then discuss the problem, with each person allowed the time and the space to air any grievances. Brainstorm possible solutions and set these out in a written agreement which can be reviewed at a set time. Ask a friend or a relative to arbitrate, for he or she is bound to see things more clearly because of being less emotionally involved. It helps, too, to focus on the simple question of whose problem it actually is. If their bedroom is untidy, if their clothes are not washed because they haven't put them in the dirty clothes basket, they have to live with the consequences. Save energy for the really important battles over health, safety and education.

Children learn most effectively by example rather than from lectures. Treating people with respect breeds respect, marshalling the courage to apologize to a young person when we have made a mistake fosters tolerance, humility and an ability to apologize. It is not an act of weakness. Accepting that you do not have complete control over a teenager's being does not mean that you lose control completely. Parents have far more power than they realize, provided that there are firm ground rules within which the child is allowed to operate and misbehave. When we feel that a teenager has overstepped the mark, the best practice is to say so, express disapproval, explain yet again the reasons for certain rules and make it clear that those ground rules are still in place. Young people listen and respect the fact that their parents have borderlines of tolerance, provided that these are clearly stated and consistent. Teenagers can accept the need for certain boundaries and when family life is founded on feelings of love and support, they do not want to feel disapproved of, or that they might lose that love and support even for a moment by transgressing those boundaries. 'She's been going on for ages about having her belly button pierced and I've always said that she can do it when she's sixteen. I think it's horrid mutilation and I don't want to have to take her to Casualty because it's infected.' Clara's daughter then went away on a school trip to France and rang up, leaving a message on the answer machine saying that she had had her belly button pierced. 'I was just furious, and amazed that my authority had not held as far as France. Then she rang up a few days later and we had this lovely chat and then I remembered and got angry and said she was lucky not to be around and she asked me if I was really cross. I said, "You know how I feel about it and you promised me you'd wait until you were sixteen." She then said she hadn't really done it, her friends had, and she wanted to test me out. If I hadn't been cross she would have done it.'

Humour can also be an invaluable tool for enhancing communication, provided it is non-judgemental. 'Soon there won't be anybody left at your school,' Barbara joked with one of her sons after a round of suspensions, provoking a wider discussion about what was going on. But she also discovered how suspension from school thrusts the responsibility right back onto the parents for something that is beyond their jurisdiction, when her own son was sent home for two days. 'If I'd let him, he'd have stayed in bed, then got up and watched telly and then gone out skateboarding with his friends at 3.30. It's so unfair, they're actually punishing you and if you have to go to work what do you do? I made him get up and go to my mother's to do the work they had set him and he was very angry at that. But when he came back he was calmer and I decided to try and stay calm too and negotiate more, not giving way, but just standing back. I said he wasn't allowed to go out skateboarding because that was part of the punishment and he kept saying, "You can't control me, why won't you let me out?" which was a complete contradiction, but obviously I was stopping him even though there was nothing physical preventing him from going out. He kept hovering in the doorway saying this and in the end he did go out, but only for twenty minutes. I realized then that it was better to do it this way and maintain my own sanity but at the same time you're not giving up trying to communicate, saying what you think should be. They do have some voice of conscience in their heads which makes them do things like come home at eleven o'clock, because they could easily not.'

Home and family life are still crucial props for teenagers. They may seem indescribably bored by everything about it, but that boredom gives them much-needed respite in their over-stimulated lives. Family life can give young people invaluable continuity in their lives when everything else seems to be changing. There is great comfort and security in those certainties and the knowledge that some family habits never change. There is great relief in being hidden temporarily from view by the great embrace of family, because teenagers are so acutely aware of their appearance and their tentative impact on the world. Family life continues to exert a powerful influence over a child's development through adolescence, even though teenagers often go to great lengths to pretend that parents no longer matter. Most teenagers continue to feel warm and close to their parents once the upheavals of early adolescence have settled down. Parents help shape an adolescent world view and a sense of identity and belief. Provided that channels of communication are kept open and parent and child effectively stay on the same side, parents offer invaluable guidance on careers, how to handle disputes and misunderstandings with friends, and fundamental information that can protect their health and safety. And when there is mutual respect and understanding in family life, teenagers are far more likely to devise their own solutions in order to minimize the upset that derives from conflict. When Vicky was seventeen she found she wasn't getting on so well with her mother because she had been going out a lot, having fun with friends. 'We kept having the same conversation about how I was never there. I didn't dread coming home but it was tense the whole time because when I was here I couldn't do my own thing without Mum wanting to know what that was. When I realized that we weren't getting on I decided to do something about it because I don't wanna lose that and decided to stop taking her for granted and just be here sometimes and watch the telly with her and things have got better as a result.'

'It's a game of keeping hold of them in the face of whatever they throw at you,' maintains Sally. 'One of his friends was kicked out by his mother while he was doing his GCSE retakes, and she is a university lecturer. What on earth is the good of that? When I hear from other people that he is so polite with such a lovely sense of humour when he is at their house I can't believe that they are talking about the same boy. But it's good to know that what you've told him has gone in and is showing somewhere even if that's not here. You just have to hang on in there and they want you to hang on in there, they're fighting to let go but they want you to hold on. It's all so uncertain for them, everyone's fighting to do well and it's so materialistic that it is hard to get the other side through, of kindness and respect for other people, but by treating him as an adult, he does give back. He uses my car as we don't go out much and I think he appreciates that as he is very careful with it. The first few times it was full of rubbish and smoke and I said that's not on and he cleaned it up. It's nice for me to know that he is now being more caring.'

Relations in loving families cannot by definition remain

cool or neutral. Conflict arises because we care, but teenagers care passionately too and value and need their parents far more than they like to let on. Parents, wounded by life with an adolescent warrior tend to see only the generational differences between them and overlook the similarities, which are often far greater. Research shows that there are substantial similarities between parents and their children usually over core issues such as politics, religion, sex and gender roles and attitudes towards work and achievement. While teenagers can see that there is a substantial generation gap in wider society, they often perceive their families differently, for they know older members as individuals with individual strengths and weaknesses rather than as stereotypes.[7]

Children may change radically as they grow up, but so too do the best parents as their children connect them to a younger, changing world. The fruits can be just as nourishing for family life as they were when the children were younger and more innocent and endearing, for teenage children are important in explaining wider aspects of social and cultural change to their parents. They challenge entrenched prejudices and conservative points of view and make human sense of what might otherwise be considered utterly alien to the middle-aged. It is far, far easier to accept and understand changing attitudes when it is your own child coming home with her belly button pierced or a lesbian girlfriend.

'I do feel that the family is an incredibly valuable practising ground, particularly at this age,' says Gillian. 'We learn so much from being with the children. They tell us exactly what they think of us, they're quite harsh and they point out hypocrisies or inconsistencies without fail. They really know what's false and that's very valuable.'

Parents grow up with their children, revisiting aspects of their own childhood, and they are capable of changing with their children, improving even simply by association with them, as Mark Twain has amusingly written: 'When I was a boy of fourteen, my father was so ignorant I could hardly stand to have the man around. But when I got to be twenty-one, I was astonished at how much he had learned in seven years.'[8]

'Parents can only help a little; the best they can do is to survive, to survive intact, and without changing colour, without relinquishment of an important principle. This is not to say they may not themselves grow,' writes the child psychologist D. W. Winnicott in his book *Playing and Reality*. It is incredibly hard being an adequate parent to adolescents when they tax our reserves of tolerance, patience and the ability to stand firm in the face of one's principles. Nobody gets it completely right, but those who tend to foster healthier adolescent development and who keep conflict to a minimum are those parents who adapt quickly and accept the inevitability of these changes, those who show their children warmth and respect, those who accept that they are fallible and make mistakes and are able to apologize to their children when they do, those who listen to their children and demonstrate a sustained interest in their lives and do not abandon expect-ations, guidance or faith in their adolescents' abilities. They also increase the likelihood that their teenagers will stay positive about school and education and make it less likely that they will seek out other sources of support through drugs or a deviant bunch of peers. If there is one consistent message from the many troubled and lonely teenagers I have interviewed it is this: teenagers want more respect, empathy and support from their parents, they want their parents to really listen to what they have to say and they want more open consultation and discussion.

6. Friends

I had a friend, one of those fellow adolescents to whom a normal boy is more faithfully devoted than to any mistress. Once turned twenty, a woman, or military service, or a profession breaks into one's life and ruins this beautiful mutual affection.

Colette, *The Tender Shoot*

My most vivid memories of secondary school during the late 1970s are of hanging out with a tight-knit gang of friends. Our territory was a particular bench in the back cloakroom, and a small patch of lawn near the back gate where we could huddle together to smoke, gossip and explore the mystery of boys. Eight or nine of us gravitated towards each other at every free break, or every free moment out of school – at each other's houses, on Hampstead Heath or at the Freemasons Arms. We wore clogs, loon pants, stripy Biba tops and Laura Ashley smocks, branded even then. By hanging out together we felt complete, superior, keenly aware of how cool and unique we were compared to the others in our year. Affiliation to this group defined us as individuals.

Memory of our conversations has evaporated with time but that deep sense of togetherness endures. By being part of a gang we threw a protective bubble around ourselves in order to find sanctuary from our parents and learn how to grow up. Through the laboratory of our friendship group we could explore emotions, learn about our bodies, exchange crucial information about sex and find the confidence to make forays into the wider world of pop concerts and pubs. As we grew older, found greater self-confidence and boyfriends, the bonds between us inevitably weakened and we have gone our separate ways. Now, as a middle-aged woman, I have a wide circle of friends – some closer than others, where there is give and take and a respect for the fact that friends have lives apart. Friendship dovetails haphazardly with family life and provides an essential escape from it. But it lacks that intense, passionate, all-consuming quality because work and bringing up children are now so all-consuming.

My experience of friendship at school is, I now discover, typical. With early adolescence, young people begin to be drawn to others of the same gender in small cliques and occupy particular areas of territory at school. A herding instinct leads young teenagers to seek out others they feel are of like mind, similarly attractive and at roughly the same stage of pubertal development. 'Everybody sticks together in these dirty little goddam cliques,' writes Salinger in *The Catcher in the Rye*. 'The guys that are on the basketball team stick together, the Catholics stick together, the goddam intellectuals stick together.'

Girls and boys divide by gender with early adolescence. They withdraw into two camps so that they can huddle, 'talk' and galvanize themselves, ready to commence battle with the opposite sex as they mature and begin to feel ready for dating as guys and dolls. They also learn very different skills through their friends. Girls need close friends to share their most secret personal thoughts with and are more likely to have a best friend; boys indulge in more competitive games with clear rules where conversation revolves around the game and those rules. As a result, boys tend to learn more about negotiating and cooperating with a group, while girls tend to learn more about communication and the importance of keeping a relationship going and develop their listening skills. Girls pick a topic and then develop their mutual understanding through analysis and comment on each other's contribution to the conversation, whereas boys like to tell stories and accentuate their own individuality by describing their own triumphs in particular circumstances rather than analysing or supporting each other's. By downplaying the seriousness of each other's problems, perhaps boys provide their own form of stoic reassurance. 'Maybe that's our way of growing up,' says Gary, who is sixteen.

'We mostly talk about girls and football and sometimes about people getting beaten up or about what we're going to do and money, but I don't really talk that deeply to my friends, I keep it to myself,' says Colin. 'I might just say, "Bad times," and leave it at that.' This can mean that boys often feel less supported through the process of growing up than girls. They can be more easily embarrassed about discussing their feelings, sexuality or contraception when it comes to dating and they find it harder to trust others with deeply personal information. And when it comes to forming relationships with girls age-old gender divides appear. Girls feel they have to work hard at boys in order to make them express their true feelings and they feel unsupported by them, whereas boys look to girls to make them feel nourished emotionally. Girls, as we shall see in the next chapter, are more experienced at forming intimate relationships because they have already been intimate with their friends, whereas most boys have yet to learn it, usually from girls.

Affiliation with a particular clique is much more important than actual friendship at this stage because association with a particular group defines who you are and affirms a young person's vulnerable sense of identity. Black and Asian teenagers tend to stick with others from similar cultural backgrounds. The prettiest, coolest girls are attracted to each other (that was my gang), sporty types stick together and so on. Dress may define the boundaries of each particular group, for early adolescents express their burning desire to be different by looking exactly like their friends. Allegiance to a particular band may define a group. Sometimes language is the defining factor. 'We've got a special language,' says Colin. 'Five pounds is a "ching". Twenty is a "scone". Girls are "beef" or "beanie". And we say "sweet mate" instead of "hello", or sometimes it's just a nod, it says so much.'

It is in adolescence that people first begin to form real and enduring friendships. In childhood we simply need someone to play with, but as adolescents we form deeper relationships where concepts of loyalty, betrayal, exchanging confidence and providing emotional support begin to matter more. As the security of parental love and protection begins to evaporate, friendships become more important. Adolescents gain confidence and a sense of social acceptance by being connected to a crowd which boosts their sense of self-esteem at a vulnerable time. Friendships provide adolescents with a valuable buffer against so many of the emotional difficulties that teenagers face. They are a sounding board for ideas, feelings and problems and they can be essential in helping adolescents understand or accept freshly discovered failings or paradoxes in their parents as well as in themselves. They are so important to a teenager's well-being, that being ostracized by friends, or loneliness, is potentially far more distressing and damaging than anything the wider peer group can do to a healthily confident and happy young person.

Parents often fear the influence of peers unnecessarily. When parents feel their adolescent children pulling away from their influence, or when they suspect that they might be getting into trouble, the tendency is to blame peer pressure. However, research shows that young people are more attracted to delinquent peer activities when there are other more fundamental difficulties in their lives at home.[1] All of the evidence suggests that peer pressure is far less significant in a young person's life than all of the other pressures they face. The peer group socializes young people in a positive way, persuading them to conform to the norms and standards of a wider community, based on care and concern for others, helping others out when they can, mutual protection and a sense of place. With fewer adults around and less of a sense of local community, adolescents depend upon strong friendship groups even more for emotional support and guidance. Now that young teenagers find themselves incarcerated within the depersonalized routines of large schools where the teachers are distant, 'securing one's place in a clique prevents a student from having to confront this sea of unfamiliar faces alone,' writes Shirley Feldman in her book on adolescent development, *At the Threshold*.

Teenagers tend to have a great deal more fun with their friends than they do with their parents. Time spent with friends is almost always the best part of an adolescent's life. Teenage friendships are like love affairs – all-consuming, passionate, tactile and uplifting, providing the emotional nourishment that teenagers need so badly now that they feel unable to turn exclusively to their parents.

'I'd do anything for this guy – I would die for this guy,' says Geoff, who is eighteen. 'I don't want it to sound homosexual, but seriously I would do anything for him and I would have to think twice about doing anything for the girls I've gone out with.' Adolescent friendship is the most intense kind. Friends are often the main point of school and having a laugh or kicking a ball around at break offers life-saving relief from the tedium of lessons. The simplest pleasures such as singing, laughing, eating a bag of chips or going to the cinema are exhilarating when enjoyed with a gang of friends. Teenagers need to connect physically to confirm those bonds and when they cannot do so physically, they connect on the telephone, for hours on end. They need to sit close together and reserve seats for one another. Girls tend to stroke and hug each other frequently; boys shove, punch, wrestle and indulge in fake karate chops. Partings are hard without some sense of continuity, some knowledge as to when they will see each other again. They like to travel together to and from school and yell at each other through bus windows when their paths part.

When I finally let my daughter have a mobile phone, placating my fears for her well-being with her need to connect not just with me but also with her friends, she spent the best part of the day sending text messages to one of her closest friends. They had nothing particular to say, just a need to reassure the other that they were there with consoling, pleasing thoughts. The best read: 'A star is like a friend, you can't see them but you know they're there.'

Belonging to something is all that matters. Young adolescents need to attach themselves to a particular group of other young people in order to feel rooted within set boundaries during the rapid physical and emotional changes inherent to growing up. The group literally defines what they think and feel and they do not feel complete or content unless they are together. It can be hard to know where the individual ends and the group begins. These cliques of early adolescence often have a hierarchy within the school and young adolescents are keenly aware of that order, where they stand in it and who is in or out. At the top of the pyramid are the 'trendsetters' (that was my gang). We were noisier, naughtier and considered ourselves braver, more attractive, cooler, and liked to make sure that we stood out above the crowd. Below the trendsetters are the 'wannabes' who aspire to be trendsetters, and then as far as the trendsetters are concerned there is everyone else, in one large pool of mediocrity.

'We once drew a Venn diagram of all our friends,' says Adam. 'I'm not in the main popular gang, there's a couple of them.'

His friend disagrees: 'I think we're quite in with them.'

'OK. Well, we're mates with them, but we're the kind of

"unknowns", the people who do something different. I'm a bit of a wannabe skater.'

'I'm a real skater,' says a third member of the clique, 'but I don't wear that many skate clothes any more. There's basically three types: there's the kevs who wear labels, the suits, the rebok classics and loafers; then there's people like us who do something different but are still friends with them; then there's those who are still in the thirteen-year-old stage of just wearing a pair of jeans and a T-shirt they picked up from somewhere like Tenerife. With the clothes comes the culture. Before I skated I was a "wannabe" skater and I've been in a rock music band when Britpop was cool. Then when everyone followed the fashion and went from Britpop to drum-and-bass and dance music, I've stayed with the rock music.'

This conversation between three sixteen-year-old boys took up a great deal of mental energy and time during one interview as they each tried to ascertain who they were by association with a clique. I felt incredibly confused by all of these definitions, but they seemed to understand what they were talking about. What was clear was that now these young men had reached mid-adolescence, they were beginning to gain some kind of perspective over the importance of their social associations. At thirteen, they just wanted to be accepted by the top group. Now at sixteen, they felt more at ease with their own individuality. 'There are some people who just aren't cool,' said Adam, 'and that's because they've tried so hard to create this identity and it's just a façade, and they're just not cool. People who are real individuals are cool, because they aren't like just a façade going to places with a gang. Now everyone's different collectively. When we go places there'll be a few skaters and some who wear their loafers and rebok classics and so on.'

From mid to late adolescence, teenagers feel more confident about who they are and what they believe in and consequently affiliation with particular cliques becomes less intense. The social circle of teenagers widens. Cliques meet up with other cliques at take-away food outlets, parks, shopping centres, parties, pubs and clubs and genders begin to mix in order to move onto the next stage of social attachment – dating.

'I used to want to be like my friends and follow them,' says Claudia, aged seventeen. 'If they went out drinking, I went with them; if they wore skimpy clothes, I wore skimpy clothes, skirts and little tops. It was a band of girls trying to get with boys. Now I'm trying to mix with other people, not stick with one group of girls all of the time and be more mobile so that I learn more from other people.'

'I went through quite a few friendship changes,' says Emily, aged fifteen. 'It's only recently that I've had a steady group of friends which has actually been expanding. You get to know so many more people. Now I have a filofax full of people that I've met from other circles and people in the year below me who I would never have talked to before but now it's OK and it's not them tagging along with us, it's an equal friendship. Maybe that's because you change so fast when you're twelve or thirteen, whereas now everyone feels more stable. It's no longer me and my five friends that are all that matters in the world. All the little groups have joined together and we're not so dependent on the same people.'

When friendships are so crucial in providing young people with feelings of security and social acceptance, they can be devastated when they are rejected, feel excluded or things go wrong. Exclusion is particularly hurtful because it forces teenagers to acknowledge that other people do not see or accept them in the way they would like to be seen. When attachments to friends are so intense and strong, betrayal hurts that much more deeply. A great deal of effort and energy goes into shoring up friendships but fallings out or disagreements are common because early adolescents still lack the social insight that is crucial to more mature relationships. Young people explore principles of fairness and justice by working through disagreements but because they are still relatively inexperienced they lack the communication skills that would help them resolve misunderstandings swiftly and effectively.

Though exclusion helps define the clan it can become so prolonged that individuals forget what the disagreement was about in the first place. 'We always fall out over sillinesses,' says Emma, who is fourteen and hangs out with two other girls in a regular gang. They were in a music class and asked to work in groups and one girl who was previously in their clique resented having nothing to do and walked off. 'She was being silly and annoying us so we stopped talking to her but instead of making up the next day we haven't talked to her for about six months. I just can't be bothered now, I've got other friends.'

Clans survive by creating an exclusive and highly specific identity and they will eject anyone they feel to be 'different', as Tobias Wolff describes in his childhood memoir, *This Boy's Life*. 'Victims are contemptible, no matter how much people pretend otherwise; it is more fun to be inside than outside, to be arrogant than to be kind, to be with a crowd than to be alone.' Loyalty is paramount. 'There was this girl hanging around alone in the playground so we said she could hang out with us,' says Emma. 'I said at one point that I hated Kelly, that she was such a cow. Then this girl went over to this larger gang of ten or so girls in our class and wanted to be in with them and told them what I'd said. So now, we're not talking to them and they're still not talking to her. I hate people like that, a backstabber. We allowed her to hang around and she did that, it's horrible.'

When social relations are so volatile, young people are keenly aware of how easy it would be to be ostracized from the pack. 'When I was about thirteen, we went round in this massive gang and I wanted to make sure that I fitted in with them,' says Karen. 'It would have been quite easy for them to push me out if I didn't look right. Clothes were the most important thing.' For boys, being seen as tough and sporty tends to be crucial. They indulge in competitive posturing and confiding secrets or problems is easily interpreted as weakness. 'It comes down to being macho,' says Gary. 'If you've got a problem you don't want to tell your mates because you might lose status, and not be the big bloke any more with your mates.' Feeling excluded from something fun on a Saturday night becomes a source of excruciating anxiety. 'When I was younger, like thirteen, little things would really upset me, like having an argument with somebody or if I was at home over the weekend and nobody phoned me,' says Emily. 'You get this fear that if you don't go out at least once or twice over the weekend then there must be something wrong with you, you must be a bit of an outcast. Now I really don't care that much, I'd ring someone up if I wanted to do something.'

Cherry is fourteen and has yet to find the more self-assured confidence of middle adolescence which Emily now enjoys. 'I feel lonely when I've been out two Saturdays in a row and the next Saturday I've got nothing to do. I'm stuck indoors and I feel angry and bored and I don't know what to do except sit in my room and watch TV.'

Young people are acutely sensitive to criticism from their friends or others of the same age because feeling accepted is of paramount importance and they judge themselves by the way they are seen by their peers. 'I've gone through this really awful stage of feeling so incredibly superficial,' says Emily, 'because this friend, who is this amazing person [no one could ever say anything bad about her] told me that she thought I was getting to be a bit like Nicola. Nicola's this really superficial girl who spends the whole time worrying about whether she's fat or talking about boys she fancies, and that really made me take a step out of my life and look at myself.'

Going out to parties can be excruciating when you don't

feel good about yourself. I remember dragging myself out because I didn't want to miss anything and then feeling the most extraordinary panic when I got there. Unable to engage socially and talk to anyone or dance, I'd long for escape. Emily is another who's shared that experience. 'Last year we were going to parties where they trashed the house and stuff and I'd get all dressed up and put on loads of make-up and then I'd come back home and be so depressed. Every time I'd go to a party I'd get hyped up, dressed up and then I'd get there and I wouldn't talk to anyone and be really miserable and sit in a corner and sulk and then go home really early.'

As teenagers grow older and feel more self-confident and certain of who they are, criticisms from friends hurt less and friendships mature. They have to reach out to one another once they are not necessarily forced together by the school environment. 'Things have got better,' says Denise, who is sixteen and recently left school for sixth-form college, 'because I've changed my attitude and if people say bad things about me I just ignore them. They're just immature and can't have a life if they need to be chatting about me. Before, I'd have got upset because it felt so personal.' She has parted from her best friend who used to go to the same school, but 'we're still close, I can talk to her about things and maybe it's getting stronger because we're going our separate ways, doing separate things so that when we talk on the phone we've got more to chat about, comparing things.'

Cliques and peer groups throw a useful protective shield around the adolescent when they are at their most vulnerable and many of the least attractive aspects of adolescent clan behaviour reflect that vulnerability. Teenagers tend to herd through the streets because they feel more insecure out alone and need to be physically attached to each other to feel safer. Adolescent homophobia and racism are common because scapegoating temporarily detracts attention from themselves.

When they are feeling vulnerable both sexes will hit out at those whom they perceive to be different or marginalized. With boys, these attacks are often physical, whereas girls are less likely to express their anger quite so directly. They use their superior communication skills for vicious verbal criticisms and unparalleled bitchiness that temporarily raises their own fragile self-esteem and guards against the possibility of being hit or excluded by others.

Appearance and merging with the crowd is everything and when the manifestations of puberty are so blatantly obvious, differences between people get highlighted. Early maturers and good-lookers tend to be pack leaders and those who are particularly immature are easy targets. 'I haven't shaved yet but I'm going to start because my friends take the mick. A lot of mickey-taking goes on and I get so much of that because I'm half Italian,' says Colin. 'It's a joke and I'm not that bothered really but sometimes it really winds me up. One boy, when I started school, wound me up so much that I just had a fight with him and that sorted it out. And then another time, after a great uncle had just died, they were winding me up with this game Super Mario and his name was Mario and that got me so angry, it almost got me into trouble.'

Appearance is every young girl's Achilles' heel, so insulting another's clothes, or their hair and using derogatory names such as 'slut' or 'tart' releases anxiety about their own appearance. Emma and her two friends have a reputation for being 'bad', 'But we're not half as bad as some of the people I know who have to live up to this bad girl image and hang out with older people and beat up girls for no reason. Some of them went up to this girl and called her a "retard" four times to her face. When someone else said something to the same girl she was reported to the teacher but because everyone's scared of this lot they don't tell on them.'

There is a very fine line between this deeply insensitive

name-calling and prolonged bullying, which can make young people very unhappy because they are so vulnerable and need to feel accepted by their peers at this age. At its very worst, bullying has driven children to suicide. Bullying is common in our schools. Several British surveys have found that approximately 23 per cent of Year 7 children report being bullied and that most do not confide in parents or teachers.[2] Large-scale Canadian surveys have found 38 per cent of schoolchildren aged five to fourteen reported being bullied 'once or twice' during that term and 15 per cent reported being bullied more than that.[3] Children play games where the target is the 'germ' and mustn't be touched. They steal trainers so that the victims have to go home in their socks. They will ring them up and tell them about a party they are not invited to and slander their name in graffiti across the lavatory doors and walls. Insults which imply that someone does not fit in are common, such as 'mental', 'loser' or 'moron', because adolescents feel the importance of being socially included so keenly. Such treatment obviously renders children distraught. Their whole lives are affected, they feel physically ill as a result and shun school, drifting into truancy if they cannot persuade parents to let them stay off sick. 'The people in my school are calling me names again. I really feel like pulling the plug on my life, I can't cope with it. What really bugs me is that they don't even know me,' writes one young Glaswegian girl, aged thirteen, for an adolescent survey.[4]

Mark's thirteen-year-old son arranged with friends to meet at his house and then go into town together one Saturday. The day before, one of them rang all of the others and told them not to come and Mark's son was left wondering where they were.

Kim is thirteen, black, and lives in Hackney, London. She was deeply upset when I met her, in floods of tears and acutely sensitive to the cruel teasing and taunting of some of the other girls. She says they pick on one in particular and call her a tramp. She knows that they talk about her, 'But I can't make out what they say.' She misses the certainty of childish play with friends in the primary school playground but at the same time has yet to find a way of being more grown-up and more accepted in her secondary school, and that's hard. The set rules of children's games make it easier for a child to participate and know what to do. 'In primary school you have games like skipping and hide and seek and you just join in and nobody cares about how you look, but at secondary school you just walk around or talk and you have to be thin. People notice how you look and want your hair to look nice. It matters how you look.'

Bullying begins in primary school but reaches its peak and becomes more subtle at early adolescence when intellectual horizons begin to expand and young people feel the effects of inclusion or exclusion so keenly. Victims have higher rates of anxiety, insecurity, their self-perception is more negative and they are more likely to be lonely at school because as the persecution increases over time, peers desert them.[5] It can also affect school work because young people do not want to draw attention to themselves by being too swotty or too enthusiastic or by asking questions when they don't understand something. Many children feel ambiguous about bullying. They may express concern about it or condemn it but then stand by and watch it happen without supporting the victim. Substantial numbers will actively join in the persecution if it is someone they don't like.[6] Many children underestimate the level of their own participation in bullying incidents but by merely laughing or offering verbal encouragement rather than actively partici-pating they spur on the more aggressive. The pressure to conform and not be excluded is so great at this age that children will join in with bullies and side with them in order not to become the victims. 'In my school you had to either be a bully or be bullied, you couldn't just go to that school and sail through,' says Jack from Edinburgh.

Adhering to the rules of the clique is as crucial with dress codes and music tastes. To be excluded is to be condemned to the diaspora. When teachers fail to intervene or punish, a bully's behaviour is seen as powerful and successful by their peers and they become role models. Children consider themselves stronger by association with them. Children without friends are more likely to be picked on. Those with even just one close friend are offered valuable protection within the cruelty of the playground.

Symptoms of bullying include not sleeping well, bed-wetting, stomach pains and headaches. If they come home with cuts and bruises, requests for even the most standard things to be replaced because they have been stolen, or if they seem to suddenly have fallen out with a group of friends, then these are also signs that something may be amiss. Bullied children are also often over-quiet and moody and may want to spend most of their time at home. If children say they are being bullied, they are, regardless of what the school says, and as parents we have a duty to listen to them and take their concerns seriously. They may feel unable to talk to teachers, in case that should expose them to even more violence or unpleasantness from peers, but parents can intervene in more subtle ways. It's important not to overreact and storm into the school demanding action. Much better to arrange a meeting with their class teacher or head of year and explain worries in a non-confrontational way. If the bullying continues, keep a diary of events and then write a letter detailing all of the incidents, however small, and ask them to monitor contact between the bully and victim. If that doesn't work, write to the head outlining events. When bullying is taking place in the playground or in changing rooms ask for supervision to be increased over the bully. If your child is particularly distressed, take them to the doctor so that this can be recorded. A letter from the doctor to the school can also be helpful. If the bullying still continues, contact an organization such as Bullying Online or a local advice centre.

Adolescents are at their most vulnerable when they feel lonely. Studies suggest that up to 20 per cent of young people feel long-term isolation and loneliness because they are unaccepted or estranged from their peers, and 'reduced friend networks' have been consistently found in emotionally distressed and psychiatrically disturbed adolescents.[7] They go to great efforts to disguise it because being alone implies social failure. Lonely children tend to be less talkative, less inquisitive and most prone to negative and gloomy thoughts. As children mature psychologically they become more aware of how others perceive them and will withdraw if they feel they are not wanted, easily losing interest in participating in group activities out of fear of further rejection.

Low levels of social support can lead to depression in girls and poor school work in boys.[8] It means that children are not developing their social skills and learning how to negotiate with and respect others, and their sense of self-worth can be badly affected. Some children just feel different and unable to fit in with the existing gangs. 'There's the skateboarders, the computer nerds and the druggies and I don't really feel that I fit in with any of them,' says Sam, who is sixteen. Others feel so ostracized and lacking in self-worth that they daren't trust new relationships. Unpopular children tend to have low self-esteem. They have been tried by a jury of their peers and found to be inadequate, and the insecurity that provokes can last a lifetime. Rebecca's best and only friend suddenly ignored her and stopped talking to her when she was fifteen. 'We used to have this thing about being the devils in the school, so when she stopped talking to me I stopped talking to everybody as a way of protecting myself, because at school you're always scared that people won't like you.' Rebecca's isolation led to an entrenched unhappiness through much of her teenage years and she still finds it hard to get on with people. 'If I'd had a lot of good friends then it would have been easier but I've never been someone with a lot of friends and I suppose I am quite exacting when it comes to people. I've noticed that I'm doing the same thing now that I'm at college, not talking to people and thinking that I don't need them. When you do that it's partly because you're afraid of people, afraid that they are not going to like me or look down on me.'

Young people who have been rejected by their peers are more likely to be disruptive and aggressive. They are also more likely to drop out of school. When those who left early were compared to those who stayed on, 46 per cent of the male early leavers were described by their teachers as socially rejected, compared with 7 per cent of those who stayed.[9] Many children with friendship difficulties grow up to be healthy, social individuals. However large numbers of adults and adolescents with mental health problems have been found to have a history of poor peer relations.

When adolescent friendships are that intense and important for self-definition and self-esteem it can be extremely difficult for young people to pull away from the crowd view and stand up for what they really believe in or want because they risk rejection and alienation. It takes confidence to be able to resist the magnetic allure of the crowd, confidence that parents can plant in their children from an early age. Joan is proud of the fact that her fifteen-year-old daughter, Suzanna, has always managed to stand up for herself and pulled away when she felt uncomfortable. 'At the end of her first year at secondary school, they went to the park for a party and there was trouble. They were being noisy and someone threatened to call the police. So she got up and came home. She knew that if the police came that would be a bad thing so she had the courage to draw back. Then she decided to break away from these people, and boy did she learn the hard way. They sent a girl who had stolen someone else's boyfriend to Coventry and she decided to side with her. She couldn't understand why they were being so horrible to her. When she was about thirteen she was fighting with us as the "enemy" and fighting with this group and no one would speak to her, which had never happened to her before, she'd always been so successful. This went on for about six months.' Suzanna wouldn't walk to school because she had no one to walk with and was clearly very unhappy but Joan resisted interfering because she felt that her daughter had made the decision to leave this gang and had to see it through to the end. 'Eventually the school got involved and the girls and their teachers yelled and roared at each other and it was wonderful because it felt like getting our child back. It was as if she had been in a cult but she has loads of new friends now.'

Caroline also found that she had no choice but to stand back when her daughter decided that she wanted to pull away from a close-knit group of friends from primary days to join a group of older girls who did more grown-up things. 'She had a very difficult time for a couple of years but I think that's what's given her confidence, because she did it herself. I couldn't prevent her from joining this new group of older girls, but I could put rules around it like, "You always have to be with somebody" or laying down times to be back. We decided to make it safer for her by giving money for taxis and insisting that she always phoned if there was a problem. We couldn't guarantee that we wouldn't be cross but we said that we'd always help.'

Young people are sometimes so intent on feeling more grown-up that the lure of the older friend is irresistible. There are so few places for teenagers to go. Pubs and clubs are forbidden to the under-sixteens, unless they have fake IDs, and money is tight for many, but the urge to be away from home is strong. What they do is secondary to the principal drive of being away from parental scrutiny and control. When young people are away from their parents they can be individual and feel more mature. Older friends with cars or flats provide an essential escape route from family life and simply being with someone that much older gives a vulnerable adolescent adult status by association and can be very seductive. This is far more common than many people realize – half of all the adolescents in one study had at least one friend over the age of twenty – and it is a relationship that is potentially far more threatening than same-age friendships because it is so often predatory.[10] There may be only a few years difference in age between a fifteen-year-old and someone who is twenty, but there is a whole world between them in terms of experience and intellectual maturity, and one easily preys on the other. They may have access to drugs and need a market to sell to. They may be interested in sex with younger, inexperienced girls, many of whom either find boys of their own age unattractive or are uncomfortable about being single and eager for sexual experience. Or, they may merely want to boost their own fragile self-esteem by being in a relationship where they have all the power. It is almost always the most vulnerable adolescents who are attracted to these power figures, the ones with absent or abusive fathers or an unhappy and unsupportive home life. It provides them with some semblance of security and a sense of being loved.

I remember two older men as being very influential in my teens. Harry had a car, a full beard and smoked copious amounts of dope. I was fifteen, he must have been about twenty. We didn't go out, he slept with me on Saturday mornings and left me with enough hash to smoke for the rest of the week. I was willing and utterly complicit, I looked forward to our meetings for those fleeting moments of emotional nourishment and of

sexual connection, even though the sex was deeply unsatisfying. But he had all the power. He came and he went. His car
and adult lifestyle gave him the freedom to do so, the freedom
I so longed for. Then there was Andrew, who must have been
twenty-two. He was good-looking, American, had money
and his own small bedsit in Hampstead and hooked on to my
gang of 'trendsetting' girls. I can't remember how we met him
but all of a sudden there he was, all of the time – on Hampstead
Heath, in pubs, sitting on the floor of our bedrooms listening
to the Rolling Stones. There was something exhilarating about
having a man that much older within our midst and we were
flattered by his attention. Now I look back at him with
hindsight, he was weird. He wanted sex with young girls rather
than women of his own age and one wouldn't do. He had to
work his way through the gang in order to feel like some sort
of sheikh with his own harem. Some of us ran home at the
first hint of danger, others succumbed – inevitably the ones who
were most vulnerable and insecure emotionally at that time.

The urge to feel and seem older is so strong with younger
teenagers that association with slightly dangerous gangs can
also be seductive. 'It made it seem like you were older when you
did rebelling-type things,' says Lucy, aged sixteen, 'sneaking out
past curfew and causing trouble. A lot of people hang around
with older friends, or older sisters and they know about all of
the privileges they get and it plays a big role, who you hang
around with.' Denise is keenly aware of the seductive power
of friends. When she was younger she used to hang around
with 'rough boys who start a fight like that, just for nothing.
It was exciting and it felt right at the time. I wanted to be in
that group because they knew lots of other people and it made
me feel a little bit older.' Now that Denise is sixteen and has
gone on to further education she tries to keep herself to herself
more 'because there are a lot of people who go to college just
to socialize. They sit downstairs instead of going to lessons and

I don't want them to distract me from doing what I want to do.'

Francesca fell in love with a thirty-year-old man when she was seventeen. She was used to socializing with older people in their twenties because her brother was eight years older than her and she spent time with his friends. 'There was this woman who I worshipped and then when I was in the pub one night I met this guy and liked him and he liked me and then I discovered that he was her husband. That gave me such an ego boost. The woman that I wanted to be, her husband wanted me! I felt like I was part of something exciting and special. But now that it's all gone wrong I wish I'd never met him. I feel as if I've wasted time because I spent time between the ages of seventeen and nineteen with him, when I should have been with other friends my own age. He wouldn't let me see them. The time when I could have been going out and having fun with friends and having loads of boyfriends I spent it with one man and got severely hurt by him.'

Peer pressure exists and exerts a powerful influence over young people but it is only potentially harmful when other sources of support or influence are wanting. When young people become embroiled in seriously deviant or dangerous behaviour (as opposed to the minor flirtations with excitement that are common, essential even, to youth), research suggests that it is family background with poor parenting marred by lack of support, monitoring or firm enough boundaries which tends to push children with low self-esteem towards the more degenerate peer group, rather than innocent, contented children being seduced away by the charms of the devil. Research consistently shows that children actively seek out and are attracted to like-minded peers.[11] They are not passive victims, but willing, complicit members of cliques or groups, and young people tend to be attracted to others who share the same values and beliefs and reinforce each other's behaviour.

One year-long study found that young people who perceived few opportunities for decision-making at home and no increase in those opportunities as they got older were more likely to be swayed by advice from their friends rather than from their parents. Those with stricter parents associated with peers who had more extreme behaviour and were more likely to consider it acceptable to break parents' rules in order to keep in with their friends, or to let school work slip in order to stay popular.[12]

Young people need to conform to some extent to the norms of their peer group in order to feel accepted. But that does not mean that they lose their sense of individuality completely. They seek out advice from friends on dress, appearance, music tastes or social difficulties because they need to belong and conform in these aspects and because they are intelligent enough to know that parents are bound to be useless on these issues. Why ask them about sex when they clearly never have it? But they often still trust parents and listen to their advice in areas where they presume them to be knowledgeable, on the really important long-term issues such as education, career, politics and moral values. Children who are self-confident and value themselves are far more likely to find the strength of mind to resist peer pressure when they feel uncomfortable with it or to walk away from situations where they feel uneasy. Teenagers who feel secure in their relations with their parents are more able to form close attachments with friends and are less attracted to influence from anti-social peers. Children who like themselves because their parents have always shown how much they value them are more likely to assume that other children will like them and be popular, and are therefore less likely to feel the need to follow the crowd in order to feel accepted and more grown-up.

It is not an either/or situation where teenagers reject everything that parents believe in or say in favour of the peer group. Parents and friends offer non-competitive sources of support to a teenager and fulfil different needs. They are just growing up and growing slowly wiser to the fact that there may be different opinions, different ways of doing things which have to be assessed so that they can decide what they really think and how they want to live. They begin to be able to understand that parents have to say and do things in order to be good parents, that they may deny them things simply because they feel it is their responsibility as parents rather than just for the sake of it (which is how a child thinks). The peer group is generally an essential socializing force for good. The child with such a low sense of self-esteem that he will do anything to be accepted by the group is the exception rather than the rule and most of the time it is the delinquent kids who seek each other out and then egg each other on. Their numbers are small, concentrated in particular areas of great poverty and deprivation and have been greatly exaggerated by media obsession with the criminality of youth. Youth culture is not one homogeneous mass of irresponsible, hedonistic and recalcitrant teenagers. There is as much variation in the values, activities and aspirations of the young as there is between adults. Teenagers pick and choose aspects from the hundreds of thousands of different cultures out there which appeal to them, and they remain essentially the same caring and considerate individuals that they have always been. They are not necessarily out raving, taking drugs and driving stolen cars at breakneck speed up the wrong side of the motorway just because they've been brave enough to have a tattoo etched onto their right shoulder.

All too often what parents and adults perceive as threatening behaviour in groups of young people is just high spirits and normal precocity as they begin to discover their independence from adult authority and stretch and beat their wings. Identifying with a core aspect of modern youth culture is an essential part of growing up. It is exciting and challenging, a way of asserting their new-found sense of strength or masculinity through collective irreverence within a wider culture that tends to infantilize or marginalize teenagers and where the adults hold all of the cards.

Crowds have great pull. Gangs offer security in numbers when they are away from home for they have nowhere else to go but out. The fourteen to seventeen age group is badly served with leisure facilities, they are too old for youth clubs and too young for pubs and clubs. They have very little money and if they are not into sports their free time is spent watching TV, visiting friends or getting up to minor pranks or crime for the sheer buzz of excitement. 'You end up getting into trouble then, if you just carry on roaring the streets and that,' says Brian, who is sixteen and lives in Cardiff. 'We used to traipse around graveyards at midnight because there was nothing else to do, we were so bored. It was better than being in the house.' Practical jokes or playing truant from school relieve the boredom of daily life, but they also enable young people to challenge the authority of adults in order to assert their own autonomy and establish their difference as they test the wider boundaries of society. Adults are the status quo, they hold all the power, so minor crime enables young people to distinguish themselves from the establishment. There are few adults today holding down responsible jobs and behaving as socially responsible citizens who would not admit to minor crimes committed during their adolescence for which they did not get caught. The short-term buzz of excitement means that they can forget temporarily the morality of their actions and feel justified because of the hostility they feel from older generations.

Parents still have a role to play in their children's social lives when they become teenagers. Adolescents need to feel that they are still welcome at home and able to bring home their friends, even if that means fifteen gangly youths squashed into their tiny bedroom. Parents go out of their way to invest in their children's social lives when they are small, inviting friends over for tea and organizing birthday parties with balloons and entertainers. Small children are allowed in even though they tread sandwiches and crisps into the carpet and smear jelly across the walls. Yet when it comes to teenagers, large numbers of parents put their foot down and forbid social gatherings under their roof. Somehow the beer can and the sheer height and volume of their bodies is now a great deal more adult and threatening. The prospect of getting them to clear it up is daunting. But forbidding it banishes young people from their homes at a time when social relations are pre-eminent, condemning them to be out more on the street and more vulnerable, given that there are so few places that young people can go. Young children are considered angelic and innocent even though their skills of deceit and manipulation are often surprisingly sophisticated, but teenagers are never to be trusted home alone. The assumption is that the carpet will be awash with beer, and cigarettes will be stubbed out on your sofa the moment your back is turned. 'It's fine if you have nice parents who'll let you have twelve people in the house but most people haven't,' says Vicky who is seventeen. 'You want to be in a big group, not just three people, you want everybody to be there and it's a lot to ask your parents but that's what you need because there isn't that much you can do outside your own home.'

All too often parents are apprehensive of their children's friends and unfairly suspect them of exerting an adverse influence. They make it seem as if they are not wanted, but welcoming them in would establish a basis of trust and respect which can be built on to encourage them to behave responsibly. Judith has always made a point of being nice to her sixteen-year-old daughter's friends. The biscuit tin is always open and she buys in extra coca-cola for them when she goes out.

'Because I've been nice to these lads I have been assured that this house will not be trashed because they like me.' When Judith and her husband go out, they often make a point of even suggesting to their daughter that she has some friends round because they know how important her social life is and how all they often need at that age is a safe place to be together. The house is always immaculate save for the smell of cigarette smoke. 'The kids are gobsmacked by this, they say this is one of only two houses in the area where they are allowed when their parents are out, which I think is shocking. It smacks of disapproval and says there is something rather grubby and disgusting and awful about being a teenager which just confirms what a lot of them feel. One boy who I really like has got himself a girlfriend who is white. Her parents came home one day and found him in her bedroom and threw him out as if he were vermin. It wasn't a colour thing, just, "What the hell are you doing here?" If anyone treats my son in that way then I will be very, very cross.'

Teenagers like to be home alone, for the same reasons that they like to gather on street corners or in shopping centres – for a sense of group autonomy. 'Free houses', where the parents are out, are at a premium. 'We go to houses where the parents are out not because we're up to something,' says Vicky, 'but because it's nice to know that you're on your own, for the privacy, that no one's listening to us and also knowing that your presence isn't causing anybody any inconvenience, particularly in small houses like this where you can hear the music and you're taking up so much space. If the parents are there and you don't know them very well you sort of have to tiptoe past them.' Some parents who find themselves at home when their children's friends are there find it best to retreat. 'I do clear off as a rule because they want me to and I want them to feel comfortable,' says Judith. 'Sometimes I feel like a bit of a housekeeper, I sneak into the kitchen muttering, "I'm just getting a piece of toast," because they're all sitting round in their nighties after a sleepover, talking about how far the tongue got down the throat and I actually don't want to be there listening to it.'

Laying down house rules so that teenagers know what to expect helps – respecting property and steering clear of no-go areas such as parents' bedrooms are obvious. Feeling offence because teenagers often fail to rise to adult standards of social behaviour is pointless. 'They sneak in and they sneak out and it feels furtive which is what I don't like,' says Rosamund, who has a sixteen-year-old son. 'A whole load of them stayed the night on the last day of GCSEs and what made me really cross was that the next day, not one of them came up and said goodbye. I didn't expect them to come up and shake my hand or anything, but for not one of them to say goodbye when they stayed the night I found shocking.'

Understanding the difference between high-spirited but essentially harmless fun and the signs of adverse peer influence enables a parent to know when it is appropriate to intervene for the child's benefit and when it is best to stay well away. Making sure that teenagers feel happy to bring their friends home is one of the best ways of monitoring their behaviour and feeling reassured. If there are worrying signs, such as evidence of heavy drinking or drug use and truancy, parents may be able to approach the whole issue with greater sensitivity because they have not previously alienated them by banning them from the house. They can be given time to see if this is a phase that just passes, and they can be warned more adequately about the dangers of being sucked into deeper trouble. Going out drinking is one thing, but piling into a 'borrowed' car at midnight with a driver who is drunk at the wheel is really not a good idea. Bunking off school once or twice for the thrill of it is one thing, but missing enough to fall behind could lead to difficulties at GCSE, AS and A levels.

Any criticism of children's friends for influencing them is likely to lead to rows or offence. Nobody likes to think that they do things simply in order to conform. Drawing attention to peer pressure merely communicates the message that you consider them weak and easily led. Grounding children all too often has the negative effect of making them see your concerns as unreasonable because you're punishing them in a way that undermines their most important concern – their social life. Instead it is better to bolster children's sense of self-esteem so that they are able to withdraw from an awkward or unpleasant situation without losing face. Sudden illness is always a good one and a code word can also be agreed on which they can use over the phone if they feel they are in trouble and need rescuing.

Adolescents form their own friendships. They struggle with social difficulties and they walk away from friendships when they have had enough. It is not a parent's right to meddle with or attempt to control that process and attempting to do so will probably only succeed in drawing the children even closer towards their peer group. Banning a fifteen-year-old from meeting up with certain friends is pointless when you both know that there is nothing that you can do to prevent that from happening. If adolescents feel that they have to reject their mother to be with their friends, that places an unnecessary emotional burden on young people who still need emotional nourishment from their parents. It's much better to foster your own changing relationship so that you stay on the same side and can influence through encouragement and words of wisdom without impeding that continuous drive for autonomy that is essential to adolescence. Before we intervene we must consider whether our own emotional needs during the gradual separation between us and our children are being confused with those of the child. Are those friends really that unsuitable or is it just that you don't like them, resent the way they take your child away from you and mourn the times that you used to spend together?

Understanding the supreme importance of a teenager's social life is essential if parents and adolescents are to stay close. 'Her social life is more important than being there for dinner,' says Judith. 'If she's hungry, I'll make her a sandwich. I also say that she doesn't have to come anywhere with us unless she wants to, that her life is as important as ours. If it's something like Grandad's seventieth birthday, I give her plenty of warning but then if she decides not to come I let her because she's got to live with the fact that she decided to be a cow.' Liberalism appears to work in Judith's case. But research backs up her experience. In families where decisions are discussed democratically, where young people feel that their friends are accepted and welcome and where they do not feel torn between them, those young people are more likely to stay close to their parents and share the same values as they grow up.[13]

Friends matter deeply to young people particularly in early adolescence because friends define who they are as they begin to separate from their parents and strive for autonomy. The peer group, that small group of highly influential friends, feels like an extension of oneself at thirteen, and makes it hard to know where the individual ends and the group begins. The thoughts and feelings of the two become enmeshed and confused. But this phase doesn't last. By middle adolescence, young people are more able to distinguish their own individuality, their own beliefs and feelings from those of their friends. Research shows that delinquent children are generally attracted to other delinquent children. Those from loving homes where parents set boundaries and encourage autonomy rarely get seduced by the rough gang intent on criminal behaviour. When children are swayed by negative peer pressure it is often because they are pushed there because of some factor in their upbringing – childhood trauma, adverse reactions to divorce,

separation and bereavement or parents who are either vindic-
tively harsh or utterly neglectful.

Friendship is a positive and essential force at adolescence,
through which teenagers explore the world and validate themselves. Friends offer essential support and guidance through
the emotional difficulties of growing up and provide a forum
for discussion and understanding of parents as conflict rises
and their inadequacies loom large. Loneliness at adolescence
is especially distressing because of the damage not being liked
does to one's fragile self-esteem and sense of identity at this
time. Friendship makes us feel valued and loved and enables
us to give and receive. Humans are social beings and through
adolescent friendships, teenagers develop all of the skills they
need for a healthy adult social life. I first met Tim when he
was fifteen and then again when he was eighteen. His teenage
years were far from difficult and when I asked him why he
thought adolescence had been a relatively smooth ride for him
he was unequivocal in his answer: 'I've always had a lot of
friends. Don't get me wrong, I value my family and they'll
always be there but having friends is the most important thing
because without friends, what are you? If you don't have
friends that you can relate to and talk to then at the end of the
day, you've got nothing.'

7. Sexuality

It was all new to him: the memorization of strategic speeches, the trial runs of possible conversations, the yogic deep breathing, all leading up to the blind, headlong dive into the staticky sea of telephone lines. He hadn't suffered the eternity of the ring about to be picked up, didn't know the heart rush of hearing the incomparable voice suddenly linked with his own, the sense it gave of being too close to even see her, of being actually *inside her ear*. He had never felt the pain of lacklustre responses, the dread of 'Oh . . . hi,' or the quick annihilation of 'Who?'

Jeffrey Eugenides, *The Virgin Suicides*

Understanding the opposite sex may be a continual mystery for adults, but for adolescents just embarking on this journey it is usually preoccupying and difficult. Looking for love, dating, what to do and how far to go are often frightening prospects for young people and riddled with embarrassment which they have to deal with largely alone. For centuries, dating had traditionally been structured and organized by parental figures with set codes of conduct. Coming-out balls, marked cards at dances and the system of chaperonage once enabled young people to follow a prescribed route through romantic exploration with a view, specifically, to finding a marriage partner. The set steps of classic dances demanded everybody's participation at a social event. They encouraged gentle physical contact with the opposite sex under the watchful eye of the grown-ups. But from the 1950s onwards all that changed. Sexual relations before marriage became widespread and more acceptable, the pill, concepts of 'free love' during the Swinging Sixties and feminism liberated women as well as many men from previous sexual constraints and the emergence of new and vibrant youth cultures segregated adolescents from adult guidance or monitoring.

Young people now explore the beginnings of sexuality alone. Children begin puberty earlier than ever and grow up in a highly sexualized culture. The age of first sexual intercourse has dropped steadily and rates of pregnancy and sexually transmitted diseases have risen sharply in much of the Western world. It is presumed that most teenagers are sexually promiscuous from an early age, when in fact nearly three-quarters of sixteen-year-old girls in Britain have not lost their virginity.[1] Some feel they should be more sexually active because of this recent myth. Many more grow up confused and ignorant of sex and relationships because adults haven't stepped in adequately to bridge the gap with more open and thorough advice to help them make sense of the sexually charged culture they now grow up in. 'My mum was really shocked when she found me reading *Just 17*. It had a sex survey in it which was about where you got your information from but my mum thought it was about sex,' says Trish, who is fourteen. 'She said, "You shouldn't know about all this, you're much too young. Why do you need to know about this?"'

Friends are of minimal use when they are also inexperienced. Exchanging genuine confidences about masturbation or intercourse is far too revealing, when friends cannot necessarily be trusted not to use that information against them, mocking them in public as either inexperienced (shameful for boys) or a slag because they are experienced (shameful for girls).

'Sex isn't something that comes up in conversation. We have got friends who are sleeping with people but it isn't something that we discuss like some major issue. When we were thirteen and went to sleepovers all we would ever talk about was periods or whose breasts were bigger and you would think that all we would talk about now is who was sleeping with who, but it hasn't happened. It's not something that you discuss, it's private. With periods it's a way of dealing with it. But having sex is something that you're either ready for or not. It's too change-able, too different for each person to be able to draw up a set code of how to do it, who to do it with and when,' says Camilla, who is sixteen.

Amanda agrees. 'It's your private life so we're not really interested in hearing about it unless you've got a problem. I find it difficult to talk to my friends because it's so private. I can talk about how I feel about a bloke but I don't think you ever tell anyone the whole extent of what you're feeling, you can't really.'

Adults tend to romanticize early sexual experience as some-thing precious and magical that has to be saved for someone special. They tend to idealize sexual exploration and forget the agony. Adolescents know that sex is the ultimate rite of passage to adulthood but often find sexual exploration frightening, with acres of opportunity for rejection when they are at their most vulnerable emotionally. Each first – first kiss, first fondling of a breast, first touch of a genital – is a landmark stage along the way, but first they need to fathom the depths of their courage just to talk to someone they fancy. 'It's difficult to know how to handle it when you think someone's good-looking,' says Dan, aged fourteen. 'I know people who just go for people and then get rejected, but I can't handle that. I personally need a bit of reassurance from their body language that I'm in with a chance.' Dates can be difficult to handle if there is no common code for sexual practice, and the gentler, more sensual aspects of simple contact, such as holding hands, may be denied when this could be misinterpreted as an invita-tion for full sexual congress. The whole idea of dating now has an old-fashioned ring to it. You 'hang out' as far away from parents as possible, at pubs or parties at 'safe houses' where the parents are out. Dancing at gigs or parties is anarchic and solo rather than the prescribed, collective rituals of yester-year. Modern dancing is also often overtly sexual, signalling availability for the more socially confident or physically able but leaving many of the less courageous isolated in the shadows. Young people have to brave prospective partners and master the subtle differences between casual conversation and flirtation on their own.

Huge increases in hormones during early puberty trigger desire and interest in sexual matters and children often feel confused about these new feelings. They don't quite know how to handle them or what to make of them. Their skin feels more sensual and easily aroused by touch. Their senses of smell and sight begin to respond to sexual stimulae, and bare flesh, breasts and genitals are now exciting rather than just interesting, a pretty face or a muscular torso triggers new thoughts and feelings in an adolescent's mind. 'Sometimes when I lie in bed at night, I have a terrible desire to feel my breasts and to listen to the quiet rhythmic beat of my heart,' writes Anne Frank in her diary in January 1944. 'I believe that it's spring within me, I feel that spring is awakening. I feel it in my whole body and soul.' Just one month later she writes, 'I feel utterly confused, I don't know what to read, what to write, what to do, I only know that I am longing . . .'

Simone de Beauvoir is even more graphic about her strong sexual desire at the age of thirteen in her autobiography, *Memoirs of a Dutiful Daughter*.

I read a fragment of a novelette in which the hero applied his burning lips to the heroine's white breast. The kiss burned right through me; I was both hero and heroine, and watcher too; I both gave and received the kiss, and feasted my eyes upon it also. If I felt such ripe excitement it was surely because my body was already ripe for it;

but my daydreams were crystallized around that image; I don't know how many times I lingered over it before I fell asleep . . . I would toss and turn in my bed, calling for a man's body to be pressed against my own, for a man's hand to stroke my flesh. Desperately I would calculate: 'girls aren't allowed to marry until they're fifteen!'

As boys and girls begin to mature, they withdraw into two distinct camps so that they can eye up and assess the opposition. Often they become suddenly mute and inept at communicating with the opposite sex, particularly if they go to a single-sex school. 'I find it really difficult, I don't know how to talk to boys,' says Trish. 'How can you even begin to get to know what they're like when you don't know what to say?' When I brought up the subject of girls with a group of fifteen-year-old boys who go to a single-sex school and asked whether they found them frightening, the cockiest replied, 'Girls aren't frightening, they're wicked, just great things.' But this was followed by a twenty-minute discussion amongst them as to how you actually get to talk to them and whether it was worth risking rejection by going in strong: 'Some people just pair off but I'm crap at it. I'm not that good at asking out a girl if I fancy her, she might say no and I'm actually quite timid.' Or, whether it was better to hide behind the mask of arrogance and pretend to be confident when you're not: 'I've kept links with the girls I knew when I was small so I've never been that worried but if I am I just have to be really arrogant and cocky. You don't have to feel confident, you just have to come across as confident so that they take an interest in you.'

'Going out' in its earliest forms in mixed-sex schools is usually just a state of being, a circuit of the playground characterized by complete silence, with little physical contact other than holding hands, and lasts a day or two if things are going really well. 'In Years 7 and 8 a lot of people had boyfriends, but it wasn't proper. You never saw each other outside school, you'd just go round at lunchtime holding hands and then maybe you'd kiss them, but you never really spoke to them or had anything to say so you'd then have to run up to your girlfriends and plead with them to talk to you because you were so desperate for conversation,' says Suzanna, aged fifteen, from Brighton. Often the objects of adolescents' desires have no idea that they are being admired because teenagers find it so hard to talk. 'I saw this bloke once who was just so lovely,' says Amanda, who is eighteen. 'I remember having to go out for dinner and he was there and I couldn't eat because I was so besotted with him and yet I've never really spoken to him, I'd just seen him in a pub. I was so in awe of him, so scared that I couldn't speak. And then before anything has happened, you see someone else.'

Huge issues over gender emerge as boys and girls adhere to sexual stereotypes in order to engage in early mating rituals. Most teenage boys have sex because of the pressure put on them by their peers. Early sexual experience is glorified as being macho. They crow about their sexual conquests, and research shows that they tend to exaggerate their achievements in sex surveys (while girls tend to reduce the number in order not to appear promiscuous). Boys like to delay intimacy with girls for as long as possible because truly amorous encounters isolate them from their peers. Dan and Ian are fourteen and close friends. 'We've agreed not to go out with anyone any more because it's just a hassle. It's too restricting because you can only be with that girl.'

'I had a girlfriend for about two months, that was the longest. The shortest was for about two and a half hours when I was at school.' Colin is sixteen and recently left school. 'I'm going on holiday for the first time with friends and we'll go clubbing, get a bit of action hopefully and then when I get back maybe I'll be able to take on something a bit more serious.'

'I'm not in a girlfriend stage because then you get redefined – you *gotta* have a girlfriend,' says Mark, aged fifteen. But this false bravado often masks a deep anxiety about making the first move and their own performance. They snigger at the mention of sex to deflect attention from the dozens of unanswered questions that mill around their heads and the acute uncertainty they feel about having to take total responsibility for sex. 'They say there are three holes down there, what happens if I get the wrong one?' asked one brave fourteen-year-old boy at the Wirral branch of the Brook Advisory Centre. The enlightened worker there managed to allay his anxiety with humour. 'Well there's a good chance that someone else will be there with you and she'll help you to get it right,' he replied.

Girls face a whole range of other pressures to conform to socially accepted stereotypes. 'Good' girls have to wait for the right man to come along, for too much sexual experience scars their reputation. They face far greater pressure these days to perform sexually because of the false presumption that everyone else is 'doing it', and they still get caught between age-old sexist assumptions: if they do it they're slags and if they don't they're frigid. 'It's always portrayed on the TV that girls are completely obsessed with whether or not they've done it but I don't think that most of the girls in my year are that preoccupied with it,' says Claudia, who is seventeen. 'But girls are bound to be more reluctant about it. If a girl sleeps with a boy or more than one she's a slut, whereas if a boy does it he's a real big guy. Being a virgin is not really a stigma at all, there's this whole thing about teenagers having sex too early and I just never find that amongst my friends because we all know that there is too much to lose.' 'Hardly any twelve-year-olds get pregnant, but as soon as you hear about one on the telly, everyone presumes that every twelve-year-old girl is having sex,' says Vicky, who is seventeen and still a virgin. 'It has a lot to do with ambition. If you wanna go places you don't get pregnant.'

And so the dance begins with boys piling on the pressure to seek out sexual experience and girls craving the same but having to resist for as long as possible in order to save sexual experience for the intimacy that comes with relationship. 'I don't really wanna be like all the girls I know who've gone a long way with boys,' says Trish, 'but I also wanna catch up and have sex because I think they have. I do feel ready for boys. I've kissed and had the opportunity for sex and said no. But the thing is, if you don't they just dump you. Sex at my age is degrading but boys just want sex.'

'A lot of the time, a girl says yes to a boy who asks her out even if she doesn't like him. If you didn't they'd say you were frigid,' says Suzanna.

Claudia was fourteen when a boy she met at a disco took her telephone number and asked her out to the cinema. 'We didn't have anything to say to each other and sat there. I kept thinking, what's he gonna do? And he didn't do anything except in the middle of the film something funny happened and we smiled at each other. Then we went home. We barely spoke and *then* I discovered that he'd told everyone that I was frigid!'

'I guess my first kiss was when I was thirteen or fourteen on holiday. He was really intense with me, he kept asking me if I was OK and then he said that I couldn't kiss properly so I used my braces as an excuse. But I didn't really go out with anyone until this year, I didn't really know anyone,' says Louisa, who is seventeen and goes to a single-sex school.

Girls have to justify and romanticize sexual fantasies and exploration through love and spend inordinate amounts of time and mental energy lounging about and longing for it. They pore over teenage magazines, romance literature and television soaps in order to feed these fantasies and learn about social and sexual interaction with the opposite sex. I spent the entire eight-hour drive up to Scotland at the start of one summer, at the age of thirteen, pining silently on the back seat for a boy who barely knew my name. I imagined impossible scenarios in which he would just happen to drop by at our remote holiday cottage, a puncture perhaps, or maybe he had noticed me after all and was having me followed at that very moment to discover my destination. Simply telling him, or indicating subtly that I liked him was way beyond the scope of my fledgling social skills. Girls fill the emotional void left by backward or not-yet-ready-for-involvement boys with plenty of physical contact with their female friends, hugging and kissing frequently as they sit on each other's laps puffing on cigarettes and exchanging interesting facts about the opposite sex not yet available to the general public. Or they form crushes on older women, often their teachers, as encapsulated by Miss Jean Brodie's remarkable hold over her thirteen-year-old charges in Muriel Spark's novel *The Prime of Miss Jean Brodie*. When there are no obvious, known sources to attach their affection to, girls readily fixate on pop stars and film idols and fall deeply in love with people they have never met. 'Linda with the Prince of Wales, and I with a fat, red-faced, middle-aged farmer whom I sometimes saw riding through Shenley,' writes Nancy Mitford in *The Pursuit of Love*. 'These loves were strong and painfully delicious; they occupied all our thoughts, but I think we half realized that they would be superseded in time by real people. They were to keep the house warm, so to speak, for its eventual occupant.'

Girls need intimate relationships with boys in order to be able to have any sort of a sexual one. They need the emotional confirmation that comes with love at an earlier age than boys, so large numbers of attractive, lovely, confident, capable teenage girls find themselves single and feeling inadequate. 'Being lonely frightens me, you can only have sex with no caring for so long because then you get called a slag and men take advantage of you,' says Stella.

'Boys are fine if you're in a steady relationship,' says Vicky. 'It's great when it gets to a comfortable stage, but all that "Will he ring me?" "Does he like me?" is a bit stressful and yet another thing to worry about. I'd fix my hopes on somebody and then when they let me down I'd think it was the end of the world. It shouldn't really matter that I haven't got a boyfriend. I know that I'll find the love of my life eventually. But it does matter, however much I try and pretend that it doesn't. When I've had a boyfriend I don't care about my body because they obviously like me for some reason, which is really tragic but that's the way it is.'

Lots of girls are too mature for the boys of their own age and too young for anything other than the most predatory older man. 'Boys my age don't really fancy me,' says Stella. 'They all want girls of a certain type, thin with long hair and light skins and I'm not like that so it's with older men that things tend to happen.'

'I can't bear blokes my own age, they're so immature. They've gotta be older,' says Vicky, aged seventeen.

When teenagers are in a relationship that matters to them and it goes wrong, both sexes can be devastated. They often lack the emotional resources to cope with the rejection, being at their most self-conscious and vulnerable self-esteem-wise. They also have little concept of how insignificant this will seem in just a few months' time. Being dumped by someone you really like hurts at any age but when you are a teenager still lacking self-knowledge or confidence in your abilities and feeling insecure about how you look or how acceptable you are to your peers, the rejection is far more painful. 'I did have a boyfriend a while ago but he was a bit strange and it adds a whole lot of extra stress when you don't need it sometimes,' says Vicky. 'If your feelings get involved it can be difficult. I've known people who have been really upset when they've been dumped and it's affected them for months and months and that's not worth it, that pain. I think you have to be careful and try and remember that you're only seventeen and it's not the end of the world if he doesn't like you back. For me it was the other way around, when we split up he was the one who was really upset and I kept ringing him up to see if he was OK and ignored myself for a while and I wasn't fine either. It cost me a month or two focusing on him and that wasn't very good for me.'

Gender differences in the way that sex is experienced and explored also emerge with puberty. Boys almost always experience their first orgasm and sexual sensations alone, through masturbation or nocturnal emissions rather than as a direct result of intimate relations with another person. Erect penises are hard to ignore. They spring from nowhere, often without any obvious provocation, and seem to many an adolescent boy to be beyond their control. 'They can kind of get in the way, I suppose, every morning I just flick it to get it to go away,' says Colin. Masturbation enables them to take back some sense of body ownership, to get to know how their new maturing genitals operate and what gives them sexual pleasure. Girls on the other hand are far less likely to have explored their bodies through masturbation and first orgasm is usually much more elusive. All statistics and surveys on sex have to be treated with a little suspicion but approximately 85 per cent of fifteen-year-old boys masturbate regularly compared to only 20 per cent of fifteen-year-old girls.[2] Without masturbation, girls are far less likely to discover the joys of orgasm or what gives them pleasure. They need boys to unlock those secrets, but few are adept or experienced enough to know how. Surveys suggest that the majority of women admit that sex during their teenage years was disappointing and that masturbation, when they discovered it, gave them far more pleasure than intercourse during those early years. Most teenage girls find it hard to really enjoy their early sexual encounters. 'So how about sex and drugs and rock and roll?' I asked a group of sixteen-year-old girls, tongue-tied and uncomfortable about broaching the subject of sex with teenagers I had never met before. 'Rock and roll's my favourite,' one answered glumly.

Adolescents need slow steady progression in their sexual experimentation in order to be able to assimilate what they have learned or felt as they experience layers of intimacy. They cannot cope with everything at once and need to feel confident about snogging and light petting before they progress to heavy petting or intercourse, or even begin to understand more complex concepts of adult sexuality such as game playing or sado-masochism. 'I've got this friend who really hacks me off because she likes to make out that she's this goddess in the bedroom.' Amanda is eighteen. 'You're curious about sex, sure, and you want to get your virginity out of the way but you also know that you have to learn how to do it. I think it's frightening, nerve-wracking learning, so I can't bear it when she sits there and gloats about it. I'd prefer just hugs, gentleness, which sounds really pathetic, but maybe that's more of a female thing.'

'What I can't figure out is if their tongues are slipping around in there the whole time, lapping on each other,' writes Mary Karr in *Cherry*, 'or if they just lip-lock and every now and again touch tongues.' When they finally hook up with someone, hours of kissing and breast or back rubbing are essential before anything more intimate can be attempted. When I was fifteen, whole afternoons of my summer holiday disappeared in the bedroom of one particular boy as we lay on his narrow bed beneath the Che Guevara poster listening to Bob Dylan and the Rolling Stones, fondling each other half dressed, sucking at each other's mouths until our lips were raw, searching for the point of the opposite sex as if we were about to be tested on it. We never discussed it or how far we would go, but somehow we knew that there was a barrier that we were not yet ready to cross. Genitals were not to be touched until we had somehow got to the heart of all this kissing. Whole hours would pass, measured in LPs and punctuated only by the rolling of joints, as we practised with tentative and clumsy hands, confirming the contours of our new physiques and attempting to discover how to find pleasure for ourselves rather than give it. There was more pretence and play-acting to our fumblings than sensuality, but neither of us could have progressed to greater things with other people without that essential experience.

Adolescents generally move through a series of stages as they practise lovemaking. First there is kissing, then petting, then heavy petting of genitals and oral sex, usually of girl on boy, followed lastly by intercourse. One recent survey of eighteen-year-olds in Britain found that 46 per cent of boys and 28 per cent of girls had engaged in oral sex with casual partners and 56 per cent of boys and 58 per cent of girls had oral sex with steady partners.[3] Similar rates have been found amongst American students.[4] Losing one's virginity is for many young people a haphazard, quick and unemotional event to cross that ultimate adult threshold rather than the all-consuming, passionate and sexually fulfilling fruits of a profound romance. For some young people losing their virginity is carefully considered and planned. 'We've discussed it, maybe when I'm sixteen, on my birthday!' says Suzanna, who has been with her boyfriend for three months. Vicky is seventeen and still a virgin. 'Knowing that other people my age have boyfriends and are possibly having sex doesn't make me feel that I must go out and sleep with someone who's horrible. It just makes me feel that I wish I could have as good a relationship as them, that I could be really happy. I want to be with someone that I really like for the whole thing.'

Others snatch at it with strangers as a bid for maturity, out of curiosity or loneliness. Stella longs for a proper boyfriend and recently lost her virginity with an older man. 'I've only had sex once and it could have been better. I went to a film afterwards and saw how it could be and thought, I can't ever do that again. We never even kissed. I told him that I was a virgin, but thought I might as well do it, get it out of the way. I didn't know who else to break it with, but at least I waited until I was sixteen.' Lacking a Romeo, I too chose to lose my virginity with someone who I thought was sexually experienced, although younger, to whom there was no possibility of making a commitment. Like Stella, as well as like countless other teenage girls, I found the experience disappointing and sexually unsatisfying. A quick kiss, a brisk and unarousing squeeze of the breasts followed by repeated battering as he attempted, for what felt like the best part of an hour, in a desperate and over-excited way, to dock successfully. He clearly knew nothing about the existence of the clitoris (neither did I) and when he finally succeeded, the knife-edge agony of his penetration was mercifully swift. He came seconds after entry, and I leaped away like a wounded animal, dribbling semen, confused, wondering what all the fuss was about, but highly conscious that I had crossed an important adult rite of passage. Many leap to the mirror immediately to see if they look any different. I snatched my clothes and walked home, proud of the damp patch between my legs and feeling much more grown-up.

Sexual congress can be so hard to navigate for young people that even established couples find it difficult. Claudia has been deeply emotionally involved with her boyfriend for the past year. 'We don't sleep together. We both want to and it's not that I don't feel ready for it yet, it's just that we're both a bit inept, it just goes really wrong. It either becomes too laughable and absurd or it's too painful. Neither of us knows what we're doing.'

'Half the time, if you really want to know the truth, when

I'm horsing around with a girl I have a helluva lot of trouble just FINDING what I'm looking for, for God's sake, if you know what I mean,' echoes Salinger's hero of *The Catcher in the Rye*.

However it happens, and whoever it is with, losing one's virginity is almost always a landmark memory, a sexual encounter that is remembered vividly, unlike many of those enjoyed subsequently. There is now a 'before' and an 'after', a firm boundary between the two states of existence and a crucial marker in time for the young person now keenly aware of the passage of time. 'Philippe searched his memory,' writes Colette in her novel about sexual awakening, *Ripening Seed*, 'without recollecting a single story in which a young man cast off the shackles of childhood and chastity as one fell blow and did not continue to be shaken by strong, almost seismic tremors for many a long day after.' Vicky says, 'My friends don't go around sleeping with people generally. Sex is quite a big thing still. But when people have been going out for a while you tend to assume that they are sleeping together. I don't know anyone who says they're going to wait until they get married. You can go round the room and think, she has or she hasn't, because we talk about it and because they are in a relationship.'

Losing one's virginity often has different ramifications for boys and girls. For boys it's usually nothing more than 'a posh wank', says Naheen who is seventeen. It is exciting. They walk away from it feeling taller, older, better, for they have usually experienced orgasm and can brag about their conquest to friends. Girls, however, rarely feel quite so good about the incident. They are unlikely to have had an orgasm and may feel anxious about pregnancy, and their news has to be kept secret from all but the most trusting friend in case they should develop a reputation. Surveys and anecdotal evidence from agony aunts show that large numbers of girls who had sex before the age of sixteen regret the incident. 'Sex is a boys' life,' says David, aged seventeen. 'They think it's a big thing if they go round the corner with a girl. They think they're "bad". They'll come back and everyone will be cheering for them. It's all a game. Boys used to bring porn to school. That's how they learn and then when they meet a girl who's coming on a bit strong they do some crazy stuff.'

'C and J have slept together and it's been all round Westminster including what rating he gave her, not that he's got anyone to compare it with. It's so pathetic,' says Claudia. Then the story may change or be repeated ad nauseam because boys feel the need so badly to be seen as men among men, as Salinger describes in *The Catcher in the Rye*:

All he did was keep talking in this very monotonous voice about some babe he was supposed to have had sexual intercourse with the summer before. He'd already told me about it a hundred times. Every time he told it, it was different. One minute he'd given it to her in his cousin's Buick, the next minute he'd be giving it to her under some boardwalk. It was all a lot of crap, naturally. He was a virgin if ever I saw one.

Boys go for the erotic experience and are able to walk away. Girls crave emotional intimacy from boys in order to justify sexual exploration, and need romance in order to feel they are not being exploited because they are still so sexually inept and unself-aware and because they are vulnerable to pregnancy. 'It's difficult because of my insecurities,' says Denise who met a boy she really likes through a chat line. 'I don't want him to use me for sex, basically. What's good is just being with him. He's assured me many times that he's not that type of boy and sometimes I do believe him but there's still an edge in me that isn't sure, even though obviously I want to find out what it's all about. But I don't want this to be a hit and run.'

The emotional and practical repercussions of intercourse

are so inconsequential for boys that girls often feel pressurized to have intercourse before they are ready. For a substantial minority of young women first sex is not voluntary, but forced on them through rape, date rape or saying 'yes' in order to please a boy when actually they mean 'no'.[5] Adolescents are particularly vulnerable to date rape because they fear getting into trouble and many teenagers are unaware of what constitutes consensual behaviour. One American study has found that large numbers of high school students condone it. Twelve per cent of girls and 39 per cent of boys felt that it was acceptable for a boy to put pressure on a girl for sex if he had spent a lot of money on her; more than one third of the boys felt that it was acceptable if the boy was so aroused that he could not stop and 54 per cent thought that pressure was acceptable if the girl changed her mind about having sexual intercourse.[6] Sometimes it is the girls who exert the pressure on boys with taunts of 'Show me how much you love me,' but usually it is the boys who become adept at emotional blackmail ('If you loved me you'd have sex with me'), and they still use the old contraceptive con-trick of 'I won't come inside you.' When they can't get what they want, many still resort to force. 'I once met this boy who was a friend of a friend,' says Claire, who is sixteen. 'He goes to me, "Do you want to go behind the bowling alley?" I was forcibly trying to get him off me. I found out later that he was the only virgin in his group of friends and they were all teasing him about it. He wanted to lose his virginity and tried the same thing with one of my friends.'

Rebecca felt pressured into having sex with her boyfriend when she was seventeen. 'I felt like I wasn't ready for it and I didn't enjoy it at all, it was just a horrible thing, so I withdrew from him but the memory stayed with me a long time.' Rebecca left her boyfriend soon afterwards and is now in another, better relationship with someone she feels is far more sexually attentive. 'But sometimes those thoughts come back. It's a tense uneasiness and a fear of not being relaxed, a fear of it not being the way that it should be. If you're nervous and thinking that you're not going to enjoy it then obviously you're tense and you're not going to enjoy it. Sometimes I also feel that there is something in men, a drive to have sex, which somehow turns them into something else, they're not the same person any more and I suppose it has to do with men being able to rape women, the humiliation of it.'

Uncertainty over sexuality and sexual orientation is common during adolescence, and many young men and women experiment with gay and lesbian activity. It is often easier to approach and accept close physical proximity with a member of one's own sex before one attempts anything more ambitious with someone from the opposite sex, and most adolescents who experiment with homosexuality grow up to be exclusively heterosexual. Mutual masturbation to the point of orgasm is common amongst boys, particularly in single-sex schools, and girls often experiment with kissing other girls. 'Loads of girls pull [kiss] another girl before they pull a guy but it doesn't really mean anything,' says Claudia, who is seventeen and goes to a single-sex independent school in London. One of the most comprehensive surveys on adolescent sexual orientation, involving 35,000 young people in Minnesota, found extensive uncertainty which gradually gives way to predominately heterosexual or homosexual identities as they become sexually experienced.[7]

For the minority of the adult population who are gay or lesbian, adolescence is riddled with far greater emotional turmoil and confusion than it is for straight people. At a time when young people are generally grappling with who they are and desperately need to feel normal and accepted as part of the gang, coming to terms with their homosexuality can be difficult, undesirable or frightening given that homophobia is, according to surveys, particularly virulent amongst teenagers.

Many homosexuals talk of an awareness of being 'different' from childhood: girls who do not want to do the things that are traditionally associated with their gender and boys who see themselves as more sensitive and less competitive than their peers may find this sense of difference develops into strong sexual attraction towards friends of the same sex during puberty, which then has to be concealed. Society's attitudes towards homosexuality have become more tolerant in recent years and some researchers believe that the average age for 'coming out' has dropped from the early twenties to the late teens as a result. But within the cruelty of the schoolyard it is still an area ripe for taunting. Any child suspected of being gay or lesbian is vulnerable to jibes of 'poof', 'queen' or a humiliating public 'outing'. 'If you don't go round obviously pulling someone at parties then you're automatically a lesbian,' says Claudia. 'I hate the way that people use the word "gay" perjoratively. They say, "That's so gay," meaning stupid, which means that they can't use "gay" in a nice way to mean someone not being straight.'

At a time when adolescents depend so heavily on their friends and peer groups for support, gay and lesbian teenagers often find that they have no one to confide in or turn to for support or advice. They may be sexually attracted to their best friend and be unable to reveal their desire to extend their happy times together to intimate sexual pleasure. They may fear queer-bashing so much at school that they join forces with a gang doing just that to conceal their own tendencies. They may not know of national or local support groups for gay and lesbian teenagers and they are unlikely to be able to confide in their parents – another source of stress that few teenagers feel able to confront before adulthood. Recent research has found that substantial numbers of gay and lesbian adolescents have been harassed and physically or verbally abused while they were growing up and this has serious implications for their mental health. A survey of gay men and lesbians in 1996 found that 48 per cent of respondents under eighteen had experienced violence, 61 per cent had been harassed and 90 per cent had been called names because of their sexuality, and that 40 per cent of these attacks took place at school. This victimization may account for the higher rates of suicide, substance abuse, running away from home, and school difficulties reported by gay and lesbian adolescents.[8] In 1993, a British study found that young gay men had significantly poorer mental health than a control group, and researchers in the United States found that 42 per cent of the gay and lesbian young people they studied had attempted suicide in the previous year.[9]

As teenagers grow older and more confident about themselves, they become more confident in their relationships. The silent hand-holding for two hours before being dumped gradually develops into conversation and more intense physical contact. Peer perception and the need to be part of the gang begin to diminish as adolescents mature and space emerges in their social lives for more intimate personal pursuits as a couple. 'When we were in Years 7 and 8, my friends had boyfriends in school. Now, those who do have boyfriends come from out of school and it's weird looking back at some of the people they were once with. How could they have been together?' says Suzanna. 'Quite a lot of my friends are now getting boyfriends, but only a few of them are in what you might call established couples.'

'I prefer being friends with people in college, because once you start going out with somebody, everybody knows and everybody wants to be in the business. There's no privacy,' says Denise. 'So I'm going out with someone I met in a chat room. Some of my friends have met him and don't like him much, but that doesn't bother me, if it was close friends it probably would matter more. We've been to a restaurant and chatted a lot. It feels normal, nice, and when I'm down it makes me happy just to think about him because he is a nice person, funny, different. I experimented a lot when I was thirteen, fourteen, fooling around for ten minutes with boys at parties but that was nothing compared to this. I don't know if I'll decide to do it with him yet, but if I do, it's my body. What's good is just being with him.'

Children grow up with contradictory messages about sex and sexuality. They are bombarded by highly sexualized imagery in the media. They grow up sensing that sex is important even though they do not necessarily understand what it means. They need more thorough and honest explanations from parents in order to help them make sense of the huge divide between the fantasies and extremes projected by television and advertising, and the stark reality of normal life. Yet even the most liberal parents still find it hard to discuss puberty and sexual relations with their children, often assuming that they know it all already, from school, their friends or the telly. Far too many children are still not prepared for puberty let alone sexual relations. Children who have never seen their parents naked have little idea of normal adult nudity, and have only the abnormal fantasies of the advertising that surrounds them to go on. 'I started growing hairs round my penis and it scared me. Am I meant to grow hair here?' says Dan, aged fourteen. A child who has never seen a tampon let alone witnessed her mother inserting one is far more likely to find periods shocking and find it harder to accept menstruation as a normal aspect of growing up than one who has.

Absurd numbers of boys are still astonished by their first nocturnal emission and shameful numbers of girls still live through Carrie-esque emotions of shock and humiliation with their first show of menstrual blood, simply because they have not been adequately prepared. When it comes to understanding how the bodies of the opposite sex change as they grow up, adolescents are even less well informed. One third of those who answered a questionnaire in *Mizz* magazine in 1997 felt that they had not received enough information to be able to cope with starting their periods, and an astonishing 4 per cent knew nothing at all before they started bleeding. Studies show that when girls say they know all about puberty and periods, closer questioning reveals that their understanding is limited and often wrong. Many think that periods clear the body of bad blood, that it comes from the bladder and that women lose pint-size mugs of blood rather than spoonfuls. They want to know whether menstrual blood drips one drop at a time or whether it gushes like a river, and sometimes question the need for pads at all because of their understanding of urinating. Why can't you just pee it all out when you go to the loo? In an Australian study one girl thought that the point of periods was to make life more interesting, and another thought menstruation enabled women to have a baby, 'because if it hadn't opened the way, then a baby wouldn't be able to get out, it'd just suffocate'.[10]

Adults are, in my opinion, duty bound to prepare their children from an early age for the physical changes of growing up, with thorough and open discussion about puberty and sexual relations. Good preparation with regular, honest conversations is the key to a smoother transition through the physical changes of puberty.[11] It helps young people understand what is happening to them and to accept many of their physical attributes which so easily get interpreted as negative, such as menstruation, body fat and body fluids. It is easy to forget about the importance of talking about puberty when they are younger and we have so much on our hands already, organizing their lives, getting them to and from school, shopping, cooking as well as attempting to earn a living. But if parents don't start talking about these issues from middle childhood, suddenly puberty is there, the bathroom door locks, embarrassments surface and open discussion seems harder. Before long a whole host of inaccurate misunderstandings have taken root in the child's mind.

Sex and sexuality are often taboo subjects between parents and their children. Adults can feel very uncomfortable with expressions of fledgling sexuality in young children and still find it hard to discuss the most basic aspects of the sexual act. 'My mum wants to meet my boyfriend,' says Denise, 'but all she says is "no hanky panky". What does she mean by that? I can't know from that how far she means because we've never talked about sex. I found out about it from elsewhere, magazines, TV, what people said.' As children grow older and display more overt and mature signs of sexual beings just talking about it can feel dangerously close to incest. The simplest touch or physical expression of affection can now be misinterpreted. 'I still squirm inwardly watching anything on the TV with the kids that has a high sexual content,' says Mark who has two children aged sixteen and thirteen. Imagining our children in the sexual act is difficult, even horrible (just as it is for teenagers visualizing their parents making love) and we feel a whole new mixed bag of emotions when girlfriends or boyfriends are first brought home – who are they/how dare they steal them away/ are they good enough for my precious child and will they expect to stay the night?

We project our own ambiguity and embarrassments over sex and sexuality onto our children. As they grow up they quickly pick up society's mixed messages. Nakedness is to be covered and toddlers are chastised for exposing themselves in public. Yet nakedness surrounds us on advertising hoardings and is used to sell everything from ice cream to jeans. Countless parents still feel uncomfortable about letting their children see them undressed and find it hard to refer to genital parts by their real names, preferring to use 'it' or 'there' instead. We call a hand a 'hand', a foot a 'foot', but a vagina mysteriously becomes a 'tinky winky'. Children take great pleasure from their own genitals, soothing themselves at night, rubbing their groins against their parents in hugs and they don't feel complicated about it until adults tell them that it's just not done in public. They are intrigued by adult body parts because they are so different to their own, they love willy and fanny jokes and find their 'poo' and their bodily functions endlessly fascinating, but adults tell them to stop being disgusting. Then as sexual feelings become more intense with adolescence, they find it very hard to simply enjoy the good feelings because adults seem to view sex as something 'naughty but nice', as something secret, private and potentially dangerous that has to be hidden silently from view.

As the borders between adult and child sexuality become hazy, with five-year-olds swinging their hips and singing 'if you wanna be my lover' and thirteen-year-olds modelling scanty adult clothes, the adult world has become increasingly unsettled and uncertain about how to approach the whole subject of sex with children. We have seen a series of moral panics and fierce debates in the past two decades in Britain around the subject of children and sex – child abuse, teenage pregnancy and paedophilia are never out of the news. There have been heated debates about lowering the age of consent for homosexuals and protecting minors from access to pornography on the internet. Battles have repeatedly been fought in the courts over the content of sex education in schools. Section 28, which states that teachers must discuss the value of 'normal' family life, was added to the Local Government Act of 1988 because of fears that local authorities were promoting homosexuality at the taxpayers' expense, and then caused massive public controversy yet again when Blair's Labour government sought to remove it. In 1984 Victoria Gillick established through the courts the right of parental consent over the provision of contraception to under-sixteens until it was overturned by three out of five law lords in 1985. These attempts at clamping down seem to indicate that society still considers that children's sexual rights need to be limited in order to conform to what adults believe constitutes a 'proper' childhood.

Yet young people have never been in greater need of honest and thorough information. The age of first intercourse has been steadily falling since the 1950s now that marriage is mercifully no longer a prerequisite for sexual activity. Three major studies conducted in Britain in 1965, 1978 and 1994 show that the numbers of teenagers aged sixteen to nineteen who lost their virginity before the age of sixteen have been rising steadily. In 1950 only 7 per cent of white American sixteen-year-olds had experienced sexual intercourse, but by 1982 that figure had risen to 44 per cent. The best current estimates we have are that by the age of fifteen, approximately one third of boys and a quarter of girls in Britain have experienced intercourse, and by the age of nineteen that figure zooms up to 86 per cent for boys and 80 per cent for girls.[12] Studies from all over the Western world consistently show that anything between one-third and two-thirds of young people regularly avoid using contraception and that rates of sexually transmitted diseases and pregnancy are soaring. HIV is now spreading faster amongst young heterosexuals than it is amongst the gay community.[13]

Young people are now sexually mature earlier, within a culture where sexual desire is a constant factor in adult films and television programmes. The negative aspects of relationships such as divorce and adultery are frequently highlighted because that's where a good story lies, and young people see adults pursuing sexual gratification without responsibility. X and R rated videos are freely available from rental shops and being watched at home without parental guidance, which means children often learn about sex from soft pornographic or violent images, without the rudiments of contraceptive planning or responsibilities towards sexual partners. For the developing adolescent lacking mature critical judgement or experience in relationships, there is no opportunity to understand the steady progression of human sexual relationships or the ways in which so-called sexual 'deviances' emerge, when television, general culture and friends are their main source of social and sexual education. 'You have so many expectations about sex from the movies and so on, but what does that do to your fantasies?' asks Gary, who is sixteen.

'It's impossible to avoid sex now no matter what you watch – except perhaps *Blue Peter*,' says Louise. This growth in sexual obsession and early sexual activity has not been matched by greater permissiveness in our attitudes towards sexual behaviour or enhancing sexual understanding. Young people are physically able to procreate from middle adolescence, yet parents and teachers, even the liberal ones, still find it uncommonly difficult to talk about the most routine aspects of sexual functioning and relationships, leaving young people confused and unsupported in one of the most important areas of their lives. The more open the climate of discussion at home, the easier it will be for children to come and ask those difficult questions, because they will sense that their ignorance will not cause shock or be laughed at. Sitting down and watching soaps with children can initiate discussion about the difficulties presented under the guise of fiction, their solutions if they exist and the way that fictional drama differs from reality. 'I've tried to keep an open dialogue going with them,' says Andrea, 'and watching *EastEnders* together is good as that sort of drama, where every complexity in relationships is portrayed, spills over into conversations.'

There is also a growing disparity between what parents imagine their children must be up to and the reality of teenage sexual fumblings and their slow learning curve to maturity. Sexual permissiveness among young people may appear to be widespread but surveys show that in fact three-quarters of girls under sixteen are not fully sexually active. Having intercourse once may log an adolescent in the statistics but that is not the same thing as having an ongoing sexual and emotional relationship. Members of older generations easily assume that the youth of today are vigorously promiscuous and amoral about sexual ethics because of the high rates of teenage pregnancy. The assumption is that they must all be doing it all the time. Put a boy and a girl in a room together and they'll be at it like dogs in seconds. However, this doesn't appear to be the case. They may be having sex earlier and admitting to a range of sexual activities but they still believe in love, romance, being faithful and the value of virginity. Young people are no different to the rest of us. Ultimately, they still want love and sex within meaningful relationships. Premarital sex may be acceptable, but one-night stands are still widely disapproved of, and losing one's virginity, the 'big V', is still a profound rite of passage and one that few approach lightly. Snogging, or pulling, may be common at parties, 'but sex is very, very, very rare,' says Matthew, aged sixteen. 'I don't think it'll ever be anything more because it's just rude at parties.'

Young girls may want boyfriends in order to feel valued and loved, but many of the teenagers I met were also intelligent enough to understand how distracting that could be. 'If I had a boyfriend now I'd get caught up more with that and not do my work,' says Emma, who is fourteen. 'Maybe I'd cut school. There's a girl I know who only comes in three days a week and spends the other two with her boyfriend. She's changed a lot, she didn't smoke before and was never this rude and I'd be scared to end up like that.' And they also look to their parents' examples for guidelines as to how to behave in relationships, far more than their parents often realize. Actions speak louder than words and it is how parents relate to and behave with their own lovers which can influence teenage attitudes more than anything else. Claudia's parents divorced and her mother was on her own until she embarked on an affair with a married man six years later. 'It upsets me as an adolescent idealist that she takes part in this affair with a pretty free conscience. It's really not what I want to hear when I've got a boyfriend, and don't like the thought of him going out with someone else at the same time. If I hadn't been going out with him I don't think it would have bothered me but now I can imagine how it might feel for the other woman. Also she's having sex and I really don't want to think about that. She says that I can't begrudge it when she's been on her own all this time, but I always expected her to be a bit less fallible, she never used to do things wrong.'

We like to think of ourselves as sexually liberated because we do not parade blood-stained sheets through the village streets after a bride's inaugural night or stone adulterers to death as they do in some Third World countries. But when it comes to talking about sex and sexuality with our children we use euphemistic half truths and hope that they get the point without too much description, or that they know it all already. It is easy to laugh at the way our parents did it, but when it comes to our own children we're often not that much more progressive about imparting accurate information, and still unwittingly communicate the message that there is something messy, dirty and slightly disgusting about sexual activity. 'We haven't done what my father did, which was to give me a rather confusing book on what banana flies did – I think they were called Basil and Betty. It was horrible,' says Mick, who has a sixteen-year-old son and two daughters. 'What we've always done is answer their questions. I've never ever sat him down and said, "Is there anything that you want to ask me?" and from what we gather from school, he seems to know.' Colin found himself having to explain to his thirteen-year-old daughter why a joke in a film about a blow job was funny. 'I got her to tell me what a blow job was and then I asked her what she thought the conclusion was – I was leading her but letting her determine the conversation because I didn't want to be telling her things that she didn't know. When I explained to her she went very silent and was slightly repelled.' Hardly surprising when her father feels that there is something so shameful about the words 'blow job' that he has to whisper it to me under his breath and has to preface the information to his daughter with, 'This is not a nice one, are you sure that you're ready for this?'

Joan has three daughters. 'My mother told me about the facts of life in front of *Come Dancing*. She said, "Darling, I think there's something you should know," as she kept her eyes firmly glued to a screen. I wasn't amazing with my own daughters but I suppose I was OK. I left Tampax lying around when they were six or seven and waited for them to come and ask. I remember when one of them was very young she asked me what Tampax were for and I said they were just something that grown-ups use. "Oh, you mean, like hard sweets," she said. We did the facts of life, but I couldn't have particularly talked about foreplay or desire but they get all that from TV. Do we even need to talk about it any more?'

I am as bad as the next person. While my younger daughter sat in the bath, aged six, I asked her if she knew how babies were made. She replied, 'With a seed from Mummy and a seed from Daddy,' which she had garnered during a particularly interesting conversation that we had had one night about genes when she had asked me why our dog looked like a dachshund and not like a monkey. But when it came to explaining how those seeds met I was utterly tongue-tied, unable to find the words to explain something in a way that she could understand. However a book came to my rescue just a few days later, one that I had forgotten we had lying around. A friend came to stay the night and when it came to choosing a bed-time story, my daughter's friend chose *Mummy Laid an Egg* by Babette Cole. I began to read – the parents in this story were telling their children all sorts of stork-like myths about how babies come into the world – and these two six-year-olds half listened as they did somersaults on the bed. Then when they heard me read a line which said, 'That's not true, we're going to tell you how babies are really made,' they stopped mucking around immediately, rushed to my side to look at the pictures and listened intently. When I returned my daughter's friend to her father the following morning, I confessed that she was now a little more knowledgeable than she had been the day before. He laughed, 'Thank God we don't have to do it!'

Some schools do a very good job when it comes to sex education, others do not, using diagrams of the human body with their underwear on, explaining reproduction in terms of rabbits, or letting the children slump in front of a video so that the teachers don't have to answer embarrassing questions in public. British schools are required by law to cover the basic biology of reproduction in National Curriculum Science and to provide a programme of sex education in secondary schools. In primary schools it is up to the governing body to decide whether to provide any sex education in addition to the National Curriculum, even though puberty is increasingly beginning there and parents can remove their child from sex education lessons in primary school. This loophole supports the view that there is something contentious or sensitive about sex and that power over this knowledge lies with the parents. The child's right to know as part and parcel of an education for life is withdrawn. A written sex education policy has been a legal requirement since 1987 but surveys have found that large numbers of schools still don't have one.

'Our sex education was pretty boring,' says Sarah. 'How to stop getting pregnant, how to put a condom on an object and basic videos of a penis and a vagina, but we didn't pay much attention because it was so boring. We knew that you could catch diseases, but we didn't have the faintest idea what they were.' Girls tend to get more in the way of sex education because of the practicalities of dealing with menstruation and pregnancy. 'The girls all went off one day during PE and we were left on our own in the hall,' says Gary. 'The girls came back looking all confused and we were left sitting there not knowing what to think. The only sex education I've had is watching insects on a video at school.'

The same gender divide tends to exist at home, with mothers offering their daughters advice over menstruation but finding it difficult to broach the subject with boys. Fathers tend to avoid the whole subject altogether and few boys are told about ejaculation and nocturnal emissions before they happen. Girls explore the existence of their vaginas from inserting tampons and the line diagrams on the instructions. They are also more likely than boys to have had intimate conversations with friends where secrets are shared. At school, few sex education lessons concentrate on anything more than the physical rudiments of pubertal development and reproduction when, as this book testifies, it is the emotional and psychological aspects of adolescence as well as establishing and maintaining sexual relationships which give young people such grief. 'Sex education never covers anything about the emotional side of relationships – the fact that you're dealing with young people in love,' says Maya, a teenage mother. And much of this sex education is too late. With earlier puberty, substantial numbers of children in Year 6 at primary school will already be well into early adolescence, some will even have started their periods. Eighty per cent of girls in one survey said that they had no, or inadequate, preparation for puberty at their primary schools.[14]

Astonishing numbers of young people are ignorant about fundamental aspects of sexual behaviour, affecting their health and safety as a result. In one survey 25 per cent of teenagers aged fourteen to sixteen thought that the pill gave protection against sexually transmitted diseases.[15] Thousands of unanswered questions mill around young people's heads. At a conference on puberty organized by the Trust for the Study of Adolescence in 1999 two school nurses listed some of the questions they are often asked. Can you have sex without getting pregnant, if so how? Roughly how long does it take to have sex? Why do people like sex? Why do some erections go out and others diagonal? Is there a bone in the penis? How long do you leave it in? Often that ignorance is compounded by lack of easy access to contraception. Fifteen per cent of girls and 25 per cent of boys said they did not use contraceptives when they had sex for the first time because they could not get hold of them.[16] Approximately three million American women do not have access to contraception – and two-thirds of these are sexually active adolescents – either because they can't afford it or need parental consent for medical prescriptions. 'Clinics are so badly publicized.' Claire is sixteen. 'I walked past mine loads of times because it's just a little shop with blinds in the windows. It's trying to discourage teenage pregnancy but it's only open on a Thursday night and it rations the number of condoms it gives out. People should be given as many as they need.' Far too many young people fall through the doors of services like Brook Advisory when a crisis propels them there, when they think they may be pregnant, rather than as a proactive preventative measure. Ignorance about emergency contraception is still widespread and the 'morning-after pill' is scandalously under-used, simply because most young people still don't know of its existence, or that it is effective for up to seventy-two hours after sexual intercourse. Contraception is not legally available to under-sixteens in Britain, and embarrassing for teenagers of all ages to acquire. Young couples also need the confidence to be able to discuss what precautions they are going to use and who's going to take responsibility for getting them before they actually do it, and often in the heat of the moment that simply isn't practical.

It is hard for children to grasp the complexities and intricacies of sexual activity and one simplified explanation of the act of reproduction will not suffice. A child's awareness of sexual activity develops patchily, in a fragmented way, and they cannot understand the full picture immediately. They build that knowledge gradually like a three-dimensional jigsaw, adding layer upon layer when they feel able emotionally to deal with it, and they need channels of communication to be constantly open so that they can ask questions when they need to. Textbooks and explanations are always two-dimensional. They gloss over the sweat and the passion, the visceral, carnal urgency of desire as well as the sounds of sighing, the smells of body fluids. When we tell them how babies are made we present sex as a mechanistic, functional action and then rarely make the leap to say that we don't just have sex to make babies, or that its principal attraction is hedonistic pleasure where pregnancy is prevented. We are failing children badly as parents and as educators through our reluctance to tackle the subject of sex thoroughly and head-on from an early age. Children are as entitled to full sex education as they are to books, food and water.

Puberty begins at primary school for more and more children, but sex education begins officially in secondary school. 'Children may look innocent and naive but most have a lot of knowledge when they're eight, nine or ten and are still uninhibited enough to be able to ask questions,' says Viv Crouch, a school nurse. 'Talking about sex at an early age does not rob them of their childhood.' Children may be sexually innocent but they are sexual beings from an early age. Some researchers maintain that small children are even capable of orgasm but not ejaculation.[17] We assume that it is only with puberty that a child will be able to fully understand sexual matters, yet research shows that it is cognitive maturity that facilitates their understanding, and clear communication from a very early age greatly enhances a child's ability to understand sexual matters. Avoiding the issue or preaching sexual abstinence is the least effective option. Those who feel guilty about having sex may well be less active sexually but, when they do indulge, research shows that they are even less likely to take precautions because using contraception means accepting that you are having regular sex.[18] Sex education should be something that is ever present at home and at school, not something that is suddenly sprung on children when they reach early adolescence and are at their most self-conscious and inhibited. Viv Crouch maintains that she can tell the difference between those children who have had some sex education at primary school and at home and those who have not. 'If sex is openly discussed from infancy these children are less embarrassed in discussions about sex in adolescence. The ones who muck about and get silly during sex education lessons are usually the ones who didn't have any sex education at junior school.'

Good sex education should be integrated into the school curriculum from Year 1 as children learn about how their bodies work, and even earlier at home. If children see their parents naked occasionally, mature adult genitals hold little mystery and they are more able to understand that one day they too will have breasts or pubic hair. Then as their horizons extend and their emotions mature they will be able to add layers to their most basic knowledge about adult bodies and the process of reproduction – that people make love because they love each other and because it is enjoyable not just in order to make babies, that it is a special and precious act to be reserved for special people, that it takes time as we grow up to get to know what we like and don't like sexually and we need to be able to assert that within a sexual relationship, that it is important to respect other people and not to hurt them, and that above all sexual acts can have long-term consequences such as pregnancy, HIV or other sexually transmitted diseases.

Parents don't need to feel that they have to hide their embarrassment about sex from their children. By admitting their embarrassment they actually draw their children closer towards them, because they too feel shy and uncomfortable and need to know that these feelings are common and mutual. Young people appreciate their parents' efforts in this respect, they don't dismiss you with a C plus when you make a hash out of a particular conversation. Laugh with them rather than at them when you are both embarrassed or they get something wrong and never make the mistake of confusing their curiosity over sex with their behaviour. When they start asking about sex they are just interested, not actively doing it. And a little revision helps. Sexuality and reproduction are intricate, complicated subjects and many adults who have been happily copulating for years would be amazed to discover their own ignorance about some very basic aspects. Reading some of the leaflets and books aimed at teenagers before embarking on a casual conversation because of something that has come up on the TV or in the newspaper ensures that you are at least accurate factually and more likely to get the right tone. Leaving that literature lying around the house so that teenagers can read it for themselves is even more effective.

Parents also need to be prepared to go into their child's school to actively assess their sex education programme. If it's a primary school without a sex education programme, then suggest they set one up. If there is a programme, go into the classroom and ask to see the resources that are used. Many schools allow parents to borrow videos and books to help their children learn at home. Ask the school what happens in their PSHE lessons (Personal, Social and Health Education) and suggest other topics and subjects for conversation that

emphasize the emotional aspects of friendships and relationships, such as jealousy, being dumped, body-image, anger,
shame and betrayal. Some intellectually broad-minded schools
organize parents' workshops, so that the parents themselves
can learn how to teach their children. If this doesn't exist in
your area ask the school and some of the older children at the
school to help you set one up. The Sex Education Forum at
the National Children's Bureau, which helps to raise public
awareness, suggests other tactics which have helped inculcate
wider discussions about sex and relationships, such as pupil
surveys about what they need and want from discussions,
inviting parents into the school to talk about being a mother
or a father, or teenaged parents to talk about their experiences.

If we were truly sexually liberated, sex education would
be considered a child's natural right, crucial for adequate
preparation for adulthood rather than slipped in between PE
and playtime by some unfortunate and untrained teacher who
happens to pull the short straw. If we were truly permissive,
masturbation would be actively encouraged in young people
as a means of sexual exploration rather than suppressed, for
children learn from an early age that it is wrong to touch their
genitals and then have to reverse that conditioning as adults.
Anthropological investigations of adolescence show that far
more societies are permissive than restrictive towards adolescent sexuality. 'The Middle Eastern village girl who should
speak to no man outside her family after puberty, and even
with kin assumes a modest demeanour, is a far cry from the
saucy girls of Polynesia, bathed, scented and decked with
flowers, strutting about or trooping to neighbouring villages
for festivities that end in amorous embraces,' write Schlegel
and Barry in their landmark survey of adolescent experience
worldwide.[19] In very permissive societies such as the Alorese
of the Pacific Islands, the Masai of Africa and the Yaruro of
South America, early sexual play amongst children is not

discouraged by adults and fingering and exploring of genitals becomes an established habit which easily extends to touching, mutual masturbation and oral–genital exploration with others during adolescence. Among the Pukapukans of Polynesia, boys and girls masturbate freely and openly in public.[20] In a large number of societies the onset of puberty and particularly menstruation is an occasion for ceremony and a period of seclusion for a girl, during which time she receives special instruction from older women on sexual matters and marriage, which often includes active demonstration in pantomime of lovemaking techniques, as well as methods of contraception and what to expect in childbirth.

Amongst the Chewa of Africa, parents believe that unless children begin to exercise themselves sexually early in life they will never have children. The older children build huts away from the village in which boys and girls practise at being husband and wife with the full approval of parents. Consequently in these societies, where adults and children sleep in close proximity, children are fully aware of the entire reproductive act, complete with grunts and groans, by the time adolescence hits, and are probably far less complicated about the sexual act than our own dear mites of the so-called 'civilized' world.

The average age of marriage in pre-industrial societies is fourteen to fifteen for girls, seventeen to eighteen for boys and the decision is usually made for them by their elders, for young people are rarely in an economic or political position to do so for themselves. While obviously it would be ludicrous and far too simplistic to expect these attitudes and practices to be adopted in the developed world, there are at least open and understood sexual rites of passage for young people to adhere to and an acknowledgement that sexual exploration goes hand in hand with puberty. In the developed West, young people have far greater powers of choice and self-determination, but those powers are not matched with sufficient information or education. These sexually explicit times impel us to radically alter our attitude towards sex education and general discussion about sexual responsibility, if young people are to flourish. When young people are asked, they say that society's mixed messages about sexual behaviour contribute a great deal to their confusion and their mistakes. They are bombarded with sexually explicit messages with the implication that to be sexually active is the norm, yet access to information is difficult and contraception is either illegal or embarrassing to get hold of. They want more sex education, they want more information and more open conversations about sex so that they can make informed decisions.

As parents it may be hard to accept that our children will grow up into sexual adults, in need of adult sexual relationships, but all of the evidence suggests that preparation in the form of thorough sex education works. One of the most consistent findings of research into the effects of sex education is that it does not lead to earlier, more precocious or more vigorous sexual activity. Early and full sex education has a protective quality, it equips and enables young people to delay full sexual intercourse until they are ready for it. A Dutch girl under the age of sixteen is ten times less likely to get pregnant than her British equivalent, in spite of the fact that she grows up in an environment where sex education is explicit from an early age and the age of consent is twelve.[21] In Sweden, where sex education is compulsory from an early age, young children have been found to be far better prepared for adolescent sexuality. More pre-adolescents surveyed in Sweden know of the multitude of reasons for coitus and the importance of contraceptive protection than those in Australia, Britain or the US, proving that quite young children are capable of understanding far more complex biological concepts than many adults give them credit for, provided they are taught in the right way.[22] Good communication between parents and children increases the chances that those young people will not rush headlong into full sexual intercourse at the age of thirteen or fourteen and will protect themselves with contraception when they do.[23] If young people grow up within a culture which views sex as something slightly smutty to be done round the back of the bike sheds, they will think of it as smutty and do it quickly round the back of the bike sheds. But if we want young people to view sex and relationships as serious and worthy of respect then we have to treat those subjects as something serious and worthy of respect in all of our conversations, and by example with our own behaviour.

Research consistently shows that young people want far more practical guidance about sexual matters than they actually get. They understandably feel that questions over who they chose as boyfriends or girlfriends and the emotional tussles that result are private and they want autonomy to be able to sort these things out for themselves. But they feel that honest and comprehensive advice about bodies and precautions falls firmly into the category of protective parental concern for health and welfare, and they want it because they know they need it.[24] They need to know that one bad sexual experience will not tarnish their reputation for life. Parents who take an honest, upfront approach with their children often find that they are able to maintain close emotional links with their children as they grow up. Mary's sons are now twenty-three and twenty-six. 'I always made sure as they grew up that they knew what was happening and that they were comfortable with their bodies. We've always been quite uninhibited. I realized when they were quite young that sex was likely to enter their relationships when they were about fourteen and was quite clear about what was and wasn't acceptable. I said that I wasn't having any casual sex in my house, that sex should be a manifestation of a proper relationship and I said always wear a condom because if you father a child, you father it for life.' Then when her son, at the age of eighteen, formed a deep attachment for a woman that Mary knew was not being very nice to him, she was able to console him. 'She did hurt him very badly and we had several evenings sitting up until 2 or 3 a.m. with him sobbing on my shoulder. Boys are so vulnerable, their hearts break very easily.'

Vicky's mother turned the wendy house at the end of the garden into a snogging shed when she discovered that her fourteen-year-old daughter was out loose with boys on the common, because she needed to know that she was safe.

Annie finds it hard to discuss sex with her thirteen-year-old daughter but the more threatening dangers of sexual harassment are discussed. 'Every now and then I try and have a conversation. She was going to a disco once and I said, "If you must snog a spotty boy in the corner keep your knickers on." She was so shocked that I could say that, but she does know how to talk about her feelings and we talk about sexual harassment which is a step forward on my own adolescence. She devises her own strategies; she said that if there was a man on the bus trying to chat her up she'd decided that she would turn to him and say, "Do you realize that I'm only thirteen?"'

Gillian discovered that the common parental fear of letting the boyfriend stay the night can have humorous overtones. Her eldest daughter brought home a boyfriend that Gillian wasn't very keen on when she was seventeen and announced that they wanted to go to bed with each other. '"I'm just telling you," she said. So I said, "Thank you for telling me but how are you going to go about this, are you kitted out?" And she said she was. So then we knew, but they were very discreet. When he finally stayed the night I couldn't bring myself to say that he could share my daughter's bedroom so I said he could sleep on the sofa bed which lives in the kitchen, even though I knew what would happen after we went to bed. In the morning we were a bit hesitant to come down for breakfast because he was still in bed and our daughter had gone to work, so we crept into the kitchen and kept our voices down. By 11.30 he still hadn't got up so I went in breezily and said, "Good morning, would you like a cup of tea?" He said he would so I craftily put it on the table so that he would have to get out of bed to drink it, and hung around to make sure that he didn't drop off to sleep again, but still he wouldn't get up. The tea was almost cold when it suddenly dawned on me that he didn't have any knickers on so I left him to it. But I did think then that it was a bit much having to tiptoe round the sleeping lover of your child, (a) who you don't approve of, (b) who you have no relationship with other than that she has, and (c) who intrudes, but then these boyfriends do, don't they? But I have to say that she is very happy and that's helped her to come to terms with who she is as a woman and being loved and it is so easy to underestimate the importance of that.'

Even potentially traumatic situations can be turned into an educational advantage. Like countless other couples, Joanna and her husband found it harder to find the time for leisurely lovemaking as their children grew older and went to bed later. On one particular night, after prolonged sexual abstinence, they pounced on each other passionately, convinced that both their children were asleep. The eldest wasn't. She ran down to the loo with a tummy ache. The next morning she was subdued and refused to go to school, and after gentle questioning admitted that she had heard them making love and thought from the noise that her mother was making that she was dying. Joanna felt terrible, guilt-ridden and anxious about damaging her child and would have done anything to put the clock back. But the silver lining to this unfortunate incident was that it provoked a week of unparalleled discussion about sex which culminated in a wonderful girlie conversation between mother and daughter in an empty restaurant one tea time when she pulled out every unanswered question in her head and demanded an answer.

'Do you roll around a lot and fall off the bed sometimes?'

'If you're really lucky.'

'Does it hurt?'

'If you're not aroused properly . . .'

Their conversation had to be whispered in hushed tones so that the waiter who was hovering dangerously close couldn't hear. Obviously in an ideal world it would have been better for her not to have heard Joanna's exultant cries, but it happened and she wasn't traumatized by it because they turned that incident to their advantage and opened Pandora's box of sexual secrets just enough to feed a child's natural curiosity.

Returning to the days of chastity, chaperonage and the sanctity of sex within marriage is unimaginable and thankfully impossible. Abstinence programmes and the use of scare tactics in the United States have been shown to produce the reverse effect, increasing the levels of unsafe sex. Conversely, sex education works and the more intensive that programme is, the more effective it is. Our attitude to sex education and its content should not be based on what adults consider to be appropriate, or on adult intuition about what children are capable of understanding, but on what children say they want and on what research shows they are capable of understanding. Young people are having sex earlier and our duty, surely, as parents and guardians is to accept that and to make sure that they are fully protected in advance and confident enough to only indulge in full sexual intercourse when they feel ready for it. We cannot shield our daughters with arranged marriages or convent life. But we can accept their burgeoning sexuality as legitimate and important, and improve the lot of our young people considerably by confronting our own sexual hang-ups and endeavouring to be more open and honest about sex and sexuality with our children from an early age. It will only be by communicating the message that sex and relationships are important and worthy of respect that young people will learn how to approach sex with greater dignity and respect for each other. Puberty is just the beginning of sexual discovery, as Susan Moore and Doreen Rosenthal write in their book *Sexuality in Adolescence*: 'Sexual conflicts are by no means over at the end of adolescence but, luckily, neither are sexual rewards.'

8. School

Schools teach boys to take themselves seriously as functions of an institution, before they take themselves seriously as persons or individuals.

Stephen Spender, *The English Adolescent*, 1948

Whenever I talk to teenagers about school, I am left with a resounding impression of its drawbacks rather than its strengths. Some love it and thrive there, but for large numbers (roughly half according to surveys) it is just something they have to get through until they are old enough to leave.[1] For the more able and privileged it is at best 'all right', a pressurized place where the completion of coursework and high grades are paramount in order to move up to the next stage. It is a place where young people derive immense support and strength from the camaraderie of friends. They survive it, they pass the benchmarks established by modern society, which supposedly give young people a valid ticket to adulthood, but much of what they learned in the actual lessons is quickly forgotten. But for the less able or for those who may be having difficulties in other aspects of their lives, school can be intimidating, alienating and unhelpful. They express their resistance to it as an institution through truancy, drop out, vandalism, exam failure and boredom.

'I just find school really boring,' says Emma, who is fourteen. 'I used to like school when I was in Year 7, I'd do my work and put my hand up in class, but now it's just so depressing. You just think, I've got double geography – YUK! It's get up, go to school, go home, get up, go to school, go home, there's never any change.'

'School work is pretty dull,' agrees Tim. 'Socially, though, it's pretty good.'

'At secondary school, I was quiet, shy at first and then I met a few people and found it easier to talk. That's the main thing I got out of it but not much else, meeting people and making friends,' says Colin, who left school at sixteen with one GCSE.

Most secondary schools are large, impersonal, densely crowded and noisy institutions with locked gates that bear an uncanny resemblance to open prisons. For far too many young people, school is just somewhere they have to be by law between certain hours of the day, full of petty rules and meaningless curricula, rather than a cosy place where they want to be because they feel it has intrinsic merit. The school day is dominated by a timetable and bells, which shunt pupils from lesson to lesson, from break to the dinner queue. One study found that children spend as much as 20 per cent of their time (i.e. one day out of every working week), just moving around the building.[2] Lessons are increasingly exercises in cramming aimed to get students through exams rather than explorations which enhance critical thinking and perception at a time in their mental development when they are particularly open to this sort of experiential stimulus, and need it to mature effectively into autonomous and responsible adults. There is little peace and quiet, no privacy for the self-conscious adolescent from the constant analysis and teasing of peers and the judgement of teachers. At a highly volatile time, their emotions are frequently being provoked, rather than soothed or explained. Anger quickly flares into fights, individuals are easily hurt by insults or alienated by tight-knit cliques and anxiety levels soar with the pressure of exams.

Far too little, it seems, has been done to meet the personal and very specific needs of a child in transition, to ease the emotional complications of adolescence that our education system is in part responsible for having created. Contemporary adolescence is now shaped by school more than at any time through history. Yet what we provide for young people in schools has never been more at odds with their current needs. At the beginning of the twentieth century most children left school and started work before the onset of puberty and their adolescence as such was shaped by the realities of the economic and social worlds they inhabited. By the time they left home adolescents were accustomed to working long hours, they knew the value of money when their earnings were so crucial to the overall welfare of their families, and their future role and sense of identity was determined largely by the social position of their birth – wealthier girls were married off, the poorer ones sent into service; boys learned their father's trade or became apprentices to learn another's. Good behaviour was rewarded financially or with swift advancement and bad behaviour was sanctioned by the threat of dismissal. With compulsory schooling, sanctions are less relevant or effective. Bad behaviour can never be effectively controlled when the punishments are public humiliation, suspension or exclusion. Good work may or may not be rewarded at some point in the future with a better job. A sense of social responsibility is harder to inculcate because schools are now so segregated from the wider community and adult example at the time in their lives when adolescents are most open to learning these values.

Nowadays children leave school well into middle adolescence, with roughly 70 per cent of all teenagers staying on after sixteen and a third moving into higher education.[3] School defines their social world when the peer group is at its most powerful, and it plays a crucial role in their emerging sense of identity. Everything that happens at school affects their belief in their own abilities, their images of life and career opportunities, and their standards of right and wrong. Adolescence is a time when human beings are easily influenced, because we need to be socialized for adult life at this time. With the declining influence of the church as a moral standard and families less able to influence their children because they are in school, education needs to take on an ever-expanding brief in order to breach the void. Our education system ought to feed all of adolescents' needs rather than just equip them with qualifications. It needs to prepare them for every aspect of adult life, nourish them emotionally and help them develop as confident, socially responsible, constructive and imaginative adults capable of at least contributing to the status quo or more. At present any child who is not academically bent immediately feels alienated in such an environment. Little attempt has been made to alter the very basis of the curriculum in order to meet the very different needs of adults in the twenty-first century, when change is fast and rampant and the social and economic fabric very different to that of the early twentieth century. A wide brief indeed, but one that needs to be addressed if we are to stem the tide of school drop out, truancy and delinquency.

School exclusions more than tripled between 1993 and 1998 with pupils from some ethnic minorities disproportionately at risk. Government statistics say that approximately 12,000 children are permanently excluded each year and that 150,000 are excluded temporarily.[4] But the actual numbers are far higher because many children are 'cleansed' from schools, with the head indicating to parents that the child must withdraw from the school to avoid the humiliation of being excluded. This means that they are not included in the official figures. Truancy is far higher amongst the poor and disaffected. Government statistics confirm that regular truancy is four times more likely in homes where both parents are unemployed.[5] There are children who go to school for the register and then walk out. There are children who rarely arrive at school before lunchtime. There are children who never go to school at all because they are needed at home to care for younger siblings. Inevitably the children with the least to gain from being at school are the most likely to stay away. 'Because we're in the intelligent sets, most of us attend lessons,' say Suzanna and Emily, who are fifteen and go to a large comprehensive school in Brighton. 'But a lot of the people who are in the lower sets are just never in school. They bunk off every lesson and there isn't much that the teachers can do about it.'

Concern over the state of education and its links with rising rates of delinquency has dominated the news in Britain for years. The statistics alone suggest that conventional education does not do enough to prepare all young people for the wide range of roles, challenges and responsibilities they will face in a modern world characterized by change. A fifth of the British working population has no qualifications. The Basic Skills Agency recently estimated that a quarter of those under twenty-five have limited mathematical competence and one fifth lack basic literacy skills. In the 1996 Skill Needs in Britain survey, 40 per cent of employers thought that among their employees aged sixteen to nineteen there was a significant gap between the level of skills and those skills needed to meet current business objectives, such as management, general communication and personal skills as well as computer literacy.[6] One study con- ducted by the Industrial Society found that 67 per cent of young people they interviewed felt that school had not prepared them for the world of work. 'In school I was told what to do, I didn't have my say,' says Colin, who has left education permanently to work for his father. 'The idea of having work handed to me with, "Do this, by then, this way," wasn't for me. I'd rather be handed the work and told, "Do this, but if you find a better way to do it then do it that way."'

'I did fine in school because I was pretty bright,' says Sam, aged sixteen, who lives in Glasgow and dropped out of school before his GCSEs. 'I only ran into problems when I began to question things, then I just began to lose interest.'

More young people than ever before gain qualifications and go on to higher education but their intellectual capacities, emotional and psychological development seem to be ever more constrained by the process. Adolescent needs are not being met and neither, increasingly, are those of society. It is loving parents who have to step into the brink and ensure that their children flourish within an outdated and often brutal education system.

The harsh way we transfer children from primary to secondary school, just at the time when puberty begins, is typical perhaps of a nation that spawned the prep school system, caning and Wackford Squeers in Charles Dickens's *Nicholas Nickleby*. With the move to secondary school, children face a barrage of change and often the greatest stress of their short lives. Most cope well with the change. It's exciting. They feel as if they are growing up and have an opportunity to redefine themselves. Starting secondary school was one of the happiest moments of my childhood because I could leave the unhappiness of primary school behind. I had few friends there and was often bullied but at secondary school I could feel older and more in control of myself and quickly made a new set of friends who knew nothing about my history. But for significant numbers of children the transition is traumatic and can lead to other difficulties as they move up through the school, such as truancy, disaffection and bad behaviour in the classroom, if they are not supported at this time.

There is a tendency to assume that children need toughening up as they get older and move to secondary school. But that change is usually much too sudden and brutal. The cosy, kind and small local school with one form teacher acting as a surrogate mum disappears suddenly at the end of Year 6. They leave a place where they felt secure with one classroom, one teacher and one desk and move to a much larger institution where they have to change rooms every fifty minutes and carry all their possessions around with them, for theft is common and lockers scarce in many schools. They now have nearly a dozen teachers, who barely know who they are for much of the first year, let alone their capabilities. They now see older children smoking or snogging in cloakrooms. 'The playground is so big and busy that if you don't meet up with your friends before you go out there you never find them,' says Daisy, aged eleven, who had just started secondary school six weeks before we met.

Each year we suddenly shift the entire population of eleven-year-olds from an environment in which they feel secure into a much larger and impersonal context, which lacks comfort and stability, sends anxieties and insecurities into orbit and then we expect them to be able to learn. Children face a whole new range of expectations and demands. They can lose much of the confidence gained from being the oldest and most privileged within their primary school, for now they are the youngest and smallest. The challenges of a new secondary school push the confident, well-supported, capable child further up the ladder to maturity, but there is considerable evidence that many children find this particular upheaval devastates their sense of self-confidence and well-being, and consequently they suffer academically as well. Up to a quarter of a million children per year seem to make no gain academically and some even regress, with less confident literacy and numeracy, as they adjust to a new way of life at school. With so many different teachers it is often hard for children to form relationships with them. They seem less friendly, more distant and less interested in them personally than their form teachers at their previous school. Young adolescents can easily move through an average school day or an entire week without having any close personal contact or conversation with a single adult at the time in their lives when they badly need to feel a tight emotional safety net around them. They need relationships with a wide variety of adults in order to learn how to become adult. They move from maths to French to English with barely enough time in each lesson to scrape beneath the surface of things or express their views. The way these subjects connect in the grand scheme of things is rarely made, for there is maths in music and architectural design, and history in English literature, but few children are given the time to garner any wider sense of perspective or understanding.

Adolescents' sense of self-esteem is extremely vulnerable, yet there is less opportunity for them to shine within a larger school that has yet to recognize their abilities. Confidence in subjects that they thought they were good at can be quickly whittled away through harsher marking of their work and the gradual realization that different teachers have different approaches. Children are thrust into a more competitive atmosphere, where they are grouped by ability and cannot help but compare themselves to their peers, and are likely to find themselves wanting. When children have moved to new schools without their friends from their primary school, they have to find new friends. It can take months to get to know their contemporaries well enough to ascertain who those friends are. Young adolescents easily feel alienated and anonymous in such an atmosphere for these conditions are not conducive to a sense of belonging, loyalty or purpose which is central to any healthy school. They are expected to cope, and for those children who are already emotionally vulnerable the additional stress and institutionalized insecurity can be enough to push them over the edge or turn them off school completely.

Children in their first year of secondary school face the pressure of change in other aspects of their lives. Many are negotiating public transport on their own for the first time as they travel further away from home to get to school. They get lost, lose their bus passes and sometimes feel scared at being out in the big wide world alone. Many mothers go back to full-time work when their children start secondary school, which means that they may not be there to talk to or help with their homework. Suddenly children are expected to help more around the house. Parents tend to be less involved with secondary schooling and children feel this withdrawal at a time when adult support at school is also lacking. Statistics show that more days are taken off 'sick' during the first year of secondary school than at any other time and many parents say that this is a difficult and stressful year for their children.[7] When too much change happens at the same time, if they find that they are having rows and feel less supported at home, if they feel insecure about their friendship networks or their bodies at the same time as living through the adjustments of secondary school, then children's ability to concentrate or to learn is bound to be affected, but little is done to address this, to school the entire physical and emotional being in a more holistic way.

In an ideal world the transition would be far smoother with Year 6 spending some of the second half of their summer term in their new schools and then going back to their primary school to discuss the experience with their teachers and friends. Year 7 and perhaps even Year 8 would be structured more like primary school with fewer teachers and greater geographic stability in one or two rooms. Teachers would meet regularly to coordinate values, rules, rewards and sanctions. In the absence of these more humane conditions, parents can help a great deal with the transition. For both parents and children the anxieties begin early in Year 6 with families looking at and choosing schools and going through application procedures. Parents and children have to go through this together, with children involved and consulted at every stage so that they can express their emotions and their desires. Once a child has a place, visit the school whenever possible on induction days, the school concert or play, the summer fair or car boot sale and sports day so that parents and children can pick up on the atmosphere and expectations and discuss them.

Moving to secondary school is an important rite of passage for both parents and their children. Parents feel their children suddenly growing older and more independent and inevitably become more anxious about their welfare. Children worry about all the unknowns, about getting there on the bus or being bullied, about making friends and losing old ones and whether or not they will be able to find their way around. Through acknowledgement of these anxieties and of the importance of the rite of passage, parents build bridges with their children and teach them ways to cope with these new, intense emotions triggered by change. The move to secondary school often coincides with the beginnings of major intellectual changes in a child's mind, which I have described in detail in Chapter 4. This means that we have a chance to teach our children something of significance at this time. We can help them devise ways of coping with the stress created by change, and these will help them to cope with the plethora of change to come as they grow up. Keep the school prospectus somewhere obvious so that they can look at it without having to ask for it. When they start school they will need organizing at first to make sure that they have the right books each morning and are not carrying everything they need for an entire week in their school bags. They will need help with homework, interest in what they are doing and greater understanding of the new challenges they face. They will also be very grumpy and tired for a while, needing early nights and masses of tolerance. Being there for them that much more than usual during those first few months of Year 7 will help them to settle quicker.

★

All learning, for people of any age, needs to be based on relationships characterized by trust and respect. Good teachers produce a sense of industry rather than inferiority, they create an atmosphere where teenagers can feel good about themselves and are, in the words of the child psychoanalyst Erik Erikson, 'mildly but firmly coerced into the adventure of finding out that one can learn to accomplish things which one would never have thought of by oneself'. 'The younger teachers are much nicer than the older ones,' says Trish, who goes to a girls' school in London's East End. 'At least they try to be your friend. Some of them try to make the lessons really interesting with lots of drama and acting out but the others are so boring that you really don't want to work in them.'

Adolescent psychological development equips young people with new skills of insight. They see through people, they witness the hypocrisies of grown-up life and sense individual weaknesses more readily. They can now tell when a teacher only has a tenuous grasp over a class and has to shout regularly to maintain order or silence and they often actively disengage with dull, dogmatic and authoritarian teaching. Teachers who try to tell teenagers how it is meet with resistance, just like parents. All too often a 'them' and 'us' atmosphere arises because the teachers so obviously hold all the power and make all the decisions. The good-looking and more youthful teachers may be idolized and become the focus of numerous fantasies; those who are less appealing are loathed, or become the butt of jokes and bad behaviour. Their physical defects get homed in on and ridiculed, and pupils have to learn how to suck up in order to get into their masters' good books. I still feel guilty about the way we tormented Miss Peake over her enormous nose in music lessons, because she failed utterly to keep the class silent enough to listen. And I still remember with great fondness my last teacher at primary school who managed to create an extraordinary spirit of cooperation within a class of highly impressionable eleven-year-olds. To the dismay of the headmistress, we were allowed to call him 'Steve'. He was on our side and he had the imaginative flair to be able to follow the children at times in order to teach them something really worthwhile. When one of the boys kicked our ball over the fence into a neighbouring garden, we rushed to Steve and maintained that fairness required the same boy to retrieve it. Steve suspended lessons for the morning and instituted a court within the classroom where he was the judge and the children had to present their case with witnesses, defence and prosecution. I cannot remember the outcome, but the electrifying atmosphere where a child's voice was heard remains a landmark memory.

We remember good teachers with great fondness, but we also remember those who intimidated us, or destroyed our natural enthusiasm for something with their dull teaching methods or their damning sarcasm. Time and time again teenagers complain about the attitudes of teachers. They may shout and intimidate students, publicly humiliate them in front of the class and easily label individuals as troublemakers and 'no hopers' or intelligent and worthy of attention. Many complain that they feel picked on, that teachers ought to listen more and shout less, and that they hate having to say 'Sir'.[8]

'The teachers really shout at you, they come really close and shout straight into your ear but if I shouted at them they'd think I was rude,' says Trish. 'It's a respect thing, they try and intimidate you by banging their fists on the table when it's not even necessary. I once said, "Could you not shout at me?" and I got into so much trouble. I said, "If you shout it's not going to get through my head any better than if you're nice to me. You'll just get a sore throat and a headache." I think they should speak with respect. If they have a right to shout at me, I should have a right to shout at them. Even though I may not show it, obviously when someone's shouting at your face and pulling at your hair it's scary.'

'If you're opinionated or confident, if you ask questions that they don't wanna answer, or can't answer, they think you're arrogant little madams. It's so annoying because you don't want to give off this image, it's just what they get,' says Emma. 'If you question a teacher or say, "That's not fair," they say, "Go to the head," or "You've no right to question me." There's counsellors but when we ask to go and see them they say, "That's not for you, they're for people with problems." I don't like my head of year so I don't go and talk to her, but there is this other teacher who is strict but she tries to hear both sides and she's a lot more understanding. She explains the decisions she makes, but others don't and think you're just being arrogant when you're trying to be confident with them. They should listen to you more before they judge you.'

Suzanna and Emily feel the same way. 'The teacher never just tells us off for talking or whatever. They always tell us that we're arrogant. They think that just because we're clever we think we're above them, that we can talk when actually we're just being naughty. It's amazing that they think that just because you're clever, you're going to have amazingly good behaviour. Why should the two go together?'

Adolescents are intelligent enough to notice when teachers apply rules in an arbitrary fashion. At Suzanna's and Emily's large, streamed, twelve-form entry comprehensive, 'They definitely give all the good teachers to the higher sets and those in the lower ones have teachers that can't control them. They choose prefects from the high sets, when it's your behaviour and what you do for the school which should determine it. People from the lower sets would do better if they were chosen, it would do wonders for their self-confidence. From their point of view we're the clever people and we're wasting our time if we don't pay attention. They're less bothered about the less clever people,' says Suzanna.

Emily was put into the lowest set for English because both

her teachers and her parents failed to recognize that she was dyslexic. 'Quite a lot of them want to work but they have behavioural problems, and the teacher didn't know what to do with them. She had four cupboards and she used to put four people inside them and then keep four outside but it didn't work because when you were inside the cupboard you didn't work, you just sat and drew.'

'One of the teachers, my head of year, pinned me to the wall when I was about thirteen, with both of her arms on either side of my head and kissed me.' Claudia was rightly appalled by this assault. 'Then she said, "By the end of the year, Claudia, you'll love me!"'

Joe just scraped through his eleven-plus in Canterbury and then dropped out of school 'before sitting GCSEs with his confidence absolutely shattered,' says his father. When he started school he played up constantly and never did any homework and then when he finally did do some the teacher was so amazed he turned the whole thing into a joke in front of the whole class. 'Well, well, Joe's done some homework,' he said before giving it a cursory glance and then tossing it out of the window. Joe's father is clear about where the blame lies for his son's adolescent difficulties. 'He is drifting dangerously in the aimless society of other lost teenage souls, smoking too much dope which further dulls his appetite for life and inevitably draws him towards criminal society. His self-esteem is extremely low and the only sensible explanation is damage by education. We aren't perfect parents, but we're stable and we're not wildly ambitious for our kids.'

Teachers are trained to teach, but they are rarely well versed in adolescent development, or equipped as therapists to be able to deal with the growing range of emotional and psychological problems that plague the nation's impoverished children and affect the way they behave in the classroom. Government statistics indicate that mental health problems and specific learning difficulties are far higher amongst children whose parents are unemployed.[9] Yet there is often no other adult, apart from teachers, who has regular contact with these children. Just like many parents, teachers often assume that teenagers need greater control and discipline as they get older and more wayward, rather than more subtle methods of manipulation which foster trust, responsibility and mutual respect. When 'difficult' boys with vulnerable self-esteem are made to feel stupid for making a mistake in front of the rest of the class, they are likely to muck about even more in an effort to protect their wounded pride in front of that precious audience rather than to reform.

Teenagers often find it hard to trust teachers with their safety when it comes to dealing effectively with bullying. Teasing is very common in schools and often leads to retaliation because adolescents cannot stand public humiliation. Playgrounds are often patrolled by ancillary staff rather than teachers, classrooms are often locked during breaks and there is no safe, quiet place to hide. For children just beginning to come to terms with their physical vulnerability and the fact that they are now prey to a whole new set of dangers as they grow up and separate from their parents' protection, bullying and victimization at school is a terrifying thing to contend with. And it is common – one survey of 1,000 students conducted in 1995 found that 580 had been bullied.[10] Victims get kicked and punched or set on by gangs and often feel that teachers do not care, or feel that they will suffer even more should they tell. 'Do you remember being told, "If you're bullied you should tell us, nobody will find out"?' asks Selina, who was severely picked on when she was thirteen. 'Well, it got to the stage where my lunch was getting stolen and things like that and I told my mum. The day after that I went to the shop at lunchtime and got two black eyes. They were suspended for bullying me but I'll never trust teachers again. Everyone knew that I must have been the one who told. Everyone knows there is bullying in schools but it won't get any better if people can't trust the teachers.'

While some teachers are slow to accept the seriousness of bullying (if it took place outside the school gates it would be classed as an assault, inside school it is easily dismissed as just something children do); others are quick to blame those whom they perceive as difficult, loud or cocky. 'I've done bad things like cut someone out or said bad things about people, but never bullying,' says Trish. 'They're so quick to blame us without ever getting our side of the story. This girl told the teacher that we were bullying her so they sent a letter home to our parents without even talking to us. This teacher in PSHE [Personal, Social and Health Education] asked everyone to anonymously write down the names of people they felt intimidated by. Who answers all the questions in class and has anyone ever said bad things about you and your work?' The next day Trish and her friends were called to their head of year and told that some of their classmates had accused them of dominating the lessons. Trish, an intelligent and articulate girl, saw things very differently. No one else puts up their hands to answer questions so she does and she rightly feels that it is up to the teachers to encourage the others to participate rather than to penalize her. 'There was one girl I wasn't speaking to and one day we got put in a group to work together. She said to the teacher, "I'm not working with her." I just ignored it and then I heard her whispering, "Why did we have to get her in our group?" I can't remember what I said to her but she went and told the teacher and I got into trouble for this, for retaliating, and she didn't. The teacher didn't think about how I might feel about what she had said about me just because I've been in trouble in the past. That sort of thing makes me really annoyed and I argue with the teachers about it, not in a rude way, not questioning their authority but saying that they ought to consider both sides. But that only gets me into more trouble for being outspoken.'

Increasingly, young people don't trust the old truths about education either, that sticking with school and gaining qualifications will guarantee you a better job and a better way of life. Finding a job and establishing one's own economic independence is becoming less easy to navigate and far more complex. The collapse of the youth labour market has meant wide-scale unemployment amongst school leavers with approximately 20 per cent of white youths aged sixteen to twenty-four out of work and even higher levels amongst black and Asian communities of 40 per cent and 35 per cent respectively. More and more sixteen-year-olds are being encouraged to stay on at school as a result of the withdrawal of state benefits to anyone aged sixteen or seventeen and the introduction of government training schemes. The numbers staying on in higher education have doubled from roughly 30 per cent in the mid-1980s to nearly 60 per cent in the mid-1990s. Playing the educational ball game and getting the necessary qualifications has become more important than ever if young people are to find a job at the end of it. Good GCSE grades are now almost a prerequisite for economic survival given that there is little unskilled work available that pays enough for independent living and no chance of moving into higher education without them. But teenagers who reject those values or find themselves alienated from school stand a far higher chance of facing long-term unemployment than those who manage to stay the course.

At the other end of the educational spectrum, life is not necessarily easier. Competition for university places grows as more and more young people apply. Pressure to know what you want to be in life begins earlier and a degree is no longer a ticket to a job. Financial dependence on the family has been prolonged with the introduction of student loans, fees, freezing of maintenance grants and the prevention of students from claiming benefits in their holidays. One fifth of education authorities in Britain do not give any assistance with travel costs or discretionary grants to students aged sixteen to nineteen, forcing many young people either to work when they ought to be studying, or to drop out. The theory is that education will eventually raise the financial status of the less well off and a small handful of success stories justifies that policy. But the reality is that large numbers of the less well off have no choice but to bail out of the system at some point while those families who can afford to keep their children on in school do so. The 'haves' gain more for their children while the offspring of the 'have nots' have little choice but to opt for low-paid or unskilled work in the expanding service sector.

The British school system is essentially an academic one and still rooted in late nineteenth-century notions of what constitutes an education. The curriculum remains pretty much the same as it has for over a hundred years. In the late nineteenth century, grade one schools taught a classical education of Latin, Greek, maths, modern sciences and languages to the offspring of the upper classes. The grade two schools taught a more liberal education of English, arithmetic, modern languages and natural sciences to the children of the middle classes, while the grade three schools taught basic literacy and numeracy to the working classes. These subjects as well as a few more, such as history, geography and design and technology, still dominate the timetables of every teenager in the land. Multi-skilled adaptability, tolerance and cooperation with all sorts of different types of people as well as the courage to take risks may be far more use to people as adults in the twenty-first century than biology GCSE but this ethos is often absent from our schools. Essential life skills such as computer literacy, money management, sex and health education, citizenship, and parenting skills are bolted onto an existing heavy schedule rather than incorporated into the fabric of the curriculum. At the time in their lives when people are preoccupied with the physical changes of puberty and sexual concerns, school skates over these. Meanwhile life outside school directly impacts on an adolescent's ability to study or work effectively in school. When young people are coping with emotional difficulties with friends, parents or boyfriends and girlfriends, they cannot switch off and compartmentalize their lives in the way that adults do and they are likely to lack the more mature skills of coping, such as perception or deflection. They are also less likely to be able to learn effectively in class. But schools rarely incorporate counselling or 'emotional intelligence' into the main body of their teaching.

Learning how to recognize and manage one's emotions is an essential aspect of growing up into an adult capable of managing relationships with friends, colleagues and lovers, as well as life's abundant difficulties. Daniel Goleman's book *Emotional Intelligence* synthesizes a mass of research on the functioning of the brain which shows just how important emotions are, and how malleable they are in childhood and adolescence. The child who has experienced trauma or depression can learn how to reduce the negative effects through therapy and can develop more positive approaches. The shy child can be gently coaxed out of his or her shell. While 'emotional intelligence' obviously begins at home, schools are vital to the process because it is there that children form their first friendships and have to learn how to function and relate without the support of their parents. 'Emerging educational work . . . and research into the factors which put young people most at risk of dangers such as child abuse, alcohol and drug misuse, teenage pregnancy and severe depression, all show emotional intelligence and literacy to be at the core of successful prevention,' writes Tom Bentley, Director of Demos, in his book *Learning Beyond the Classroom*. Yet the emotional issues that drive adolescents so profoundly are rarely addressed. Teenagers are understandably preoccupied with the physical changes of puberty and their emerging sexuality. Friendship problems, peer pressure, difficulties at home, anxiety over coursework or future directions, preoccupy young people but are rarely addressed, or assimilated into the core culture of the school. They are chucked together under the general label of PSHE, Personal, Social and Health Education, in less than an hour a week.

If young people felt there was a point to going to school, if they felt enabled and encouraged there, if they were given challenging things to do which they felt were worthwhile, they would learn more and rates of truancy and drop-out would undoubtedly be far lower. Tinkering with literacy hours or a national curriculum may help, but only an education system which is both 'broader and deeper' will adequately prepare young people for adult life in the twenty-first century, writes Tom Bentley: 'Broader, because it must include a wider range of learning experience, experience of roles and situations which mirror those we value in society. Deeper, because it must nurture a greater understanding in young people: understanding of themselves, their motivations and goals in life, and of the subjects and disciplines they study.'

A sense of achievement is an essential means of propping up their self-confidence and self-esteem, but without clear goals other than the acquirement of GCSEs, young people have no way of knowing whether they are actually achieving anything. 'In science we're investigating stuff like the different temperatures of magnesium or the oscillation of a pendulum. I mean do we really care? I suppose all of it is a tiny bit relevant to life but why do we need to know about the reproductive life of a fungus?' asks Emma. 'In maths I can understand why you need to know how to add and subtract, but why do you need to know all that x = stuff? No one ever bothers to explain why it's important or useful.'

Emma enjoys aspects of the curriculum where she can actively participate, such as drama, music, PE or social studies, and dislikes the subjects in which she feels less competent. Her friend Trish feels the same way. 'Some of the stuff they teach you like history I don't like. I don't care what happened in the past really – that may be ignorant of me. But I do like PE and drama a lot because I'm good at it. The stuff I'm good at I enjoy.' Trish may be ignorant in the academic sense, but she isn't stupid. She is articulate, intelligent and very self-aware. But like countless other adolescents, she needs to participate actively in the subject, she needs interaction and dialogue with her peers, team-work and an immediate sense of achievement in order to learn and develop. Subjects such as PE, drama and social studies, which both girls say they also enjoy, encourage this kind of active participation from students.

Research consistently shows that when young people are engaged with 'extracurricular' activity, those efforts impact positively on their academic performance, for the confidence that comes from playing the recorder in a concert or scoring a goal triggers the same self-belief needed to sit down and write that history essay. They need to 'do' things in order to 'know'. Yet it is these extracurricular subjects that are fast disappearing from Britain's state schools as education authorities are forced to make cuts by selling off playing fields and disbanding music and drama groups, as well as anything else that does not fall within the parameters of the National Curriculum, because they do not have the funds or the time in the average school day. For many children these activities also provide a valuable release from the pressures of the day and their demise inevitably raises the emotional temperature.

'Most disruptive behaviour is because the children are angry,' says Julie, who has been an art teacher for thirty years and has taught in the East End of London for the past fifteen. 'The school I teach in was built for 600 and we have 900 girls now.

It's a very pressurized place and then, if they go home to horrid flats where they have to share their bedroom with two or three others and there's no garden, no park nearby, they're squashed, there's no space or privacy. Sitting quietly painting in the corner might be the only peace they get in the day. Calming down through creativity is essential in a place like ours, but art is also important for skill-building, especially for those who may be dyslexic or find the other things they learn in school too hard. They want you to show them how, not just for you to say, "Draw some flowers." I'm doing a project on families with Year 8 and I showed them a general trick to help them draw noses and that makes them feel good at something. It builds their self-confidence and that helps their self-esteem, and everyone else sees what they're doing and they will praise each other when something is good. It goes up on the walls all over the building. Some of those kids don't get praise like that from their peers in their other lessons because they're not working together and the work doesn't show.'

Teenagers need stimulating challenges. They need to experiment in order to learn and they need to participate actively in that learning with goal-setting and teamwork as they develop their research skills and devise ways to achieve their objectives, seeking out the help they need from more experienced adults. When teenagers are challenged in this way, they develop their brains in ways which equip them for adult life and raise their self-esteem when they succeed. But there is little room for this type of active learning within the narrow confines of our current curriculum. Exams teach children how to focus, concentrate and work to a deadline, but they also constrict the developing adolescent mind when it is at its most malleable and creative. Adam has taught English to teenage boys for the past thirty years. 'I think the exam system, the obsession with testing and monitoring has become quite lunatic in this country. A two-year GCSE course cuts out that very important developmental year when they are fourteen to fifteen. That used to be the period where they explored all sorts of things and found out more about themselves. They also developed certain academic skills in various subjects. Crudely, in my own subject, a boy who had found a talent for storytelling in a rather black-and-white form in the first, second and third years could then in the fourth year expand that talent and make it a bit more sophisticated. And for boys who were good at acting, there would be time for them to explore that side. It was a year of growth and development. Now there is always the shadow of coursework, projects and things related to GCSE. Prescribed learning rather than explored. That has hit the sixth form now as well, because classically the first year was always the time when having done your GCSEs you could then have another year of exploration and development. You shed a lot of subjects and you could spread your wings and contribute to the life of the school as something more than an exam factory. But that's much harder now with the new AS syllabus.'

'The academic pressures have increased hugely,' says Julie, 'and for the non-academic girl that's hard. There are girls in our school who only just know English, who are studying French. Some of them should be able to drop things, why are they doing three sorts of science? The pupils we have who are extremely low ability are never going to do much more than work in a shop however much you teach them. They're doing tons of science and they ask, "Why do we have to do so much science? Why can't we do more art, Miss?" When I first started teaching, those kind of girls would have done child development, cookery, English, maths and some music, but now that end of the scale has suffered and they're more stroppy and disruptive as a result and I can understand why. They can hardly write and they're trying to do physics? They're not stupid, they know what level they're at. When you teach basic life skills, such as how to look after a child, you are also subtly teaching them how to look after themselves and that's all missing now, basic life skills.'

Adam teaches in a very different environment, where the boys are financially privileged and far more academic, for it is a selective, independent school. Yet he feels too that our contemporary schooling fails to equip boys adequately for adult life. 'Passing your GCSEs is just exam results. Then you have your sixth form when you're still a teenager and have bags of energy. Then it's your gap year if you're lucky and then it's university. It goes on for such a long time that the prospect of coming out and facing the idea of being an adult is, I think, traumatic. I don't know how you do this but I think they need to learn far more about being independent, developing initiative and responsibility at an earlier age. There's also a certain kind of boy who really takes off when he's given people to look after and is absolutely marvellous at it. That kind of situation, where you are putting yourself last, is a very educative one.'

Adolescents have very specific intellectual and emotional needs yet all too often these are rarely addressed because of the authority-based and conforming nature of school. Adolescents vary far more than young children in the pace of their psychological and emotional development, yet we still group them according to age, unfairly pitting the late developer against the more advanced. They are struggling at this age to take some sort of control over their lives and their destiny in order to grow up effectively, yet school disempowers them. A sense of autonomy and responsibility is rarely fostered by encouraging teenagers to take an active part in the running of their school.

School fosters acquiescence rather than autonomy. Just as a child embarks on this seismic psychological transformation, lessons become more prescribed and less exploratory, with little time for small group work and fewer discussions. Teachers hurtle through the curriculum and try to unify thought with spoon-fed facts, for the easiest way to get children through exams is to cram and test, cram and test. Teenagers genuinely find it harder than adults to concentrate for long periods of time when they have little opportunity to explore or discover for themselves or even to communicate, for silence is usually required to maintain order and get through the syllabus. The current strictures of education mean that it is almost impossible for young people to set themselves tasks, to discover things for themselves and find ways of achieving their aim through research and teamwork, practices which encourage the development of cooperation and responsibility between peers, and enhance self-knowledge or awareness of the strengths and weaknesses of others. Original thought is discouraged, as a child's emerging powers of adult thinking are channelled with structure, discipline and routine.

Schools which recognize the importance of extracurricular subjects and encourage active learning tend to find that their overall exam results improve. My daughter's secondary school, a banded comprehensive, now has performing arts college status with two orchestras and a thriving arts programme, when just four years ago it had none. The percentage of five A*–C pass rates at GCSE rose from 75 per cent in 1998–9 to a staggering 92 per cent just two years later, the most improved school in London. Active learning projects, where young people are allowed to work in teams to achieve clearly defined goals, such as making a video or staging a fashion show or an exhibition, enhance adolescent intellectual development. Teenagers set their own objective and then have to find ways of achieving it. They have to research, ask questions and listen to teachers because they have something to offer them by way of expertise, rather than just sit and listen passively and silently in rows because teachers are authority figures. In order to achieve their objective they have to learn how to work as a team in which everyone has strengths and weaknesses that have to be played to for the overall benefit of the project, and consequently they begin to recognize their own strengths and weaknesses. They will probably need to go outside school, approaching organizations and individuals who may be able to help them with either advice, products or funds, and learn a great deal more about the reality of the world outside and how to function successfully within it as a result. When it finally comes to staging their objective they have to solicit an audience from the wider community of the school or their neighbourhood, and the resulting praise and recognition of their achievement is the greatest prize.

All adolescents benefit from aspects of active learning, but it can also provide an essential, positive focus for disaffected kids. I will never forget one particularly powerful and poignant evening researching for this book at Notting Hill's community centre, The Tabernacle. It was the premiere screening of a film made by excluded children, called *The Real Notting Hill*. Their youth worker had encouraged them to take part in the Duke of Edinburgh Awards, where young people have to undertake a series of challenges, and they had spent months writing the script, auditioning for the parts and learning how to film and edit. The film showed life as it really is for the disaffected and largely black youth community of North Kensington who channelled their fear, boredom and chronically low self-esteem into car theft, pranks and parties. It was honest, shocking at times, and very funny. But the most moving moment of all came when the young film-makers made their way up onto the stage to receive their certificates in front of an audience of friends, relations and members of the local youth service. These were young people who had rarely felt the praise of success in their short lives. They looked bemused, but their pride at the applause was palpable.

Many teachers are aware of the benefits of active learning but are too harassed and short of time within the current strictures of our curriculum to give space to these types of activities within the average school day. 'Some of the girls haven't been out of Hackney, they don't even know where Oxford Street is. We used to have time in the past to take them out during the day to see things, in a more spontaneous way, but we can't do that now because there's always something pressing: SATs or curriculum to get through,' says Julie. Cash-strapped schools with a large intake of poor children from a local catchment area of inner city estates find it impossible to offer these sorts of extras when often they haven't enough money for books and basic learning materials – yet these are the kids who would most benefit from more active participation. However, good schools with sufficient budgets do try to integrate active participation from young people in as many small ways as possible, through school councils, activity weeks, outward-bound courses and after-school clubs. When young people are appointed as prefects or sports captains or given responsibilities for tidying or decorating their classrooms or looking after text books, papers and younger members of the school, an important message is also communicated – that they are trusted, valued and have a genuine sense of place within the school community. Research shows that the schools which actively strive to create an overall climate where individuals are valued in all of these ways, tend to be the ones where the children are more likely to succeed, irrespective of their backgrounds or the social make-up of the intake.[11] Good schools bear a striking resemblance to good parents, where adults consistently have adolescents' best interests at heart. Teenagers need to feel the warmth that comes from a sense of belonging, they need to be challenged with high expectations, and set standards with clear guidance about what is expected of them, as well as receive buckets of praise.

In an ideal world, school would be a hive of exciting cross-curricular activity where children longed to be to escape the boredom and more ridiculous restrictions of home. It would be an empowering, inspiring place, where young people could learn about themselves, their strengths and weaknesses, as well as how to tackle and solve problems and operate effectively within an adult world riddled with emotional complexity and conundrums. It would be a place teeming with adults from all walks of life, keen to do their bit for the next generation rather than segregated from reality by a sixteen-foot barbed wire fence. The problems of education are deep-rooted and complex. They will not be easily resolved without radical change and that is unlikely in the near future. In the absence of an enlightened revolution in education, parents have little choice but to step into the brink, given that the pressures young people face are now so complex and education matters so much more to their long-term economic prospects. There is little certainty for young people any more, no clear-cut route through one of the most important transitions of adolescence to economic independence. When I was a child parents rarely got involved with their child's life at secondary school and young people went to university to get away from home, to discover who they were, to read books and discover the pleasure of sex, drink and drugs. The tendency for parents now is to assume the same, to withdraw from their school life once they no longer need chaperoning and to play down worries about future careers. But times have changed, the pressure to succeed and compete is greater than ever, and adolescents haven't developed the emotional resources to be able to cope with all of this on their own.

Teenagers need to feel that their parents are interested in their life at school, with regular conversations about the work they are doing, the relationships they are developing with teachers and friends. They need praise for good work and enthusiastic support when they fail to gain the recognition or marks they hoped for because adolescent thinking precludes wider concepts of the arbitrariness of judging unless it is pointed out to them. When young people are successful at something they tend to attribute their triumphs to ability rather than the results of hard work. When they are less successful, they also tend to blame themselves, their own inner failings, and easily stop trying, believing themselves to be 'bad at maths' or 'hopeless at science' unless it is actively and constantly pointed out to them that good marks and success are the fruits of hard work. Doing homework for a child or checking it over before it is handed in actively undermines the child's emerging sense of independence and autonomy. They need to devise independent working methods, meet deadlines and feel the pride that comes from those achievements, however small. Active, ongoing discussion about what they have to do in a general way keeps channels of communication open and gives parents valuable information about how their own child may be coping with subjects and assignments.

If they are not learning study or revision skills at school, they need to learn them at home. The more mature adult mind finds it easier to prioritize tasks, to identify what may be the most significant factors to a particular subject and what needs highlighting, and may be more skilled at constructing an essay given that they have had more experience. By offering constructive suggestions as to how they might go about doing the work, books they could use, aspects of their own experience that they could bring into their work, parents trigger thoughts and communicate the valuable message that they care. If they are doing particular projects, trips to relevant museums, historic sites or nature reserves may help fuel their enthusiasm, and simple things like helping them to look up something when they can't find the answer will do wonders for their self-confidence. When young children are enthused with a love of learning and an understanding of how to learn from a very early age, they are more likely to stay educationally motivated as teenagers. There are now some charities which are dedicated to raising the self-esteem of disaffected children by providing a place for children to learn through an active contribution. Kids Club Network and Education Extra organize out-of-school activities. Children's Express, a children's news agency, develops young people's research and literacy skills by working on real stories which are sold to the media, and Community Music captures teenage musical talent and enthusiasm in much the same way. Local drama or music groups can do wonders for a child's self-confidence, enable new friendships and bust up the rigid age categories of school.

By engaging in conversations about school and listening to what young people say, parents are more likely to identify problems before they become too big. If there is active engagement over homework, parents can pick up on falling marks or difficulties with particular subjects before that annual parent–teacher meeting when the English teacher points out that Johnnie's spelling and understanding of basic grammatical structure has shown a marked deterioration over the previous year. If there has always been extensive and open discussion about school at home, young people feel able to say, 'It's soooo boring', 'It's soooo hard, I can't keep up', 'My friends will laugh at me', or 'The maths teacher hates me', and parents are already being given crucial clues as to potential danger spots. Is that expression of boredom really masking a fear of failure or a fear of appearing to do well in front of friends? Studies show that low self-esteem, particularly amongst boys, impacts on their attitude to school and performance there. One study of 1,400 boys aged thirteen to nineteen found definite links between low self-esteem, feeling alienated through bullying, racism, ridicule or injured pride, and academic failure.[12] Complaints over the high level of work may mean that a conversation with the teacher is essential in order to establish whether the child is in the right set or needs extra help. Hostility towards a particular teacher may indicate that there is a personality clash that needs active interference for it to be resolved.

Parents naturally shy away from involvement with secondary school. They shiver with reminiscences of their own school days and it can be hard to talk to teachers as equals when so many of one's most vivid and influential years were spent either enthralled by them or terrified of their power. But we have to pluck up the courage to march into our children's school as often as possible in order to safeguard their interests. Secondary schools rarely reach out to parents before children show distinct signs of difficulties such as truancy or repeated reluctance to complete homework. 'It's administratively easier without the parents,' says Martin, a teacher and father. 'It's a lot easier if you're a teacher and know how the system works, how teachers behave, and schools put up the barriers. Children easily get labelled as tidy, messy, disorganized, hard-working and bright, lazy or stupid, and parents need to get in early to make sure that the right labels get attached, particularly if their child has special needs.'

Schools will listen to parents who reach out to them and regular contact will enable them to monitor an individual child's progress more closely or at least identify them amongst a large crowd. If there is evidence of bullying or victimization, if a child is being placed in a stream for a particular subject but becomes demotivated, if there is evidence of unhappiness, underachievement or boredom, then shying away from tackling the issue with teachers or the head at the earliest opportunity may make those problems more entrenched and harder to resolve. And if parents help improve life for teenagers at school in ways which they cannot do for themselves, family relationships improve, trust and confidence are made that much stronger as young people feel that their parents are truly on their side.

Karen felt ambivalent about the attitude of some of the

teachers at her son's school. 'There were signs that we might be heading for trouble when the school asked to see us, they said that Jack's attitude could "do with a bit of improvement" but I thought, well, he's a teenager. The mum in me thought, don't you talk about my son like that, but the other part of me thought, well, these people are trying to teach him.' When Karen discussed this with her son she sensed that there was a definite personality clash with a particular teacher, and she called a meeting with the school and insisted that her son be there too. 'He needed to hear what they were saying and I needed to know whether or not that was true in his eyes. I got quite cross with the school at that point because I witnessed the interaction between them, and Jack was right. He is not the adult in this situation, after all, and I backed him to the hilt. It helped our relationship enormously for him to see that I wasn't always going to take the grown-up side.'

There are all sorts of other ways that parents can maintain links with their child's secondary school, over and above the obvious annual parent–teacher meetings. If every working parent volunteered at some point to come into the school and talk about their jobs and how they got there, that would give students invaluable advice and potential role models. They could teach or tutor special skills, or arrange for group visits to their place of work and work experience. Parents could start up mentoring schemes, where children are twinned with an adult for regular conversations and advice about school, home life, careers or just how life is in general. This would give young people valuable time with a dispassionate adult who is not a relative or a teacher. They could indulge their own hobbies by volunteering to run after-school clubs in tennis, chess or drama. These activities enhance young people's cognitive welfare through active participation, they mix up children of different ages, forcing them to act as a team, and they enable young people to break away from peer group pressure and form new friendships. It's tough I know. Time is the one thing most of us haven't got and just when freedom seems to be there, glimmering on the horizon, when our children are able to do so much more for themselves, somehow we have to get more involved. But there is so much more at stake now, qualifications matter more now than they ever did and children easily become disaffected within an educational system that tends to view youth *en masse* rather than as individuals with different capabilities. Just the odd hour a term, a year even, brings parents into valuable contact with their child's world at school. All of the research indicates that this involvement has a positive effect on children and their education. It shows them that you care, that you value learning and school as a place to be, it gives you an 'in' for conversation when you get home and it will provide invaluable glimpses of the culture and environment at that particular school.

Parents need to be especially attentive during exam time, which is a notoriously difficult period for young people. Childline gets hundreds of calls each year about exam stress alone, and one in twenty of these callers have contemplated suicide. Adam feels that the pressures have noticeably increased during his time as a teacher. 'They have a battered quality about them which increases with the public pressures put on them by the exam system, which have become much worse in the past few years. The problem is going to have to be addressed quite soon but it won't be until something dreadful happens like a string of suicides. I watch them as they go in to sit their exams and even such a brilliant army of generals as I have had this past year, you can see their vulnerability fill the room. You want to say, "Don't worry, it'll be all right. We'll take care of you and guide your pen if need be," because they now live with this terrific build up of victimhood through the exam system.'

Teenagers need extra support at home during exam time. They may need help with drawing up revision timetables and structuring their day. They are bound to need extra cups of coffee and high-protein snacks, lifts in the car and even extra cash to dissuade them from spending valuable revision time earning money. They need to be cajoled to switch on in the mornings and encouraged to switch off with regular breaks. They need time for fun and, above all, they need their parents to relax about the results. Exam results are just that – results from an arbitrary test rather than utterly reflective of a child's strengths and weaknesses. Adolescents have to shut themselves away from their friends to revise when they most need them for support. Consequently they need extra support from their parents to see them through rather than pressure to do well. They need to talk about something other than exam results at dinner time and they need concrete discussion about possible scenarios when the results come in. If 'the' results (not 'your' results) are great, what next? And if they are not quite so good, explore the options such as resitting exams or switching courses.

Schools rarely have the time to provide enough constructive advice about future careers. In the past, large numbers of young people followed prescribed paths to adulthood. Now young people have to make their own decisions, and rightly so, but the emotional baggage associated with those choices can be difficult. They sense that they alone are responsible for their future economic viability, but are not necessarily able to deal with the increased anxiety and uncertainty that accompanies those choices. 'I used to know what I wanted to do, be an epidemiologist in tropical areas,' says Claudia. 'Then when I came to thinking about how I'd do it, a degree in medicine, I couldn't help thinking that I'd be a terrible doctor. If someone said, "You're going to do these A levels and then you're going to go to this university," I'd do them and enjoy them because I enjoy everything. It really wouldn't matter what they were. But having to make those choices all by yourself is so difficult.

It's really horrible when that could affect the rest of your life. How on earth can you really know?'

When young people spend such a large amount of time at school, their career aspirations and hopes are fostered there, their sense of identity moulded by subject preferences and competencies exhibited in that arena. If they enjoy French they could teach it. If science and dissection thrills them they can imagine life as a doctor, a vet or a surgeon. Otherwise their dreams ride on their hobbies. 'First I wanted to be a professional footballer and then I was a bit more realistic when I got to be twelve and wanted to be a tennis player. But now that's out of the window 'cos I can't be bothered. It's too much work, too much hassle.' Tim was sixteen when I met him. 'At the moment I want to be an actor, but it's hard to know. I'm learning Spanish, so if I go on with that, that ought to set me up with a few pounds, but I don't want to be a businessman. I definitely know that I don't want to go to work every day in a suit to the city.'

'I reckon I'd make quite a good doctor,' says Kate, who is sixteen. 'I'm never ill, I don't need much sleep and I reckon I'm quite nice to people when they're ill. It's not necessarily good A levels that will make you a good doctor but that's what they look for and only a third of all applicants get accepted. It does worry me that I don't know what I want to do. I think I'll just do A levels in something that I enjoy, like philosophy, and then just see. But I don't want to have to study again. I don't want to have to study my whole life.'

Francesca, aged nineteen, knew that she had what it took to get into medical school but realized that she was pursuing that course to fulfil her parents' expectations rather than her own desires. 'I felt like I was letting everybody down when I decided to do drama instead of medicine. A lot of people I know were desperate to do medicine but couldn't get the grades but I knew I could do it. I feel like I'm throwing away a good job for some Mickey Mouse degree that lots of people could get, with no guarantee of a job at the end of it. But when I thought about doing medicine I thought, this just isn't me. The whole dilemma of thinking that this could be the biggest mistake of my life and I've only got a few weeks to make the right decision – that's very scary.'

Sophie finds the prospect of determining her future daunting. 'I really want to work outdoors and I'm really worried that unless I work out all the options for working outdoors now, lots of doors will be shut for me. I haven't even got a geography GCSE. You seem to have to decide before you do A levels.'

'The future is a big worry,' says Ed, who was fifteen when I met him and about to embark on GCSE revision. 'Nothing interests me to do with work. When I had to pick my A levels it wasn't, "I really want to do this," it was, "I want to do this more than anything else that's available." Actually, I don't want to do anything. When it comes to getting a job, I don't know what to do. I reckon I'm going to end up doing some really boring job and it's going to be just like school only you start earlier and end later, with shorter holidays.'

Ed's friend Jamie is more certain of his likes and dislikes. 'I really want to be an architect because my two loves are art and music. And I'll be a freaky deaky music producer on the side, and I'll be really cool and smoke dope with my children and I won't be married and we'll say poems to each other.'

Their friend Sam, who is far less confident and outspoken, knows categorically that he wants to be a journalist but doesn't believe that he can make it. 'That's what I want, but the best things never happen.'

Adolescents need more support and guidance from parents now that youth unemployment is with us, the routes to economic independence are more diverse and so many of the old bridges into adult life that we relied on have disappeared. If parents do not acknowledge that it is hard, and hard for everybody, teenagers easily feel as if they are the only ones with these problems. Discussion which focuses on aspects of life which are within their control, such as studying for exams and filling in application forms for jobs or colleges, will help, so too will discussion about the way that there are so many other factors which will always be beyond their control – widespread unemployment, what individual colleges or employers actually look for in people. Their lives will be full of decision-making like this with new possibilities on the horizon and they need to know that everybody makes mistakes in life at some point and then has to find ways to put them right. We all have regrets but we rarely close doors permanently, and by making decisions we open up new possibilities. We literally move on. The world of work has changed. Young people face a whole new set of dangers and opportunities, which demand flexibility, a wider range of skills, the ability to be able to adapt quickly to new challenges, and the courage to take risks. The links between school and work seem weak and getting to know who you are is not helped by the uniform nature of most schools. To expand their horizons they need to understand more about what it is that other adults do for a living. They need discussion which stirs the imagination with questions about what sort of a person they would like to be or where they see themselves in five or ten years' time. And they need to know that they are supported in their dreams, however unrealistic those may be.

We dampen young people's natural enthusiasm and optimism with pessimistic predictions about how difficult it is to succeed outside in the real world, instead of constantly encouraging them to try to go for it, to cast their fears of failure to one side, because not to try at all is the ultimate failure. They need to be assured that it is fine not to know what they want to do or be and they need their shadowy sense of self-confidence bolstered at all times with the certain knowledge that the people they care about believe in them and their abilities. But there are also ways in which we paradoxically raise young people's expectations at a time when they are most impressionable without being realistic about the options. 'A lot of our girls have been told throughout the school that they can do whatever they like in this world,' says Julie. 'But they're often not educated enough and then when they get to sixteen and realize that they haven't got the grades they're going to need to go to university, they're terribly disappointed. Widening people's horizons is important, but we also have to be careful not to give them false hope about what they actually can do.'

When schools fail to prepare the less academic child for the wider ramifications of adulthood, they are just buildings where children have to be, warehouses for containment until they are old enough to take their place in the adult world. For many, that's where the real learning begins. Colin feels he is learning far more of worth now that he is working at his father's business installing coffee machines. 'I'd rather go into the workplace and communicate with people, that's what I'm best at, talking. The teacher just says, "Man, you're too mouthy." But at work I'm learning some computer skills, how to book in orders, talking to customers. I'm learning every aspect of the business and how to deal with customers, which is one of the main things in business. You've got to learn how to communicate properly with customers otherwise the business is going to go downhill. If you talk to them rudely they're not going to want to do business with you. You don't learn that at school, you're just told what to do, whereas here I feel more in control. There's less pressure. You do a job and when that's done you find something else to do and I'm getting money at the end of the week, like I'm nineteen, twenty. I feel so much more grown-up at work. I'm doing trainee warehouse work now with my dad and I'm going to go on to be an engineer on the coffee machines. I want to start at the bottom and work my way up, to prove to everyone else that I can do it, that it's not just because my dad's the manager. That it doesn't mean I can walk it.'

Alice's son decided he wanted to work during his gap year and walked up and down Oxford Street until he found a job. 'He grew up when he left school, took on responsibility, good timekeeping and doing what was expected of him. He had done that in school but it wasn't born individually because he was always with his chums. Once he left school he was on his own and it was up to him to turn up and be answerable for his actions alone. He also wore a suit for the first time. He wore a blazer at school but otherwise he was always in sports gear and trainers. Seeing him go off to work in a suit, he looked like a man, for the first time!'

For the more academic children intent on working their way through the system, the pressures at school are often compounded by pressures to perform at home. Understandably, parents worry about how their children will ever become financially independent within such an uncertain climate. They long for stability for them and spend years coaxing and cajoling them through the education system in order to give them more choices as young adults and a better chance of earning decent money. They want more for their children than they ever had. But too much pressure to get through the system can be counter-productive. Children need to be encouraged through the system, but they should never be pressurized into doing what parents think is best for them. Francesca's parents are wealthy property developers and have given both their children the best fee-paying education. They always assumed that their son (now twenty-seven) would be a lawyer and that Francesca would become a doctor. Their son dropped law for music and Francesca sat three science A levels, got a place to read medicine at university and then flunked out and decided to do drama instead. 'Biology, chemistry and physics A levels bored me completely. I've always been into singing and drama since I was very young so I decided, this is the rest of my life and I've got to do something I enjoy. When I thought about it I couldn't see myself as a doctor at all and it was pressure from my parents, what they expected of me. When I told my father that I wasn't doing medicine, he said, "We were counting on you to make something of your life now that your brother hasn't." My mother got really upset and said, "You're both such failures. You've ruined your lives because you were meant to be doing law and medicine."'

Parents who encourage their children's independent dreams and resist the temptation to pile on the pressure often find that their children work out their own futures in their own time. Linda has two daughters who are now in their thirties. The eldest left school at sixteen and earned her own living, making and selling jewellery, while she was living at home. The youngest left school at eighteen when she fell in love with a riding instructor in Wales and went to live there. 'We saw lots of other parents putting on the pressure academically and we always said, "We don't care what you do. If you want to join a circus that's brilliant by us. If you're passionate about something just do it." So when they said, "University? I don't think so," we had to accept that. We always felt that the most important thing to teach children is to be able to make decisions for themselves and stand by those decisions. We always wanted to teach them independence and independent thinking so when they turned out to be totally independent buggers at sixteen we felt that we had in some ways brought it on ourselves.' However, this acceptance of their children's independent difference worked as a strategy on two levels. Neither daughter went seriously off the rails and both returned to education in subsequent years when they felt ready for it. The eldest studied art and then did her Masters in English, while the youngest daughter has just graduated in law at the age of thirty.

Teenagers need time to vegetate and withdraw and work things out for themselves, time which is rarely afforded within an increasingly pressurized and competitive system. Inevitably the numbers of those who burn out or flunk out have risen. Sally's son got into the top sixth-form college in Cambridge, but came home after just a month and said that he wasn't going back. 'He's so articulate and bright but he just wanted to get out there and work, he was fed up with being bossed around.' The college advised her to let him take a year out and he went to work at Pizza Hut. 'I had to swallow all my joy about him getting in to do A levels. I never had any of that and I always felt that it was a great shame and I could have done so much more with my life if I'd had a few more certificates. No matter how hard you try not to, you know what you want them to do. It's all based on yourself half the time and not on them. That's what you have to try and do, base it on them, sit and listen to them and when they're talking crap you have to accept it and that's the hardest thing.'

After a year at Pizza Hut, Sally's son went back to college, even though Pizza Hut was so pleased with his efforts that they wanted to put him through a management training course. 'He's grown up this past year and proved that he can hold down a job. It sounds awful but I made him contribute financially. I wanted him to know that in order to earn good money you need qualifications, but he loved working, he thrived on it, even though he had less money for clothes and things than when he was at school.' After just a term he began to question again the point of further studying when he might still have to do a management training course after A levels. '"Why don't I just do that now?" he said. We're supporting him financially now but he says he misses working. He likes having his own money. I think that's quite a grown-up thing to feel. He just wants to get out and be his own person and I think, why am I battling with him?'

All of the evidence from academic research as well as my own with parents, teenagers and teachers suggests that our education system is not meeting the emotional and psycho-social needs of far too many adolescents. Now that so many children spend so much of their adolescence at school, we have to question the whole nature and purpose of education in order to equip them adequately for adulthood. Is it just there to provide young people with qualifications or should it bring out the best in our young people for the benefit of future society as well as the individuals that we entrust into its care? If we encourage individual talents instead of always trying to hone their minds into old ways of doing and seeing things, if we encourage the resilience and flexibility of young people, we not only equip them more effectively for the complexities of life but also raise the possibility of future generations finding solutions for the increasingly complex problems of the modern world, such as pollution, poverty, globalization and peaceful stability. 'I think schools are failing children but it's the system rather than individual schools,' says Adam. 'What is being created is a vicious circle involving parental expectation. Parents become convinced that their child has got to be a high achiever so they endorse the system and won't speak out against it. All the new pressures just get taken on board, that's what you have to do in order to get through the hoops and nobody will speak out in the way that one might hope for that child, what does that child want? It's sort of a conspiracy really between government, schools and parents and I suppose society as a whole. But I don't think if they sat down and thought about it seriously society necessarily wants this. We need young people's initiative and new ways of thinking to move on as a society but we're dampening that at the moment because there's so much short-termism, we still fail to think of education as our most important resource.'

9. Youth in Crisis

Every kind of vice gets its claws into adolescence, like the hundred little hooks of a burr sticking into one's hair.

　Colette, *Green Sealing Wax*

Adolescence is the time of life when people are most interested in taking risks and testing the boundaries of the world outside as well as their own limits. Throughout history countless young people have drunk alcohol to the point of vomiting semi-consciousness or indulged in petty crime, but the vast majority of these hoodlums grew up into sober, law-abiding, hard-working citizens all the same, just as they do today. Richard Wagner took part in a violent student demonstration and was a chronic gambler; Graham Greene played Russian Roulette five times at the age of seventeen; Napoleon seriously contemplated suicide at sixteen after the death of his father; Beatrice Webb stole chloroform from the family medicine cupboard 'as a vaguely imagined alternative to the pains of life and the *ennui* of living'. Crowds of marauding youths were rife in seventeenth-century London and in 1857 state militia were called out to quell the violence of adolescent street gangs in New York City.[1] The fourth-century bishop St Augustine stole at the age of sixteen, 'not urged on by poverty, but from a certain distaste for well-doing . . . for I pilfered that of which I already had sufficient, and much better, nor did I desire to enjoy what I pilfered, but the theft and sin itself.'[2] OK, so they were only pears from a tree, but for a man of his religious sentiments this was a considerable crime.

Experimentation with danger is crucial to the adolescent experience. Adolescents drink and take drugs as an act of rebellion, as a sign of maturity and because they make life more fun. They drink and take drugs out of boredom, loneliness and because they have the time to do it. 'It's not pressure, like I can't take my life any more so I'm going to go out and get stoned.' Jack, who is sixteen, has a daily dope-smoking habit verging on addiction. 'Everyone smokes. It's just our social thing. If we're at school we smoke, and if we're in the holidays we smoke, because it's fun and when you've done it a few times you think, "I could be like this or I could be stoned." It just gives you a better outlook.'

They drink and take drugs because their friends do it at a time when they are most vulnerable to peer pressure, and because the experiences associated with these risks give them tales to tell and earn them stripes for bravery or endurance – the day they nearly got busted, or did and escaped with a warning, or the day they were so drunk that five friends had to carry them home. 'My mum thinks we drink beer, when most people drink spirits,' says Suzanna, aged fifteen. 'A lot of my friends have been sick and passed out from drinking and it's quite a normal thing. If you're at a party there will be at least three or four people who will get sick. Some people do it to forget everything else or because they want to be having fun. Some feel terrible at the time but they'll laugh about it afterwards. I always end up holding their hair back over the bath and we kind of laugh about it afterwards and in a way it's almost funny.'

However there have been substantial rises in the rates of drug and alcohol use, depression, suicide, pregnancy, eating disorders and self-harm amongst young people in much of Western Europe and America since the 1950s, which indicate that young people are now dealing with difficulties that they cannot manage alone. Damage to health associated with alcohol and drug use, violence, and sexually transmitted diseases, all of which affect young people far more than any other sector of the population, appears to be increasing. Between 1960 and 1980 there was a decline in the mortality rate for every other age group except for adolescents.[3] Rates of juvenile crime have been rising since the Second World War and young people are now also increasingly the victims.[4] Anorexia was rare until the 1960s. Now it is spreading like a virus among young women. The Mental Health Foundation estimates that one in twenty women will suffer some symptoms of an eating disorder and one in a hundred will need medical treatment. Of these, 20 per cent will die and many more will suffer lasting health consequences. Rising numbers of people aged ten to twenty-five are suffering from psychosomatic health problems such as headaches, stomach aches and sleeping difficulties, and roughly half of all teenagers report difficulty in dealing with stressful situations at home and at school.[5]

Modern adult perception of youth is that it is in crisis, with stories of aberrant, delinquent, drunken or pregnant teenagers in the media daily, and it can be hard for parents to gain a true perspective over what is going on in their own teenager's life when the overall picture is so negative. Many young people try soft drugs but most don't use them regularly or move onto harder substances. Many young people drink but then so do many adults. Many indulge in petty crime or daredevil acts of delinquent bravado and then quickly grow out of it. The vast majority of young people manage to negotiate the transition to adulthood without causing too much damage either to themselves or to other people. However, a small but significant and rising number of young people do 'go off the rails' in adolescence and I will be exploring the most likely causes later in this chapter. Parents need to be able to distinguish between normal experimentation and depressive or avoidance behaviour, which needs help. That means understanding why adolescents feel the need to take risks, and opening our eyes and ears to what is really going on in their lives. And it means using discussion, empathy and education from an early age to keep them safe rather than the methods our parents were more likely to have employed such as denial or autocratic punishment.

The ubiquitous presence of drugs inevitably raises parental anxieties. 'The drugs are out there, they're exposed to them, and trying to steer your kids past that I think is a nightmare,' says Sally, whose eldest son is nineteen. 'He's all right but it's probably luck more than anything else. You can do all you like for your kids but at the end of the day there's luck – who they meet, what they've got and whether they go down one of those bad paths.'

However, luck is actually the least likely factor influencing a child's experimentation with hard drugs. Soft drugs such as cannabis are now cheap and easier than alcohol for under-sixteens to obtain. 'There is no drugs problem at school,' one sixteen-year-old boy from London told me. 'They're easy to get.' Yet rates of addiction to hard drugs have remained remarkably and consistently low at somewhere between 1 and 3 per cent since the 1970s.[6] It is the consumption of drugs that are more easily sanctioned by adults such as cannabis and alcohol that has risen dramatically, with teenagers experimenting at an increasingly early age.[7] Surveys in the UK have found that of children aged fifteen to sixteen roughly a third admitted to smoking cannabis; between 5 per cent and 10 per cent say they have tried amphetamines and solvents, hallucinogens and ecstasy and less than 1 per cent have used heroin or cocaine.[8]

Drugs and alcohol are rarely problematic for happy children. All the available research suggests that the majority of children who develop serious hard-drug habits exhibited problems way before the onset of adolescence. When children lack love or suffer neglect, when they are victims of abuse, mental illness, bereavement or divorce without sufficient support, when there is economic hardship in areas of high unemployment, these conditions provide fertile ground for problems during adolescence. Disadvantaged children are up to one hundred times more likely to become high-risk problem teenagers than those from financially advantaged backgrounds.[9] Too much freedom or authoritarian constraint from parents can also lead to health risk activity in adolescence. When parents have given their children too much freedom, teenagers may need to latch onto the rituals, the rigid framework and the firm sense of control that eating disorders, drugs or self-harm give. When parents have been over-controlling, young people may use these activities as a means to break free. Some children also have such low self-esteem that they set themselves up for abandonment and abuse because they feel they deserve it.[10] Others are so spoilt and over-indulged that they are more likely to turn into teenagers who are always searching for another high to feel good than children who have had limits imposed on their desires.

In small doses, experimentation with danger helps young people to grow up. Drugs appeal to young people because they can enhance the senses and make colours more vivid, music more tuneful, give lyrics more depth and make sex more sensual. They ease difficulties in social situations and trigger conversations about morality, relationships and the rights and role of the individual, which in turn help adolescents to understand abstract concepts and themselves more clearly. 'I want to take acid because I want to see what my subconscious comes up with,' one fifteen-year-old boy told me as we sat in his mother's sitting room with several of his friends one afternoon during the Easter holidays. Their conversation had been guarded until I sensed that they were keen for me to go so that they could roll a joint. When I told them to go right ahead and ignore my presence, they talked more freely about drugs, their attractions and dangers. 'That's quite an intelligent point of view,' Jack replied to his friend's comment about taking LSD. 'I have tried quite a few illicit drugs and one of the main reasons was that I wanted to be more creative. I wanted to see what I could do and expand it. Being drunk is totally different. It gives you a sort of safe feeling. But it would really worry me if I only ever drank to get drunk. It would scare me and I would psychoanalyse myself because getting drunk all the time would tell me that I'm trying to escape from something. Whenever I do drink I'm quite happy to have escaped from something.'

Pushing new and volatile emotions to extremes helps teen-agers to recognize and master them. Risky activities push you to the limits and force you to think quickly in order to look after yourself, for adolescents are now acutely aware for the first time of the fact that they hold their own life in their hands. Contemplation of suicide is therefore a common and natural consequence of this new-found awareness.

Graham Greene's gambling with Russian Roulette at the age of seventeen followed a number of other sensation-seeking dices with danger and self-destruction:

My heart was knocking in its cage and I felt that life contained an infinite number of possibilities. It was like a young man's first experience of sex – as if in that Ashridge glade one had passed a test of manhood. I went home and put the revolver back in the corner cupboard.

The heightened sensations that come from the adrenaline rush of danger or drugs help young people along the road to self-definition. By crash-dieting and anorexia, adolescents attempt to control the contours of their bodies. By wounding or cutting themselves, young people sever childhood innocence and perfection for good, they assert self-autonomy and perform their own initiation ceremony. 'It was like a symbol,' says Rebecca, aged twenty. 'If I could withstand this pain I could stand all the other pain that other people can inflict.' Alcohol and drugs relieve anxieties and focus people's minds on the pleasure of the here and now rather than the terrifying prospect of an uncertain future. They allow young people to return to the more carefree, emotion-led sensations of childhood that they are used to. They bind people together, replicating the feelings of confidence, peace and security that they used to get from their parents, and they allow them to fool around and just be silly, just as they used to as kids. 'One of the reasons that I drink and a lot of people drink, I think, is that it almost gives you an excuse to act without thinking,' says Joe, who is sixteen. 'It's like socially acceptable to drink and be stupid. People can go out and do stupid things and say "I was drunk," and that's OK.'

All of the teenagers I talked to were highly aware of the presence of drugs and the attractions of alcohol. The ones who were most educated about drugs and their dangers seemed to be most in control. 'I smoke draw, we all do,' says Tim. 'I told my mum and dad and they said, "OK, but be careful." Mum's read somewhere that it can reduce your short-term memory and that worries me a bit but it's a social thing – it's easy to get. I haven't done E or speed or cocaine but it's easy to get if you go to certain clubs. If I wanted to get it I'd just ask around. I feel slightly nervous about harder drugs, I'm dead set against heroin but I think E is probably pretty safe. A few people have taken it in my year but not a lot. I know my limits, how much I can take when you're talking about draw.' They acknowledged that hard-drug use was rare and did not feel pressure to try them. 'About five people in our whole year have taken drugs harder than marijuana,' says Harry, aged fifteen. 'There's a bit of cocaine but nobody looks down or up at them for that. I think I probably will try E because it's supposed to be wicked but I won't do it until I'm like clubbing a lot and I'm confident enough to let myself go. Cocaine is such a stupid '80's drug. Speed is the one that most people seem to move onto after draw but apparently it has such a bad come-down that it isn't worth it.'

The vast majority seemed aware of the dangers of addiction or excessive drinking. They enjoyed the experimentation, the 'highs' of indulgence. New powers of perception and awareness equip young people with greater understanding of the chance nature of life and their own individual power in controlling their fate. Dabbling with risky activities enables adolescents to explore the extremes of this new state of being, to test their own limits and means of coping, or to soothe the fears and anxieties that loom as more adult responsibilities and pressures take hold. Young people also harbour genuinely different attitudes towards health and risk to those of their parents. Adults tend to value health, a good night's sleep, exercise and a balanced diet as they get older. Their adolescent children have never felt so good. They are at their peak vitality and rarely think of ill-health as a potential hazard when their bodies bounce back so quickly from hangovers.

Parents devise routines to protect their own health interests; adolescents despise routine as middle-aged and boring. Parents are programmed to see the dangerous consequences of trying an illegal drug or smoking cigarettes that much more clearly when they have spent years protecting their offspring's interests. But when social acceptance, physical appearance, having a laugh and staying cool in tricky social encounters matter so much more to teenagers, the potentially damaging health consequences of indulging in substances couldn't be further from their minds. They need quick-fix answers to their immediate needs. Crash-dieting to the point of anorexia may be detrimental to a girl's health, but not in her eyes if the end result means that she can feel good about her appearance at the time of her life when she is most self-conscious. Mobile phones may or may not be responsible for an increased risk of brain tumours, but what's that compared to the acute teenage need to communicate with their friends when they are apart? The potential long-term health consequences of smoking cannabis or excessive drinking are not foremost in young people's minds when they are at a party and eager to get that immediate high, fit in with the crowd or pluck up the courage to talk to someone they fancy. Adolescents feel that whether or not they drink or take drugs is principally a question of personal choice. It's a crucial marker in their growing autonomy rather than a question of pandering to any wider sense of morality. And they never quite believe that anything bad could happen to them, as David S. Kogan writes in his diary, published in 1955: 'I have indulged in a typical adolescent experience today. Was one of seven ASC boys who piled into an old, smoking, bumpy '29 jalopy and toured around Yonkers for about half an hour. It's fun and thrilling, but I suppose quite dangerous. Nevertheless, everyone feels that HE won't get hurt.'[11]

When they face so much change and uncertainty, any potential long-term or disastrous consequence of the risky activity is negligible compared to the immediate relief or exhilaration they gain from it. 'Drugs are definitely dangerous,' says Jack. 'It's whether you really care – if you weigh up the fun you can have and the possible badness, you go for the fun. My mum knows that I don't smoke but she would be really annoyed if she found out that I smoke dope. She's a doctor. I understand how she feels, I think. If they were our age, our parents would probably be smoking as well but there's another twenty years between this age and theirs, during which time you mature, grow out of it and start seeing the bad sides, and that's what we don't appreciate.'

Kate, who smokes, can see the immediate dangers of being allowed to come home at any time of night. 'But with smoking, no one actually thinks they are going to die, you don't think about the health risks. The reason for taking any sort of drug is curiosity. I didn't have my first cigarette because I thought it was cool. I wanted to know what it was like and then if you enjoy it you carry on doing it. Most of the things that harm you are enjoyable. If I'm in a really bad mood and I storm out of the house I want a cigarette, and that's quite depressing really. There's something middle-aged about needing a prop, like having a stiff drink when you come back from work, when I'm only sixteen!'

Colin also talks about the benefits of drink and drugs rather than their dangers. He's had a hard year with his parents splitting up. 'I've smoked cigarettes for about a year, and now dope, sometimes every day. I'm not hooked, I can go without it, but when it's about it calms you down and makes life more fun, but I don't think it's anything big. I've started drinking and I get sick but I wake up the next day and I'm all right. When I'm drunk I can talk to anyone, dance with anyone. I'm more lively, completely changed. As I get older and more confident I reckon I'll become more lively without the drink.'

Drug consumption, particularly alcohol, has been rising rapidly amongst all age groups since the Second World War, so it would be naive to expect teenagers to be somehow exempt from this trend. Most of these socially sanctioned 'vices' begin at home. Children's first alcoholic drink is usually sampled with their parents. Those who smoke are more likely to have children who smoke. Addictions to gambling are usually triggered by parents who see nothing wrong with a harmless flutter on games machines in the arcades, or on the Grand National. Doing things to fit in with the gang may seem immature and adolescent, but numerous adults find it hard to resist a drink at parties, fashion trends in clothes or interior décor, dining in restaurants that newspapers tell them it is cool to be seen in, or seeing the films that everyone else is talking about. When young people strive to express their individuality by dressing in a particular way or riding a motorbike, these are merely fledgling but important attempts at asserting their status within society just as adults do.

However, the fact that adolescents are drinking more and smoking cannabis at an earlier age is a cause for concern. Among children in England aged eleven to fifteen alcohol consumption more than doubled during the 1990s, and they are drinking more often, with the proportion who drink at least once a week rising from 13 per cent in 1988 to 20 per cent in 1996. In the 1980s approximately 1,000 children under fifteen were admitted to British hospitals with acute alcohol poisoning each year. While these figures are not collected routinely, research from the Royal Liverpool Children's Hospital Accident and Emergency department shows a ten-fold increase in such admissions between 1985 and 1996.[12]

In early adolescence, the mind and body develop vigorously and both alcohol and drugs affect general growth and may interfere with hormonal activity. Research on animals strongly suggests that the harmful effects of alcohol or drugs are greater during periods of critical brain and body development.[13] The adolescent brain is different to that of an adult. It is 'built to learn', able to change in response to experience, and the presence of chemicals could affect the way that permanent connections between nerve cells are made in the developing mind. Studies on the influence of alcohol in people between the ages of twenty-one and twenty-nine by American professors of pharmacology and psychology found that learning abilities were impaired to a greater degree among the youngest. They were unable to test teenagers for legal reasons, but suspect that the younger the subject, the greater the mental function is impaired by alcohol.[14]

Early adolescents have less body mass than adults and drugs work that much more quickly, pushing them quickly over the edge. They may drink less often than adults, but when they drink they tend to drink a lot, and intoxication is far more dangerous for children and adolescents who are vulnerable to hypoglycaemia, hypothermia and breathing difficulties.[15] The long-term consequences of alcohol abuse, such as liver damage, are well known, but very few people realize that alcohol can be lethal with just one single overdose. High concentrations of alcohol shut down the parts of the brain that control breathing, and can paralyse the muscle that closes the windpipe when we eat and drink. When young people are so drunk they vomit, they are also at risk of suffocation. Alcohol also heightens confidence and aggression, which quickly translates into violence amongst gangs of youths and injury, even death, from car crashes. Suicide in older male teenagers is strongly linked to alcohol abuse, with up to one-third of young suicides intoxicated at the time of death.[16] Alcohol is often a pre-requisite for sex, increasing the likelihood that young women in particular will engage in unprotected intercourse and may therefore suffer from the consequences – pregnancy and sexually transmitted diseases.

Psychoactive drugs interact with the neurochemistry of the brain just at the time when it is radically changing shape and some studies have indicated that these substances can impair short-term memory, the ability to store new information and problem-solving abilities. Stoned young people easily avoid tackling difficulties head-on and learning from them, by rolling another joint. Alcohol is water-soluble and passes out of the body through sweat and urine within hours. But THC, the active ingredient in cannabis, is fat-soluble and hangs around the body for weeks before it is finally eliminated. It heads for the organs – the brain and the sex organs – and may disrupt menstrual cycles and reduce sperm counts. It has been found to widen the spaces between neurons in the brain, which slows down brain messages and makes it harder for people to study, concentrate and revise for exams or maintain previous dexterity in physical sports. Regular use also appears to reduce motivation. These effects can linger long after the pleasurable effects of being stoned have worn off. The cannabis young people smoke today is approximately four times stronger than the dope their parents may have smoked when they were young, and one deeply inhaled joint can cause as much damage to their lungs as an entire packet of cigarettes.

'I know that he smokes dope, which is a big worry because we didn't smoke dope at that age. It wasn't common then but now it is and you don't know how it is affecting their concentration at school,' says Barbara, whose elder son is fourteen and has told her that he smokes. 'You lay down these rules that seem pathetic in some ways – no dope in the house and no smoking on weekdays – but I'd be very surprised if he took any notice of it. There's one mother who's either never in or doesn't care so that's where they go. But then you don't know how paranoid you're being. It could be all in your head. Perhaps it's all much more harmless than you think it is, but you don't really know.'

Rosamund's son developed an addiction to dope when he was fifteen. 'He told me about it last summer and I took it fairly lightly because he trusted us enough to tell us and I know that everyone does it. But it became the main focus of his life, far more important than anything else. We then got worried and he did disastrously in his mocks. He then asked to go and see the doctor because he felt so ill from so much smoking, and knew that he'd overstepped it and stopped. But by that time all patterns of work had gone and he was in with a crowd who were not working, so I don't hold out much hope for many passes. It's an entirely different mindset from an adult who might have a drink at a party or smoke a joint because it's going round. It becomes an obsession, all they want to do. They just smoke until they pass out and then they wake up not looking too happy or well.'

Looking back on my own adolescent relationship with cannabis resin, it is clear that I was overusing it as an emotional prop. At the time I thought I was being ultra-cool. It was exciting carrying dope around London and smoking it illicitly whenever possible. It made life more fun and enhanced social and sexual pleasures. But there is a sliding and degenerative scale between the exhilaration of experimentation and abuse, and I crossed over that boundary by constantly looking forward to the next opportunity to get stoned. I smoked enough to be able to forget my problems, my lack of sense of direction. I smoked so much that I now wonder whether I merely froze my difficulties while I was growing up rather than resolved them and question sometimes whether there isn't a part of my brain that is now missing as a result. To this day, the smell of it simply makes me feel sick.

It is important to get the problem of drugs into perspective. We may all be only a few hundred yards away from scoring illegal drugs, but that does not mean that young people want them or take them. 'There are drugs,' says Amanda, aged eighteen, 'but mainly dope which I have tried, but I'm not that interested in. I have friends who deal it and that doesn't seem that shocking and I have another friend who does harder drugs, but the majority just don't do them.' 'Drugs aren't difficult to find if you want them but there isn't a major drugs culture at school, of pushing at the school gate,' says Tim.

Most adolescents have the confidence, self-esteem and sense of self-preservation to avoid their parents' worst nightmares although they may dabble on the fringes, by smoking the occasional joint at parties or even getting seriously stoned with ten other people in a girlfriend's bedroom on a Saturday afternoon. Generally speaking, if they are drinking and smoking socially rather than on their own then there is less to worry about, for the social indulgence either fades or moderates while the solitary indulgence is a sign of deeper unhappiness and can become entrenched as they grow older.

The most effective thing that parents can do is to keep channels of communication open so that there can be honest discussion about the detrimental effects of smoking or drinking too much. Adopting a judgemental policy of 'just say no' will push children further away from your influence, because they can see that reality is very different and they are bound to know people who are drinking and smoking cannabis. However, parents can decide what they consider to be acceptable and once they have drawn that line they need to be consistent about it. They can discuss regularly the extreme dangers of drinking and driving, in quite brutal terms, so that their children understand the risks they run once they accept a lift home from a driver who has been drinking. They can highlight the ways in which alcohol can kill and affect their mental development. They can talk about the acute sensitivity of the adolescent brain and the need to keep it safe while it is still growing and changing. Parents need to be aware of the differences between experimentation and abuse (outlined in Appendix 2) and act swiftly once the danger signals appear. Cannabis may be ubiquitous, but it is still illegal. It is also, contrary to the Sixties myth, addictive in much the same way that tea, coffee and alcohol become a daily prop in countless people's lives.

If parents suspect that their children are abusing drink or cannabis to the point of addiction or may even be indulging in harder drugs then they have to take action. Three or more of the following danger signs, according to the adolescent psychologist Laurence Steinberg, indicate that there may be drug abuse:

- possession of drug paraphernalia
- preoccupation with drugs in conversations and jokes
- dramatic changes in school performance
- physical symptoms such as bloodshot eyes, dilated pupils, persistent hacking coughs and colds, greater lethargy and fatigue, memory lapses and poor physical coordination, changes in appetite and weight
- changes in behaviour such as greater dishonesty, increasing and inappropriate anger, hostility, irritability, secretiveness and greater mood swings, indifference to grooming and hygiene.

If there are several warning signs, parents have to accept that their child may have a drug problem, which is harder than it sounds when parents so easily interpret this as failure on their part. But parents do not make teenagers take drugs – they make that decision for themselves. Not stepping in to help them when they may have got into something too deep and may not be able to help themselves is, however, a great failing of parental responsibility. If teenagers admit that they have a problem then you are halfway there to solving it and can help enormously at home with discussion, negotiation and the establishment of a contract of behaviour where you lay down standards, monitor their activities closely and withdraw privileges if that contract is broken. When they do well, praise must be heaped upon them and their behaviour rewarded with something they really want. Sometimes it is this closer contact and support from a parent, with better communication and understanding, that teenagers needed so badly in the first place, and the lack of it may have contributed to their dependency on drugs as an emotional prop. Outside professional help, from your GP principally, is also essential.

Telling young people not to drink or take drugs simply won't work these days. Frightening them with scare stories merely obliterates their confidence in your judgement. When they take their puff on their first joint and discover that they quite like the effects, that their head doesn't explode and that they do not become severely addicted, suffering instant withdrawal symptoms, your argument will be severely discredited. It's much better to arm them with accurate information about drugs in general. Paracetamol may be in every bathroom cabinet to ease headaches but an overdose with as few as fifteen to twenty tablets can cause death through liver damage. Alcohol can be doubly dangerous if it is mixed with other drugs that cause sedation, such as Valium or some cold medicines. They need to understand the damaging consequences of over-indulgence as well as the gradual insidious nature of addiction. They also need to know what to do should they be with people who are near-comatose from drink or drugs.' "Just say no to drugs" is crap because you've got to know about your body and what they do to them and where to go if you're in trouble,' says Judith, who writes novels for teenagers and has two teenage children of her own. 'It's also important not to be judgemental so that you keep the channels of communication open. So if, for instance, they come home and say a friend has taken ecstasy don't go, "Oh my God!" with shocked outrage. Just say, "Oh has she, how do you feel about that?"'

Parents need to protect their children from the dangers of substance abuse by considered and informed advice about the known effects on health and cognitive development. Parents who try to stay on the same side by listening to what their children have to say rather than condemning their behaviour outright, are far more likely to have their children confide in them when they genuinely need help. They are then able to help them with tactics and strategies to say 'no' to drugs when they are offered them, without losing face. Parents can analyse the way alcohol is advertised as healthy and sexy in order to help them understand that it isn't. They can talk about the ways that drink and drugs ease anxieties, but there are times when those anxieties are crucial to our natural self-protective instincts. While they may reduce pain temporarily, they do not make our problems go away. They can also keep up the encouragement of as many extra-curricular activities and hobbies as possible, such as sport, music, dance and drama clubs and give hope to their special interests or ambitions. Busy children do not have the time to drift through adolescence or to waste on drugs. They are also likely to have higher self-esteem because they can excel at something and are less likely to need them. 'I don't worry about drugs because he enjoys music and sport and he's always saying, "Why would anyone want to do it when it makes you feel so awful?" If you drink a lot or do drugs, you're not going to be able to play tennis,' says Jill. 'Also my brother has been severely alcoholic and they've seen the effect that it's had on him and we talk about that quite a bit, so I think they are quite aware of what the awful consequences of getting addicted to something are.'

Infancy used to be the most dangerous stage of being a child, with high rates of mortality and vulnerability to serious illness. Now it is adolescence, with rising rates of drug and alcohol abuse, eating disorders, deliberate self-harm and suicide amongst young people. All of these afflictions are linked with depression, which is a regular complaint for adolescents, although rarely recognized as such. One adolescent psycho-therapist I met told me that ME is also now an increasingly common presentation of depression in adolescent referrals.

It is often hard to tell the difference between depression and the mood swings which most parents associate with normal adolescent development. However, depression is common, affecting anything between 33 per cent and 40 per cent of adolescents with low self-esteem and a sense of nothing to look forward to.[17] Depression is rare in children, but as the changes of adolescence pile on the pressure, rates soar. One large-scale study on the Isle of Wight in 1986 found a three-fold increase in depressive feelings between the ages of ten and fifteen.[18] Several studies have found that up to half of those who are depressed meet the criteria for a diagnosis of major depressive disorder but are often ignored because adults assume adolescence to be a time of emotional turmoil.[19] The statistics, as well as anecdotal evidence from those working with young people, indicate that rates of depression are higher today among young people than they were for their parents at the same age.

Rebecca became severely depressed at fifteen when her best and only friend stopped talking to her, so she withdrew and stopped talking to everybody, including her parents. 'It started as a protection thing because it seems easier if you say you don't care, if you don't try, so I isolated myself. Also it was a way of not taking responsibility for your own being. You're sad and unhappy because everybody else is being nasty but you don't have to do anything, just blame everyone else. It never occurred to me that it was down to me to do something about it.' Rebecca developed glandular fever, lost a lot of weight and then liked the feeling of being empty so much that she became anorexic. When her weight fell to seven stone she got frightened and began to eat again. She also began cutting her forearm with a razor blade. 'It was a lonely time but you enjoy being lonely in a slightly sick way. I felt like I was better than everyone else because I had my own world that no one else knew about. With hindsight it was a totally close-minded way of being, not looking outside of yourself, not wanting time to move on or anything to change, not engaging with life or the world because it didn't occur to me to cope with it.'

The fact that suicide rates amongst young people are rising, while those amongst other age groups have remained stable or fallen, gives us the most accurate indication that all is not well with the adolescent state of mind. In America the adolescent suicide rate quadrupled between 1955 and the end of the 1970s, and then tripled between 1970 and 1990, and similar increases have been found in seventeen European countries.[20] The completed-suicide rate for males aged fifteen to twenty-four has increased by 75 per cent in Britain and Europe since the mid 1980s.[21] It has been estimated that the real suicide rate could be up to three times higher but is masked by uncertainty over the actual circumstances of death and by taboo, for many parents are reluctant to admit that their children may have killed themselves.[22] There have also been rises in the attempted-suicide rate, known as Deliberate Self-harm, which is the most common reason for acute hospital medical admission in young people. One study in Oxford discovered a 28 per cent increase between 1985 and 1995.[23] The highest rates of suicide are found among girls aged fifteen to nineteen and the attempted rates are three times higher amongst girls than boys, but young men are usually more successful when they attempt suicide because they tend to choose more violent and immediate methods. Depression rates are also about three times higher in girls than in boys. 'In 1995 more teens and young adults died from suicide than from cancer, heart disease, AIDS, pneumonia, influenza, birth defects and stroke combined,' writes Kay Redfield Jamieson in her book on suicide, *An Unquiet Mind*.

Young people are increasingly depressed for good reasons. Many more young people are undoubtedly better off than previous generations; more qualify from higher education, they are better informed and have more money. But now that we live in such a complex society which changes so swiftly they also confront numerous new external pressures, demands, expectations, risks and uncertainties that previous generations never had to contend with. There is a direct relationship between social change and the nature of adolescent development. With puberty beginning earlier and economic dependence extending well into their early twenties, young people spend far too long as adolescents in transition without autonomy. They grow up within a consumer society which incites them to be acquisitive before they have the financial means to be so, and they face a bewildering array of lifestyle options. They are denied genuine responsibilities or rites of passage which connect them to wider society and make them feel valued and older, and all too often are left bereft and unsupported through the genuine, inherent difficulties of growing up. More and more teenagers may be passing their exams, but the increased emphasis on testing in schools and the pressure to pass piles yet more stress onto stressful lives. With changing work patterns for men and women, and the growing concept that jobs are no longer for life, young people have trouble imagining their futures. Adolescents have to deal with the temptations and pressures of drugs, alcohol, tobacco and sexual activity at a distressingly early age. They also grow up now well aware that they are not safe, with bullying and sharp rises in mugging, often with knives, at school or on the streets.

One quarter of our young people experience parental divorce and subsequently live with a great sense of emotional abandonment. Young girls who have suffered adversely from the effects of divorce or an absent father are apparently more likely to engage in promiscuous behaviour, and boys lack positive role models and more easily succumb to the lure of the male gang. Child poverty has increased threefold in the past twenty years at a time of unprecedented materialism amongst the young. Young people are marginalized from society without an adequate voice. They are excluded from adult society and privilege and are more isolated from adult example and support in schools than they have ever been throughout history although the pressures have increased hugely and they need adult wisdom for greater understanding of those pressures and support. All of these factors can make life very hard for young people, harder than ever to navigate alone, and a small but rising number are consequently finding growing up too much to bear. 'We live in a much more stressful world now,' says Nicky, a Relate counsellor who works with children of divorcing parents. 'It's faster-moving, with expect-ations to do more in less time. There's positive aspects to that, but many negative ones as well and many children are now growing up with great stress and pressure. I take my hat off to them, for most are managing against considerable odds, but others are not coping well at all. They live on the margins.'

Any radical change can be stressful and adolescents face numerous adjustments, often at the same time. They have to prove their worth in almost every aspect of their lives – socially, sexually, in their educational achievements and in their general efforts to wrest a sense of autonomy and independence from their parents. The biological upheaval of puberty may play a part in the rise of depression, as does an individual's inherent genetic predisposition, for those with a family history of depres-sion are more likely to succumb. But both of these factors appear to be secondary to the wider social and cultural shifts that puberty provokes, particularly in girls. Girls have to contend with a whole new set of contradictions which do not generally affect boys, and it is these new cultural pressures which seem to send depression rates of adolescent girls soaring way above that of boys. Girls are also more likely than boys to have been sexually abused as children, a leading cause of depression in adolescence. Sexually abused children display more emotional and behavioural difficulties than their counter-parts during adolescence. They are also more likely to engage in promiscuous, criminal or self-destructive behaviour.[24] Sexu-ality is burgeoning and important, but they now have to appear as 'good' girls, restrained rather than tarty. They jostle with new concepts of femininity, which means abandoning the selfishness of childhood and being self-sacrificing and kind, putting the needs of others before their own. And young women now grow up facing a whole new set of demands; they have to become someone career-wise, they now expect and are expected to earn their own living without putting off the boys they so badly want to be loved by, they have to look good, they have to be good, and they have to succeed on their own merits. They either conform to stereotype, or fail to try by withdrawing into depression and anger.

Boys face additional pressures in becoming 'men' on top of all the normal adjustments of adolescents described in this book. Adam, a teacher for thirty years, is passionately devoted to the welfare of boys. 'I have taught girls as well and noticed that the way they managed adolescence was so much more competent partly because the presence of the mother is so vital and there is a wisdom which is passed on that doesn't exist between males. It seems to be much more traumatic for boys, a phase of complete awkwardness or dysfunction. Fathers don't pass on much wisdom to their sons. There is the idea of what a "man" ought to be, a construct that fathers maybe pass on. There is terrific investment of hopes that they make in their sons, of "what I want my son to be". There is also the whole idea of the son as already a man before he has had time to be an adolescent, to be a boy. It manifests itself in the whole culture of laddishness. The idea that you declare your masculinity through grossness, a coarseness and aggressiveness.'

With so many new and conflicting pressures, it is hardly surprising that frustration and anger are rife among young people. They express that anger through graffiti, aggression, violence, crime and delinquency. Or they turn it against the self through drugs, anorexia, promiscuity, self-mutilation, depression and ultimately suicide. When young people seem isolated, depressed or down, it is crucial that parents try to talk to them about how they are feeling and acknowledge the pressures they live with in being young. If their children refuse to talk to them, parents need to swallow their hurt pride and encourage links with other close adult friends their children like, so there are at least opportunities to talk to someone else about how they are feeling and get support. If parents are worried that their children might be suicidal, ask them if they have contemplated it and never, ever dismiss casual talk of killing oneself as adolescent fantasy. Discuss it seriously and then try to find ways of temporarily lifting their gloom, encouraging childish pleasures in play, taking them to the football, to a fairground, ice skating or shopping.

When young people indulge in common adolescent behaviours such as shoplifting, spraying graffiti or bunking off school, they express their frustration and boredom. They do these things to see if they can get away with them, and raise their vulnerable self-esteem through the temporary high of achievement, as Tobias Wolff describes in his memoir *This Boy's Life*:

When I finally managed to steal something I figured I was getting away with it because I was sharp, and not because these women had been on their feet all day and were too tired to deal with a shoplifter. Instead of making us more careful, the interest of the police in what we'd done elated us. We became self-important, cocksure, insane in our arrogance. We broke windows. We broke streetlights. We opened the doors of cars parked on hills and released the emergency brakes so they smashed into the cars below.

Girls more readily turn their anger against the self than boys do. Rather than shout or fight, ask for what she wants or say 'no' to what she doesn't, an unhappy girl will reach for food or the razor blade. 'I'm a constant eater, I eat when I'm angry, when I'm sad, when I'm depressed, when I'm bored,' says Stella, aged sixteen. 'If I'm at home then I just eat everything. I tried bringing it up once but it's just too difficult and anyway food's so good, I want to hang on to it.' Ann Cox, author of *Autumn Dawn: Triumph Over Eating Disorders*, writes of how her comfort-eating soon led to eating disorders which enabled her to focus on something other than her emotional needs. 'There was an emptiness there, a great lack of confidence, of self-esteem, so I tried to fill that emotional void with food. It's so easy to get caught up in the symptoms when you're ill because you've taken, albeit subconsciously, the focus off the real issues in life. So I wasn't anxious about my parents, I wasn't worried about my friends. I was able to solve all of those concerns with a twenty-four-hour obsession with food, weight, shape and size.'

Eating disorders such as anorexia and bulimia are dramatic, shocking and very obvious manifestations of extreme adolescent unhappiness. Food itself is rarely the problem though, but a means of avoiding other problems and one of the most common traits found amongst sufferers is a chronic lack of self-worth. Psychologists generally believe that there is never one sole cause for eating disorders, but a jigsaw of causes. There may be childhood trauma, family dysfunction or a history of eating disorders. Some believe that anorexics need to cling on to childhood by literally reversing the physical development of their bodies, for the extra layers of fat laid down with puberty disappear and periods cease. By becoming ill they perpetuate childhood dependency on their parents. Others maintain that anorexics are making a desperate bid for autonomy as they wrest control of their bodies away from over-controlling parents, since food is the source of maternal nourishment and they now determine what food goes in and what shape they become. They battle daily with food, rather than with their parents, denying themselves much of the nourishment that they so badly need. Some researchers have found higher rates of anorexia amongst teenagers who have mothers who strive constantly for perfection, are preoccupied with dieting themselves, and in homes where food is a constant source of obsession.

The one thing that is clear about the rise of eating disorders is that they coincide with wider aspects of cultural and social change in the West, such as rates of obesity, snack foods and television. Children eat more junk and exercise less as they sit slumped in front of the TV. Advertising of snack foods triggers their appetite, and the fact that children of all ages are getting fatter may in itself be contributing to rising rates of eating disorders, for young people need to devise more radical means of control to eliminate the possibility of getting fat. Never before have young people been so bombarded by images of fit, beautiful, thin and successful people, and inevitably adolescent girls, who are at their most self-conscious and vulnerable about their image, their bodies and their self-esteem at this age, are affected.

Young women say that it is this constant exposure to images of unnaturally stick-thin women that is the strongest force in their striving for the thin ideal.[25] 'You see all these pictures of really thin women and they say, "This is really beautiful, this is what you should look like," and then you think, I wish I was like that and how can I get thin?' says Emma, who is fourteen. Many have yet to gain the wider skills of perspective, self-knowledge and success in some other area of their lives which help to compensate for looks in more mature women. All they can do is control how they look through dress and what they eat. 'If I'm on a diet I just stop eating, sometimes I don't eat anything but yoghurt for about three weeks,' says Emma. 'Every time I weigh myself and see that I'm putting on weight I just stop eating or go swimming.'

Numerous personal accounts by anorexics and bulimics confirm that both cultural and private concerns shape eating disorders. 'I was influenced by media images, but I know that my internal struggle was much more personal,' writes Maya.

She was bulimic in her teens. 'The childlike ideal for me was connected to my awareness and uncertainty about the process of turning from a girl into a woman. Coming up against so many responsibilities and expectations made me want to slow everything down. Terrified of making visible mistakes I just wanted to be small, still a child . . . Being ill and vulnerable in this way was a call for help at a time when asking directly seemed difficult and I couldn't articulate what it was I wanted.'[26]

Dr Dee Dawson who runs Rhodes Farm, which specializes in eating disorders, believes that many parents need to take action far sooner when they suspect their children are starving themselves. 'We have met many parents who have wasted months and in some cases years of their child's young life taking one step forward and two back, always giving her one last chance and believing her promises to eat tomorrow,' she writes in her thoroughly helpful book *Anorexia and Bulimia − A Parent's Guide to Recognizing Eating Disorders and Taking Control*. She recommends that all parents talk to their children about the extreme physical dangers of eating disorders and the effect that deprivation will have on their growing bodies, possibly for life. Children with eating disorders need close surveillance. They need the responsibility and decision-making as to what to eat taken out of their hands and they need professional guidance soon, not nine or twelve months down the line when their fragile bodies have been starved of nutrients, protein and energy foods. A visit to the doctor may be all that parents need to back up a programme at home which encourages their child to gain weight and grow. If that fails the teenager will need to be admitted to a specialist unit either in the NHS (which inevitably has a long waiting list) or at a private clinic. Adult psychiatric units are terrifying places and need to be avoided at all costs: adolescents with eating disorders need specialist units and they need to be nourished as children.

Self-harming is another way of releasing the pressure of

inner emotional pain. 'I have come to regard self-harm as morbid forms of self-help,' writes Armando Favazza, a psychiatrist who specializes in young people who self-mutilate, 'because they provide rapid but temporary relief from distressing symptoms such as mounting anxiety, depersonalization, racing thoughts and rapidly fluctuating emotions.' Claudia, like several of her classmates at an independent school in London, tried cutting. She says that she was going through a particularly bad time at home with her foster sister. 'I really liked it, it gave me a sense of satisfaction, of well-being and it stopped me feeling so frustrated. It seemed like a really good way to purge the bad feeling. My mum got really upset and said, "Come and hurt me. Don't hurt yourself." But it's not the same. For me it was a control thing. There were all these things happening that you couldn't control, but this you could control and you could see it as well. I was proud, that I managed to do that.' Claudia and her friends say that cutting was particularly prevalent in her class the previous Christmas when they began to plan fund-raising for a sports trip to New Zealand. The entire spring term they had to do weekly fund-raising work and extra netball training for the trip on top of their coursework, homework, choir and instrument practice. 'The whole thing was like "heavy pressure" and then when that faded, the craze for cutting seemed to disappear, except for one girl who got into it heavily on all her arms and legs.'

'Sometimes I injure myself to make myself numb because I can't deal with what I'm feeling,' writes Daphne, who is sixteen and lives in Canada. 'I mostly do it when I'm angry.'

Promiscuous sex can also be a way of easing the hopelessness and inertia of depression. Jeannie Milligan, psychotherapist at the Tavistock Centre in London, told me about a young girl who had been abused as a child, and then had promiscuous sex from a young age. 'She could seduce anyone in a pub, and used that power. She had sex not for the sex but because it made her feel powerful and in control. Sex often fills the same hole as drugs. If you're uncertain about who you are, it's a piece of action. It's exciting, dangerous, challenging, and they chase sex as a way of being loved, but rarely get it and then get caught in a repetitive syndrome. It's the wrong solution to the problem. There isn't much difference between sex and eating being misused. They're both used as a means of avoiding something else, attacking your body because you're feeling unloved.'

As children grow older and begin to 'put away childish things', the adult world they are about to join draws closer and even the most confident teenager, keen to assume adult privileges, finds the prospect of fighting his corner in that world scary at times. Countless teenagers, who do not engage in crime, drug use or cutting, complain about feeling constantly tired, bored, without any sense of direction and purpose. Stella is just one example of many I met. She is sixteen and recently began studying for A levels at a further education college in South London. Her attendance is erratic and the college have written to say that she will have to leave if things don't improve. She works in Boots four days a week from 3.30 p.m. to 6.30 p.m. and feels shattered most of the time – she sleeps for hours and watches TV in her room. 'The pay is really bad, £3.44 an hour, and I feel like they're draining all my energy. By the time I get home I'm permanently tired. Going out is too much effort, I'd rather stay at home.' Her parents split up when she was twelve, her mother recently married again and she has a half-brother who is two years old. She doesn't see her dad, pretends that she doesn't care about the fact that she hasn't got a regular boyfriend, or that she might be pregnant from a casual sexual experience, and has lost contact with many of her old friends by moving on. She has yet to make new friends about whom she feels confident enough to 'bring home'. She is depressed and with good reason. She has thought about suicide but says that she couldn't possibly do something so cruel to her mother. 'College misfired from the start. They expect a lot from you with essays and deadlines, I can do the work, it's just really hitting me, the pressure. I know I have potential, I just don't know what I'm doing with it, I'd like to be rich, win the lottery, if I dropped A levels now there'd be nothing else to do and I don't want to work in Boots for the rest of my life. Mummy says I'm depressed and asks me what I want to do, but I don't know what I want to do, that's the whole problem. If I thought that I could do something I'd probably get down to college and do it.'

Support is limited. She hasn't dared approach a counsellor at college, her mother cares but has yet to break through. She doesn't feel as if anybody is there for her. 'My twin brother is in the same boat, I know, but he has a girlfriend and even though he doesn't talk to her he knows she's there for him and I feel like I haven't seen Denise [her closest friend] for ages. Sometimes I see friends but I feel alone, sometimes it all feels too much.' She cannot conceive of a way of improving her life all by herself, and given the mountain ahead of her one can well understand why she would rather go to bed. She wants quick solutions to her problems, she wants to win the lottery, get rich; she needs certainty in her life and feels unable to make important decisions all by herself. The lyrics of pop songs by stars such as Eminem speak to her more readily, he alone seems to understand, empathize and express how she feels even though they have never met. 'I'd like things to happen to me, I'd like it to be decided for me what I should do and I know that's not going to happen. It's the decision and whether or not it's a good one.'

It is this isolation, this alienation from adult example and guidance at such an influential age, which lies at the root of so many of the difficulties young people face. At the beginning of the twentieth century, most adolescents learned how to be adult in the real world from a much wider range of role models, earning a living as apprentices or domestic servants. Compulsory education, with rising numbers of young people in the past forty years staying on in full-time education until they are eighteen or in their early twenties, means that whole generations of young people have been segregated from the outside world in an unprecedented way. At school they observe a handful of teachers each week, from whom they learn coursework rather than essential life skills, and they spend most of their time with their peers. At home they spend more time listening to the television than they do to their parents. The one-way nature of this dialogue does little to enhance their critical skills for they do not have to argue back or think on their feet, or consider other people as they would in a live, two-way conversation.

Adolescents have never been so isolated from adult examples in order to learn how to be responsible and cope with the conundrums of modern life with the minimum of stress. They are rarely given active challenges either at school or at home which involve them in their local community and make them feel valued and of consequence. One survey of over 30,000 young people found that connectedness, a sense of 'belonging to a community of others' was the strongest protective factor against emotional distress or disturbed behaviours such as drug use or consistent truancy.[27] Nearly half of all young people who attempt suicide have had reduced contact with adults through regular truancy or with only one parent at home.[28] A substantial number of young people who engage in high levels of problem behaviour such as delinquency, crime, sexual promiscuity and substance abuse have been found to have detached links with adults, through low parental supervision, erratic or harsh discipline, marital disharmony or outright parental rejection.[29]

The reduced contact that results from divorce inevitably contributes to the isolation of adolescence. Summary reviews

of studies show that children are more likely to develop problems during late childhood and adolescence, such as school
failure, delinquency, precocious sexual behaviour and substance abuse, if their parents are divorced.[30] One large study of
14,000 teenagers in the Netherlands found higher levels
of loneliness, depression and suicidal thoughts as well as suicide
attempts among children from single-parent households and
stepfamilies than among those still living with both parents.[31]
It is the reduced contact with important adults resulting from
divorce which appears to be at the heart of the matter. 'It's
harder for me to get my needs met, therefore it's harder to
meet his needs,' says Helen, a single mother with a teenage
son living in Manchester. 'I just don't have the time or the
money.'

Sometimes there are distinct advantages to the new extended
family networks that have been produced by divorce and re-
marriage. I sought sanctuary at my father's flat whenever things
got rough at home and found the space there to breathe
and be myself. If children are lucky enough to have good
relationships with step-parents, they have other adults to learn
from and provide support. My relationship with my first
stepmother was an essential lifeline. She provided me with
different models of femininity, intimacy and support without
ever trying to replace my mother, and I still value that relationship even though she is no longer living with my father. But
there are countless other, less happy circumstances where
children lose more than they gain. Children of divorce not
only lose a parent on a day-to-day basis, but they often lose
them to another family, with step-siblings to compete with.
Negotiating stepfamily life can be fraught with practical and
emotional difficulties. Ties with grandparents and aunts and
uncles on the paternal side are weakened if the mother has
custody, and while there may be a greater extended family
around through re-marriage, these relationships are often

emotionally complicated with both children and new spouses resenting the other.

Fathers play a major role throughout a child's upbringing but the absence of a good relationship with fathers can deny an adolescent boy a role model at the time in his life when he most needs one. Rosamund attributes some of her son's difficulties with excessive dope-smoking and educational failure to a difficult relationship with his father. 'I certainly feel that if his father had been less explosive and around more instead of a workaholic a lot of these problems would have been made easier. There have been times when they haven't spoken for months and I don't think his father realizes how damaging that's been. I have to be careful because I want their relationship to survive so I haven't told him half the things that our son has told me about how he feels about his father because it's too painful. He feels that he's never here and when he is, he erupts with this fierce, unpredictable temper. The families where the fathers are strong and around are getting through it but I can see one common factor in that all of Karl's friends who have got into trouble do not have their fathers around. They need them so badly at that age, yet where are they when they need them?'

Adolescence is now defined by a devastating combination of factors. Teenagers are denied clear social and economic roles and the opportunity to make a contribution to society at the time in life when people most need to prove their worth and learn responsibility and respect towards others. They are denied recognition, honour and respect for the monumental changes they live through with adequate rites of passage, enabling them to move more easily from the clear definitions of childhood into adulthood. They are excluded from politics, their views rarely consulted in policy formation in spite of the healthy idealism and enthusiasm to make the world a better place which is inherent to this age. They are bombarded by sexual imagery but are ill-prepared for the onset of sexuality. They are widely feared and disliked, blamed for most of society's ills – crime, drugs, disorder, lack of respect or consideration. They are rarely supported enough with the difficulties they face at home or at school, such as divorce or separating parents, inner city poverty and its effects, bullying and increased academic pressure. Without adequate support and clear frames of reference as to what it is to be an adult and how to get there, adolescents easily fall prey to other influences, to drugs and the power of the media.

When I was a child, television was limited to children's hour before the six o'clock news with special dispensation to watch *Top of the Pops* and *The Man from U.N.C.L.E.* on a Thursday evening. Today, children grow up with twenty-four-hour exposure to media with cable, breakfast and daytime television and video. We have no concrete evidence to prove whether this is beneficial or harmful, but common sense would suggest that it is bound to be a mixture of the two and that children are influenced by it as they grow up. We have also witnessed, in the past two decades, an unprecedented rise in the commercialization of childhood and these new industries depend heavily on the purchasing power of the young, reaching them through the media. A sophisticated marketing and retail industry has made vast profits out of the young through sales of magazines, alcopops, pop music, clothes, jewellery, make-up, mobile phones, snack foods, videos and even cosmetic surgery. Two-thirds of all the music CDs and tapes sold in the US are bought by young people aged ten to twenty-four.[32] The film *Titanic* became one of the highest grossing films largely because crowds of teenage girls went to see the film four or five times. For every film aimed at adults there are at least four aimed at the youth market.

Even aspects of their social relationships are now being influenced by what they see on television. 'I can see that the arguments they have with each other at school are direct copies of the types of conversations they see on programmes like *Jerry Springer*, all that aggressive, in-your-face type language,' says Julie. 'It wasn't like that when I first started teaching. They pick up a lot from the telly, especially at that age when they don't want to be influenced by their parents and they haven't got the money to go anywhere or do anything.' Adam agrees: 'What they see on the television is bound to affect them and create role models, things like *Men Behaving Badly* or some of Harry Enfield's grosser comic creations, which they are sophisticated enough to be able to laugh at and put themselves at a distance from, but another side of them wants to emulate that. It may sound conservative blaming the media but the point is that the stable door has been opened, the horse has bolted and you're never going to be able to round them up again, so what do you do? You've got to provide more support, more frameworks and basically they need listening to. It's terribly important just to be there for them, that's one of the most important parts of my job – being there to listen, talking to them and being a friendly presence.'

With such unprecedented social change producing new pressures on the young, adolescents need greater involvement from the adults that surround them to help them make sense of it. The greater the insecurity they face in the outside world, the more they need to feel that parents and interested adults can contain that insecurity with reassurance and guidance. All of the troubled teenagers I have talked to have craved greater empathy and understanding, principally from their parents, during the great changes of adolescence. 'I just wish she'd listen, really listen', 'I wish I could talk to them', 'If only I felt they really understood' were phrases that came up over and over again. Feeling misunderstood is a crucial aspect of adolescence as teenagers strive to establish their individuality. But when that misunderstanding mutates into isolation, teenagers are left bereft and alone. If support from teachers and the wider community is lacking, teenagers inevitably focus more on all the ways that their parents fail them and are likely to say so. When communication breaks down completely with a troubled teenager, parents can find it harder to get through because there are fewer adults around that they can rely on to help them. But we have to be brave enough to reach out and simply ask others for help during those times and not consider it an act of weakness or failure, because as parents we always have to do what is right for our children. Rosamund began to despair that she would ever be able to break the cycle of educational failure and daily dope-smoking in her sixteen-year-old son on her own. So she drove him to a sixth-form college where he could re-sit his GCSEs and take A levels. Karl was so adamant that he was going to agricultural college that he refused to get out of the car. Rosamund went into the college and explained to the head, who then went out to the car and crouched down to talk to Karl through the car window. 'He told him that he knew that he wanted to go to agricultural college, but that if it didn't work out as he wanted, he was welcome to come here and re-sit his exams and take A levels. Karl listened and there were tears in his eyes. That man had connected, he needed a grown man to break through and sort things out for him, otherwise he's just marooned, lost and isolated and feeling as if he has to sort everything out for himself, which he can't.'

There has always been a tendency to blame minor crime, misdemeanour and vandalism on the young, and the statistics back up this assumption. Of recorded crimes 45 per cent are committed by people who are under twenty-one. For most young people these acts of minor rebellion are thrilling activities that make the adrenaline rush, relieve the boredom and harness all that restless energy. Surveys show that approximately one-third of adult males have some form of criminal record picked up while they were young. The vast majority of adolescent naughtiness evaporates with adulthood and only a small number become hardened criminals or repeated offenders, and many of these exhibited signs of criminality way before the adjustments of adolescence.

However, the growth of youth crime mirrors the growth of other psychosocial disorders in young people and supports the theory that it is segregation from adult example and alienation from adult privilege in this extended period of adolescence that is perhaps the root cause. Researchers and social psychologists acknowledge that the main reason why the vast majority of young people desist from crime as they grow up is because they understand the importance of social ties. They do not want to lose a sense of connectedness with those they care for by crossing too far over a boundary to a place from which they cannot return. Strong social bonds tend to sit hand in hand with conformity and a need to seek out friends and lovers who reinforce those ideals. Weak social bonds tend to lead to delinquency and a choice of friends who may weaken those essential, benign social bonds still further.[33] Those with lower IQs have been found to be at increased risk of delinquency and a significant minority of children aged sixteen and seventeen are not participating in any form of education, employment or training. Each month in Britain 12,000 of them apply for severe hardship payments and many of these are either homeless or excluded from mainstream society.[34] If young people are bored to the point of educational failure at school there is little else to capture their energy or enhance their enthusiasm and offer them a smoother passage to adulthood. They are thrust out into the world defenceless, and are far more likely to drop out and turn to less socially acceptable uses of their time.

Rising rates of child poverty also sever children's links to the wider community. Over the past two decades the social geography of Britain has changed, with wealth and poverty increasingly polarized in different areas. Increasing numbers of young people now grow up in places where far too many of the adults are unemployed, schools are drained of investment and middle-class involvement and where the local community offers sparse opportunities. Lack of qualifications severely reduces a young person's chances of employment and social inclusion in later life. Poverty also has a disproportionate impact on child mental health. The Office for National Statistics has found that when both parents were unemployed, 20 per cent of their children were suffering from mental health problems, they were four times more likely to truant, three times more likely to have a specific learning difficulty and ten times more likely to get into trouble with the police.[35]

More and more children grow up in vast, impersonal cities with rapid demographic change, where crime rates are higher. If neighbours keep changing, or they themselves have moved several times, their sense of being connected to a community is bound to be weakened, and their sense of responsibility towards others reduced. If there is high local unemployment or job instability, impetuous or disheartened young people quickly adopt the attitude 'Why bother?' Poverty plays an insidious and complicated role in disrupting adolescent development. Adolescents are far more connected and dependent on their local neighbourhood than either children or adults. Adults are at work or at home, small children at school or at home. But adolescents make forays out alone into their local neighbourhood, to the streets, parks and shopping centres, or go out with their peers in order to find some private space for themselves and explore. Most of the crimes committed by young people are localized, less than half a mile from their homes. With urbanization and the clustering of the very poor and ethnic minorities on inner-city estates and in tower blocks where crime rates are higher, children grow up with reduced chances of a relatively smooth transition to successful adulthood regardless of their own individual family circumstances. In areas with high crime rates parents are often more distrustful, less forthcoming and inevitably mix less with local people. There are fewer resources such as local businesses, libraries, or safe outdoor spaces for children. Adolescents from impoverished areas are far more likely to drop out of school or become teenage parents. School drop-out often leads to delinquency and association with deviant peers. Gangs thrive and severely disheartened youth easily turn to drugs, which are more easily available in these areas. They are far more likely to be exposed to violence, which can harden young people at such a volatile and vulnerable age. Studies have found that witnessing violence is significantly associated with higher rates of depression and hostility, and breeds yet more violence as a short-term fix.[36]

Wider adult society fails to provide a safety net for young people who develop problems during adolescence. There are few refuges for teenagers who find life at home too much to bear and hostels are not allowed to admit those under sixteen. Counselling, therapy and drug treatment for adolescents are thin on the ground. Under-eighteens are not covered by adult drug-addiction treatment schemes and there are very few NHS in-patient centres for those with severe eating disorders. Twenty per cent of the population in the UK is under twenty, yet children and adolescents receive only 2 per cent of the mental health budget. One-fifth of poor children have been found to be mentally ill, yet substantial numbers of health authorities do not even have a policy for child mental health and there is a national shortage of child psychiatrists and therapists.[37] Those who need help usually have to wait months for their first appointment after being referred by their GP. Children with learning difficulties need to be 'statemented' before they can receive help and this bureaucratic procedure can be inordinately slow. But children slip very quickly from learning difficulty to disaffection and truancy, and once they have taken this route it takes a long and concerted effort to set them onto a more positive path. When child abuse comes to the attention of social services, they are often so short of accommodation that they have to leave the child at home, after telling the parents of their concern, which only lays the child open to more abuse for having 'told'.[38] All too often, troubled children have no one to turn to other than their parents, who are usually part of the problem, or their friends, who can offer immediate comfort but few long-term solutions.

Teenagers live in limbo, longing for adult privilege during a prolonged state of adolescence and economic dependence on their families. When they feel excluded from a world which flaunts its riches, nicking a mobile phone or a car instantly gives them status symbols of adult power. When they feel bored and undirected, joy-riding or violence feels real and thrilling. When they hurt inside, hitting someone else makes them feel better because all of the anger and irritation is somehow thrust temporarily into another human being. Shoplifting leaves a girl feeling full and powerful inside, as well as the proud owner of a garment she couldn't have afforded to buy.

Countless teenagers simply want money. Money is the one thing that will guarantee a better life, eliminate their impotence and guarantee the lifestyle that the media constantly tells them is necessary. I felt more than a little gloomy at the response when I asked Emma what she was going to do for her fourteenth birthday: 'We're gonna go to Harrods and pretend that we can afford to buy stuff, just look. Then we'll go to the cinema and try to get into a 15.' And her dreams for the future consist of materialism: 'I'd like all my clothes to be designed by Stella McCartney, a nice car, a nice house and be famous even though you can't buy it.' She dreams of going to the States and genuinely believes that life will be better there.

Each child locks onto a dream of escape. Fantasies of winning the lottery, becoming a star or travelling the world prevail and who can blame them when the adult society they are so eager to join has so emphasized the benefits of material gain. 'They are a bit silly about what they can do,' says Julie. 'Loads of girls in our school fall for those awful ads telling them to spend £250 on photographs so that they can be models. I've told so many, "Don't waste your money," but they say, "But I'm going to be in a catalogue." That's another £250 that they can't afford.'

Older generations lament the loss of old-style values amongst the young. But the rapid rise in the number of psychosocial disorders and crime amongst teenagers is in fact a sign that we, as adults, are failing children badly as they enter adolescence. At this highly vulnerable time they need greater investment in their welfare from society as a whole and more support from individual adults and parents if they are to stand the best chance of managing the pressures they live with now. They need their confidence enhanced so that they can develop positive ways of managing and expressing their anger. They need their personal skills honed so that they know how to introduce themselves to someone they have never met, so that they know how to negotiate or disagree with someone in a conversation, and so that they develop a sense of assertiveness. Adolescents need a sense of framework around them as so many of the certainties of childhood begin to disappear. They need quite clear boundaries to operate within and they need them constantly highlighted. Some create that framework visually through clothes, with the black cowboy hat and boots they always wear, or the uniform of a clique, defining who they are by association. I spent most of my adolescence hugging a full-length light blue velvet coat to disguise my discomfort with my rapidly changing body. Others define themselves within different frameworks – with the rituals of dope-scoring and joint-rolling, with obsessive control of their bodies through the rituals surrounding eating or not eating, or by the four rigid walls of their depression. 'All adolescents are extremely conservative,' says Adam. 'They need structure, they're desperate for the outline, for someone to say "no" to them. That doesn't mean they need a mindless authoritarianism, because they need to be encouraged to ask questions and have doubts and to hang on to the idea that your most priceless gift is being able to think and decide for yourself. But they do like the outline all the time, often on the most banal level. I set out the GCSE syllabus at the beginning of the year, but they will go on asking about this through the year with a kind of desperation, as if they were on the edge of a cliff and this was the rope. So you tell them again and again and there's this extraordinary relief when you do.'

Adolescents lack this framework from wider society. The law is unclear about where autonomy begins and true childhood ends. Sixteen-year-olds can win the lottery and pay emergency tax but they can't vote or claim state benefits until they are eighteen. The law says that sixteen-year-olds must be accompanied by an adult when they go to the doctor, yet 50–60 per cent of fifteen-year-olds go on their own.[39] Sexual intercourse with someone under sixteen is unlawful, yet doctors regularly dish out contraception to under-sixteens who are having sex and need protection. Sex may be legal for sixteen-year-olds but they can't go into an X-rated movie until they are eighteen. In some areas of Britain, under-sixteens need permission from their parents to have their body pierced, but in other areas everyone over twelve can puncture or tattoo their body without their parents' consent. Adults openly indulge in huge quantities of alcohol, yet it is proscribed in young people and while they are free to drink at home underage drinking in pubs is an offence. We also often transmit contradictory messages about values, encouraging the idea of

monogamous marriage and having children, when young
people confront a reality where nearly half of all marriages end
in divorce and other systems such as homosexual partnerships
and childless couples exist.

Modern Western society also offers little in the way of rites
of passage which give young people clear markers along the
path to adulthood and public recognition of their growing
status. Countless initiation ceremonies in pre-industrial societies around the world challenge adolescents with tasks, risks,
rituals and ordeals to prove their growing responsibility to the
community. Nelson Mandela describes in his autobiography,
Long Walk to Freedom, how he was circumcised at sixteen with
other boys of the same age. They were secluded in special
huts and all the villagers gathered there the night before the
ceremony for dancing and singing. During the circumcision
they had to shout, 'I am a man,' after their foreskin was severed
without anaesthetic, and not show pain. The boys were then
given new names and instructed to bury their foreskins that
night. They lived in the huts while their wounds healed.

At the end of our seclusion, the lodges and all their contents were
burned, destroying our last links to childhood, and a great ceremony
was held to welcome us as men to society . . . Though it was
forbidden to look back while the lodges were burning, I could not
resist. When I reached the area, all that remained were two pyramids
of ashes by a large mimosa tree. In these ash heaps lay a lost and
delightful world, the world of my childhood . . . Now I was a man
and I would never again play *thinti*, or steal maize, or drink milk
from a cow's udder. I was already in mourning for my own youth.
Looking back, I know that I was not a man that day and would not
truly become one for many years.

As Mandela acknowledges, it takes more than ceremony and
painful initiation to grow up. But without ceremony, tradition

or honour from the wider community symbolizing the para-
doxical losses and gains integral to any life stage, young people
find it harder to know whether they have crossed any sort of
border at all. Rites-of-passage ceremonies give young people
a clear, designated place within the community and firm
guidelines over their identity, their social roles and personal
boundaries. They involve the whole community, publicly
separating the youth from family, and give community elders
an opportunity to pass on secrets, skills and stories which
make young people feel honoured and included. Tribal people
confront the extremes of adolescence with extremes. They do
not try to avoid them as we do. The angry colours of red and
black are common in initiation ceremonies, as are leaping
dances, a sense of mystery, magic and spiritual solemnity. Tribal
societies 'waited until their children reached the intensity of
adolescence,' writes the anthropologist, Michael Ventura, 'and
then used that very intensity's capacity for absorption, its
hunger, its need to act out, its craving for dark things, dark
knowledge, dark acts, all the qualities we fear most in our kids,
the ancients used these very qualities as teaching tools.'[40]

Passing one's GCSEs or A levels doesn't exude quite the
same mystique or trigger any obvious major change in social
status, responsibilities or privileges. Exams are stressful, competitive challenges and results have to be earned but they are
not placed within a wider context of values or morality. Driving
lessons stand out in an adolescent's mind as a crucial step
towards independence. They have to learn in very structured
terms how to relate to other adults on the road, and passing
one's test offers a genuine challenge, a recognizable ticket to
adulthood as well as a licence for greater mobility. When
teenagers go on outward-bound courses or take driving lessons
they are forced to take risks in order to achieve a defined
objective. When they are challenged as adults, they behave
more like adults. When they are allowed to experience the

edge of danger within a controlled environment they are less likely to need to seek out that edge for themselves. 'I don't think of my A levels as an achievement other than that it shows that I was able to do it,' says Rebecca, aged twenty. 'I want to be someone who makes decisions for themselves and doesn't let circumstances carry them away. I also need to do things which I find frightening and would never imagine doing. I've always wanted to go on a boat trip round England and this summer I'm going to try and find a way of doing it rather than just to think it's practically difficult. That would make me feel stronger and as if I had really achieved something.'

In the Western world attaining adult status is an individual matter, borne alone rather than collectively, and something that tends to be bestowed with age rather than earned. Without clear rites of passage or a common sense of purpose, young people work out their own, through distinctive dress, tattooing and piercing. When they gather in gangs they devise their own initiation ceremonies for membership, such as becoming blood brothers, and they test individual courage. Sexual intercourse, that first cigarette, beer or puff on a joint are exciting, dangerous activities but they also signify monumental leaps into the adult world. Teenage pregnancy can also be seen as attempts at self-initiation in some respects, for motherhood gives young girls a profound sense of purpose and signifies maturity. With fewer guidelines and structures from wider adult society, adolescents have inevitably found the lure of strong organizations seductive. Hitler and Stalin capitalized on the adolescent need for structure with the creation of Hitler Youth and the Soviet Komsomol system. These organizations severed children from their families and made them feel adult. They harnessed youthful energy and gave it direction with simplistic answers to their uncertainties. Countless lost and undirected adolescents still latch on to the occult, cults such as the Moonies and Guru Maharesh Gi and new-age theories, for the security they give through simplistic, quasi-spiritual answers to life's conundrums.

We provide structure for adolescents through the timetabled routine of the school day but that isn't enough to ease them through what can be a prolonged and difficult transition. We need radical investment and change in the nature of education to meet the specific psychological and emotional needs of adolescents and to prepare them better for aspects of adult life in the twenty-first century. We need to include adolescents more in what goes on in the rest of society, rather than to warehouse them in schools until they are chronologically old enough to take part. They need to be consulted and involved with politics, institutions and their local community to build up their sense of purpose and trust. Young people have as good a sense of right and wrong as anybody else and often their political and social idealism makes them a great deal more moral than many of their apathetic elders. Yet this enthusiasm is not harnessed politically. Of those under twenty-five 43 per cent did not vote in the 1992 general election in Britain because they felt alienated, outsiders, and have learned through experience that politics has little to offer them. People under the age of thirty show markedly lower levels of trust in fellow citizens than do older age groups, and trust in institutions such as the police, parliament, the monarchy and the church is at an all-time low.[41] Trust in others and a sense of responsibility grow in children and young people who are trusted and respected.

When puberty is distressing or difficult, adults are at fault for failing to prepare children adequately. When self-doubt takes hold, adults are to blame for abandoning children at their most vulnerable stage, when wider adult perspective, insecurity and a sense of existential aloneness emerge. When there is large-scale educational failure and disaffection, adults are at fault for failing to equip young people adequately with the skills they need for a fast-changing world. When teenage boys release their aggression in violent ways, adults have failed to encourage them from an early age to express their emotions in other ways or failed to see how much they hurt inside. When teenage girls develop eating disorders or become over-anxious about the way they look, adults have created the world which young women aspire to succeed in, where beauty and thinness matter most. When teenage girls get pregnant because they think that it never happens the first time, or because they were too embarrassed to go to a clinic to get contraception, adults have failed to prepare them with adequate and open information about protection.

It now takes young people longer to mature into rational adults and to assimilate adult behaviour because there is so much more to growing up these days. The job of being a parent to teenagers has never been harder, simply because adolescence is tougher and longer and society fails to provide adequately for our young people. Parents have to find untouched and monumental resources of resilience and tenacity in order to fight through all the narcissism, the grumpiness, the intolerance, the negative peer pressure and the drug culture, at the same time as loosening the lead that connects them to home just enough to equip them with life skills without leaving them feeling bereft emotionally and without the boundaries they need at this age. It's a difficult balance and understandably many do not feel up to the job. Parents are blamed and blame themselves for every minor transgression their child makes, but the truth is that they cannot do it alone. Family life is integrally connected to and influenced by life outside, by the local economic and social environment, by cultural values, by the state of local schools and by the media.

All we can do is to fortify the human presence around teenagers so that there are more than enough friendly adults to support and guide them when the going gets tough. Just as the research of the past twenty years indicates factors which can damage a child's development, so too it can pinpoint influences for the good. All of the evidence suggests that when young people feel strong connections to adults they can trust, they feel protected from harm and develop better coping skills for stressful situations. When young people know that they have people they can turn to who will listen, who are interested in them, who will advocate on their behalf, love them and protect them, they are able to feel more secure in a precarious, changing present and feel some sense of confidence that their future may be bright. Loving, interested and involved parents are crucial, but so too is as wide a range of other interested adults as possible now that parents cannot provide all the answers. Aunts, uncles, grandparents, former nannies and babysitters as well as family friends can offer adolescents invaluable support and connection to the wider world, and their links need to be encouraged wherever possible.

Adolescence can be a difficult time for both parents and their children. When the foundations are strong, families are more likely to have an easier time of it. But if life has been less kind and parents experience great difficulty with their teenagers then they have to find the courage to seek out help from other adults such as doctors, friends and therapists. This does not mean that we are bad parents, or that we have failed, merely that we are moulded by life's circumstances and need the support of others to raise our children well. Most young people, mercifully, do eventually come out the other side relatively unscathed. Many of the parents I talked to who had experienced problems with their teenagers going off the rails, found that these problems ironed themselves out with time, or once their child had found a different framework to cling to. Ian's son, who refused to do his homework, argued vehemently with his parents and was expelled from a liberal school, responded better to the greater structure and discipline of an independent boarding school.

Gillian's daughter's anorexia began to wane after she dragged her to the doctor on false pretences. 'He gave her a very stern ultimatum, that if she didn't put on some weight by the end of the summer, we would all have to go into family therapy. But I also think that starting my job at the end of the summer and withdrawing a bit from her helped. I used to be so focused on what she was eating and whether there was any sign of change, but with this job I didn't have the time to think of her and that helped her slowly and gently to deal with it. Then in January she screamed with joy from the bathroom when she had her period again.'

Rosamund's son began to bridge the emotional divide with his father by working for him during the summer after his failed GCSEs. He then changed schools and found a new girlfriend. 'He's not stupid,' said Rosamund, 'he could see that everything could so easily go badly downhill. Things can go wrong very quickly and at the time you don't believe it, but things can get better quickly too.'

Antonia's niece, who left home after a screaming row at the age of fifteen, turned up on her aunt's doorstep a year later on her birthday with a giant pot plant. Antonia had been deeply worried about her. She had failed most of her GCSEs, been drinking and sleeping on a friend's floor. 'But she did it, she pulled herself up, got herself a job and sorted herself out and I'm very proud of her for that. She's done well for herself with only one GCSE. She's living at her boyfriend's parents' house and they clearly adore her. Now she's got nothing to feel guilty about or beholden for and in a funny way I now feel beholden to her because she bit the bullet and came back and my God that must have been difficult, but she did it and I respect that enormously.'

Adolescence can be a traumatic and difficult time for young people but it is grown-ups who have the power to make it better for them. Levels of distress are far higher amongst young people than they need be simply because adults often fail to see young people's difficulties as genuine or to give them adequate support. They are so desperate and needy, but it was Adam, a teacher, who managed to find the words to express just how vulnerable they are. 'It's terribly important for them to feel that there is a bulwark of human presences around them to support them through this particular period. I remember seeing a picture of walking wounded from the Somme arriving at Victoria Station and there were these awful figures with bandages over their eyes and lying on stretchers. We've got to see adolescents in that way because at their worst they are walking wounded and you have to see them through the condition and ensure that there will be one or two things that they can look back on without unhappiness or embarrassment during those teenage years, because it's a much less pleasant time for them than you might imagine.'

10. Leaving Home

I knew everything in this room, inside out and outside in. I had lived in this room for thirteen of my seventeen years. Everywhere I looked stood something that had meant a lot to me, that had given me pleasure at some point, or could remind me of a time that was a happy time. But as I was lying there my heart could have burst open with joy at the thought of never having to see any of it again.

Jamaica Kincaid, *Annie John*

Leaving home marks the beginning of the end of adolescence. For the young adult, it is an important rite of passage. The future now stretches out before them with the promise of opportunity, freedom and independence. 'I look forward to leaving, I wouldn't want to move far away but to have my own place,' says Karen, who is sixteen. 'I'd feel that I was more in control and didn't have to do what I was told so much. My parents treat me like an adult at home but it's just that you can't ever really grow up when you're at home.'

An entirely different set of mixed emotions surfaces, however, in the parents. There may be pride in their children's achievements, a sense of shared excitement at their future plans, as well as deep anxiety about their welfare when they go so far away from home to university or abroad for their gap year. There may be a deep sense that it is too soon for them to go: 'You can't go, darling, I haven't finished you yet,' one mother said to her eighteen-year-old son as he left. 'I kept on thinking things like, "We should have gone to the theatre or on holiday more, you don't know everything that you need to be on your own,"' says Imogen, whose eldest son had just left for South America in his gap year. The relief that comes with the freedom from responsibility sits uneasily beside a deeper sadness which feels close to a grief of surprising intensity. 'I was as upset at the prospect of him going as I was when my father was dying. I couldn't stop crying and would wake up at 5.30 in the morning in floods of tears, worrying about whether he was going to be all right when he was going to be so far away. It signals the beginning of the end of the family, you know. I've seen him almost daily for the past eighteen years and there's now this horrible awareness that when he comes back it will be different. I know this is a cut-off point and I feel as though it's never going to be the same again. No one ever told me it would be like this.'

After they have gone there is an eerie silence around the house. Their childhood bedroom still houses some of their least wanted things and their spirit still lingers. While the young adult looks forward unequivocally, the parent cannot help but look back. 'It feels like the end of an era, a bit like dying or going into an old people's home, and that life will never be the same again,' says Joan, whose eldest daughter is about to leave their home in Brighton to go to university. 'They're no longer here. They'll come home but it'll only be like an interval in their lives and you forget so much of the past. I don't remember them being small much, which is sad. I can't think what we did at the weekends; swimming, I suppose. I was watching neighbours through the window the other day, packing up to go down to the beach with their children. I haven't done that in years now and remembered how we used to do that when our girls were small, and go to the park. It just seems like such a long time ago now.'

Leaving home is perhaps the most assertive and sudden way of growing up, but it is not the only way. The most obvious indications of maturity include economic self-sufficiency and a stable sexual relationship, but feeling really 'grown-up' comes gradually from experience accumulated over time. It can take a great deal of practice with temporary flings before one finds a suitable partner. Young people spend years learning how to earn and manage money while they are being supported by their parents before they are grown-up enough to be financially self-sufficient. Knowing oneself properly is only possible after much soul-searching and experimentation. 'I wouldn't say I was grown-up, but I've come a long way,' says Tim, now eighteen. 'I've finished school and I'm a lot more independent than I was at fifteen, I drink and smoke a hell of a lot more as well. I also wouldn't have been able to have this conversation with you three years ago. I'm a lot more confident now.'

Freddie is twenty-six, lives in his own flat, earns a good living and has a girlfriend, but he still doesn't feel like a grown-up. 'I'm more grown-up than I was when I went to university, but I'm not really there yet. I don't have any responsibilities.'

Those who have to return home after graduation because they cannot afford independent living inevitably feel less grown-up, particularly when they are still uncertain as to what they want to do in life. Nick, who is twenty-four, travelled through America picking up casual work for six months after he finished university. He had to return home when his money ran out and now lives with his parents and has a permanent job. 'I feel grown-up because I've got more money now in my pocket and I could buy a car if I wanted to or even rent a flat, although that would cripple me financially. But at the same time I don't feel grown-up because I live at home and doss about too much and don't really know what I'm doing with my life, and that really worries me. I feel I ought to know by now.'

Young people grow up in some areas before others and those who have had a difficult time during adolescence, those who have stunted their development through drugs, depression or eating disorders inevitably take longer to mature. Just being old enough to look back on those experiences with some sense of perspective is a major achievement. 'I feel grown-up in relation to the way I was because when I talk to people who are younger I can see that I see things in a much broader way than they do. I also used to think that I was being really independent when I wasn't talking to anyone,' says Rebecca, who isolated herself with severe depression at fifteen and is now much happier with a boyfriend she really likes. 'But what really shows that you're strong and autonomous is being in a relationship and being OK with it, making it work because if there are weaknesses in you then relationships won't work. I don't feel completely grown-up yet. Sometimes I think I'm not twenty at all but younger. I still feel as if I'm not taking as much control of things as I should.'

'I feel a lot stronger now, more stable and I don't panic about things or cry and go bonkers so easily,' says Francesca, who was in a clinic for eating disorders for four months when she was sixteen, fell in love with a much older man when she was seventeen and feels she took far too many amphetamines. 'Sometimes I think I'm nineteen, how did that happen? But I do feel much more responsible now and controlled in general. I can control what I eat now and keep it down. I'm not such a party animal and I don't take drugs any more, so that feels like growing up.'

Just as it is hard to know where childhood ends and adolescence begins, so it is also hard and getting harder to know where adolescence ends and adulthood begins. They overlap and slide into one another, with young people maturing physically, emotionally, psychologically and socially at different times. They may be in an established and nourishing sexual relationship and working, yet still living at home. They may be taking responsibility for sick or disabled parents, or younger siblings while they are still at school and unable to earn a living. They may be old enough to vote and face prosecution in an adult court, yet they are still not necessarily equipped through the education system to support themselves by finding a job. Or they may be living away from home and earning a good living, but still lacking the emotional maturity to establish a lasting sexual relationship, or to separate effectively from the legacy of their childhood by establishing an equal relationship with their parents. The urge to be looked after and not have to accept the consequences of one's actions because one's parents are still there to shoulder them lurks ominously beneath the need to strike out and forge an independent path.

It takes our children far longer to achieve complete autonomy than it did for previous generations. The socio-economic climate in which they grow up helps to prolong the process. In the 1960s and 1970s jobs were far more secure, and housing relatively cheap. When teenagers of my generation left for university, they left home for good and a degree guaranteed a job of some sort. Now rising numbers have to return home after they have graduated and face the uncertainty and humiliation of unemployment. The vast majority now graduate with debts; they may have student loans of up to £7,000 as well as overdrafts and credit card bills to service and most simply can't afford the financial down payment for independent living. 'I've only had this job for six months and I've got a lot of debt, so financially it wasn't really viable to live anywhere else,' says Rupert, who has been living at home for the past year after finishing university.

'The older generation wouldn't consider wasting money on the kind of rents they charge now, particularly in London,' says Nick. 'They say get a mortgage but where are you going to get £5,000 to £10,000 as deposit? Where are you going to get a 100 per cent mortgage?' But Nick also admits that there are distinct advantages to staying at home. 'I'm living at home because I can't afford to live on my own in London. I'd love to move out. But it is easy living with Mum and Dad. You get your laundry done and a meal on the table and although I pay them some rent it's not that much.' Rupert's parents live in Islington. 'I like living here. All my friends are local and most of them are living at home too. Friends who have moved out are earning £250 to £300 a week. Half of that goes on rent for crummy rooms miles away from anyone they know and the rest goes on food and bills. I'd have to spend an extra £150 a week and move away from my friends all for a little bit more independence. When I get enough here it doesn't seem worth it. I've got a telly here, a fridge, a bathroom nearby and my parents hardly ever come up here except perhaps to say goodnight and this has to be one of the nicest bedrooms I'll ever have, so why leave it?'

Those who go straight to work from school are even less likely to be able to afford complete self-sufficiency away from home, for first earnings are considerably lower for those without a degree and cheap accommodation or state provision is scarce and getting scarcer. In 1970, unemployment in Britain was 2.5 per cent and most school leavers could go straight into a job or an apprenticeship. In 1987, one-third of school leavers were in full-time employment compared to just 8 per cent ten years later. The percentage of unemployed teenagers aged sixteen to nineteen rose from 13 per cent to 19 per cent between 1990 and 1997 despite higher educational achievement.

Young people have little choice these days but to stay at home, and many more now do so until their early twenties. Government legislation in 1988 exacerbated youth dependency on parents by withdrawing automatic entitlement to state benefits for most of those aged sixteen and seventeen. Single people under the age of twenty-five receive less housing benefit for accommodation in the rented sector (the only housing they have access to) than older people. This can have a crippling effect on their ability to find somewhere independent to live. Leaving home now is rarely a one-way process, with roughly half of all those who leave having to return. One study found that half of all men aged twenty-three to twenty-four and one-third of women of the same age were still living at home.[1] Britain's largest national annual survey, published as *Social Trends*, found that one in ten people aged thirty to thirty-four were still living at home in 2000. Similar trends have been found in much of the rest of Western Europe and the US. This dramatic shift means that parents and their children have to maintain good enough relations to be able to live under the same roof, which can be particularly difficult when parents quickly develop assumptions based on their own very different experience of adolescence.

Parents tend to expect their children to be out of both the nest and their hair long before they are actually capable of standing alone. They can feel as if they have failed to raise them adequately as independent beings, and do not know how much support to give to help them in the best way possible. Should they be doing more to force them out, and if they stay should they be paying rent or contributing more by doing the cooking or their own washing? 'I left home at eighteen and had a job and flats and travelled but it was easy then, although we didn't realize it at the time,' says Linda who has just celebrated her sixtieth birthday and has two daughters, aged thirty and thirty-one. 'So I guess you just have a pattern in your mind that that's what kids do, they go and then never come back but ours kept coming back. We weren't unsympathetic, however; it is very, very hard for them to set up on their own, particularly in London where rents are so expensive.'

'I didn't long to get rid of them because I enjoyed their

company,' says Mary, whose grown-up sons went to university in London and continued to live at home. The eldest finally left at the age of twenty-four. 'But at times I wondered whether this was going to go on for ever. When are they ever going to be bringing some money home? They said they couldn't afford to move out and of course they couldn't.'

Linda's elder daughter moved away from home when she was seventeen but then moved back in when she went to university as a mature student at the age of twenty-three. 'She used to come back with all her stuff in black bin bags most summers when she was at art school in Manchester, but then there was this one summer when she arrived with her boyfriend and then never moved out again. We kept thinking, they've got to go, but there they were, charming, sweet people to have around *but* . . . There was all this cooking at all hours, this mess all over her bedroom floor. It was more like living with lodgers than family life. You're supposed to want them around because they're your kids but actually you just want to push them out the door. When we were with friends, inevitably the conversation would come round to How to Get Rid of the Kids. I remember one friend said, "You just stop feeding them." But another couple we knew even went to the lengths of selling their house and buying a two-bedroomed flat so their girls had to go. I think they helped them financially to get their own place.'

'I found the peace and silence just blissful when they were both gone,' says Stephanie, whose elder son is now in his third year at university. Her second child is at boarding school doing A levels. 'I love it when they come back but there's a price. There's noise and the phone going constantly, and lifts to the tube station. Their friends come and stay and I'm delighted to see them but guess who has to do all the shopping and cooking? You get used to the silence and forming a new relationship with your partner and then they come back with their laundry needs, possibly some foreign parasite from their gap year, boyfriends and girlfriends, emotional problems, financial needs. I thought I might actually have some money this autumn, but no, it's never going to end it seems.'

Parents easily assume that when their children move back home after university they can simply move back to how things were before they left. But their children have meanwhile got used to living independently, coming and going as they please, and inevitably parental nags and gentle reminders provoke rows reminiscent of early adolescence. 'You have to renegotiate your perception of your authority,' says Stephanie. 'You try and re-establish some family rituals like Sunday lunch and you make it for four people and they never turn up. I was horrified to discover that his table manners had completely deteriorated while he had been away, eating with his fingers on gap year. Then of course when I pointed out that you don't eat risotto with a knife and fork the vehemence of his argument was overwhelming: "You don't have the right to tell me what to do." You feel suddenly diminished in your stature as an adult because you're now more or less on the same level and I can't direct him any more. You have to be far more tactful, stand back and find new checks and balances, new ways of still being a parent.'

'It was hard when they came back, particularly with the younger one,' says Linda, whose younger daughter moved into their cottage in Wales when she was eighteen. 'She smoked and we didn't and there'd be things like cleaning the riding boots on the kitchen table. I'd be thumping the table and saying, "Look this is our house and if I say I don't want smoking in the bedrooms because it's an old house with obvious dangers, I mean it." She'd then turn round and say, "Don't think you can tell me what to do. This is my house as well." Then you get into all those awful arguments of, "You don't pay board, you don't have a right to say this is your house." I would endlessly be saying, "Why don't you PLEASE leave home?" every time we had a row which was always about stupid domestic things.'

The novelist Isla Dewar described in the *Guardian* how her sons returned home after leaving for university:

While they had been fending for themselves, I had been discovering the joys of self-indulgence. I left the loo door unlocked. I could wander about in whatever state of undress I wanted. I could eat an apple for supper. But now, as they filled the house with their new lives, mine got shoved aside. Football roared on the telly. The rooms were filled with the bass thump of their music. I started wearing headphones. Friends and girlfriends came to stay. I was catering for the masses. For a few years, I had shopped for two; now I was heaping the trolley high again.

Like countless other mothers, Isla found that the teenage rows returned when she tried to assert her needs and had to negotiate and find new levels of tolerance as Mum once again. 'We came to new agreements. They helped with the laundry, the shopping and the cooking and were content to phone friends after six in the evening. I put up with the football. And I quite like Primal Scream anyway.'

Alice's eldest son moved back home after he had graduated from Sussex University. 'When he came back it wasn't very different from the way it was before. But I had to remember not to worry too much when he was out. As long as my children are living here I want to know where they are and when they are coming back but of course when he was not here it didn't worry me at all, it was totally up to him. So I had to learn how to bite my tongue and not say, "When are you going to be back?" and reckon that he was past all that. When he comes in from work he has a shower and I'm learning not to say, "We're about to eat," because he just wants a bit of space before he's ready to eat. He'll get something for himself later, and wash it up. But he will strip off all his dirty clothes and just leave them on the landing. So I still gather those up and stuff them in the washing machine.' Her son now has a good job in marketing. Alice and her husband supported him through university by paying for his accommodation plus an allowance and she is now happy to let him live at home without paying anything towards rent and food. 'I left home at eighteen when I went to university and never went back. I seem to remember that I had my fees and accommodation paid for and there was a small maintenance grant so my parents hardly had to contribute anything at all. But it's much harder for them now. So as long as he needs to be at home and help to shed that burden of debt, we'll give it. It would be mean not to.'

Adolescents also feel a mixed set of emotions over leaving home and having to return. Leaving for university or going abroad for their gap year can be exhilarating and eagerly anticipated but it can also provoke great anxiety and uncertainty. Teenagers often feel intense, conflicting emotions for the first time in their lives when they are forced to leave friends and lovers as they forge off on their own. Tim was a week away from leaving home for the first time to go to South America on his gap year when I met him for a drink. 'To be honest, I'm shitting bricks about going. I don't know what to expect, it's all so alien. I'm smoking more than I should be and that's not good. It feels like a giant countdown. I've never been away for so long before and now I've got this girlfriend and I don't want to leave her. I look at the second hand of my watch and think I'll never live that moment again and in a way I wish I didn't have a girlfriend because it would be easier to go.'

Teenagers often seem to regress before they leave home, and become argumentative or difficult as they face the prospect of leaving the security of their childhood for good. They need extra support at this time, in much the same way as they did when they started secondary school or sat exams. They really welcome regular contact – letters which chat merrily about life at home and reassure them that nothing has changed, small presents or extra cash when they least expect it and masses of encouragement and enthusiasm for their achievements when they telephone. Rebecca left home for Paris during her gap year, first as an au pair and then to study French, but found it a very lonely experience and the depression she had lived with earlier in her adolescence resurfaced. 'There weren't any people I liked in my classes and I put on a lot of weight so I wasn't happy about that. I also didn't get as much out of Paris as I should have, so I was mostly on my own and the same thing happened – I didn't take control of things and use the time there, I just got sucked into being unhappy. The best time was when Dad came out for a weekend and we did things together, and then coming home was good, it's so much easier here.'

When they settle away from home and make friends at university, teenagers genuinely spread their wings for the first time away from parental monitoring, and that is often liberating and enabling. 'You have the best time,' says Nick. 'You meet the best people, you get your independence and it gives you the excuse to go out and do a lot of drinking.' There are no sanctions any more, no one to answer to and countless students discover the space to think and drift and grow up that they were denied at school because of the pressures inherent to the exam system. 'Leaving for university was exciting,' says Rupert. 'I didn't find the thought of actually going nerve-wracking but it was only when I actually got there that I realized that I would have to stand on my own two feet and that took some getting used to. At school you'd get a timetable on the first day but at university you have to compile your own timetable. You have to sign up for things like the computer school in order to learn how to use them and look after your own deadlines. You have to join the library and learn how to use it because it's fifty million times bigger than the one at college. You have to get insurance for your room in case someone breaks in. You have to do the shopping every week. I went to uni with a fork, knife and spoon, a little bag of food and one bag of clothes and there were all these other people arriving with boxes of things and I thought, why have they got all this stuff? Then I realized that you have to set up home here and that's fun.'

Leaving university and the security of the education system for the big wide world can be a daunting experience. When young people have to return home to their parents after years of independent living and being close to their friends, they can feel a sense of failure, as if this is somehow a regressive step back into childhood dependency. 'I'd like to be living on my own because it's oppressive here, it's too sort of safe and like home and you can easily fall into the trap of letting your parents do things for you and not taking responsibility,' says Rebecca. She felt that she had to return home after her first year at university in London because her parents live in London as well and had paid for her to live out in halls of residence and she feels guilty about taking more money from them than they can spare. 'You want to move out and be more independent but actually moving out makes you more financially dependent on your parents because they have to shell out more, so you're actually helping them out by staying at home.'

'It was weird coming back and not seeing my friends day in day out, and going back into that home thing of being back in time for dinner and phoning to say when you're not going to be back,' says Nick. 'Sometimes when you've had a hard day all you wanna do is come in, chuck your bag down, slouch in front of the telly and not talk to anyone but that's not possible with Mum around asking questions like, "How was your day?" And because it's family, people take things out on each other. If my dad's in a mood he'll take it out on me. If I've worked hard all week I want to lie in at the weekends but he's always on about getting up and getting on with things. When I went on holiday there were all these comments and jokes about how I could stay in bed until eleven o'clock there but what business is it of theirs if that's the case? No matter how old your kids are, parents are going to be telling them things but when you're still living at home you can't avoid it.'

Francesca moved out for six months at the age of seventeen to live with her older boyfriend in his flat and then had to move back home when the relationship ended. She had been earning her own money in bars and then as a stripper to pay her college fees of £1,000 a term and found the whole thing very hard going. 'I panicked really because I was working so hard, studying all day and then I'd go to the pub and work there until closing time for £22 a shift. My boyfriend wanted me to pay towards the rent as well and I thought, what am I going to do? I can't live on this money and I'm too tired, I can't study at night and I'm too tired to concentrate during lessons. Then when I went back home I was livid for a bit at having to move back and having to ask them for money when I had been earning my own. I was really furious, I'd throw it back into their faces when they gave me any saying, "I don't want your money, I don't need it," and then they'd slip it into my bag. I felt they were invading my independence but now I will take any help I can get because I know how tough it is out there.'

It stands to reason that if more young people have to stay at home for longer, more are also going to have to leave suddenly when levels of conflict become unbearable. The Children's Society estimates that by the age of sixteen, one in ten children will have run away for at least one night, with those from single parent homes, stepfamilies, adoptive families and foster homes tending to leave at an earlier age than those with both biological parents at home. Many of those who run away repeatedly or never return home are fleeing from physical violence, sexual abuse or extreme hostility from parents or step-parents. They are likely to end up on the streets when there is nowhere else for them to go. The charity Centrepoint, which provides temporary shelter for young people at risk, has seen a steady rise in the numbers of the young and vulnerable coming through its doors in recent years. Their physical health is generally poor and they are twice as likely to suffer from psychiatric disorders as those who have not been homeless. The adolescents sleeping on the streets today are reminiscent of the street children, the Artful Dodgers, of Victorian times. But today's runaways are emotional rather than economic migrants, seizing independence with both hands in order to escape violent, unloving or abusive parents, and in search of other sources of support. They leave home as a means to grow up, rather than as a consequence of having done so. When home life is really bad, young people will do anything to get out. They will shack up with someone just because they have their own place. They will squat, living in appalling conditions or take to the streets. 'For the first time in my life I was part of a society that accepted me for myself, with people who'd look out for me if anything went wrong,' says Beverley who, having been sexually abused by her father, ran away repeatedly from the age of twelve. 'The street brings people together and you look out for each other. Nobody else will.'

Claire moved out when she was fifteen because her father had been beating her up for years. 'I feel I can get on better with my family if I'm not actually living with them. I miss my mum, my brother, the cat and the fish. We have a huge house, a big garden, two cars in the drive, but I'd rather be on the streets than living at home. That says a lot.'[2]

Some teenagers are kicked out by their parents after huge rows, when their levels of tolerance are pushed to breaking point. Others leave abruptly after arguments when they cannot stand their parents' bickering or their hypocrisies any longer, or when their choice of friends or lovers arouses such hostility from their parents that they feel they have to leave in order to be with them. They feel a burning urge to get away when relations with their parents are bad and are unlikely to improve, or when they are simply sick of the relentless tedium, the constant sameness of life at home. Leaving home should never be a dramatic, sudden severing of relations. True independence is not snatched suddenly in one moment, but gained gradually over the years within the family home, as children begin the inexorable process of learning how to fend for themselves. When young people leave home by running away in the dead of night, or after a screaming row, they are running away from difficulties or a level of familial conflict that they can no longer bear.

Francesca left suddenly when she was asked to leave and handed a suitcase to pack by her parents. They really didn't like the fact that she was in a relationship with a thirty-one-year-old man and forced her into a position where she had to choose. 'The atmosphere was awful at home, screaming rows all the time, sometimes we screamed until we couldn't speak. Every day there'd be something, just walking into the kitchen to get a cup of tea and they'd be swearing at me saying he was a dirty old man and I was a fool. I didn't know how to make it right at home apart from leaving him, which I wasn't going to do. They couldn't handle it so they kicked me out and made me choose between him and them and said they never wanted to see me again. They were trying to scare me and they didn't mean it, but it did hurt badly. At the time I had an African grey parrot who was like my best friend in the whole world and they wouldn't let me take him with me. So a week later I broke in when they were out and took him anyway.'

When my mother asked me to go and live at my father's when I was seventeen, I felt an overwhelming sense of relief at being granted the licence to leave. The rows and misunderstandings had become so entrenched that it was better to go, and leaving gave me greater independence and a sense of autonomy. However, in hindsight it would perhaps have been better if our relationship had been less confrontational during my adolescence. A gradual severing of relations is always better than leaving abruptly after major rows and conflict. Young people need to be able to retain respect and affection for their parents in order to be able to leave without guilt or blame. And I felt masses of both, unable to return or visit without feeling a sense of burden.

It may seem like something of a paradox, that keeping them close must hinder their development as individuals and that they have to be eased out in order to learn how to stand on their own two feet. But adolescents develop their own sense of identity and individual way of doing things from their sense of belonging to family and place. They need to feel able to come and go and that their family home is there for them as long as they need it. The most wayward, argumentative adolescents who are hard to live with tend to be the ones who most need the framework of a stable family life around them. When things get really difficult, leaving temporarily for a gap year or a summer travelling with friends helps to ease relations and equip teenagers with essential life skills. 'You grow up a lot during your gap year after being in school for so long with all that routine,' says Amanda, who is eighteen. 'You have to structure your own day and find work.'

'We were having some really big rows before he went off to India at the end of university,' says Mary. 'But maybe that was just because there wasn't enough space between us. We'd been cooped up together in this flat while he was at university and his going away rejuvenated everything and it was much better when he came back.'

Young people need the support of family around them for far longer than previous generations simply because they are growing up in a more complex, pressured world and it takes longer. 'I love living here,' says Rupert, who has been back at home after university for a year. 'I suppose by moving back I have allowed myself to become slightly less emotionally tough, but I like having the safety guard of knowing that Mum, Dad and my brother are around. I like coming home because it's secure. Last year's been quite a struggle, not having a job, coming back from uni, everything changing, so I'm probably not emotionally ready and certainly not financially ready. I'd have more fun with friends and stuff if I moved out but the pitfall would be that I wouldn't be as stable as I'd like to be at this point of my life. I don't have the structure of education any more and I'm not sure whether I want to make a career of marketing yet and push at it for ten years. I'm using home as my source of stability at the moment so that even if I didn't have my job I'd still be fine. It gives me more options like travelling, trying for other jobs, or saving for a down payment on a flat. Plus this is the time when I can live at home so why not enjoy it?'

When young people feel able to leave and return and that home is a stable place from which to break free, they are much more likely to move towards a more balanced and adult understanding of their parents, which is yet another sign of maturity. 'It's more like being friends with my parents now,' says Rupert. 'It's almost like being a lodger although that's too unfamiliar but I have so much freedom that I can get on with my parents rather than feeling that I have to battle with them. I have friends who've moved back home whose parents think they can recreate the old family ways again with Friday night dinners and stuff. Then it's just an immediate battle with the kids out of the house as much as possible and the parents resenting it with, "You just treat this place like a hotel." Sometimes I have the odd frustrating, "When are you coming home?" but so long as you manage it OK that's fine. I say when I'm going out and I love coming home. It's nice to see Mum and Dad, plus there's all those little luxuries like getting fed and all your clothes coming back clean and ironed. Wow!'

'It's a step forward to be able to live with your parents and be OK with it,' says Rebecca. 'But what's really important to me is being autonomous and that would show I was really strong if I could be autonomous and still live at home. It's a bit ridiculous to think that you can't be grown-up just because you're still living at home.'

'I feel I understand a lot more about my parents and their relationship and that's another way in which I feel more grown-up,' says Tim. 'Before, they were just my parents, now I can see how they get on. I spent a week last summer driving round France camping with the old man and that was brilliant because we really talked about things. I can go out for a drink with my mum or my dad now and really talk about adult things. When you're a teenager it's really all about you and they're just your parents who get in the way but now I see them more as individual equals, we get on better and that makes it easier for me to leave.'

When Francesca's relationship with her older boyfriend ended, she had no choice but to return home but now finds the atmosphere and family relations so improved that she plans to stay there while she is at college studying drama. The boyfriend had behaved very badly, and 'cheated on me, so I was able to tell them how awful he was and they were shocked and very supportive. Before when I was living at home my parents would always want to know where I was going and what I was doing and I'd be like, "UUGH, please shut up and leave me alone, I can look after myself." But since I've been back they've got used to me being my own person. They've had six months of not knowing what I've been doing and my mother won't even ask me now and it's quite funny really because sometimes I feel quite offended by that. "Don't you care about me or where I'm going?" I never ever thought that I'd actually appreciate my parents being like that. My whole outlook is completely different.'

If young people are still based at home through their late teens and early twenties, they are more able to look back over their adolescence and understand how hard things must have been for their parents. It means they can resolve some of the crises of their adolescence before moving on. 'I've got a lot more respect for them now,' says Francesca. 'They were right all along about the boyfriend and they were very concerned about me, it must have been awful for them. I had long pink extensions, piercings everywhere and was taking speed and then this older man shows up. They were right about everything really, except for the medicine thing, that's where they slipped up, expecting me to be a doctor. It's great being at home now, my friends are always welcome and I'm really lucky. Lots of people don't have parents as understanding as they are.'

'I do feel sorry for my parents now for the way I was,' says Rebecca, who suffered from severe depression in her mid-teens. 'I thought they didn't know but obviously they did and it must have been awful for them, knowing that I was feeling so bad and that I didn't want to talk to them. I didn't think of anyone else at all, it's a very selfish way of being, depression. I didn't want anyone to reach me. I didn't want anyone to scoop me up. I also thought that no one knew that I was cutting myself. Now I've discovered that they knew about that too and that must have been awful for them as well.'

Parents also begin to notice a genuine shift in their children's attitudes when they are still living at home. They become more considerate and helpful as they get older. 'I'm still Mum, but I'm more of a friend now as well,' says Alice. 'But every now and then I sense that things are beginning to shift the other way around in that he looks after me. He'll say things like, "Don't worry, Mum, I'll do that." If I'm going out he'll ask if I'm going to be all right, or "Are you driving or taking a taxi home?" This year, for the first time in ages, we're having a big family holiday. We've taken a house in France and Rupert is hiring a car and driving down to stay with a friend for a few days before going on somewhere else. That feels quite grown-up, he's coming because he wants to and doesn't feel he needs to prove anything.'

However hard it may be for parents to have their children living at home as young adults, it is now an essential and typical aspect of family life. You haven't failed as a parent if your children still want to be at home at twenty. You have succeeded in making their home a place they still want to be, where they feel able to shelter as they slowly accumulate the emotional and psychological skills essential for healthy adult life. Stephanie, like countless other parents, has found that her children still display typical adolescent reactions of recalcitrance and rebellion and still need guidance over basic aspects of personal hygiene and some of the social and emotional ramifications of having a love life even though they are twenty-two and nineteen. 'Trying to teach a ten-year-old about bad breath is pointless but it really matters when you're nineteen. They still need us around, we have a moral imperative to find new ways of being a parent. They don't have that ease and confidence yet that comes from being truly adult. But it is easier in some ways because they can discuss things in a more adult and less obvious way now.'

Our children are always our children, however old they may be and if this is what they need growing up in today's socio-economic climate, then this is what we, as parents, have to provide. It means adjusting our attitudes to living with adolescents and accepting that they may display typical adolescent behaviour at times through their early twenties. It means finding new and more respectful, adult ways of relating to our children with new contracts formed by mutual consent over cooking, clearing up, washing and whether or not they pay rent. And it means giving up aspects of our home for their benefit, treating them as if they were adult lodgers, welcoming their friends and lovers in order not to make the experience of having to live at home more humiliating than it need be.

Times have changed. We have to support our children emotionally, practically and financially in whatever way we can for far longer than we were ever supported at their age. Old-style notions of the short sharp shock, where the young are kicked out in order to fend for themselves, and are denied any form of financial assistance so that they have to provide for themselves, are no longer appropriate or helpful. 'I'm not ready to move out,' says Rupert, aged twenty-two. 'I'm certainly not ready financially and probably not emotionally either because this last year has been quite a transitional period. I've just lost the whole of the education system and don't have any other structures around me.' His mother teaches at a university and sees the consequences of lack of parental support because students are now supposed to be 'adult'. 'I have students who work all the hours they can to pay their way because they get no support from home at all. Some work so hard to support themselves that they have to miss lectures and fall behind with their essays, which defeats the object of the exercise. Some of the parents of those I teach have no idea what's going on in their child's life. There's the Eton end with stacks of money and the other end where there's no money and the parents are out working all the time. But at both ends of the spectrum they're not there for the kids, and that's what they are often, still kids.'

In many ways we have come full circle and returned to earlier pre-industrial aspects of family life, where young people stayed dependent on their families well into their twenties until they were fully able to support themselves. This extended adolescence can help mitigate the feelings of sadness and loss that so many parents find painful as their children grow up, for they never actually go completely, but leave for longer and longer periods before they come home again. Leaving anything, whether lovers, friends, jobs or schools, is hard for human beings. Saying 'goodbye' to a stage of one's life arouses mixed emotions of excitement and fear, loss and regret. Leaving home and moving away from the daily protection of parents is a monumental step for young people and the whole process of adolescence prepares them psychologically, physically and emotionally for it. Parents also experience intense emotions of sadness and loss as their children get ready to fly from the nest, but these are not sudden, new emotions. They accumulate gradually over the spectrum of a child's life. From the moment the umbilical cord is cut, parents begin the inexorable process of letting go, through weaning, teaching them how to feed themselves, or holding their hands as they learn to walk. Then there is starting nursery, sleepovers with friends, that first school trip and moving to secondary school, long before parents contemplate the prospect of life without them around at all. Every parting lays the emotional foundations for what is to come. You have to let them go so that they will want to come back.

'Letting go happens on so many different levels,' says Helen, a single mother with a fifteen-year-old son. 'I think about how it will be when he goes and I'll have to let go of the most important intimate relationship in my life, and I'll have no safety net.' As we begin to let go of our children we have to find other ways to fill the gaps in our own lives that they leave in their wake. Gillian has four children between the ages of twelve and eighteen. 'It was such a major rite of passage to have no children at primary school any more. The next big leap will be when they've all done A levels and then I think I'll have had enough. Well, I hope it'll feel like that rather than sitting here mourning the loss of something. If you have to mourn, perhaps you haven't made the most of it. You can't regret the passage of time because that's a fact and if it's the emptiness, the fact that they leave, well, fill it up with something else. If it's the fact that you're growing old, well, you do. I may think differently in eight years' time, but there is plenty of time to prepare for it.'

Parents do not lose their children as they grow older provided that they do not antagonize or alienate them, or hold them so close that they have to fight or flee to the furthest corners of the world in order to get away. When parents and their children are more at ease with the continual changing nature of family life and parents accept their child's growing autonomy, adolescence tends to be easier to deal with and relationships deepen and eventually become more equal and satisfying. 'It's got better and better since they were small,' says Mary. 'As they've got older, they've become human beings. They're intelligent and interested in things, we discuss things and they're quite politically aware which I'm pleased about. It is different to a conversation with a friend because you can go further with them. With friends you temper your conversation and hold a bit back because you don't want to hurt their feelings unnecessarily, but with my boys I can get to the bone of things and know that it'll never come to the point when they won't talk to me for the rest of their lives.'

When parents accept and tolerate the gradual and inexorable parting of the ways and yet still manage to find the strength not to show that it hurts and to make their teenage children feel welcome, they continue to bring aspects of their lives home. Some things now are always secret and rightly so, but others are generously shared. 'It goes back to this business of feeling that home is a safe enough place to take risks in, knowing that no matter how awful you are you're still loved. I still feel that with my own mum and dad,' says Karen. As teenage children grow older they bring home aspects of the world outside that parents would never encounter otherwise and make life more interesting. The dinner table becomes a meeting ground of multiple realities provided that young people feel welcome there. With something constructive to offer on both sides, they nourish each other, with parents able to offer the wisdom that comes with hindsight and their children able to challenge prejudice or presumptions with fresh insight.

'I'm glad it's over. The journey took a long time and on the way I lost my youth,' writes Polly Devlin in her autobiography *Only Sometimes Looking Sideways*:

The people I have back are amazing individuals. I am no longer the oracle or the nerd, the diviner or the know-nothing, neither the solution nor the problem. Now I'm a person they love. But where once I went ahead and they followed, now I follow in their footsteps, an old page-girl to their young Wenceslas. I have all the time in the world and all the space I could need. But I want them back.

Others fill the gap left by their children leaving with simple pleasures. 'When the youngest one left for Zimbabwe, I didn't have a sense of loss, just a sense of being really pleased for him and that it was time for him to go,' says Mary. 'Then when the eldest one went off to India I was living on my own for the first time in my life because I went straight from my own parents' home to married life. I loved it, I felt like a new person, reborn! I used to cook the most wonderful meals just for me, all the things that my children never liked.'

And those like Gillian, who miraculously find that they are still in a loving relationship after decades of tending primarily to the needs of their young, can find that there are new depths of experience to explore within that relationship: 'I was fifty in January and we went on holiday for two weeks on our own. It was wonderful, away from children and work and money problems and it was just so easy to be together again. And I thought, this is all right, we can do it, we will carry on where we left off because there is still enough dormant there to be explored. The children have been such a great intrusion in our relationship that we haven't had enough time just to be alone together. We will go walking, or look at pictures together and he was telling me about his work which normally he hasn't got time for and I haven't got the time to listen to. There isn't much time to do things leisurely with a family of six and that's something I look forward to, immensely.'

'It takes a while to get used to not having the kids around so much but we now have these amazing walks together up on the Downs. We take a picnic and look for orchids. We just have a lovely time together as a couple,' says Flora.

Linda agrees. 'Nobody warned us about this but I remember we both had this sudden realization of, "We're free!" We were only in our fifties and suddenly we understood that we could do whatever we liked all over again, just the two of us. We could make choices without having to think about the kids and that was just a brilliant moment.'

Writing this book has been far more painful for me than I ever imagined it would be. I set out to understand the nature of adolescence so that I might be better prepared for the years to come with two teenage daughters and for the inevitable hurt that their rejection might provoke. But by seeking ways of being a better parent I also revisited aspects of my own childhood, perceived it in new ways and know myself a little better.

Every single presumption I have had about the nature of adolescence has been challenged during these years of intense research and writing. I know now that adolescence is not some mad, uncontrollable monster that takes hold of the innocent, perfect child but an essential crucible of human development, which equips young people with all of the intellectual, physical and emotional skills necessary for successful adult life. It is not sudden, either, but builds gradually provided that the foundations laid through childhood are solid enough to take the load. The kind and sensitive child remains kind and sensitive beneath the essential solipsism of adolescence. Carefree, cocky and amusing children will retain that basic outlook in spite of the mixed emotions and sudden glooms of emerging adult perspective, provided that they are allowed to mature at their own pace and are supported through emotional difficulties. 'They are very much who they always were, exactly the same people,' says Gillian who has four teenage children. 'Only more so as they grow older because they are getting to know who they are and where their strength lies. But then our lives have been really stable with no unemployment or divorce. We've always lived in this house and schools have been fine so they have had this rather gentle passage through a very happy childhood.'

I also understand now that adolescence need not be impossibly difficult for parents and their children provided it is handled well, with parents continually reminding themselves that they are the grown-ups and that teenagers, however big or capable they seem, are essentially children with a profound need for love, support and guidance. The vast majority of young people grow up into adulthood through a haphazard adolescence, nudged or blown by circumstance, with coincidence determining much of their future careers, friendships, relationships and paths. Adult life is rarely planned, things usually happen to people, as John Lennon once said, 'when they are busy making other plans'. It is this shift between the structured order of family life and education, and the random nature of real life, complete with risk, danger and uncertainty, that young people and their parents have to come to terms

with. Most make it through and take much of their adolescence with them because it is such a vivid, exciting and
spiritually liberating time, when true friendships and first love
affairs are first formed, when the sensuality of the body is fully
explored, when parents are first seen as individuals with their
own strengths and weaknesses, and when one's own unique
sense of self takes shape. But as the world changes in faster and
more complex ways, huge chasms of misunderstanding have
emerged between generations. The most damaging modern
myth of all is that teenagers need to be misunderstood, for this
excuses adults from fulfilling their responsibilities to the young.
Adolescents need to be misunderstood just enough to safeguard
their privacy and sense of emerging autonomy. But that split
between generations should never be allowed to grow so wide
that it becomes a ravine that parents cannot cross to reach their
children, for then the young merely feel abandoned. Then
they feel lost within a world in which they have no place and
cannot master, and they seek out other emotional props which
are potentially far more damaging than parents.

I have been reminded of the sheer emotional fragility of
growing up through countless conversations with teenagers.
Many were so lost and unhappy I wanted to take them home.
Others were lucky enough to ooze a social self-confidence,
but all of them tussled with the vast and complex nature of the
modern world and their tiny place within it. Young people
grow up now within an extended adolescence, still dependent
in some measure and uncertain as to who they are and what
they want from life until their late twenties or early thirties.
They take longer to grow up because they face far more
complex pressures, expectations and demands from education,
the media and family life than those faced by their parents
when they were young. They also have to contend with a
whole new range of risks and temptations. As modern life
becomes more complex and changes with such speed that few

of us recognize the world that our children are now growing up in, it is more important than ever to remember our own difficulties of growing up and to talk to our children so that we understand theirs. With so much uncertainty generated by the swift pace of change, young people need a firmer framework of support and guidance around them. They need better education about sex and drugs from an early age to prepare them for the riskier years of adolescence. They need greater discussion, intellectual challenge and empathy to help them make sense of the world they inhabit. Young people need to be trusted more and considered in stereotypes less. They need to grow up within a modernized education system which truly has their best interests at heart. They need far more emotional support than many usually get from either the state or adults in general for the increasingly common traumas of childhood – family breakdown and the formation of new families, the effects of poverty and unemployment, loss, bereavement, neglect or abuse.

My elder daughter is now in early adolescence and much of what I have researched over the past four years is coming to life in my own home. Most of my fears for her future and mine have been laid to rest because of this book. I no longer fear the rifts and separations of living with two teenage daughters, I feel ready for them, equipped with greater understanding as to the reasons why they might say or do all those things that teenagers say or do. When my daughter is emotional or devious I stand back and question why. When she is angry with me I refuse to take it personally, questioning instead why she might be feeling so angry with herself. I now understand that teenagers need structures, a surround that seems to contain them within family life while everything else changes and I am not afraid of providing that scaffold for as long as they need in order to grow up strong and well. I also understand that when teenagers fight, flout parental authority or embark on self-destructive behaviour these are often ways of seeking out those boundaries for themselves, just as younger children scream and whinge for attention. I do not expect the worst in the years to come but should there be difficulties I will deal with them, hopefully with enough strength to resist the indulgence of guilt or self-blame, and with enough speed to safeguard my daughters' best interests. Young people need a strong sense of separateness between their world and that of their parents, which means that I have to resist burdening them with my own feelings of guilt, anxiety, anger, frustration and loss as they grow up. I have to grow stronger and wiser as they grow older, to shoulder the slings of insult and rejection, and find other sources of emotional support, and other things to do. But perhaps the most important lesson of all is not how to deal with the years to come but to make the most of the times we have as a family now, for I too have that sense that there are only a few years of complete togetherness left. So we will take all those holidays that we probably can't afford for those memories and those photos. We will indulge those dreams and fulfil some of those silly fantasies so that we all have something precious to look back on.

Childhood does not vanish completely with adolescence. Teddy bears share beds with boyfriends. Mementoes from friends, photographs and even the odd toy sit cosily on desks and shelves beside ashtrays and bank statements. Childhood and adolescence linger on into adulthood and we all carry around with us those memories for the rest of our lives. Our experiences of childhood and adolescence determine who we are as adults and that is where the unexpected pain of writing this book lies for me. I have wrestled with a few childhood ghosts and feel wiser, older as a result. With greater self-awareness I feel more able to sever my life story from that of my daughters. With two happily married parents my daughters are growing up in a far more stable family unit than I enjoyed, and there is far more love, understanding and fun alongside all the normal squabbles and turmoil of family living than I felt I had as a child. Their adolescence will never be a repeat of mine, but their own entirely, and my fears that they might repeat my self-destructive path are more than likely groundless. 'What the troubled adolescent is often up against is some failure of resolution in the adolescent development of their own parents,' says Andrew Cooper, Professor of Social Work at the Tavistock Centre in London. We are all guilty of this weakness in some measure, for growing up, true growing up takes most of us more than a lifetime. Perhaps it is only by looking deeper into ourselves as our children grow that we can lay those ghosts to rest and prevent ourselves from repeating the patterns of the past and so become better parents. I now feel more up to that task.

Appendix 1
Physical and Sexual Development During Puberty

Contrary to myth, puberty begins at approximately the same time in both boys and girls, usually between the ages of ten and fourteen. Sperm production and menstruation begin at approximately the same age. However boys and girls follow two distinctly different paths of physical and sexual development which leads people to believe that girls mature earlier than boys. Girls develop visibly earlier with breasts and greater height occurring at the beginning of the pubertal process while boys tend to have their growth spurt towards the end when their genitals have reached near-adult size. Other obvious physical signs of masculine maturity, such as muscles, extensive facial hair and a deeper voice, also tend to happen nearer the end of puberty.

Puberty is divided into five stages. Stage one is the undeveloped child. Stage five is full sexual maturity. From the age of about eight, the pituitary gland begins to pump rising amounts of sexual hormones to the sexual organs of both boys and girls, even though the child still looks physically like a child. In stage two, the breasts begin to bud in girls and the scrotum begins to enlarge in boys and there may be a few wisps of pubic hair in girls. In stages three and four the genitals in both sexes enlarge and grow darker in colour. Pubic hair grows thicker and curlier in girls and begins to appear in boys from stage four. Each child moves through these stages at slightly different speeds. Some develop a mass of pubic hair or pendulous breasts very quickly. Others seem to take for ever to grow at all. It can take anything from just a year to six for children to mature but the average appears to be about four years.

Girls

The first sign of puberty in girls is usually a sudden growth spurt which occurs at a mean age of 9.6 years, six to twelve months before breast budding. At its peak the average growth rate is 7.1 cm per year for girls. After this growth spurt, which rarely lasts more than a year, growth slows down again to 1–3 cm a year. Most girls reach their full adult height within one to three years after their first period.

Breasts begin to bud and may hurt, and there may be a few wisps of pubic hair, although in one-fifth of girls the appearance of pubic hair occurs before breasts swell. The vulva matures; the outer lips get fleshier and may touch each other. The inner lips grow and become more noticeable and may protrude beyond the outer lips. The whole area becomes darker in colour and moist. It takes approximately four to four and a half years for breasts to mature fully. First menstruation occurs in stage four, usually about two years after breasts have begun to grow, and after girls have done most of their growing in height. Some girls begin menstruating earlier and that is perfectly normal, but if a girl begins to menstruate before she has begun to develop breasts at all then she should see a doctor. Sometimes girls worry when they notice a little whitish fluid coming from their nipples. This is normal, the body's way of keeping the ducts open, but if the colour gets darker then that might be a sign of infection and needs medical attention. Vaginal discharge is also likely to appear one to two years before first menstruation but if that becomes a much darker colour, itchy or particularly smelly then that too may be a sign of infection and needs medical attention.

Girls can accept these changes more easily if they understand that there are reasons for all of them. Pubic hair, larger fleshier lips to the vagina and regular discharge protect that vulnerable and important area from infection, just as eyelashes do with the eyes. A little extra fat around the thighs and bum is all part and parcel of becoming a woman, for a certain amount of body fat is essential for menstruation. With puberty girls need to understand the importance of regularly examining their breasts for lumps (breast cancer is very rare in teenagers but getting them into the habit now may just help to save their lives with earlier diagnosis as they get older). Vaginal self-examination should also be encouraged so that girls can see and explore their own changing genitals. This is crucial to healthy adolescent sexual development but much simpler for boys to achieve when their genitals are external and far easier to see and get hold of!

Boys

In stage two, the testicles get larger and the scrotal sac begins to hang lower and become looser and more wrinkly. Often boys and their parents fail to notice that this has happened because the changes seem so slight. The penis is still the same size and there is rarely any pubic hair until boys reach stages three or four. The scrotal sac usually begins to change colour too at this stage, growing more reddish in fair-skinned boys and darker in others. In stage three the penis begins to get bigger as well and one testicle may hang lower than the other one, usually on the left. This is so that the testicles are not crushed against each other during walking. Boys are capable of sperm production between the ages of twelve and fourteen, long before they have achieved their main growth spurt and reached stage five. Boys may start their growth spurt later than girls but they grow taller, faster. At its peak the average growth rate for boys is 9 cm a year. By the age of fifteen, the average boy is heavier, taller and stronger than the average girl of the same age.

During early puberty 50–85 per cent of boys notice changes in their breasts. They develop tender swellings under the nipples which get wider and darker but these usually disappear within a year as production of testosterone accelerates. They are not turning into girls or developing cancer. Boys also worry about being wimpish and small but it takes far longer for them to reach adult masculinity. The average healthy boy reaches 91 per cent of his adult height at fourteen, but only gets 72 per cent of his total muscle mass at this age. It takes four more years to reach just 91 per cent of his adult value.[1] Many men don't develop their full beard until ten years after they have completed puberty and reached their full adult height.

Physical Development

It isn't just the sexual bits that change and develop during puberty; the entire physical being of a child is affected. The heart doubles in size, increasing blood pressure. The lungs expand to fill their widening rib cage and some scientists believe that the brain also has a growth spurt with a 5–10 per cent increase in size.[2] The body doesn't grow uniformly during puberty. The head, hands and feet reach adult size first, followed by the arms and legs, giving teenagers that gangly, awkward look. Feet tend to grow most at roughly nine years, hands at ten and arms at twelve. Teenagers can be very clumsy during early adolescence. Their hands, feet and limbs easily get in the way of things when they are changing so quickly and have yet to assimilate these new physical attributes mentally. Shoulders widen in boys and hips widen in girls after the limbs have stretched, and the final part of the body to lengthen is the trunk. Interestingly, a girl's pelvis is not affected by the initial growth spurt in the rest of the skeleton and follows its own slower pattern of development, reaching full adult size at the age of seventeen or eighteen. While adolescent girls may be able to get pregnant, they are not physically at their prime for reproduction until this late stage. Adolescent girls have a higher percentage of spontaneous abortions, complications during pregnancy and low birth weight babies with higher rates of mortality across rich and poor countries.

Bones become denser and harder through puberty and the skin becomes rougher particularly around the upper arms and thighs. There are subtle changes to the face too, as it becomes more angular and less childlike and chubby. The forehead becomes higher and the lower part of the face gets longer as the chin juts forward more. The mouth widens and the lips become fuller. Muscles grow too and both sexes discover a marked increase in their physical strength and endurance. The average teenager puts on about ten pounds a year between the ages of ten and fourteen, and body weight can double between the ages of ten and eighteen.

There is a marked increase in bodily hair in both sexes. Hair darkens and grows thicker on limbs and begins to appear under arms and facially on boys. Some girls also grow a fine down on their top lips and may find the odd hair on their breasts. Glandular activity increases too with oilier skin and increased perspiration under the arms, in the groin area and on the palms and feet. This does settle down towards the end of adolescence and there should be no need for deodorants or antiperspirants provided that teenagers wash with soap once or twice daily, eat healthily and remember to change their socks. Perspiration also increases because of anxiety and teenagers have numerous things to feel nervous or worried about. Sometimes just acknowledging that you are feeling anxious when your palms get sweaty helps to minimize the sweating. If young people feel that they have to use anti-perspirants to raise their confidence socially then that is understandable, but it is worth pointing out that these substances block pores and the natural pheromones which contribute to sexual attraction, provided that they are not so overpowering that they repel. The deodorants that should be firmly discouraged are the vaginal ones, for they interfere with the natural chemical balance of the vagina and irritate it. Healthy vaginas are moist with a mild and arousing smell and girls need to understand that this is not only normal but essential for a healthy sex life.

Appendix 2
Common Health Problems

Diet

Teenagers living through such rapid growth are in great need of a healthy balanced diet. They need extra protein and iron to build muscle, and calcium to build bones and strengthen teeth. They also need a great deal of carbohydrates for energy. Yet all too often it is in these years that eating patterns alter radically and can affect their health. In the US and Canada 11 per cent of girls aged eleven to fourteen and 14 per cent of girls aged fifteen to nineteen are iron deficient, weakening their immune system and impairing their mental abilities as a result. Of American children aged six to seventeen, 35 per cent already have two heart disease factors and 42 per cent have raised cholesterol.[3]

Teenagers easily slip away from the family meal table and eat on the run or alone, bunging something in the microwave when they get in. Girls in particular skip meals such as breakfast, crash-diet because they are worried about their weight gain and then fill up on the empty nutrition of junk or snack food. Food in secondary schools is often lamentably bad, a self-service selection where children help themselves to chips rather than fruit and vegetables. Fast-food outlets, processed food and microwaves have altered Western eating habits and had a profound effect on adolescent health, for teenagers are keen to assume control over their own bodies and one major step towards greater autonomy is determining what they eat, when. Children are fatter and less fit than they were just twenty years ago. Metabolism, the rate at which calories are burned, drops by about 15 per cent in adolescence. This drop, combined with the general rise in the consumption of snack and junk foods as well as the substantial fall in exercise levels, has led to startling levels of obesity and the foundations of ill health.

During this time of rapid growth, young people should have, ideally, six portions of starchy foods such as rice, bread, potatoes and pasta, five portions of fruit and vegetables, and two portions of dairy and animal or vegetable protein per day. Salt, caffeine and canned sugary drinks can interfere with the absorption of calcium from their diet. A fresh orange before a meal ups the absorption of iron, calcium and other minerals because of its high vitamin C content. Building up stores of iron through diet and natural supplements such as Floridix is essential for girls before their periods start and then subsequently as menstruation settles into a regular pattern.

Healthy eating habits are established in early childhood with plenty of fresh fruit and vegetables, home-prepared food rather than convenience or processed food, and sugar or junk snacks considered treats rather than daily fodder for those energy lows. However, there are things that parents can do to help their teenagers eat well once they begin to spend less time eating at home. Breakfast is usually a meal they are there for and can be made more substantial with tasty fruit, pancakes or omelettes. Keep the fridge, freezer and cupboard stuffed with healthier grazing food that is easy for them to prepare when they eat without you, and leave plenty of fresh fruit on the kitchen table. Establish regular family feasts where you all eat together and their favourite dishes are provided, and make sure their friends are welcome as well.

Acne

Eight out of ten teenagers suffer from mild skin problems during adolescence and they are most common between the ages of fourteen and seventeen. They are not caused by bad diet or too much chocolate as the myth suggests but because oil glands work overtime during this period and produce excess amounts of an oily substance called sebum. Sebum helps keep skin soft but too much can clog the pores and cause blackheads, white heads or spots when the pore becomes infected. Black-heads are not dirt clogging the pores, but sebum which turns black when it comes into contact with oxygen. White heads form when sebum gets trapped below the surface of the skin. Most teenagers have problems with these but when they get serious trouble with spots it is called acne. Oil glands are situated all over the body but they are particularly numerous on the face, neck, back, shoulders and upper chest, and conse-quently acne can develop in all of these places, not just the face. Stress can also provoke acne and many teenagers find that they develop lots of spots just before an important or anxious-making event such as exams or a date.

Spots cannot be completely prevented but certain habits will help to keep them to a minimum. Frequent hair washing will prevent extra oil from adding to that on the skin, and daily washing will help remove excess oil and unplug pores. Washing with hot water helps to open the pores and rinsing with cold helps to close them again. Chemists sell several types of facial washes for teenagers which can be helpful in severe cases but must always be tried on a small section of skin first in case they produce an allergic reaction. They contain strong abrasives which remove skin as well as oil and have been known to lighten the skin of black teenagers. In very severe and prolonged cases of acne, young people should be encouraged to visit their GP who can in turn refer them to a dermatologist who can provide more individual and specific help. Spots are a major source of unhappiness to many teenagers and need to be taken seriously rather than dismissed.

Growth Pains

Approximately one in five young people experience aches in their shins, calves or thighs. These pains usually happen at night and can wake them up but only last for a few minutes. These pains can be alleviated through massage, deep heat treatments and hot-water bottles or in extreme cases with painkillers.

Menstrual Problems

Menstruation may be discussed more openly today than it was a generation ago, but large numbers of young women (and men) are still not adequately prepared with the full facts. They pick up snippets of information from friends, television, sex education classes and their parents but often still find the reality of menstruation upsetting and disgusting because it is still a taboo subject. Studies show that large numbers of girls are deeply excited over the prospect of having periods before they have started because menstruation represents such a major rite of passage to adulthood. However, when those periods actually start, confidence levels plummet and negative feelings soar because the reality is so often different to the scant, two-dimensional descriptions they have been given. Adults often think that teenage girls become more moody when their periods start. In actual fact, adolescent girls usually tend to be far more moody, vague and volatile before their periods begin. It is the slow adjustment to life as it now is – the embarrassment of buying or secreting sanitary towels in their bags, anxieties over leaking in public, feeling unclean and that everyone knows they are having their periods – which makes them feel more ugly, more self-conscious and less confident.

Menstruation is viewed in the West as a private 'hygienic crisis' rather than celebrated as an important event. It is often referred to euphemistically as 'coming on' or negatively as 'the curse', and tampons and sanitary towels are shoved to the back of the bathroom cabinet. Menstrual blood is considered dirty and associated with other bodily waste while male sperm has far more powerful and positive associations. Research shows that early maturing girls who have not discussed puberty with their mothers are far more likely to view the onset of menstruation as negative.[4] They need to be made aware of the fact that their entire physical being can be affected by their periods, not just their genitals, and that there may be discomfort such as tender breasts, stomach ache, headache, feeling bloated and shifts in energy levels.

Mothers in particular can help their daughters understand the way their bodies are changing by talking openly about their own menstrual cycles. Girls need to be encouraged to keep track of their menstrual cycle in a diary or calendar so that they know when their periods are likely to happen and can chart their energy levels. It helps young girls a great deal if they understand that if they are feeling particularly lethargic, emotional or unwell that is because they are about to menstruate and not because there is something else wrong. Hot-water bottles, pampering, sofa beds in front of the telly can help when young women feel particularly sore or down. They also need regular reminders that exercise, good diet, plenty of sleep when they are feeling pre-menstrual as well as extra fluids help to minimize the more negative aspects and raise their spirits. Accepting menstruation is part and parcel of accepting womanhood, and we can do a great deal to help young girls cross that threshold by encouraging them to take care of themselves emotionally and spiritually in addition to managing the more obvious practical aspects.

Depression

Adult mental health problems such as schizophrenia and Bipolar Disorder often first appear during adolescence and it is also a time when various psychiatric conditions can change. Adolescence, for instance, is when autistic children are most likely to develop epileptic fits for the first time.[5] General depression is rare in young children, but as the mind matures, pressures increase and young people have to adjust to all of the physical, emotional, social and psychological changes described in this book. Understandably many feel down or depressed at times. When teenagers just feel down they can be helped a great deal through friendships, participation in activities such as sports or hobbies which encourage positive rather than negative feelings, and having a trusted adult around who they can confide in. But sometimes this is not enough and clinical depression sets in, resulting perhaps from a family history of depression or difficult aspects of childhood such as bereavement, divorce, failing to achieve something, or deep regret over something they have done. Entrenched, clinical depression rarely disappears by itself.

Recognizing depression in teenagers can be difficult because adults expect teenagers to be moody and emotionally unstable. Adolescents can also present a range of symptoms which adults don't necessarily recognize as typical depression. They may be bored and restless, always searching for new sources of stimulation in an attempt to avoid feeling anxious or empty. They may be constantly 'wiped out', needing ten or twelve hours sleep a night and still feel exhausted in the morning.

They may be complaining of headaches and stomach aches or have difficulty concentrating at school. They may reject people completely and isolate themselves or, conversely, dread being alone and panic when parents are late home from work.

But it is even harder for teenagers to understand that they may be depressed when they have never felt this way before, and they need adults to discuss their problems seriously and to show support. Five or more of the following symptoms, according to the National Mental Health Association, may indicate that there is depression, particularly if they last for more than two weeks:

- depressed mood for most of the day, tearful, sad or irritable
- poor performance at school
- withdrawal from friends and activities
- sadness and hopelessness
- lack of enthusiasm, energy or motivation
- anger and rage
- overreaction to criticism
- feelings of being unable to satisfy ideas
- poor self-esteem and guilt
- indecision, lack of concentration or forgetfulness
- restlessness and agitation
- changes in eating or sleeping patterns
- substance abuse
- problems with authority
- suicidal thoughts or actions

Depressed teenagers need prompt professional help, they can't just 'snap' out of it. If their depression is not recognized, discussed and supported at home, with outside help if possible, depressed teenagers easily seek escape from their feelings through drugs, alcohol or sex and increased risk-taking. They can also be rash and impulsive when it comes to suicide.

They have no idea that a small dose of paracetamol or barbiturates can be lethal.

Therapy and medication are the two main treatments and if GPs are slow to refer or families cannot afford private help, some organizations such as the Tavistock Centre in London operate self-referral schemes for adolescents so it may help to phone around.

Adults, particularly parents, find it hard to believe that adolescents could be so depressed that they would contemplate taking their own life. However, any expression of suicide, of 'I wish I were dead' or 'You'd be better off without me' must be taken seriously. Adults may think their children's negative interpretation of their life is unrealistic, but from the adolescents' point of view it is a sign that they feel so desperate that they have exhausted all other options. It is indeed a cry for help and one that has to be heard.

Researchers have identified four factors which place an adolescent at risk of a suicide attempt: being under stress, particularly at school or in romance; living with family conflict or disruption such as unemployment, serious illness, relocation or divorce; a history of suicide in the family; and emotional problems such as depression or substance abuse. The more risk factors, the higher the chances of a suicide attempt. Preoccupation with death in music, art or writing, making a will or giving away prize possessions, loss of interest in personal safety or a series of 'accidents' are distinct warning signs as are all of the other symptoms of depression listed above which have to be taken seriously.

How parents react to suicide attempts is crucial. Parents are often so shocked and outraged that they get angry or even ridicule the adolescents for causing so much trouble by trying to draw attention to themselves. Such a reaction will only distance the teenagers and may even provoke them into trying harder to kill themselves the next time. Instead parents have to swallow their anger, their own guilt and sense of self-blame in order to reach out and show concern for their children's problems and a willingness to examine the attitudes and events that led to the suicide attempt. Such support and under-standing, with constructive ideas as to how to change things in future for the better, will help those children to approach their problems more constructively and to embrace the need for counselling or therapy.

Suicide attempts seem to have a viral quality to them, they can spread and infect other vulnerable young people. So if a young person at school has killed himself or herself, or is known to have attempted suicide, then it is imperative that parents discuss the reasons or the problems openly with their teenagers.

Drugs

In order to be effective at drug education, parents need to familiarize themselves with the drugs that are available, their effects and the patterns of drug use amongst the young. When young people drink or experiment with drugs, the vast majority fall into the categories at the beginning of the fol-lowing list. However, if young people also have emotional problems at home or at school and parents are not monitoring their children closely, they can swiftly move up the scale to addiction:

Non-users – hate the idea of polluting their bodies or losing control over their minds and never plan to use drugs.
Experimenters – try the occasional drink or joint but don't really like the effects.
Recreational users – will indulge socially but won't buy drugs them-selves and are unlikely to try anything stronger than drink or cannabis.
Regular users – actively seek drugs by buying their own. They party

and socialize most weekends, frequently get drunk or stoned and may take or consider taking stronger drugs such as cocaine or ecstasy. But they do still care about their school work and what their parents think of them and try to limit their drinking and drug-taking so that it does not affect the rest of their lives.

Abusers – extend weekend activities to every evening or afternoon. They may drink or get high by themselves and use these depressants or stimulants as a means of escape. They may lose interest in activities that they used to enjoy, skive off from school, use harder drugs and steal from their parents or sell drugs to pay for them. When young people are using drugs habitually and relying on them in this way they are usually lying to themselves as well as their parents, pretending that they do not have a problem and that they could stop if they wanted to.

Addicts – use drugs just to feel normal and neglect other aspects of their lives such as personal appearance, education, and they cease to care what other people think of them.

Inhalants and solvents

Inhalants are one of the first drugs that children try. Glues, cleaning fluids, aerosols, petrol, correcting fluid, paint, nail polish and room fresheners can induce feelings of power, euphoria and excitement when they are inhaled directly into the lungs. But they also produce blurred vision, slurred speech, streaming eyes, stomach pains, breathing and circulation difficulties, a buzzing in the ears and clumsiness. They can also kill, and solvents contribute to more deaths among those under twenty than any other drug. These are highly toxic chemicals and never intended for human consumption. They can cause long-term damage to the organs and nervous system. Death can even be caused by a sudden rush of adrenaline to the heart because some inhalants make the heart more sensitive to adrenaline. Paint stains on fingers and mouth, excessive vomiting and watery eyes may be signs of paint spray or inhalant abuse. Long-term effects are short-term memory loss, emotional instability, cognitive impairment, loss of sense of smell. These are dangerous poisons which are easily available to young people and should be locked away if possible. Children need to understand how dangerous these chemicals are, and that they can cause death.

Cannabis

Cannabis is now widely available, on almost every street corner. It is smoked usually with tobacco and comes either as a grass-like substance, or as a darker lump, and is known by a variety of names including dope, draw or weed. Short-term effects are euphoria, relaxation, breakdown of inhibitions, impaired coordination, increased appetite and the giggles. Too much can induce trance-like states, stupor and panic. Excessive consumption may reduce motivation, create panic or anxiety attacks and paranoia. There may also be short-term memory loss, particularly of new information, which can continue for several weeks after last consumption. The long-term effects of continued, excessive use are not known but may be associated with psychosis, infertility and heart and lung disease.

Ecstasy

Ecstasy is commonly known as E and is a form of amphetamine – Methylenedioxymethamphetamine (MDMA). Short-term effects include increased alertness, excitement and euphoria, dryness in the mouth, tingling skin and an increased heart rate. The drug can increase emotional and sensual feelings and heighten sexual activity but it can also cause erectile failure in men and delay orgasm in both sexes. It can also cause disorientation, clumsiness, nausea and vomiting, and the subsequent hangover can enhance underlying depression. Ecstasy works by releasing massive amounts of the chemical serotonin in the brain. The latest medical research on animals and humans shows that repeated use kills the parts of nerve cells that release serotonin, and we don't know when or if recovery occurs. Young people should also be made aware of the fact that they can never know what is really in the tablets they are buying – they could be horse tranquillizers. The massive release of serotonin can raise body temperature and the small number of deaths from ecstasy appear to have been caused by excessive rehydration, drinking too much water to quench an insatiable thirst.

Hallucinogens

Hallucinogens alter the way a person perceives the world, thinks and feels. Effects can last up to eight hours and include hallucinations and increased energy; colours intensify, vision, hearing and touch are distorted. LSD (Acid) is not an addictive substance and has not directly killed anybody but long-term use can cause flashbacks, intensify psychosis, depression and paranoia in those who are predisposed to these conditions and it can give people 'bad trips', with panic attacks and heightened anxiety. The most dangerous hallucinogens are PCP, Ketamine and the belladonna alkaloids, because they affect the organs as well as mental function and can kill.

Amphetamines

'Speed' or 'uppers' usually come as tablets or as a powder which is frequently mixed with other non-drug substances such as glucose or milk powder. The drug reduces appetite and the need to sleep and increases a sense of alertness. Amphetamines raise blood pressure, cause rashes and can lead to tooth decay. They also reduce calcium levels and can cause liver damage and malnutrition with long-term use. Speed is highly addictive, with users needing to up their dose and suffering withdrawal symptoms such as depression, fatigue and sleep disturbances which can last for weeks.

Cocaine

Cocaine raises a general sense of well-being and alertness in users but the effects usually last less long than those associated with amphetamines, unless, as is often the case, the drug is cut with speed. The need for sleep and food is also depressed. Excessive amounts can produce sweating, dizziness, irritability, a dry mouth and trembling hands, and blood pressure can rise enough to produce a stroke. Cocaine is highly addictive and long-term use can lead to damage of the nasal septum (the drug is usually sniffed), impotence, heightened anxiety and risk of infection with AIDS if the drug is injected.

Narcotics – Heroin, morphine, opium, methadone

Heroin comes in the form of an off-white or brown powder which can be smoked, sniffed or dissolved and injected. With opiates pain and anxiety are reduced and the pupils of the eyes are constricted. With larger doses the user becomes sleepy, the cough reflex is suppressed and breathing is depressed. Blood pressure falls and the entire metabolism slows down. Narcotics are highly addictive and one overdose can cause convulsions and death. It is important that young people understand that these drugs are strictly controlled because they are so addictive and dangerous, and that when they are used medicinally their purity is monitored. The drugs on sale on the black market are almost always heavily cut with other substances which could in themselves be extremely dangerous.

Appendix 3
List of Organizations

General

Trust for the Study of Adolescence
23 New Road, Brighton BN1 1WZ
Tel. 01273 693311
www.tsa.uk.com
 Researches and promotes adolescent concerns with a wide range of publications and conferences.

National Children's Bureau
8 Wakley Street, London EC1V 7QE
Tel. 020 7843 6000
www.ncb.org.uk
 Undertakes research, provides information through its information service as well as seminars and training.

Bereavement

Child Bereavement Trust
Aston House, High Street, West Wycombe, High Wycombe, Bucks HP14 3AG
Tel. 01494 446648
Information and support line: 0845 357 1000
www.childbereavement.org.uk

Compassionate Friends
53 North Street, Bristol BS3 1EN
Tel. 0117 966 5202
www.compassionatefriends.org
   Nationwide self-help organization.

Cruse–Bereavement Care
Cruse House, 126 Sheen Road, Richmond, Surrey
TW9 1UR
Tel. 020 8940 4818
Bereavement line: 0845 758 5565

Winstons Wish
The Clara Burgess Centre, Gloucestershire Royal Hospital,
Great Western Road, Gloucester GL1 3NN
Tel. 0845 2030405

Bullying

Anti-Bullying Campaign
185 Tower Bridge Road, London SE1 2UF
Tel. 020 7378 1446
www.bullying.co.uk
   Gives telephone advice to parents and children.

Depression and Mental Health

British Association for Counselling
1 Regent Place, Rugby CB21 2PJ
Tel. 01788 578 328
www.bac.co.uk
   For advice and information about local practising counsellors.

Childline

Royal Mail Building, Studd Street, London NW1 0QW

Tel. 020 7239 1000

Helpline: 0800 1111 (24 hours, 365 days)

www.childline.org.uk

For young people who want to talk to a trained counsellor. All calls are free and confidential. Also provides leaflets and books for parents and professionals.

Institute of Family Therapy

24–32 Stephenson Way, London NW1 2HX

Tel. 020 7391 9150

Clinical service for families experiencing problems including those posed by adolescence.

Mental Health Foundation

20–21 Cornwall Terrace, London NW1 4QL

Tel. 020 7535 7400

www.mentalhealth.org.uk

PAPYRUS (Prevention of Suicides)

Rossendale GH, Union Road, Rawtenstall, Rossendale BB4 6NE

Tel. 01706 214449

Parents for the prevention of suicide.

Relate: National Marriage Guidance

Herbert Gray College, Little Church Street, Rugby, Warwickshire CV21 3AP

Run education courses for schools and other groups of young people whose parents are separating or divorcing.

The Samaritans
Helpline: 08457 909090
www.samaritans.org
24-hour telephone helpline for those who feel desperate or suicidal.

The Tavistock Centre
120 Belsize Lane, London NW3 5BA
Tel. 020 7447 3781

Young Minds
102–108 Clerkenwell Road, London EC1M 5SA
Tel. 020 7336 8445
Information service: 0800 018 2138
www.youngminds.org.uk
   Aims to raise awareness about the emotional and behavioural problems of children and young people.

Youth Access
2a Taylors Yard, 67 Alderbrook Road, London SW12 8AD
Tel. 020 8772 9900 (9.30 a.m.–4 p.m.)
   For addresses of nearest counselling or advice centres for young people.

Drink

Accept
Tel. 020 7371 7477
   Advice and support for individuals and their families.

Al Anon/Alateen Family Groups
61 Great Dover Street, London SE1 4YF
Tel. 020 7403 0888
   Alateen provides support for teenagers with alcoholic relatives.

Alcoholics Anonymous
Tel. 020 7833 0022 (10 a.m.–10 p.m.)
www.alcoholics-anonymous.org.uk

Drinkline
Helpline: 0800 917 8282 (9 a.m.–11 p.m. Mon–Fri; 6 p.m.–
11 p.m. Sat–Sun)
  National helpline with information about local groups.

National Association for Children of Alcoholics
Helpline: 0800 289 061

Drugs

ADFAM
Waterbridge House, 32–36 Loman Street, London SE1 0EE
Tel. 020 7928 8898
Helpline: 020 7928 8900
  Offers information and confidential support to families of
drug users.

Crimestopper Snap – Say No and Phone Campaign
Tel: 0800 555111 (freephone)
www.crimestoppers-uk.org/snap.asp
  Nationwide crimestopper campaign which you can call
anonymously if you know someone who supplies drugs or
commits crimes.

Drugscope
32–36 Loman Street, London SE1 0EE
Tel. 020 7928 1211
www.drugscope.org.uk

National Drugs Helpline
Tel. 0800 776600 (freephone)
    24-hour, 365 days a year, confidential service available in English and other languages offering information, advice and counselling.

Release
388 Old Street, London EC1V 9LT
Advice line: 020 7729 9904 (10 a.m.–6 p.m. Mon–Fri)
24-hour emergency line: 020 7603 8654
Drugs in Schools: 0345 366666 (10 a.m.–5 p.m. Mon–Fri)
www.release.org.uk
    Confidential service for legal problems over drugs. Offers emergency help.

RE-SOLV: The Society for the Prevention of Solvent and Volatile Substance Abuse
30a High Street, Stone, Staffordshire ST15 8AW
Tel. 01785 817855
www.re-solv.org
    Produces teaching materials that encourage young people to resist experimentation.

Eating Disorders

Eating Disorders Association
1st Floor, Wensume House, 103 Prince of Wales Road, Norwich NR1 1DW
Helpline: 01603 621414
Youth Helpline: 01603 765050 (4 p.m.–6 p.m. Mon–Fri)
    Helps and supports all those affected by anorexia and bulimia.

Education

Advisory Centre for Education
Aberdeen Studios, 22–24 Highbury Grove, London N5 2EA
Tel. 020 7354 8321 (2 p.m.–5 p.m.)
www.ace-ed.org.uk

Campaigns for changes in state schools in order to make them more responsive to the needs of pupils and parents. Provides free advice and information.

National Confederation of Parent/Teacher Associations
2 Ebbsfleet Estate, Stonebridge Road, Gravesend, Kent DA11 9DZ
Tel. 01474 560618
www.ncpta.org.uk

Promotes partnership between pupils, parents and teachers, home and school.

Family Life

Contact a Family
170 Tottenham Court Road, London W1P 0HA
Tel. 020 7383 3555
www.cafamily.org.uk

Brings together families whose children have disabilities. Advice for those who want to set up a local support group.

Children's Society (Church of England Children's Society)
Edward Rudolf House, Margery Street, London WC1X 0JL
Tel. 020 7841 4400
Enquiries: 020 7841 4436

Publications, information packs; also runs family centres and social projects.

Dial UK

St Catherines, Tickhall Road, Doncaster DN4 8QN
Tel. 01302 310123
www.members.aol.com/dialuk/index.htm

Telephone advice lines and drop-in information service for people with disabilities and their families or carers. Call this number for details of your local branch.

Divert

33 King Street, London WC2E 8JD
Tel. 020 7379 6171
www.diverty.org

Works with young people at risk and runs mentoring schemes.

Family Rights Group

The Print House, 18 Ashwin Street, London E8 3DC
Tel. 0207 923 2628
Advice line: 0800 7311696 (1.30 p.m.–3.30 p.m. Mon–Fri)
www.frg.org.uk

Advice and support for families whose children are involved with social services.

Family Service Units

207 Marylebone Road, London NW1 5QP
Tel. 020 7402 5175

Nationwide support for families with problems.

Gingerbread

16–17 Clerkenwell Close, London EC1R 0AA
Tel. 020 7336 8183
Advice line: 020 7336 8184

For advice and local support groups for one-parent families.

Invalid Children's Aid Nationwide

4 Dyers Building, Holborn, London EC1N 2QP

Tel. 08707 777444

www.ican.org.uk

Free help and advice for parents with disabled children. They specialize in speech and language disorders.

National Association for Gifted Children

Elder House, Milton Keynes MK9 1LR

Tel. 01908 673677

www.rmplc.co.uk/orgs.nagc/index.html

For support groups, advice and information.

NCH Action for Children

85 Highbury Park, London N5 1UD

Tel. 020 7226 2033

www.nchafc.org.uk

Runs family centres, specialist services for children with disabilities and their families, as well as a unique network of child sexual abuse treatment centres.

National Council for One Parent Families

255 Kentish Town Road, London NW5 2LX

Tel. 0800 0185 5026

Information service for lone parents.

NSPCC

42 Curtain Road, London EC2A 3NH

Tel. 020 7825 2500

Helpline: 0808 8005000 (24 hours)

www.nspcc.org.uk

Parentline Plus

(incorporates Parentline, The National Stepfamily and Parent Network)

Unit 520 Highgate Studios, 53–57 Highgate Road, London NW5 1TL

Tel. 020 7209 2460

National Helpline: 0808 8002222 (9 a.m–9 p.m. Mon–Fri; 9.30 a.m–5 p.m. Sat; 10 a.m.–3 p.m. Sun)

www.parentlineplus.org.uk

Runs very effective short parenting courses and a helpline.

Parents Anonymous

Manor Gardens Centre, 6–9 Manor Gardens, London N7 6LA

Tel. 020 7263 8918

Telephone counselling service.

YMCA Parenting and Education Support

Dee Bridge House, 25–27 Lower Bridge Street, Chester CH1 1RS

Tel. 01244 403090

www.ymca.org.uk

Develop locally based initiatives to help parents. Have set up a 'dads and lads' club session where fathers and sons come together to participate in sporting activities.

Gambling

Gamblers Anonymous

Tel. 020 7384 3040

www.gamblersanonymous.org.uk

GAM CARE

Tel. 0845 6000 133

Helps young people who have a gambling problem.

Health

Acne and Rosacea Support Group

1st Floor, Howard House, The Runway, South Ruislip, Middlesex HA4 6SE

Tel. 020 8841 4747

   Support and advice to sufferers.

Blackliners

Unit 46, Eurolink Business Centre, 49 Effra Road, London SW2 1BZ

Helpline: 020 7738 5274

Enquiries: 020 7738 7468

www.blackliners.org

   Advice, care, practical help and emotional support on issues relating to HIV/AIDS to people of Black African, Asian and Caribbean origin.

National Aids Helpline

Tel. 0800 567123 (free and confidential, 24 hours)

NHS Direct

Tel. 0845 4647

www.nhsdirect.nhs.uk

Terrence Higgins Trust Helpline

Tel. 020 7242 1010 (12 p.m.–10 p.m.)

www.tht.org.uk

   For advice and information on HIV/AIDS.

Women's Health

52 Featherstone Street, London EC1Y 8RT

Tel. 020 7251 6333

Health enquiry line: 020 7251 6580 (9.30 a.m.–1.30 p.m. Mon–Fri)

Sexual Health

Brook Advisory Service
165 Grays Inn Road, London WC1X 8UD
Tel. 020 7284 6000
Helpline: 020 7617 8000
Young people's helpline: 000018203 (free and confidential)
www.brook.org.uk
   Counselling and advice service.

Family Planning Association
2–12 Pentonville Road, London N1 9FP
Tel. 0207 837 5432
Helpline: 020 7837 4044 (9 a.m.–7 p.m. Mon–Fri)
www.fpa.org.uk
   Information on all aspects of family planning and sexual health including advice for parents on how to talk to their children about sexual matters.

Genito-urinary medicine clinic (GU M)
   Local clinics can be found in the local phone book under G, S for sexually transmitted diseases, or V for Venereal Diseases Clinic. They are also known as STDs or special clinics. They provide counselling on sexual problems, information about contraception, pregnancy, infections and other matters for people of all ages.

Sex Education Forum
8 Wakley Street, London EC1V 7QE
Tel. 020 7843 6051
www.ncb.org.uk/sexednl.htm
   Advice on good practice for sex education for schools and parents with leaflets and booklists.

Sexual Assault

Rape Crisis Helplines
In telephone directory for local helpline or dial 192, Directory Enquiries, and ask.

Survivors (Male Rape)
Tel. 020 7833 3737 (7 p.m.–10 p.m. Mon–Fri)

Victim Support
Tel. 020 7735 9166
For all victims of crime.

Sexuality

FFLAG Friends and Families of Lesbians and Gays
PO Box 153, Manchester M60 1LP
Helpline: 0161 628 7621 or 0161 748 3452 or 01392 279546
(10 a.m.–10 p.m. daily)
www.fflag.fsnet.co.uk
Information and confidential support for parents and their children.

Allsorts Youth Project
PO Box 3211, Brighton BN1 1AS
Tel. 07932 852533
www.freshweb.co.uk/allsorts
Run weekly drop-ins for anyone under twenty-six.

Jewish Lesbian and Gay Helpline
Tel. 020 7706 3123 (7 p.m.–10 p.m. Mon and Thurs)

Lesbian and Gay Switchboard
Tel. 020 7837 7324 (24 hours)

TS/TV (transsexual and transvestite) Helpline
Tel. 0161 274 3705

Smoking

Quit – The National Society for Non-smokers
Victory House, 170 Tottenham Court Road, London
W1P 0HA
Tel. 020 7388 5775
Quitline: 0800 002200 (1 p.m.–9 p.m.)
   Literature and information on quitting. Helpline staffed by
trained counsellors.

The Law

Children's Legal Centre
University of Essex, Wivenhoe Park, Colchester, Essex
CO4 3SQ
Tel. 01206 872446
Advice line: 01206 872446

Notes

Chapter One

1. *Adolescence*, Laurence Steinberg (5ᵗʰ edition, McGraw Hill, 1999)
2. *Adolescence*, John W. Santrock (McGraw Hill, 1998); *At the Threshold – The Developing Adolescent*, edited by S. Shirley Feldman and Glen R. Elliott (Harvard University Press, 1990)
3. *Adolescence*, Laurence Steinberg; *Social Networks and Social Influences in Adolescence*, John Cotterell (Routledge, 1996)
4. *Adolescence*, Laurence Steinberg

Chapter Three

1. *Young People in 1997*, J. Balding (Schools Health Education Unit, 1998)
2. *Facing it Out – Clinical Perspectives on Adolescent Disturbance*, edited by Robin Anderson and Anna Dartington (Duckworth, 1998)
3. *The Unexpected Legacy of Divorce – A 25 Year Landmark Study*, Judith Wallerstein, Julia Lewis, Sandra Blakeslee (Hyperion, 2000)
4. *Adolescence*, Laurence Steinberg
5. *At the Threshold – The Developing Adolescent*, edited by S. Shirley Feldman and Glen R. Elliott
6. *Adolescence*, John W. Santrock
7. *How We Feel – An Insight into the Emotional World of Teenagers*, edited by Jacki Gordon and Gillian Grant (Jessica Kingsley, 1997)

Chapter Four

1. *Frontiers*, BBC Radio 4, 7 June 2000; 'Rebels With a Cause', John McCrone (*New Scientist*, 22 January 2000)
2. ibid.
3. *Young People, Health and Family Life*, Julia Brannen, Kathryn Dodd, Ann Oakley, Pamela Storey (Open University Press, 1994)
4. *The Nature of Adolescence*, John Coleman and Leo Hendry (3rd edition, Routledge, 1999)
5. *Adolescence*, John W. Santrock
6. *Adolescence*, Laurence Steinberg
7. *The Universal Experience of Adolescence*, Norman Kiell (University of London Press, 1964)
8. *The Construction of the Self*, Susan Hayter (The Guildford Press, 1999)

Chapter Five

1. 'Exploring Teenagers' Accounts of Bad Communication: A New Basis for Interaction', John Drury, et al. (*Journal of Adolescence*, Vol. 21, No. 2, 1998)
2. *Adolescence*, Laurence Steinberg; *At the Threshold – The Developing Adolescent*, S. Shirley Feldman and Glen R. Elliott
3. *Psychosocial Development During Adolescence*, Gerald R. Adams, Raymond Montemayor, Thomas P. Gullotta (Sage, 1996)
4. *Growing Up Forgotten*, Joan Lipsitz (Transaction Books, 1980)
5. 'Adolescents' Perceptions of their Parents' Disclosure to Them', Kim Gale Dolgin and Nicci Berendt (*Journal of Adolescence*, Vol. 20, No. 4, 1997)
6. *The Adolescent in Family Therapy*, Joseph A. Micucci (Guildford Press, 1998)
7. *Child Influences on Marital and Family Interaction – A Lifespan*

Perspective, edited by Richard Lerner and Graham B. Spanier (Academic Press, 1978)

8. *Adolescence*, John W. Santrock

Chapter Six

1. *Social Networks and Social Influences in Adolescence*, John Cotterell; *At the Threshold – The Developing Adolescent*, edited by S. Shirley Feldman and Glen R. Elliott

2. 'The Effectiveness of Peer Support Systems in Challenging School Bullying: The Perspectives and Experiences of Teachers and Pupils', Paul Naylor and Helen Cowie (*Journal of Adolescence*, Vol. 22, 1999

3. 'Peer Involvement in Bullying: Insights and Challenges for Intervention', Paul O'Connell, Debra Pepler and Wendy Craig (*Journal of Adolescence*, Vol. 22, 1999)

4. *How We Feel – An Insight into the Emotional World of Teenagers*, edited by Jacki Gordon and Gillian Grant

5. 'The Effects of an Anti-Bullying Intervention Programme on Peers' Attitudes and Behaviour', Veerlie Stevens, Paulette Van Oost and Lise De Bourdeaudhuij (*Journal of Adolescence*, Vol. 23, 2000)

6. 'Peer Involvement in Bullying: Insights and Challenges for Intervention', Paul O'Connell, Debra Pepler and Wendy Craig

7. *Social Networks and Social Influences in Adolescence*, John Cotterell

8. ibid.

9. *Adolescence*, John W. Santrock

10. ibid.

11. ibid.; *At the Threshold*, edited by S. Shirley Feldman and Glen R. Elliott; *Adolescence*, Laurence Steinberg

12. *Psychosocial Development During Adolescence*, Gerald R. Adams, Raymond Montemayor, Thomas P. Gullotta

13. ibid.

Chapter Seven

1. *The Nature of Adolescence*, John Coleman and Leo Hendry
2. *All Grown Up And No Place To Go*, David Elkind (Perseus Books, 1998)
3. *Sexuality in Adolescence*, Susan Moore and Doreen Rosenthal (Routledge, 1993)
4. *At the Threshold – The Developing Adolescent*, edited by S. Shirley Feldman and Glen R. Elliott
5. *Sexuality in Adolescence*, Susan Moore and Doreen Rosenthal
6. *Adolescent Sexuality*, Thomas P. Gullotta, Gerald R. Adams, Raymond Montemayor (Sage, 1993)
7. ibid.
8. *Adolescence*, Laurence Steinberg
9. *The Nature of Adolescence*, John Coleman and Leo Hendry
10. 'Girls' Understanding and Social Construction of Menarche', S. M. Moore (*Journal of Adolescence*, Vol. 18, No. 1, 1995)
11. *Adolescent Health*, Patrick C. L. Heaven (Routledge, 1996)
12. *Adolescence*, Laurence Steinberg; *Encyclopedia of Adolescence*, edited by Richard M. Lerner, Anne C. Peterson, Jeanne Brooks-Gunn (Garland, 1991); *Sexuality in Adolescence*, Susan Moore and Doreen Rosenthal
13. ibid.
14. *This is the Time to Grow Up: Girls' Experiences of Menstruation in School*, S. Pendergrast (Health Promotion Research Trust, 1992)
15. *Young People and Health: Health Behaviour in School-aged Children* (HEA, 1999)
16. *Adolescence*, Laurence Steinberg
17. *Patterns of Sexual Behaviour*, C. Ford and F. Beach (Harper and Row, 1951)
18. *Adolescence*, Laurence Steinberg

19. *Adolescence – An Anthropological Inquiry*, Alice Schlegel and Herbert Barry (Free Press, 1991)
20. *Patterns of Sexual Behaviour*, C. Ford and F. Beach
21. *Leading Lads*, Adrienne Katz (Oxford University, 1999)
22. *Children's Sexual Thinking*, Ronald and Juliette Goldman (RKP, 1982)
23. *Adolescent Sexuality*, Thomas P. Gullotta, Gerald R. Adams, Raymond Montemayor
24. *Children's Sexual Thinking*, Ronald and Juliette Goldman

Chapter Eight

1. *Young People's Leisure and Lifestyles*, Leo B. Hendry (Routledge, 1993)
2. *National Curriculum: National Disaster?*, Rhys Griffith (Routledge, 2000)
3. *The Real Deal – What Young People Really Think about Government, Politics and Social Exclusion*, Tom Bentley and Kate Oakley (Demos, 1999)
4. *The Schools Report*, Nick Davies (Vintage, 2000)
5. ibid.
6. *Learning Beyond the Classroom – Education for a Changing World*, Tom Bentley (Routledge/Demos, 1998)
7. *National Curriculum: National Disaster?*, Rhys Griffith
8. *How We Feel – An Insight into the Emotional World of Teenagers*, edited by Jacki Gordon and Gillian Grant
9. *The Schools Report*, Nick Davies
10. *The Nature of Adolescence*, John Coleman and Leo Hendry
11. *At the Threshold – The Developing Adolescent*, edited by S. Shirley Feldman and Glen R. Elliott; *Fifteen Thousand Hours: Secondary Schools and Their Effects on Children*, Michael Rutter, et al. (Open Books, 1979)
12. *Leading Lads*, Adrienne Katz

Chapter Nine

1. *Adolescence and Culture*, Aaron H. Esman (Columbia University Press, 1990)
2. *The Universal Experience of Adolescence*, Norman Kiell
3. *Health Risks and Developmental Transitions During Adolescence*, edited by John Schulenberg, Jennifer L. Maggs and Klaus Hurrelmann (Cambridge University Press, 1997)
4. *Psychosocial Disorders in Young People – Time Trends and Their Causes*, edited by Michael Rutter and David J. Smith (John Wiley, 1995)
5. *Health Risks and Developmental Transitions During Adolescence*, edited by John Schulenberg, Jennifer L. Maggs and Klaus Hurrelman; *Adolescence*, Laurence Steinberg
6. ibid.; *Psychosocial Disorders in Young People – Time Trends and Their Causes*, edited by Michael Rutter and David J. Smith
7. ibid.
8. *Alcohol Concern*, Factsheet 8, Young People and Alcohol, 2000
9. 'Adolescent Resiliency to Family Adversity', David Fergusson and Michael T. Lynskey (*Journal of Child Psychology and Psychiatry*, Vol. 37, No. 3, 1996)
10. *Crossroads – The Quest for Contemporary Rites of Passage*, edited by Louise Carus Mahdi (Carus Publishing, 1996)
11. *The Universal Experience of Adolescence*, Norman Kiell
12. *Alcohol Concern*, Factsheet 8
13. *You and Your Adolescent*, Laurence Steinberg and Ann Levine (Harper Perennial, 1991)
14. *Just Say Know – Talking with Kids about Drugs and Alcohol*, Cynthia Kuhn, Scott Swartzwelder and Wilkie Wilson (Norton, 2002)
15. *Alcohol Concern*, Factsheet 8
16. *Facing it Out – Clinical Perspectives on Adolescent Disturbance*, edited by Robin Anderson and Anna Dartington
17. *Adolescence*, Laurence Steinberg; *Psychosocial Disorders in Young*

People – Time Trends and Their Causes, edited by Michael Rutter and David J. Smith

18. ibid.

19. *The Adolescent in Family Therapy*, Joseph A. Micucci

20. *Adolescence*, Laurence Steinberg; *Psychosocial Disorders in Young People – Time Trends and Their Causes*, edited by Michael Rutter and David J. Smith

21. *Facing it Out – Clinical Perspectives on Adolescent Disturbance*, edited by Robin Anderson and Anna Dartington

22. 'Suicide Among the Young – The Size of the Problem', Nicola Madge and John G. Harvey (*Journal of Adolescence*, Vol. 22, No. 5, 1999)

23. 'Deliberate Self-harm in Adolescents in Oxford 1985–1995', Keith Hawton, Joan Fagg, et al. (*Journal of Adolescence*, Vol. 23, No. 1, 2000)

24. 'Sexual Abuse and Adolescent Maladjustment: Differences between Male and Female Victims', Nadia Garnefski and Ellen Arends (*Journal of Adolescence*, Vol. 21, No. 1, 1998)

25. '"I would rather be size 10 than have straight A's": A Focus Group Study of Adolescent Girls' Wish to be Thinner', Marika Tiggemann, Maria Gardiner and Amy Slater (*Journal of Adolescence*, Vol. 23, December 2000)

26. *A Message for the Media – Young Women Talk*, edited by Jane Waghorn (Livewire, Women's Press, 1999)

27. 'Social Relationships and Health: The Meaning of Social "Connectedness" and How it Relates to Health Concerns for Rural Scottish Adolescents', Leo B. Hendry and Marylou Reid (*Journal of Adolescence*, Vol. 23, December 2000)

28. *At the Threshold – The Developing Adolescent*, edited by S. Shirley Feldman and Glen R. Elliott

29. *Psychosocial Disturbances in Young People – Challenges for Prevention*, edited by Michael Rutter (Cambridge, 1995)

30. *At the Threshold – The Developing Adolescent*, edited by S. Shirley Feldman and Glen R. Elliott

31. 'Adolescents from One Parent, Step-parent and Intact Families;
    Emotional Problems and Suicide Attempts', Nadia Garnefski and
    Renee F. W. Diekstra (*Journal of Adolescence*, Vol. 20, No. 2, 1997)

32. *Adolescence*, John W. Santrock

33. *Psychosocial Disorders in Young People – Time Trends and Their
    Causes*, edited by Michael Rutter and David J. Smith

34. *Changing Experiences of Youth*, edited by Daren Garratt, Jeremy
    Roche and Stanley Tucker (Sage, 1997)

35. *The Schools Report*, Nick Davies

36. *Adolescence*, Laurence Steinberg; 'Exposure to Violence, Depres-
    sion and Hostility in a Sample of Inner City High School
    Youth', Anne Moses (*Journal of Adolescence*, Vol. 22, No. 1,
    1999)

37. *The Schools Report*, Nick Davies

38. 'Betrayed – The Politics of Child Mental Health in Britain',
    Camila Batmanghelidjh (*International Journal of Psychology*,
    Spring 2000)

39. 'Adolescent Sexuality and Public Policy: The Role of Cognitive
    Immaturity', Sue Stuart-Smith (*Politics and the Life Science*, Sept.
    1996)

40. *Crossroads – The Quest for Contemporary Rites of Passage*, edited
    by Louise Carus Mahdi

41. *Learning Beyond the Classroom – Education for a Changing World*,
    Tom Bentley

Chapter Ten

1. *The Nature of Adolescence*, John Coleman and Leo Hendry

2. *Street Life*, edited by Jane Cassidy (Livewire, 1999)

Appendices

1. *Patterns of Human Growth*, Barry Bogin (Cambridge, 1999)

2. *At the Threshold – The Developing Adolescent*, edited by S. Shirley

Feldman and Glen R. Elliott; *Adolescence*, Laurence Steinberg

3. *Encyclopedia of Adolescence*, edited by Richard M. Lerner, Anne C. Peterson and Jeanne Brooks-Gunn

4. *Adolescent Health*, Patrick C. L. Heaven

5. *Changing Youth in a Changing Society*, Michael Rutter (Nuffield Provincial Hospitals Trust, 1979)

Bibliography

Adams, G.R., et al., 'On the Dialectics of Pubescence and Psycho-social Development', *Journal of Early Adolescence,* Vol. 12, No. 4, 1992

Adams, Gerald R., Montemayor, Raymond and Gullotta, Thomas P., *Psychosocial Development During Adolescence*, Sage, 1996

Alasker, F.D., 'The Impact of Puberty', *Journal of Child Psychology and Psychiatry*, Vol. 37, No. 3

Alcohol Concern, Factsheet 8 on Young People and Alcohol, 2000

Anderson, Robin and Dartington, Anna, *Facing it Out – Clinical Perspectives on Adolescent Disturbance*, Karnac, 1998

Balding J., *Young People in 1997*, Schools Health Education Unit, 1998

Bank, Melissa, *The Girls' Guide to Hunting and Fishing*, Viking, 1999

Batmanghelidjh, Camila, 'The Politics of Child Mental Health in Britain', *International Journal of Psychology*, Spring 2000

Beckworth, Carol and Fisher, Angela, *Passages – Photographs in Africa*, Abrams, 2000

Belsky, Jay, Steinberg, Laurence and Draper, Patricia, 'Childhood Experience, Interpersonal Development and Reproductive Strategy: An Evolutionary Theory of Socialization', *Child Development* 62, No. 4, 1991

Bentley, Tom, *Learning Beyond the Classroom – Education for a Changing World,* Routledge/Demos, 1998

Bentley, Tom and Oakley, Kate, *The Real Deal – What Young People Really Think about Government, Politics and Social Exclusion*, Demos, 1999

Berne, Suzanne, *A Crime in the Neighbourhood*, Penguin, 1997

Bettelheim, Bruno, *Symbolic Wounds – Puberty Rites and the Envious Male*, Thames and Hudson, 1955

Bettelheim, Bruno, *The Uses of Enchantment – The Meaning and Importance of Fairy Tales,* Vintage, 1989

Beyer, Christine E., et al., 'Gender Representation in Illustrations, Text and Topic Areas in Sexuality Education Curricula', *Journal of School Health*, Vol. 66, No. 10, 1996

Blatchford, Peter, *Social Life in School*, Falmer Press, 1998

Blum, R., 'Poverty and Neglect – Deprived Youth in Varied Societies', *Journal of Adolescent Health and Welfare,* Vol. 10, No. 3, 1997

Blume, Judy, *Are You There, God? It's Me, Margaret,* Gollancz, 1978

Bogin, Barry, *Patterns of Human Growth*, Cambridge, 1999

Boulton, Michael J., 'Concurrent and Longitudinal Links between Friendship and Peer Victimization: Implications for Befriending Interventions', *Journal of Adolescence*, Vol. 22, 1999

Braid, Helen (ed.), *A Stranger at My Table*, Women's Press, 1997

Bramen, J. and Stone, P., *Child Health in Social Context,* Health Education Authority, 1996

Brannen, Julia, Dodd, Kathryn, Oakley, Ann and Storey, Pamela, *Young People, Health and Family Life*, Open University Press, 1994

Breakwell, Glynis M. and Millward, Lynne J., 'Sexual Self Concept and Sexual Risk Taking', *Journal of Adolescence,* Vol. 20, 1997

Brown, Lyn Mikel and Gilligan, Carol, *Meeting at the Crossroads – Women's Psychology and Girls' Development*, Harvard, 1992

Brumberg, Joan Jacobs, *The Body Project – An Intimate History of American Girls*, Vintage (US), 1997

Buchanan, Christy M., *Adolescents After Divorce*, Harvard, 1996

Cassidy, Jane (ed.), *Street Life*, Livewire, 1999

Cicchetti, T. and Toth, S. (eds.), *Adolescence: Opportunities and Challenges*, Rochester (NY), 1996

Coleman, John, *Key Data on Adolescence*, TSA, 1997

Coleman, John and Hendry, Leo, *The Nature of Adolescence*, Routledge, 1999

Colette, *Claudine at School*, Secker & Warburg, 1956

Colette, *Ripening Seed*, Penguin, 1959

Colette, *The Collected Stories of Colette*, Secker & Warburg, 1984

Copeland, E.P. and Hess, R.S., 'Differences in Young Adolescents' Coping Strategies Based on Gender and Ethnicity', *Journal of Early Adolescence*, Vol. 15, No. 2

Copley, Beta, *The World of Adolescence – Literature, Society and Psychoanalytic Psychotherapy*, Free Association Books, 1993

Cornwall, Gretchen T., et al., 'Changing Family Context of Early Adolescence', *Journal of Early Adolescence*, Vol. 16, No. 2

Cotterell, John, *Social Networks and Social Influences in Adolescence*, Routledge, 1996

Csikszentmihalyi, Mihaly and Larson, Reed, *Being Adolescent*, Basic Books, 1984

Cummings, E. Mark, and Vogel, Dena, 'Children's Responses to Different Forms of Expression of Anger Between Adults', *Child Development*, 60, 1989

Dalsimer, Katherine, *Female Adolescence – Psychoanalytic Reflections on Works of Literature*, Yale University Press, 1986

Davidson, Gina, *The Trials of a Teenage Terror*, Virago, 1996

Davidson, Gina, *What Treasure Did Next*, Virago, 1996

Davies, Nick, *The Schools Report*, Vintage, 2000

Dekovic, Maja and Meeus, Wim, 'Peer Relations in Adolescence: Effects of Parenting and Adolescent's Self-Concept', *Journal of Adolescence*, Vol. 20, No. 2, 1997

Dolgin, Kim Gale and Berendt, Nicci, 'Adolescents' Perceptions of their Parents' Disclosure to Them', *Journal of Adolescence*, Vol. 20, No. 4, 1997

Drury, John, et al., 'Exploring Teenagers' Accounts of Bad Communication: A New Basis for Interaction', *Journal of Adolescence*, Vol. 21, No. 2, 1998

Dudman, Martha Tod, *Augusta, Gone*, Simon & Schuster, 2001

Einon, Dorothy, *Child Behaviour*, Viking, 1997

Elkind, David, *All Grown Up And No Place To Go*, Perseus Books, 1998

Eminson, Mary, et al., 'Physical Symptoms and Illness Attitudes in Adolescents', *Journal of Child Psychology and Psychiatry*, Vol. 37, No. 5

Emler, Nicholas, *Self-Esteem – The Costs and Causes of Low Self-Worth*, Joseph Rowntree Foundation, 2001

Epstein, Jonathan S. (ed.), *Youth Culture – Identity in a Post-Modern World*, Blackwell, 1998

Erikson, Erik, *Identity – Youth and Crisis*, Faber, 1968

Erikson, Erik, *Childhood and Society*, Vintage, 1995

Esman, Aaron H., *Adolescence and Culture*, Columbia University Press, 1990

Eugenides, Jeffrey, *The Virgin Suicides*, Abacus, 1993

Fasick, F.A., 'The "Invention" of Adolescence', *Journal of Early Adolescence*, Vol. 14, No. 1

Feldman, S. and Elliott G. (eds.), *At the Threshold – The Developing Adolescent*, Harvard University Press, 1993

Fergusson, David and Lynskey, Michael T., 'Adolescent Resiliency to Family Adversity', *Journal of Child Psychology and Psychiatry*, Vol. 37, No. 3, 1996

Flannery D.J. (ed.), 'Affective Expression and Emotion in Early Adolescence', *Journal of Early Adolescence*, special issue, Vol. 13, No. 4

Ford, C. and Beach, F., *Patterns of Sexual Behaviour*, Harper and Row, 1951

Fournier, Alain, *Le Grand Meaulnes*, Penguin, 1966

Francis, Paul, *Help Your Kids Stay Drug Free*, Harper Collins, 1999

Frank, Anne, *Diary of a Young Girl – The Definitive Edition*, Viking, 1997

Frankel, Richard, *The Adolescent Psyche*, Routledge, 1998

Franklin, Miles, *My Brilliant Career*, Longman, 1901

Furlong, Andy and Cartmel, Fred, *Young People and Social Change*, Open University Press, 1997

Garber, Marjorie, *Coming of Age in Shakespeare*, Methuen, 1981

Garnefski, Nadia and Arends, Ellen, 'Sexual Abuse and Adolescent Maladjustment: Differences between Male and Female Victims', *Journal of Adolescence*, Vol. 21, No. 1, 1998

Garnefski, Nadia and Diekstra, Renee F.W., 'Adolescents From One Parent, Step Parent and Intact Families: Emotional Problems and Suicide Attempts', *Journal of Adolescence*, Vol. 20, No. 2, 1997

Garratt, Daren, Roche, Jeremy and Tucker, Stanley (eds.), *Changing Experiences of Youth*, Sage, 1997

Gillies, Val, Ribbens McCarthy, Jane and Holland, Janet, *Pulling Together, Pulling Apart – The Family Lives of Young People*, Joseph Rowntree Foundation, 2001

Gilligan, Carol, et al. (eds.), *Making Connections – The Relational Worlds of Adolescent Girls at Emma Willard School*, Harvard, 1989

Gillis, John R., *Youth and History – Tradition and Change in European Age Relations 1770–Present*, Academic Press, 1974

Gillis, John R., *A World of Their Own Making*, Harvard, 1996

Goldman, Juliette and Goldman, Ronald, *Children's Sexual Thinking*, RKP, 1982

Gordon, Jacki and Grant, Gillian (eds.), *How We Feel – An Insight into the Emotional World of Teenagers*, Jessica Kingsley Publishers, 1997

Gowers, S. G., et al., 'Premenarcheal Anorexia Nervosa', *Journal of Child Psychology and Psychiatry*, Vol. 32, No. 3, 1991

Green, J., 'A Survey of Sex Education in Primary Schools in the Northern Yorkshire Region', *International Journal of Health Education*, 35/3, 1997

Greenfield, Susan A., *The Private Life of the Brain*, Penguin Press, 2000

Griffin, Christine, *Representations of Youth – The Study of Youth and Adolescence in Britain and America*, Polity Press, 1993

Griffith, Rhys, *National Curriculum: National Disaster?*, Routledge, 2000

Gullotta, Thomas P., Adams, Gerald R., Montemayor, Raymond, *Developing Sexual Competency in Adolescence*, Sage, 1990

Gullotta, Thomas P., Adams, Gerald R., Montemayor, Raymond, *Adolescent Sexuality*, Sage, 1993

Hall, G. Stanley, *Adolescence – Its Psychology and Its Relations to Physiology, Anthropology, Sociology, Sex, Crime, Religion and Education*, D. Appleton, 1904

Hambly, W. D., *The History of Tattooing and its Significance*, H. F. G. Witherby, 1925

Harris, M. L. L., et al., 'Changes in the Male Voice at Puberty', *Archives of Disease in Childhood*, Vol. 77, No. 5, 1997

Hawton, Keith, et al., 'Deliberate Self-Harm in Adolescents in Oxford 1985–1995', *Journal of Adolescence*, Vol. 23, No. 1, 2000

Hayman, Susie, *Living With a Teenager – A Survival Guide for Parents*, Piatkus, 1998

Hayter, Susan, *The Construction of the Self*, The Guildford Press, 1999

Health Education Authority, *Young People and Health: Health Behaviour in School-aged Children*, 1999

Heaven, Patrick C.L., *Adolescent Health*, Routledge, 1996

Hendry, Leo B., *Young People's Leisure and Lifestyles*, Routledge, 1993

Hendry, Leo B. and Reid, Marylou, 'Social Relationships and Health: The Meaning of Social Connectedness and How it Relates to Health Concerns for Rural Scottish Adolescents', *Journal of Adolescence*, Vol. 23, 2000

Hennieson, Clem and Roker, Debi, 'Support for the Parents of Adolescents: A Review', *Journal of Adolescence*, Vol. 23, 2000

Hesse, Hermann, *Demian*, Picador, 1995

Hetherington, E. Mavis and Kelly, John, *For Better or For Worse*, Norton 2002

Houppert, Karen, *The Curse – Confronting the Last Taboo: Menstruation*, Profile, 2000

Humphries, Stephen, *Hooligans or Rebels – An Oral History of Working Class Childhood and Youth 1889–1939*, Blackwell, 1981

Ingersoll, Barbara D., *Lonely, Sad and Angry – A Parents' Guide to Depression in Children and Adolescents*, Doubleday, 1995

Jackson, Sandy and Rodriguez-Tome, Hector (eds.), *Adolescence and its Social Worlds*, Lawrence Erlbaum, 1993

Jamieson, Kay Redfield, *Night Falls Fast – Understanding Suicide*, Macmillan, 2000

Jones, Gill, *Leaving Home*, Open University Press, 1995

Jones, Gill and Wallace, Clare, *Youth, Family and Citizenship*, Open University Press, 1992

Kagan, Jerome, *The Nature of the Child*, Basic Books, 1984

Kaplan, Louise J., *Adolescence: The Farewell to Childhood*, Aronson, 1986

Karoly, Paul and Steffen, John, *Adolescent Behaviour Disorders: Foundations and Contemporary Concerns*, Lexington Books, 1984

Karr, Mary, *Cherry*, Picador, 2001

Katz, Adrienne, *The Can Do Girls*, The Body Shop, 1998

Katz, Adrienne, *Leading Lads*, Oxford University, 1999

Kelley, Peter, 'Talking Dirty – Children, Sexual Knowledge and Television', *Childhood*, Vol. 6, No. 2

Kiell, Norman, *The Universal Experience of Adolescence*, University of London, 1964

Kim, K. and Smith, P.K., 'Childhood Stress, Behavioural Symptoms and Mother–Daughter Pubertal Development', *Journal of Adolescence*, Vol. 21, No. 3, 1998

Kincaid, Jamaica, *Annie John*, Picador, 1985

Kindlon, Dan and Thompson, Michael, *Raising Cain*, Michael Joseph, 1999

Kleinbaum, N.H., *Dead Poets Society*, Bantam, 1989

Kloep, Marion, 'Love is All You Need? Focusing on Adolescents'

Life Concerns From an Ecological Point of View', *Journal of Adolescence*, Vol. 22, No. 1, 1999

Krausman, Ilan and Amos, Ben, *Adolescence and Youth in Early Modern Europe*, Yale University Press, 1994

Kroger, Jane, *Identity in Adolescence*, Routledge, 1996

Kuhn, Cynthia, Swartzwelder, Scott and Wilson, Wilkie, *Just Say Know – Talking with Kids about Drugs and Alcohol*, Norton, 2002

Lara, Adair, *Hold Me Close, Let Me Go*, Broadway Books, 2001

Larson, Reed and Richards, Maryse H., *Divergent Realities – The Emotional Lives of Mothers, Fathers and Adolescents*, Basic Books, 1994

Lau, Sing and Lau, Winnie, 'Outlook on Life: How Adolescents and Children View the Life-Style of Parents, Adults and Self', *Journal of Adolescence*, Vol. 19, No. 3, 1996

Laursen, B., Coy, K.C., and Collins, W.A., 'Reconsidering Changes in Parent–Child Conflict Across Adolescence: a Meta Analysis', *Child Development*, Vol. 69, No. 3

Le Stevens, Veerle, Van Oost, Paulette and De Bourdeaudhuij, Lise, 'The Effects of an Anti-Bullying Intervention Programme on Peers' Attitudes and Behaviour', *Journal of Adolescence*, Vol. 23, 2000

Lebert, Benjamin, *Crazy*, Hamish Hamilton, 2000

Lee, Harper, *To Kill a Mockingbird*, Minerva, 1991

Lerner, Richard, *America's Youth in Crisis*, Sage, 1995

Lerner, Richard and Spanier, Graham B., *Child Influences on Marital and Family Interaction – A Lifespan Perspective*, Academic Press, 1978

Lerner, Richard, Peterson, Anne C. and Brooks-Gunn, Jeanne (eds.), *Encyclopedia of Adolescence*, Garland, 1991

Levi, Giovanni and Schmitt, Jean-Claude, *A History of Young People in the West Volume 1: Ancient and Medieval Rites of Passage*, Belknap Press of Harvard University, 1997

Levi, Giovanni and Schmitt, Jean-Claude, *A History of Young People*

in the West Volume 2: Stormy Evolution to Modern Times, Belknap
Press of Harvard University, 1997

Levi-Warren, Marsha, *The Adolescent Journey – Development, Identity
Formation and Psychotherapy*, Aronson, 1996

Lewis, Sydney, *'A Totally Alien Life Form' – Teenagers*, The New
Press, 1996

Lindon, Jennie, *Growing Up: From 8 Years to Adulthood*, National
Children's Bureau, 1996

Lindsay, Geoff (ed.), *Problems of Adolescence in Secondary School*, Croom
Helm, 1983

Lipsitz, Joan, *Growing Up Forgotten*, Transaction Books, 1980

Lurie, Alison, *The War Between the Tates*, Heinemann, 1974

MacFarlane, Aidan and McPherson, Ann, *Teenagers – The Agony,
The Ecstasy, The Answers*, Little Brown, 1999

Madaras, Lynda, *What's Happening to my Body? A Growing-up Guide
for Parents and Daughters*, Penguin, 1999

Madaras, Lynda and Saavedra, Dane, *What's Happening to my Body?
A Growing-up Guide for Parents and Sons*, Penguin, 1989

Madge, Nicola and Harvey, John G., 'Suicide Among the Young –
The Size of the Problem', *Journal of Adolescence*, Vol. 22, No. 5

Mahdi, Louise Carus, *Crossroads – The Quest for Contemporary Rites
of Passage*, Carus Publishing, 1996

Malo, J. and Temblay, R.E., 'The Impact of Paternal Alcoholism and
Maternal Social Position on Boys' School Adjustment, Pubertal
Maturation and Sexual Behaviour: A Test of Two Competing
Hypotheses', *Journal of Child Psychology and Psychiatry*, Vol. 38,
No. 2, 1997

McCullers, Carson, *The Member of the Wedding*, Penguin, 1962

Mead, Margaret, *Coming of Age in Samoa*, Marrow, 1928

Merke, D.P. and Cutler, G.B., 'Evaluation and Management of
Precocious Puberty', *Archives of Diseases in Childhood*, Vol. 75,
No. 4

Merton, Bryan and Parrott, Allen, *Only Connect*, DFEE, 1999

Meschke, L.L. and Silberreisen R.K., 'The Influence of Puberty, Family Processes and Leisure Activities on the Timing of First Sexual Experience', *Journal of Adolescence*, Vol. 20, No. 4, 1997

Meyerson, Simon (ed.), *Adolescence – The Crises of Adjustment*, George Allen and Unwin, 1975

Micucci, Joseph A., *The Adolescent in Family Therapy*, Guildford Press, 1998

Mitchell, Kirstin and Wellings, Kaye, 'Sexual Intercourse: Anticipation and Communication. Interviews with Young People in England', *Journal of Adolescence*, Vol. 21, No. 6

Mitford, Nancy, *The Pursuit of Love*, The Folio Society, 1991

Mitterauer, Michael, *A History of Youth*, Blackwell, 1992

Montgomery, Marilyn J. and Sorell, T., 'Love and Dating Experience in Early and Middle Adolescence: Grade and Gender Comparisons', *Journal of Adolescence*, Vol. 21, 1998

Moore, S.M., 'Girls' Understanding and Social Construction of Menarche', *Journal of Adolescence*, Vol. 18, No. 1, 1995

Moore, Susan and Rosenthal, Doreen, *Sexuality in Adolescence*, Routledge, 1993

Moses, Anne, 'Exposure to Violence, Depression and Hostility in a Sample of Inner City High School Youth', *Journal of Adolescence*, Vol. 22, No. 1, 1999

Mueller, Walt, *Understanding Today's Youth Culture*, Tyndale, 1994

Munro-Prescott, Heather, '"A Doctor of Their Own" The Emergence of Adolescent Medicine as a Clinical Sub-Speciality 1904–1980', A Dissertation presented to the Faculty of the Graduate School of Cornell University, 1992

Myers, Bob, *Raising Responsible Teenagers*, Jessica Kingsley Publishers, 1996

Myers, Bob, *Parenting Teenagers*, Jessica Kingsley Publishers, 1996

Nabokov, Vladimir, *Lolita*, Penguin, 1980

Naylor, Paul and Cowie, Helen, 'The Effectiveness of Peer Support

Systems in Challenging School Bullying: The Perspectives and Experiences of Teachers and Pupils', *Journal of Adolescence*, Vol. 22, 1999

Newberger, Eli, *The Men They Will Become – The Nature and Nurture of Male Character*, Bloomsbury, 1992

Newton, Miller, *Adolescence*, Norton, 1995

O'Connell, Paul, Pepler, Debra and Craig, Wendy, 'Peer Involvement in Bullying: Insights and Challenges for Intervention', *Journal of Adolescence*, Vol. 22, 1999

Offer, Daniel and Ostrov, Eric, *The Adolescent – A Psychological Self Portrait*, Basic Books, 1981

Patton, G.C., et al., 'Menarche and the Onset of Depression and Anxiety in Victoria, Australia', *Journal of Epidemiology and Community Health*, Vol. 50, No. 6

Pawlby, Susan J., Mill, Alice, Taylor, Alan and Quinton, David, 'Adolescent Friendships – Mediating Childhood Adversity and Adult Outcome', *Journal of Adolescence*, Vol. 20, 1997

Pendergrast, S., *This is the Time to Grow Up: Girls' Experiences of Menstruation in School*, Health Promotion Research Trust, 1992

Perkins, David, *Outsmarting IQ: The Emerging Science of Learnable Intelligence*, Free Press, 1995

Phillips, Asha, *Saying No – Why It's Important for You and Your Child*, Faber, 1999

Pilcher, Jane, 'Contrary to Gillick: British Children and Sexual Rights Since 1985', *International Journal of Children's Rights*, 5, 1997

Pipher, Mary, *Reviving Ophelia*, Vermillion, 1996

Pollock, Linda A., *Forgotten Children – Parent–Child Relations from 1500–1900*, Cambridge University Press, 1983

Postman, Neil, *The Disappearance of Childhood*, Coronet, 1985

Pugh, Penelope and Webley, Paul, 'Adolescent Participation in the

UK National Lottery Games', *Journal of Adolescence*, Vol. 23, No. 1, 2000

Rich Harris, Judith, *The Nurture Assumption – Why Children Turn out the Way They Do*, Bloomsbury, 1998

Richardson, Ken and Sheldon, Sue, *Cognitive Development to Adolescence*, Open University, 1988

Rodgers, B. and Pryor, J., *Divorce and Separation: The Outcomes for Children*, Joseph Rowntree Foundation, 1998

Rodriguez-Tome, H., et al., 'The Effect of Pubertal Changes on Body Image and Relations with Peers of the Opposite Sex in Adolescence', *Journal of Adolescence*, Vol. 16, No. 4, 1993

Rosenthal, Doreen A. and Feldman, S. Shirley, 'The Importance of Communication: Adolescents' Perceptions of Parental Communication about Sexuality', *Journal of Adolescence*, Vol. 22, 1999

Rutter, Michael, *Changing Youth in a Changing Society*, Nuffield Provincial Hospitals Trust, 1979

Rutter, Michael, et al., *Fifteen Thousand Hours: Secondary Schools and Their Effects on Children*, Open Books, 1979

Rutter, Michael (ed.), *Psychosocial Disturbances in Young People – Challenges for Prevention,* Cambridge, 1995

Rutter, Michael and Smith, David J. (eds.) *Psychosocial Disorders in Young People – Time Trends and Their Causes*, John Wiley, 1995

Salinger, J.D., *The Catcher in the Rye,* Penguin, 1958

Salmivalli, Christina, 'Participant Role Approach to School Bullying: Implications for Interventions', *Journal of Adolescence,* Vol. 22, 1999

Santrock, John W., *Adolescence*, McGraw Hill, 1998

Schlegel, Alice and Barry, Herbert, *Adolescence – An Anthropological Inquiry,* Free Press, 1991

Schulenberg, John, Maggs, Jennifer L., and Hurrelmann, Klaus, *Health Risks and Developmental Transitions During Adolescence*, Cambridge University Press, 1997

Seidman, D.S., 'Birth Weight, Current Body Weight and Blood Pressure in Late Adolescence', *BMJ*, Vol. 302, No. 6787, 1991

Shucksmith, Janet and Hendry, Leo B., *Health Issues and Adolescents – Growing Up, Speaking Out*, Routledge, 1998

Shulman, Shmuel and Seiffge-Krenke, Inge, *Fathers and Adolescents*, Routledge, 1997

Spark, Muriel, *The Prime of Miss Jean Brodie*, Penguin, 1961

Spruijt-Metz, Donna, *Adolescence, Affect and Health*, Psychology Press, 1999

Stanhope, R; Albavese and Shallet, S., 'Delayed Puberty', *BMJ*, Vol. 305, No. 6857, 1992

Staton, Thomas F., *Dynamics of Adolescent Adjustment*, Macmillan, 1963

Steinberg, Laurence, *Adolescence*, McGraw Hill, 5th Edition, 1999

Steinberg, Laurence and Levine, Ann; *You and Your Adolescent*, Harper Perennial, 1991

Strong, Marilee, *A Bright Red Scream – Self Mutilation and the Language of Pain*, Virago, 2000

Stuart-Smith, Sue, 'Teenage Sex', *BMJ*, Vol. 312, 1996

Stuart-Smith, Sue, 'Adolescent Sexuality and Public Policy: The Role of Cognitive Immaturity', *Politics and the Life Science*, Sept. 1996

Sullivan, Caroline, *Bye Bye Baby*, Bloomsbury, 1999

Taris, W.T. and Semin, G.R., 'Does Adolescents' Sexual Behaviour Affect Their Sexual Attitudes?', *International Journal of Adolescence and Youth*, Vol. 5, No. 3, 1995

Thomas, Keith, 'Age and Authority in Early Modern England', in *Proceedings of the British Academy*, Vol. B2, 1976

Tiggemann, Marika, Gardiner, Maria and Slater, Amy, '"I would rather be size 10 than have straight A's": A Focus Group Study of Adolescent Girls' Wish to be Thinner', *Journal of Adolescence*, Vol. 23, 2000

Varma, Ved (ed.), *How and Why Children Fail,* Jessica Kingsley Publishers, 1993

Waddell, Margot, *Inside Lives*, Karnac, 1998

Waghorn, Jane, *A Message for the Media – Young Women Talk*, Women's Press, 1999

Wallerstein, Judith, Lewis, Julia and Blakeslee, Sandra, *The Unexpected Legacy of Divorce – A 25 Year Landmark Study*, Hyperion, 2000

Winnicott, D.W., *Playing and Reality*, Penguin, 1971

Wolf, Anthony E., *Get Out of My Life But First Can You Drive Me To The Mall?*, The Noonday Press, 1991

Wolff, Tobias, *This Boy's Life*, Bloomsbury, 1989

Wolpert, Lewis, *Malignant Sadness*, Faber, 1999

Youniss, James and Smollar, Jacqueline, *Adolescent Relations with Mothers, Fathers and Friends*, University of Chicago Press, 1985

Permissions

Index